D0404912

Webster's
Rhyming
Dictionary

Webster's Rhyming Dictionary

Created in Cooperation with the Editors of
MERRIAM-WEBSTER

FEDERAL
STREET
PRESS

A Division of Merriam-Webster, Incorporated
Springfield, Massachusetts

This edition published by
Federal Street Press
a Division of Merriam-Webster, Incorporated
PO Box 281
Springfield, MA 01102

ISBN   978-1-59695-112-9

2nd Printing   Craftline Graphics, Fort Wayne, IN   7/2013

Printed in the United States of America

Contents

How to Use This Book

Welcome to Webster's Rhyming Dictionary, where you'll find over 40,000 rhyming words—enough to last you the rest of your life.

We've tried to make this book as easy as possible to use. However, it works quite differently from an ordinary dictionary, so please read these brief instructions to be sure you make the best use of it you can.

All the entries in this book are for *rhyming sounds*. All rhyming sounds begin with a vowel, so every entry begins with *A, E, I, O, U,* or *Y.*

All rhyming sounds also begin with an accented syllable. The rhyming sounds listed here all have one syllable, two syllables, or three syllables.

If a word has only one syllable, that syllable is always accented (as in *bee* and *sea*). A two-syllable word may be accented on either its first syllable (as in *beta* and *data*) or its second syllable (as in *agree* and *must-see*). A three-syllable word may be accented on its first syllable (*attitude, gratitude*), its middle syllable (*illusion, seclusion*), or its last syllable (*anymore, tug-of-war*).

Though the rhyming sounds in this dictionary are never more than three syllables long, the words themselves may have six or more syllables. In every entry, the words are divided into sections according to number of syllables; each section begins with a small bullet (•). So, for instance, the y^1 entry starts with a group of one-syllable words, which is followed by five more bulleted sections, the last one consisting of six-syllable words.

Some words have two accented syllables, with one of them almost always stronger than the other. Notice that when you say the word "middle," you put no accent at all on the second syllable, but when you say "schoolkid," you put a strong accent on its first syllable and a weaker accent on its second syllable. In this book, the rhyming sound always begins with the *last* accented syllable, whether or not that syllable is the one with the strongest accent. So *schoolkid* is shown at the id^1 entry—that is, the entry for its weakly accented syllable.

Many rhymes can be spelled in several different ways. For example, the rhyming sound that is often spelled *-eek* (as in *creek*) can also be spelled *-eak* (as in *peak*), *-ique* (*mystique*), *-ic* (*chic*), or *-ik* (*batik*). So how do you find a rhyme for a particular word? Just look up the spelling of its rhyming sound.

Let's suppose you need a rhyme for *equator*. All you need to do is notice how its rhyming sound is spelled. Since the rhyming sound always begins with the last accented syllable and always begins with a vowel, the rhyming sound of *equator* is obviously spelled *-ator*. And sure enough, the entry **ator** shows all the rhymes for *equator*, no matter how their endings are spelled: *crater, freighter, creator*, etc.

But suppose you had instead wanted a rhyme for *later*, and had looked up the spelling for its rhyming sound, *-ater*. There you would have found two separate entries, **ater¹** and **ater²**. Next to **ater¹** you would have seen the pronunciation \ȯt-ər\, and next to **ater²** you would have seen the pronunciation \āt-ər\. Looking at the Pronunciation Symbols table on page viii, you would have seen that only the second pronunciation matched the pronunciation of *later*. But you might not have even needed to look up the pronunciation symbols, since you would have noticed immediately that the words listed at **ater¹**—words such as *daughter* and *water*—didn't rhyme with *later*. Moving on to **ater²**, you would have seen that no words are listed there at all, but that it instead simply contains the direction "see ATOR." Turning to **ator**, you would have found all the words that rhyme with *later*, regardless of how they were spelled.

Now suppose you need a word to rhyme with *dance*, and you've found the list you were looking for at **ance³**. But maybe none of the words there is quite what you want. This time you're in luck: there are some other possibilities. At the end of the entry, you'll see the following note: "—*also* -s, -'s, *and* -s' *forms of nouns and* -s *forms of verbs listed at* ANT⁵." In other words, at **ant⁵** you can find some nouns and verbs that might do the trick. Turning to **ant⁵**, you see that it lists such nouns as *aunt* and *confidant*, which would rhyme with *dance* in their plural form (*aunts, confidants*), in their possessive form (*aunt's, confidant's*), or in their plural possessive form (*aunts', confidants'*). You would also see such verbs as *enchant* and *gallivant*, which in the first-person singular (*enchants, gallivants*) would also rhyme with *dance*.

Not everyone pronounces all words the same way. So, for example, you will see words like *drawn, gone*, and *yawn* at both **on¹** and **on³**. Usually only one pronunciation will seem right for you.

These few instructions should be all you need to make the best use of the dictionary. We hope you'll keep it close at hand to jog your memory, enlarge your lyrical vocabulary, and expand your poetic ambitions.

Pronunciation Symbols

ə	banana, collide, abut
ə	preceding \l\ and \n\, as in battle, mitten, and eaten; following \l\, \m\, \r\, as in French table, prisme, titre
ər	further, merger, bird
a	mat, gag, sap
ā	day, fade, aorta
ä	bother, cot, father
au̇	now, loud, Faust
b	baby, rib
ch	chin, nature \'nā-chər\
d	did, adder
e	bet, peck, help
ē	fee, easy, media
f	fifty, phone, rough
g	go, big
h	hat, ahead
i	tip, banish, active
ī	site, buy, deny
j	job, gem, judge
k	kin, cook, ache
k̲	German ich, Buch
l	lily, pool
m	murmur, dim
n	no, own
ⁿ	preceding vowel or diphthong is pronounced with the nasal passages open, as in French un bon vin blanc \œⁿ-bōⁿ-vaⁿ-bläⁿ\
ŋ	sing \'siŋ\, finger \'fiŋ-gər\, ink \'iŋk\
ō	bone, know, beau
ȯ	saw, all, caught
ȯi	coin, destroy
p	pepper, lip
r	red, car, rarity
s	source, less
sh	shy, mission, machine, special
t	tie, attack, late
th	thin, ether
t̲h̲	then, either
ü	rule, fool, union \'yün-yən\, few \'fyü\
u̇	pull, would, book
v	vivid, give
w	we, away
y	yard, cue \'kyü\, mute \'myüt\
z	zone, raise
zh	vision, azure \'a-zhər\

A

a¹ \ä\ aah, ah, baa, bah, blah, bra,
fa, ha, la, ma, moi, nah, pa, rah,
shah, ska, spa • aha, Allah, blah-
blah, Casbah, chutzpah, Degas,
faux pas, feta, gaga, goombah,
grandma, grandpa, ha-ha, hoopla,
hurrah, huzzah, oompah, pooh-
bah, ta-ta, Utah, voilà • Akita,
aloha, baklava, brouhaha,
Chippewa, coup d'état, guarana,
la-di-da, ma-and-pa, Mardi Gras,
Omaha, Ottawa, panama,
Panama, polenta, Shangri-la,
tempura • ayatollah, je ne sais
quoi, phenomena
a² \ā\ see AY¹
a³ \ȯ\ see AW¹
aa¹ \a\ see AH³
aa² \ä\ see A¹
aag \äg\ see OG¹
aal¹ \āl\ see AIL
aal² \ȯl\ see ALL¹
aal³ \äl\ see AL¹
aam \äm\ see OM¹
aan \an\ see AN⁵
aans¹ \äns\ see ANCE²
aans² \änz\ see ONZE
aard \ärd\ see ARD¹
aari \är-ē\ see ARI¹
aaron \ar-ən\ see ARON²
aarten \ärt-ᵊn\ see ARTEN
aas \äs\ see OS¹
aatz \ätz\ see OTS
ab¹ \äb\ see OB¹
ab² \äv\ see OLVE²
ab³ \ab\ blab, cab, crab, dab, drab,
fab, flab, gab, grab, jab, lab, Lab,
nab, scab, slab, stab, tab • Ahab,
backstab, confab, prefab, rehab,
smack-dab • baobab, taxicab
aba \äb-ə\ casaba • Ali Baba

abah \äb-ə\ see ABA
abard \ab-ərd\ clapboard, scabbard
—*also* -ed *forms of verbs listed at*
ABBER²
abbard \ab-ərd\ see ABARD
abbas \ab-əs\ see ABBESS
abbat \ab-ət\ see ABIT
abbed¹ \ab-əd\ crabbed, rabid
abbed² \abd\ blabbed, stabbed
—*also* -ed *forms of verbs listed at*
AB³
abber¹ \äb-ər\ see OBBER
abber² \ab-ər\ blabber, crabber,
gabber, grabber, jabber, stabber
• backstabber, land-grabber
abbess \ab-əs\ abbess • Barabbas
abbet \ab-ət\ see ABIT
abbey \ab-ē\ see ABBY
abbie¹ \äb-ē\ see OBBY
abbie² \ab-ē\ see ABBY
abbit \ab-ət\ see ABIT
abbitt \ab-ət\ see ABIT
abble¹ \äb-əl\ bauble, cobble,
gobble, hobble, Kabul, squabble,
wobble
abble² \ab-əl\ Babel, babble, dab-
ble, gabble, rabble, scrabble,
Scrabble • hardscrabble • psy-
chobabble, technobabble
abbler \ab-lər\ babbler, dabbler,
scrabbler
abbly \ab-lē\ see ABLY
abbot \ab-ət\ see ABIT
abby \ab-ē\ abbey, Abby, blabby,
cabbie, crabby, flabby, gabby,
grabby, scabby, shabby, tabby
abe¹ \āb\ babe, nabe
abe² \ab\ see AB³
abe³ \ä-bə\ see ABA
abel \ā-bəl\ see ABLE
aben \äb-ən\ see OBIN

aber[1] \ā-bər\ see ABOR
aber[2] \äb-ər\ see OBBER
abes \ā-bēz\ see ABIES
abi[1] \äb-ē\ see OBBY
abi[2] \əb-ē\ see UBBY
abi[3] \ab-ē\ see ABBY
abid \ab-əd\ see ABBED[1]
abies \ā-bēz\ rabies, scabies • antirabies
—also -s, -'s, and -s' forms of nouns listed at ABY
abile \ab-əl\ see ABBLE[2]
abit \ab-ət\ abbot, habit, rabbit • cohabit, inhabit, jackrabbit
able \ā-bəl\ Abel, able, Babel, cable, fable, gable, label, Mabel, sable, stable, table • disable, enable, round table, timetable, turntable, unable, unstable, worktable
abled \ā-bəld\ fabled, gabled
—also -ed forms of verbs listed at ABLE
ablis \ab-lē\ see ABLY
ably \ab-lē\ chablis, drably
abor \ā-bər\ labor, neighbor, saber • belabor
abot \ab-ət\ see ABIT
abre \äb\ see OB[1]
abul \äb-əl\ see ABBLE[1]
abulous \ab-yə-ləs\ fabulous • fantabulous
aby \ā-bē\ baby, maybe • crybaby
ac[1] \ak\ see ACK[2]
ac[2] \äk\ see OCK[1]
ac[3] \ȯ\ see AW[1]
aca[1] \äk-ə\ see AKA[1]
aca[2] \ak-ə\ alpaca • Strait of Malacca
acable \ak-ə-bəl\ see ACKABLE
acao \ō-kō\ see OCO
acas \ak-əs\ fracas • Caracas
acca[1] \ak-ə\ see ACA[2]
acca[2] \äk-ə\ see AKA[1]
accent \ak-sənt\ accent • relaxant
acchus \ak-əs\ see ACAS
accid \as-əd\ see ACID

acco[1] \ak-ə\ see ACA[1]
acco[2] \ak-ō\ see AKO[2]
ace[1] \ās\ ace, base, bass, brace, case, chase, face, grace, Grace, lace, mace, Mace, pace, place, race, space, Thrace, trace, vase • abase, airspace, backspace, birthplace, boldface, bookcase, bootlace, briefcase, crankcase, debase, deface, disgrace, displace, dogface, efface, embrace, encase, erase, fireplace, footrace, lactase, misplace, nutcase, outpace, outrace, paleface, replace, retrace, shoelace, showcase, showplace, slipcase, someplace, staircase, suitcase, typeface, unlace, wheelbase, workplace, worst-case • about-face, aerospace, anyplace, commonplace, cyberspace, database, double-space, everyplace, hyperspace, interface, interlace, interspace, lowercase, marketplace, pillowcase, single-space, steeplechase, triple-space, uppercase
ace[2] \ā-sē\ see ACY
ace[3] \äs\ see OS[1]
ace[4] \äs\ see OS[1]
ace[5] \äch-ē\ see OTCHY
ace[6] \äs-ə\ see ASA[1]
aceable \ā-sə-bəl\ placeable, traceable • embraceable, erasable, replaceable, untraceable • irreplaceable
acean \ā-shən\ see ATION[1]
aced \āst\ based, baste, chaste, faced, haste, laced, paste, taste, waist, waste • bald-faced, barefaced, bold-faced, distaste, foretaste, lambaste, moonfaced, rad waste, shamefaced, snailpaced, slipcased, stone-faced, straight-faced, straitlaced, toothpaste, two-faced • aftertaste, poker-faced • scissors-and-paste
—also -ed forms of verbs listed at ACE[1]

aceless \ā-sləs\ baseless, faceless, graceless

aceman \ā-smən\ baseman, spaceman

acement \ā-smənt\ basement, casement, placement • displacement, replacement • bargainbasement

acency \ās-ᵊn-sē\ adjacency, complacency

acent \ās-ᵊnt\ adjacent, complacent

aceor \ā-sər\ see ACER¹

aceous \ā-shəs\ see ACIOUS

acer¹ \ā-sər\ pacer, racer, spacer, tracer • defacer, eraser • steeplechaser

acer² \as-ər\ see ASSER

acet \as-ət\ asset, facet, tacit

acewalking \ās-wȯ-kiŋ\ racewalking, spacewalking

acey \ā-sē\ see ACY

ach¹ \äk\ see OCK¹

ach² \ak\ see ACK²

ach³ \ach\ see ATCH³

acha \äch-ə\ cha-cha, gotcha

ache¹ \āk\ see AKE¹

ache² \ash\ see ASH³

ache³ \äch-ē\ see OTCHY

ache⁴ \ach-ē\ see ATCHY

ached \acht\ attached, detached • unattached
　—also -ed *forms of verbs listed at* ATCH³

acher \ā-kər\ see AKER¹

achet \ach-ət\ see ATCHET

achi \äch-ē\ see OTCHY

achian \ā-shən\ see ATION¹

achm \am\ see AM²

achment \ach-mənt\ see ATCHMENT

acho \äch-ō\ macho, nacho • gazpacho

acht \ät\ see OT¹

achtsman \ät-smən\ see OTSMAN

achy \ā-kē\ see AKY

acia \ā-shə\ geisha • acacia, Croatia, Dalmatia

acial \ā-shəl\ facial, glacial, racial, spatial • biracial, palatial • interracial, multiracial

acian \ā-shən\ see ATION¹

acias \ā-shəs\ see ACIOUS

acid \as-əd\ acid, flaccid, placid • antacid, nonacid

acie \ā-shə\ see ACIA

acier¹ \ā-shər\ see ASURE¹

acier² \ā-zhər\ see AZIER

acile \as-əl\ see ASSEL²

acing \ā-siŋ\ bracing, casing, facing, lacing, racing, spacing, tracing • all-embracing, self-effacing
　—also -ing *forms of verbs listed at* ACE¹

acious \ā-shəs\ gracious, spacious • audacious, bodacious, capacious, curvaceous, fallacious, flirtatious, Ignatius, loquacious, mendacious, pugnacious, rapacious, sagacious, tenacious, ungracious, vivacious, voracious • disputatious, efficacious, ostentatious, perspicacious

acis \as-ē\ see ASSY

acist \ā-səst\ see ASSIST

acit \as-ət\ see ACET

acity¹ \as-tē\ see ASTY²

acity² \as-ət-ē\ audacity, capacity, pugnacity, rapacity, sagacity, tenacity, veracity, vivacity • incapacity • overcapacity

acive \ā-siv\ see ASIVE

ack¹ \äk\ see OCK¹

ack² \ak\ back, black, Braque, clack, crack, flak, hack, jack, Jack, knack, lack, Mac, Mack, pack, plaque, quack, rack, sac, sack, shack, slack, smack, snack, stack, tach, tack, thwack, track, wack, whack, wrack, yak • aback, Amtrak, attack, backpack, backtrack, Balzac, bareback, blackjack, blowback, bushwhack, buyback, callback, carjack, coatrack, cognac, come back, comeback, cossack, cut back, cutback, drawback, fall back, fallback, fastback, fast-track, fatback, feedback, flapjack, flashback, fullback, greenback, halfback, half-track, hardback, hatchback, hayrack, haystack, hijack, hold back, horseback, humpback, hunchback, Iraq, jam-pack, jet-black, kayak, Kazak, kickback, knapsack, knickknack, laid-back, macaque, Muzak, one-track, outback, payback, pitch-black, play back, playback, racetrack, ransack, restack, roll back, rollback, runback, sad sack, set back, setback, shellac, sidetrack, sixpack, skyjack, slapjack, Slovak, smokestack, snap back, snowpack, softback, sumac, swayback, swept-back, switchback, tarmac, throwback, thumbtack, ticktack, touchback, unpack, wisecrack, wolf pack • almanac, applejack, back-to-back, bivouac, bric-a-brac, canvasback, cardiac, crackerjack, cul-de-sac, diamondback, gunnysack, Kodiak, lumberjack, maniac, medieval, mommy track, moneyback, multitrack, off-the-rack, paperback, piggyback, Pontiac, quarterback, running back, single-track, Union Jack, zodiac • Adirondack, biofeedback, counterattack, demoniac, insomniac • egomaniac, hypochondriac, pyromaniac, sal ammoniac • megalomaniac

ackable \ak-ə-bəl\ packable, stackable

ackal \ak-əl\ see ACKLE

acked \akt\ see ACT

acken \ak-ən\ blacken, slacken

ackened \ak-ənd\ blackened, slackened

acker \ak-ər\ backer, clacker, cracker, hacker, jacker, lacquer, packer, slacker, stacker, tracker

• attacker, backpacker, bushwhacker, carjacker, firecracker, graham cracker, hijacker, kayaker, linebacker, nutcracker, safecracker, skyjacker, wisecracker • soda cracker
—*also* -er *forms of adjectives listed at* ACK[2]

acket \ik-ət\ bracket, jacket, packet, racket • dust jacket, flak jacket, life jacket, straitjacket • bomber jacket, dinner jacket, yellowjacket

ackey \ak-ē\ see ACKY

ackguard \ag-ərd\ see AGGARD

ackie \ak-ē\ see ACKY

acking \ak-iŋ\ backing, blacking, cracking, packing, smacking, tracking, whacking • bushwhacking, kayaking, meatpacking, nerve-racking, safecracking, skyjacking
—*also* -ing *forms of verbs listed at* ACK[2]

ackish \ak-ish\ blackish, brackish

ackle \ak-əl\ cackle, crackle, grackle, jackal, shackle, tackle • debacle, ramshackle • block and tackle, tabernacle

ackly \ak-lē\ blackly, slackly • abstractly, compactly, exactly • inexactly • matter-of-factly

acko \ak-ō\ see AKO[2]

ackson \ak-sən\ see AXON

acky \ak-ē\ Jackie, khaki, lackey, tacky, wacky • Nagasaki, tickytacky

acle[1] \ik-əl\ see ICKLE

acle[2] \äk\ see OCK[1]

acle[3] \äk-əl\ see OCKLE

acle[4] \ak-əl\ see ACKLE

aco \äk-ō\ see OCCO

acon[1] \ā-kən\ see AKEN

acon[2] \ak-ən\ see ACKEN

acque[1] \ak\ see ACK[2]

acque[2] \äk\ see OCK[1]

acquer \ak-ər\ see ACKER

acques \äk\ see OCK[1]
acre[1] \ā-kər\ see AKER[1]
acre[2] \ak-ər\ see ACKER
act \akt\ act, backed, bract, cracked, fact, packed, pact, stacked, tact, tracked, tract • abstract, attract, class act, compact, contact, contract, crookbacked, detract, distract, enact, exact, extract, humpbacked, hunchbacked, impact, intact, outact, playact, protract, react, refract, retract, subtract, swaybacked, transact • artifact, cataract, counteract, eye contact, inexact, interact, noncontact, overact, reenact, subcompact, subcontract, vacuum-packed • matter-of-fact, overreact, ultracompact
— *also* -ed *forms of verbs listed at* ACK[2]
actable \ak-tə-bəl\ compactible, contractible, distractible, exactable, extractable, intractable, retractable
acte[1] \äkt\ see OCKED
acte[2] \akt\ see ACT
acted \ak-təd\ abstracted, impacted
—*also* -ed *forms of verbs listed at* ACT
acter \ak-tər\ see ACTOR
actery \ak-trē\ see ACTORY
actible \ak-tə-bəl\ see ACTABLE
actic \ak-tik\ tactic • climactic, didactic, galactic • chiropractic • anticlimactic, intergalactic
actical \ak-ti-kəl\ practical, tactical • impractical
actice \ak-təs\ cactus, practice • malpractice
actics \ak-tiks\ tactics
—*also* -s, -'s, *and* -s' *forms of nouns listed at* ACTIC
actile \ak-t°l\ tactile • pterodactyl
acting \ak-tiŋ\ acting • exacting, self-acting

—*also* -ing *forms of verbs listed at* ACT
action \ak-shən\ action, faction, fraction, traction • abstraction, attraction, contraction, diffraction, distraction, extraction, inaction, infraction, live-action, reaction, refraction, retraction, subtraction, transaction • benefaction, chain reaction, counteraction, interaction, satisfaction • dissatisfaction, overreaction, self-satisfaction • affirmative action
actional \ak-shnəl\ factional, fractional
active \ak-tiv\ active • attractive, inactive, proactive, reactive • hyperactive, interactive, overactive, psychoactive, retroactive, unattractive • radioactive
actly \ak-lē\ see ACKLY
actor \ak-tər\ actor, factor, tractor • contractor, detractor, fudge factor, protractor, reactor, subtracter • benefactor, chiropractor, malefactor, subcontractor
actory \ak-trē\ factory • olfactory, refractory • satisfactory • unsatisfactory
actous \ak-təs\ see ACTICE
actress \ak-trəs\ actress • benefactress
actual \ak-chəl\ actual, factual • contractual
acture \ak-chər\ fracture • compound fracture, manufacture, simple fracture
actus \ak-təs\ see ACTICE
actyl \ak-t°l\ see ACTILE
acular \ak-yə-lər\ oracular, spectacular, vernacular • unspectacular
acy \ā-sē\ Basie, lacy, racy, spacey, Stacy, Tracy • prima facie
acyl \as-əl\ see ASSEL[2]
ad[1] \ä\ see A[1]

ad² \äd\ see OD¹

ad³ \ad\ ad, add, bad, bade, brad, cad, Chad, clad, dad, fad, gad, glad, grad, had, lad, mad, pad, plaid, rad, sad, scad, shad, tad, trad • Baghdad, Belgrade, comrade, Conrad, crash pad, crawdad, doodad, dryad, egad, footpad, forbade, gonad, granddad, ironclad, keypad, launchpad, maenad, mouse pad, naiad, nomad, notepad, reclad, scratch pad, Sinbad, touch pad, triad • armorclad, Galahad, Iliad, legal pad, Leningrad, lily pad, Stalingrad, Trinidad, undergrad, Volgograd • jeremiad, olympiad, Upanishad

ada¹ \äd-ə\ nada • armada, cicada, Granada, Masada, Nevada, tostada • empanada, enchilada, yada yada • Sierra Nevada

ada² \äd-ə\ Ada • armada, cicada, Grenada

adable \ād-ə-bəl\ gradable, tradable • persuadable, upgradable • biodegradable

adah \äd-ə\ see ADA²

adal \ad-ᵊl\ see ADDLE

adam \ad-əm\ Adam, madam • macadam

adan¹ \ad-n\ see ADDEN

adan² \äd-n\ see ODDEN

add \ad\ see AD³

adden \ad-ᵊn\ gladden, madden, sadden • Aladdin

adder \ad-ər\ adder, bladder, gladder, ladder, madder, sadder • air bladder, fish ladder, gallbladder, puff adder, stepladder • Jacob's ladder

addie \ad-ē\ see ADDY¹

addik \äd-ik\ see ODIC

addin \ad-ᵊn\ see ADDEN

adding \ad-iŋ\ padding
—also -ing forms of verbs listed at AD³

addish¹ \äd-ish\ see ODDISH

addish² \ad-ish\ see ADISH

addle \ad-ᵊl\ addle, paddle, saddle, straddle • astraddle, dog paddle, sidesaddle, skedaddle, unsaddle

addler¹ \äd-lər\ see ODDLER

addler² \ad-lər\ paddler, straddler

addock¹ \ad-ik\ see ADIC

addock² \ad-ək\ haddock, paddock

addy¹ \ad-ē\ baddie, caddie, caddy, daddy, faddy, laddie, paddy • granddaddy, tea caddy

addy² \äd-ē\ see ODY¹

ade¹ \ād\ aid, aide, bade, blade, braid, fade, glade, grade, jade, laid, made, maid, paid, raid, rayed, shade, spade, staid, suede, they'd, trade, wade • abrade, afraid, air raid, arcade, Band-Aid, barmaid, Belgrade, blockade, bridesmaid, brigade, brocade, cascade, Cascade, charade, clichéd, cockade, crusade, decade, degrade, dissuade, downgrade, evade, eyeshade, fair-trade, first aid, grenade, handmade, handmaid, homemade, housemaid, inlaid, invade, limeade, low-grade, man-made, mermaid, milkmaid, nightshade, nursemaid, old maid, parade, persuade, pervade, postpaid, repaid, sacheted, self-made, stockade, sunshade, switchblade, tirade, unbraid, unmade, unpaid, upbraid, upgrade, waylaid • accolade, Adelaide, aquacade, balustrade, barricade, cannonade, cavalcade, centigrade, chambermaid, colonnade, custom-made, dairymaid, escapade, esplanade, everglade, foreign aid, hearing aid, legal aid, lemonade, marinade, marmalade, masquerade, Medicaid, meter maid, motorcade, orangeade, palisade, promenade, ready-made, renegade, retrograde, serenade, tailor-made, unafraid, underlaid, visual aid

—also -ed *forms of verbs listed at* AY[1]

ade² \äd\ see OD[1]

ade³ \ad\ see AD[3]

ade⁴ \äd-ə\ see ADA[2]

adely \ad-lē\ see ADLY

aden¹ \ād-ᵊn\ laden, maiden • handmaiden • overladen

aden² \äd-ən\ Aden • Baden-Baden

ader \äd-ər\ aider, blader, grader, Nader, nadir, raider, seder, trader • crusader, day trader, evader, fair trader, free trader, horse trader, invader • masquerader, serenader

ades¹ \ād-ēz\ ladies, Hades

ades² \ādz\ AIDS • Cascades • Everglades • jack-of-all-trades *—also* -s, -'s, *and* -s' *forms of nouns and* -s *forms of verbs listed at* ADE[1]

adge \aj\ badge, cadge, hajj, Madge

adger \aj-ər\ badger, cadger

adh \äd\ see OD[1]

adhe \äd-ē\ see ODY[1]

adian \ād-ē-ən\ Acadian, Arcadian, Barbadian, Canadian, circadian • French Canadian, Trinidadian

adic \ad-ik\ haddock • nomadic, sporadic • seminomadic

adie \ād-ē\ see ADY

adies \ād-ēz\ see ADES[1]

ading \ād-iŋ\ braiding, shading • degrading, unfading *—also* -ing *forms of verbs listed at* ADE[1]

adir \ād-ər\ see ADER

adish \ad-ish\ faddish, radish • horseradish

adium \ād-ē-əm\ radium, stadium • palladium

adle \ād-ᵊl\ cradle, dreidel, ladle

adley \ad-lē\ see ADLY

adly \ad-lē\ badly, Bradley, gladly, madly, sadly • comradely

adness \ad-nəs\ badness, gladness, madness, sadness

ado¹ \äd-ō\ bravado, mikado • avocado, Colorado, Coronado, desperado, El Dorado • aficionado • incommunicado, Llano Estacado

ado² \ād-ō\ credo • Alfredo, Laredo, tornado • desperado, El Dorado

ados \ā-dəs\ see ADUS

adrate \äd-rət\ see ODERATE

adrian \ā-drē-ən\ Adrian, Adrienne, Hadrian

adrienne \ā-drē-ən\ see ADRIAN

adt \ät\ see OT[1]

adual \aj-əl\ see AGILE

adus \ā-dəs\ Barbados *—also* -s, -'s, *and* -s' *forms of nouns listed at* ADA[2]

ady \ād-ē\ lady, Sadie, shady • bag lady, first lady, landlady, milady, old lady, saleslady • dragon lady, leading lady, painted lady

ae¹ \ā\ see AY[1]

ae² \ē\ see EE[1]

ae³ \ī\ see Y[1]

aea \ē-ə\ see IA[1]

aean \ē-ən\ see EAN[1]

aedal \ēd-ᵊl\ see EEDLE

aedile \ēd-ᵊl\ see EEDLE

aegis¹ \ā-jəs\ see AGEOUS

aegis² \ē-jəs\ see EGIS

ael \āl\ see AIL

aeli \ā-lē\ see AILY

aelic \al-ik\ see ALLIC

aemon \ē-mən\ see EMON[1]

aen \äⁿ\ see ANT[1]

aena \ē-nə\ see INA[2]

aenia¹ \ē-nē-ə\ see ENIA[1]

aenia² \ē-nyə\ see ENIA[2]

aens \äⁿs\ see ANCE[1]

aeon \ē-ən\ see EAN[1]

aera \ir-ə\ see ERA[2]

aere¹ \er-ē\ see ARY[1]

aere² \ir-ē\ see EARY

aerial¹ \er-ē-əl\ see ARIAL

aerial² \ir-ē-əl\ see ERIAL

aerie[1] \ā-rē\ airy, fairy
aerie[2] \er-ē\ see ARY[1]
aerie[3] \ir-ē\ see EARY
aero[1] \er-ō\ see ERO[2]
aero[2] \ar-ō\ see ARROW[2]
aeroe[1] \ar-ō\ see ARROW[2]
aeroe[2] \er-ō\ see ERO[2]
aery[1] \ā-rē\ see AERIE[1]
aery[2] \er-ē\ see ARY[1]
aesar \ē-zər\ see EASER[2]
aestor \ē-stər\ see EASTER
aet \āt\ see ATE[1]
aetor \ēt-ər\ see EATER[1]
aeum \ē-əm\ see EUM[1]
aeus \ē-əs\ see EUS[1]
af \af\ see APH
afe[1] \āf\ chafe, safe, strafe, waif
  • fail-safe, unsafe, vouchsafe
  • supersafe
afe[2] \af\ see APH
afel \äf-əl\ waffle • falafel • Belgian
  waffle
afer \ā-fər\ strafer, wafer
aff \af\ see APH
affable \af-ə-bəl\ affable, laughable
affe \af\ see APH
affed \aft\ see AFT[2]
affer[1] \äf-ər\ see OFFER[1]
affer[2] \af-ər\ laugher, staffer
affic \af-ik\ see APHIC
affick \af-ik\ see APHIC
affir \af-ər\ see AFFER[2]
affle[1] \äf-əl\ see AFEL
affle[2] \af-əl\ baffle, raffle
affy \af-ē\ daffy, taffy
afic \af-ik\ see APHIC
afir \af-ər\ see AFFER[2]
aft[1] \äft\ waft
  —also -ed *forms of verbs listed at*
  OFF[1]
aft[2] \aft\ aft, craft, daft, draft, graft,
  haft, raft, shaft, Taft, waft • abaft,
  aircraft, campcraft, camshaft,
  crankshaft, downdraft, driveshaft,
  handcraft, life raft, redraft, skin
  graft, spacecraft, stagecraft, state-
  craft, updraft, witchcraft, wood-

craft • fore-and-aft, handicraft,
hovercraft, landing craft, under-
staffed, watercraft • antiaircraft
  —also -ed *forms of verbs listed at*
  APH
after \af-tər\ after, crafter, drafter,
  grafter, laughter, rafter • here-
  after, thereafter • handicrafter
aftsman \af-smən\ craftsman,
  draftsman, raftsman • handcrafts-
  man • handicraftsman
afty \af-tē\ crafty, drafty
ag \ag\ bag, brag, crag, drag, fag,
  flag, gag, hag, jag, lag, mag, nag,
  rag, sag, shag, slag, snag, stag,
  swag, tag, wag • air bag, beanbag,
  brown-bag, dirtbag, dishrag, dog
  tag, do-rag, fleabag, flight bag,
  gasbag, grab bag, handbag, ice
  bag, jet lag, mailbag, mixed bag,
  outbrag, phone tag, price tag,
  ragtag, red flag, sandbag, school-
  bag, sight gag, sleazebag, tea bag,
  time lag, tote bag, washrag, wind-
  bag, zigzag • carpetbag, doggie
  bag, duffel bag, garment bag,
  litterbag, lollygag, punching bag,
  saddlebag, scdlccbag, chopping
  bag, shoulder bag, sleeping bag
  • capture the flag, overnight bag
aga[1] \ä-gə\ bodega, omega
  • rutabaga
aga[2] \eg-ə\ see EGA[1]
agan \ā-gən\ see AGIN
agar[1] \äg-ər\ see OGGER[1]
agar[2] \əg-ər\ see UGGER[1]
agate \ag-ət\ see AGGOT
age[1] \äj\ dodge, lodge, raj • barrage, collage, corsage, dislodge,
  garage, hodgepodge, massage
  • camouflage • espionage
age[2] \äzh\ barrage, collage, corsage, dressage, garage, massage,
  mirage, montage, portage • as-
  semblage, bon voyage, camouflage, decoupage, fuselage,
  sabotage • espionage

age³ \āj\ age, cage, gage, gauge, page, rage, sage, stage, wage • assuage, backstage, birdcage, engage, enrage, front-page, ice age, Iron Age, new age, offstage, onstage, Osage, outrage, rampage, rib cage, road rage, school age, soundstage, spaceage, teenage, uncage, upstage • batting cage, center stage, disengage, legal age, mental age, middle age, multistage, underage • coming-of-age, minimum wage

age⁴ \āg\ see EG¹

age⁵ \äg-ə\ see AGA¹

aged \ājd\ aged, gauged • engaged • middle-aged
—*also* -ed *forms of verbs listed at* AGE³

agel \ā-gəl\ bagel, Hegel • finagle, inveigle

ageless \āj-ləs\ ageless, wageless

agen¹ \ā-gən\ see AGIN

agen² \ä-gən\ see OGGIN

ageous \ā-jəs\ aegis • courageous, contagious, outrageous • advantageous, noncontagious • disadvantageous

ager¹ \ā-jər\ major, pager, sager, wager • New Ager, teenager • golden-ager, middle-ager, preteenager, Ursa Major

ager² \äg-ər\ see OGGER¹

agey \ā-jē\ see AGY

agga \äg-ə\ see AGA¹

aggar \äg-ər\ see OGGER¹

aggard \ag-ərd\ blackguard, haggard, laggard

agged \ag-əd\ cragged, jagged, ragged

agger \ag-ər\ bagger, dagger, lagger, stagger, swagger, • three-bagger, two-bagger • carpetbagger, cloak-and-dagger

aggie \ag-ē\ see AGGY²

agging \ag-iŋ\ bagging, flagging, lagging, nagging • unflagging • carpetbagging
—*also* -ing *forms of verbs listed at* AG

aggle \ag-əl\ gaggle, haggle, straggle, waggle

aggly \ag-lē\ scraggly, straggly

aggot \ag-ət\ agate, maggot

aggy¹ \äg-ē\ see OGGY¹

aggy² \ag-ē\ baggy, craggy, scraggy, shaggy

agh \ä\ see A¹

agi¹ \äg-ē\ see OGGY¹

agi² \ag-ē\ see AGGY²

agian \ā-jən\ see AJUN

agic \aj-ik\ magic, tragic

agile \aj-əl\ agile, fragile, gradual

agin \ā-gən\ pagan, Reagan • Copenhagen

aging \ā-jiŋ\ aging, raging, staging • unaging
—*also* -ing *forms of verbs listed at* AGE³

agion \ā-jən\ see AJUN

agious \ā-jəs\ see AGEOUS

agm \am\ see AM²

agman \ag-mən\ bagman, flagman

agne \ān\ see ANE¹

ago¹ \äg-ō\ Chicago, farrago • Santiago

ago² \ā-gō\ farrago, Tobago, virago • San Diego • Tierra del Fuego

ago³ \äŋ-gō\ see ONGO

agon \ag-ən\ dragon, flagon, wagon • bandwagon, chuck wagon, Pendragon, snapdragon • covered wagon, paddy wagon, station wagon

agonal \ag-ən-ᵊl\ diagonal, hexagonal, octagonal, pentagonal

agoras \ag-ə-rəs\ Protagoras, Pythagoras

agot \ag-ət\ see AGGOT

agrance \ā-grəns\ flagrance, fragrance

agrant \ā-grənt\ flagrant, fragrant, vagrant

agster \ag-stər\ dragster, gagster
agua \äg-wə\ Managua
  • Aconcagua, Nicaragua
ague[1] \āg\ see EG[1]
ague[2] \äg\ see OG[1]
aguey \eg-ē\ see EGGY
agy \ā-jē\ cagey, stagy
ah[1] \ä\ see A[1]
ah[2] \ȯ\ see AW[1]
ah[3] \a\ baa, nah
aha \ä-hä\ aha, Baja
aham \ā-əm\ see AHUM
ahd \äd\ see OD[1]
ahdi \äd-ē\ see ODY[1]
ahdom \äd-əm\ see ODOM
ahib \äb\ see OB[1]
ahl \äl\ see AL[1]
ahler \äl-ər\ see OLLAR
ahlia \ä-lē-ə\ see ALIA
ahma[1] \äm-ə\ see AMA[1]
ahma[2] \am-ə\ see AMA[2]
ahman[1] \äm-ən\ see OMMON
ahman[2] \am-ən\ see AMMON
ahn \än\ see ON[1]
ahms \ämz\ see ALMS
ahnda \än-də\ see ONDA
ahr \är\ see AR[3]
aht \ät\ see OT[1]
ahua \ä-wə\ see AWA[1]
ahum \ā-əm\ Graham, mayhem
ahveh \ä-vā\ see AVE[1]
ai[1] \ā\ see AY[1]
ai[2] \ē\ see EE[1]
ai[3] \ī\ see Y[1]
ai[4] \ȯi\ see OY
a'i \ī\ see Y[1]
aia[1] \ā-ə\ Hosea, Isaiah, Judea
  • Himalaya, Mauna Kea
aia[2] \ī-ə\ see IAH[1]
aiad \ī-əd\ see YAD
aiah \ā-ə\ see AIA[1]
aic \ā-ik\ archaic, Hebraic, Judaic,
  mosaic, prosaic • algebraic, for-
  mulaic
aice \ās\ see ACE[1]
aiche \esh\ see ESH[1]
aid[1] \ād\ see ADE[1]

aid[2] \ed\ see EAD[1]
aid[3] \ad\ see AD[3]
aida \ī-də\ see IDA[2]
aide[1] \ād\ see ADE[1]
aide[2] \īd-ē\ see IDAY
aiden \ād-ᵊn\ see ADEN[1]
aider \ād-ər\ see ADER
aiding \ād-iŋ\ see ADING
aido \ī-dō\ see IDO[1]
aids \ādz\ see ADES[2]
aiety \ā-ət-ē\ see AITY
aif \āf\ see AFE[1]
aig \āg\ see EG[1]
aight \āt\ see ATE[1]
aighten \āt-ᵊn\ see ATEN[1]
aightly \āt-lē\ see ATELY[1]
aign \ān\ see ANE[1]
aigne \ān\ see ANE[1]
aignment \ān-mənt\ see AINMENT
aik \īk\ see IKE[2]
aika \ī-kə\ see ICA[1]
ail \āl\ ail, ale, bail, bale, braille,
  Braille, dale, Dale, fail, flail, frail,
  gale, Gale, Gayle, grail, hail, hale,
  jail, kale, mail, male, nail, pail,
  pale, quail, rail, sail, sale, scale,
  shale, snail, stale, tail, tale, they'll,
  trail, vale, veil, wail, whale, Yale
  • airmail, assail, avail, bake sale,
  betrayal, bewail, blackmail, bob-
  tail, broadtail, bud scale, cattail,
  chain mail, Clydesdale, coattail,
  cocktail, contrail, curtail, derail,
  detail, dovetail, downscale, duck-
  tail, e-mail, entail, exhale, fan
  mail, female, fire sale, fishtail,
  folktale, full-scale, guardrail,
  handrail, hangnail, impale, inhale,
  junk mail, mainsail, outsail, pass-
  fail, pigtail, portrayal, presale,
  prevail, renail, resale, retail, right
  whale, Scottsdale, shirttail, slop
  pail, small-scale, snail mail, sperm
  whale, strong gale, tag sale, tell-
  tale, thumbnail, timescale, toe-
  nail, toothed whale, topsail,
  travail, unveil, upscale, voice

mail, wage scale, wassail, white
sale, white whale, wholesale, yard
sale • Abigail, altar rail, antimale,
Chippendale, Chisholm Trail,
coffin nail, cottontail, express
mail, fairy tale, fingernail, garage
sale, ginger ale, Holy Grail,
humpback whale, killer whale,
monorail, nightingale, old wives'
tale, paper trail, pilot whale,
ponytail, Richter scale, rummage
sale, supersale, swallowtail, tattle-
tale, tooth and nail, vapor trail
• certified mail, Fort Lauderdale,
Oregon Trail, registered mail,
Santa Fe Trail, self-betrayal,
sixpenny nail, tenpenny nail
ailable \ā-lə-bəl\ mailable, sailable,
salable, scalable • available, resal-
able, unsalable • unassailable,
unavailable
ailand \ī-lənd\ see IGHLAND
aile \ī-lē\ see YLY
ailed \āld\ mailed, nailed, sailed,
scaled, tailed, veiled • detailed,
pigtailed, unveiled • ponytailed
—also -ed forms of verbs listed at
AIL
ailer \ā-lər\ bailer, baler, jailer,
mailer, sailor, scaler, tailor, Taylor,
trailer, wailer, whaler • black-
mailer, derailleur, detailer,
e-mailer, house trailer, retailer,
self-mailer, wholesaler • semitrailer
—also -er forms of adjectives listed
at AIL
ailey \ā-lē\ see AILY
ailie \ā-lē\ see AILY
ailiff \ā-ləf\ bailiff, caliph
ailing \ā-liŋ\ failing, mailing, rail-
ing, sailing, veiling, whaling
• boardsailing, prevailing, retail-
ing, unfailing • parasailing
—also -ing forms of verbs listed at
AIL
aille[1] \āl\ see AIL
aille[2] \ī\ see Y[1]

aille[3] \īl\ see ILE[1]
aille[4] \ä-yə\ see AYA[1]
ailles \ī\ see Y[1]
ailleur \ā-lər\ see AILER
ailment \āl-mənt\ ailment • derail-
ment
ailor \ā-lər\ see AILER
ails \ālz\ see ALES[1]
aily \ā-lē\ daily, gaily, scaly • Israeli
• ukulele
aim \ām\ see AME[1]
aimable \ā-mə-bəl\ see AMABLE
aiman \ā-mən\ see AMEN[1]
aimant \ā-mənt\ see AYMENT
aiment \ā-mənt\ see AYMENT
aimer \ā-mər\ framer, gamer,
lamer, tamer • disclaimer, pro-
claimer • Hall of Famer
aimless \ām-ləs\ see AMELESS
ain[1] \ā-ən\ see AYAN[1]
ain[2] \ān\ see ANE[1]
ain[3] \en\ see EN[1]
ain[4] \in\ see IN[1]
ain[5] \īn\ see INE[1]
ain[6] \aⁿ\ see IN[4]
aina \ī-nə\ see INA[1]
ainable \ā-nə-bəl\ stainable, train-
able • attainable, containable,
explainable, obtainable, restrain-
able, sustainable • unattainable,
uncontainable, unobtainable
aine[1] \ān\ see ANE[1]
aine[2] \en\ see EN[1]
ained \ānd\ brained, caned,
craned, drained, grained, pained,
stained, strained, veined • bird-
brained, bloodstained, coarse-
grained, contained, harebrained,
ingrained, lamebrained,
restrained, tearstained, unfeigned,
unstained, untrained • feather-
brained, multipaned, scatter-
brained, self-contained,
unexplained, unrestrained
—also -ed forms of verbs listed at
ANE[1]
ainer \ā-nər\ drainer, gainer,

planer, stainer, strainer, trainer
• abstainer, campaigner, com-
plainer, container, explainer, no-
brainer, obtainer, retainer
• aquaplaner, entertainer
—*also* -er *forms of adjectives listed
at* ANE[1]

ainful \ān-fəl\ baneful, gainful,
painful • disdainful

aininess \ā-nē-nəs\ braininess,
graininess

aining \ā-niŋ\ complaining, sustaining, weight training • self-
sustaining, uncomplaining
—*also* -ing *forms of verbs listed at*
ANE[1]

ainless \ān-ləs\ brainless, painless,
stainless

ainly \ān-lē\ mainly, plainly,
sanely, vainly • humanely, in-
sanely, profanely, ungainly • in-
humanely

ainment \ān-mənt\ arraignment,
attainment, containment, detain-
ment • edutainment, entertain-
ment, infotainment,
self-containment

aino \ī-nō\ see INO[1]

ains \ānz\ reins • cremains, Great
Plains, remains
—*also* -s, -'s, *and* -s' *forms of nouns
and* -s *forms of verbs listed at* ANE[1]

aint \ānt\ ain't, faint, feint, mayn't,
paint, quaint, saint, taint • ac-
quaint, complaint, constraint,
greasepaint, oil paint, repaint,
restraint, war paint • head restraint, patron saint, plaster saint,
self-restraint • Latter-Day Saint,
luminous paint

ain't \ānt\ see AINT

ainting \ān-tiŋ\ oil painting, wall
painting • finger painting
—*also* -ing *forms of verbs listed at*
AINT

aintly \ānt-lē\ faintly, quaintly,
saintly

ainy \ā-nē\ brainy, grainy, rainy,
zany • Khomeini • Allegheny

ainz \īnz\ see INES[3]

aipse \āps\ see APES

air[1] \er\ see ARE[4]

air[2] \ir\ see IRE[1]

aira \ī-rə\ see YRA

aird \erd\ see AIRED

aire[1] \er\ see ARE[4]

aire[2] \ir\ see EER[2]

aire[3] \ir\ see IRE[1]

aired \erd\ laird • fair-haired, im-
paired, long-haired, prepared,
shorthaired, unpaired, wirehaired
• multilayered, underprepared,
unimpaired
—*also* -ed *forms of verbs listed at*
ARE[4]

airer \er-ər\ see EARER[1]

aires[1] \er\ see ARE[4]

aires[2] \ar-ēs\ see ARES[2]

airess[1] \er-əs\ see ERROUS

airess[2] \ar-əs\ see ARIS[2]

airie \er-ē\ see ARY[1]

airing \er-iŋ\ see ARING[1]

airish \er-ish\ see ARISH[1]

airist \er-əst\ see ARIST

airly \er-lē\ barely, fairly, rarely,
squarely

airn \ern\ see ERN[1]

airo \ī-rō\ see YRO[1]

airs \erz\ theirs • downstairs,
nowheres, somewheres, up-
stairs • foreign affairs, musical
chairs
—*also* -s, -'s, *and* -s' *forms of
nouns and* -s *forms of verbs listed
at* ARE[4]

airy[1] \er-ē\ see ARY[1]

airy[2] \ā-rē\ see AERIE[1]

ais \ā\ see AY[1]

aisal[1] \ā-zəl\ see ASAL

aisal[2] \ī-səl\ see ISAL[1]

aisant \ās-ᵊnt\ see ACENT

aise[1] \āz\ see AZE[1]

aise[2] \ez\ see AYS[1]

aiser[1] \ā-zər\ see AZER

aiser[2] \ī-zər\ see IZER
aisian \ā-zhən\ see ASION
aisin \āz-ᵊn\ see AZON
aising \ā-ziŋ\ blazing, glazing,
   hazing, phrasing • amazing, ap-
   praising, fund-raising, hair-rais-
   ing, stargazing, trailblazing
   • crystal gazing
   —*also* -ing *forms of verbs listed at*
   AZE[1]
aisle \īl\ see ILE[1]
aisley \āz-lē\ paisley, nasally
aisne \ān\ see ANE[1]
aisse \ās\ see ACE[1]
aisson \ās-ᵊn\ see ASON[1]
aist[1] \ā-əst\ see AYEST
aist[2] \āst\ see ACED
aist[3] \äst\ see OST[1]
aisy \ā-zē\ see AZY
ait[1] \ā\ see AY[1]
ait[2] \āt\ see ATE[1]
ait[3] \īt\ see ITE[1]
ait[4] \at\ see AT[5]
aite \īt\ see ITE[1]
aited \āt-əd\ see ATED
aiten \āt-ᵊn\ see ATEN[1]
aiter \āt-ər\ see ATOR
aith \āth\ eighth, faith, Faith,
   wraith • good faith
aithe \āth\ see AITH
aiti \āt-ē\ see ATY
aitian \ā-shən\ see ATION[1]
aiting \āt-iŋ\ see ATING
aitly \āt-lē\ see ATELY[1]
aitor \āt-ər\ see ATOR
aitour \āt-ər\ see ATOR
aity \ā-ət-ē\ deity, gaiety • spontaneity
aius \ī-əs\ see IAS[1]
aiva \ī-və\ see IVA[1]
aive \āv\ see AVE[2]
aix \ā\ see AY[1]
aize \āz\ see AZE[1]
aj \äj\ see AGE[1]
aja[1] \ä-hä\ see AHA
aja[2] \ī-ə\ see IAH[1]
ajan \ā-jən\ see AJUN

ajj \aj\ see ADGE
ajor \ā-jər\ see AGER[1]
ajun \ā-jən\ Cajun • contagion
ak[1] \äk\ see OCK[1]
ak[2] \ak\ see ACK[2]
aka[1] \äk-ə\ Dhaka, Oaxaca, Osaka
   • Lake Titicaca
aka[2] \ak-ə\ see ACA[2]
akable \ā-kə-bəl\ breakable, shak-
   able • mistakable, nonbreakable,
   unbreakable • unmistakable
akan \ak-ən\ see ACKEN
akar \äk-ər\ see OCKER
ake[1] \āk\ ache, bake, Blake, brake,
   break, cake, drake, Drake, fake,
   flake, Jake, lake, make, quake,
   rake, sake, shake, sheikh, slake,
   snake, spake, stake, steak, take,
   wake • air brake, awake, back-
   ache, beefsteak, caretake, cheese-
   cake, cheesesteak, clambake,
   cupcake, daybreak, disc brake,
   earache, earthquake, fast break,
   firebreak, fish cake, forsake,
   fruitcake, green snake, hand
   brake, handshake, headache,
   heartache, heartbreak, hotcake,
   housebreak, intake, jailbreak,
   keepsake, king snake, milk snake,
   mistake, muckrake, namesake,
   opaque, outbreak, outtake, pancake, partake, pound cake, pre-
   bake, rat snake, remake, retake,
   rewake, seaquake, sea snake,
   shortcake, snowflake, sponge
   cake, toothache, uptake, wind-
   break • bellyache, coffee break,
   coral snake, Crater Lake, double
   take, garter snake, give-and-take,
   Great Salt Lake, Great Slave
   Lake, griddle cake, hognose
   snake, johnnycake, make-or-
   break, minute steak, overtake,
   parking brake, patty-cake, piece
   of cake, plumber's snake, rat-
   tlesnake, station break, stom-
   achache, undertake, water snake,

wedding cake • Salisbury steak, tension headache, upside-down cake • emergency brake, Lady of the Lake, potato pancake

ake² \ak\ see ACK²

ake³ \äk-ē\ see OCKY

aked \ākt\ awaked, half-baked, sunbaked
—also -ed *forms of verbs listed at* AKE[1]

aken \ā-kən\ bacon, Macon, shaken, taken, waken • awaken, forsaken, mistaken, retaken, unshaken • godforsaken, over-taken, undertaken

aker¹ \ā-kər\ acre, baker, breaker, faker, maker, Quaker, shaker • backbreaker, caretaker, car-maker, dressmaker, filmmaker, gill raker, glassmaker, heartbreaker, homemaker, house-breaker, icebreaker, jawbreaker, kingmaker, lawbreaker, lawmaker, mapmaker, match-maker, muckraker, noisemaker, pacemaker, peacemaker, print-maker, sailmaker, saltshaker, shirtmaker, shoemaker, snow-maker, steelmaker, strikebreaker, tiebreaker, toolmaker, watch-maker, windbreaker, winemaker, wiseacre • automaker, bellyacher, circuit breaker, coffee maker, moviemaker, papermaker, pepper shaker, troublemaker, undertaker • cabinetmaker, policymaker

aker² \ak-ər\ see ACKER

akery \ā-krē\ bakery, fakery

akes \āks\ cornflakes, Great Lakes, sweepstakes
—also -s, -'s, *and* -s' *forms of nouns and* -s *forms of verbs listed at* AKE[1]

ake-up \ā-kəp\ break up, breakup, make up, makeup, rake up, shake-up, shake up, take up, wake-up

akey \ā-kē\ see AKY

akh \äk\ see OCK[1]

aki¹ \äk-ē\ see OCKY

aki² \ak-ē\ see ACKY

akian \äk-ē-ən\ see OCKIAN

aking \ak-iŋ\ see ACKING

ako¹ \äk-ō\ see OCCO

ako² \ak-ō\ wacko • tobacco

aky \ā-kē\ achy, cakey, flaky, shaky, snaky • headachy

al¹ \äl\ doll, loll, sol • atoll, Baikal, cabal, chorale, Nepal, real • aerosol, femme fatale, parasol, Portugal, protocol, Senegal • Ne-anderthal

al² \el\ see EL[1]

al³ \ȯl\ see ALL[1]

al⁴ \al\ gal, pal, Val • canal, chorale, corral, decal, locale, morale • femme fatale, rationale • Guadalcanal

ala¹ \äl-ä\ à la, Allah, gala

ala² \äl-ə\ Allah, gala • Kampala, koala, Valhalla • ayotollah, Guatemala

ala³ \ā-lə\ gala • Venezuela

ala⁴ \al-ə\ Allah, gala • Valhalla

alable \ā-lə-bəl\ see AILABLE

alace \al-əs\ see ALIS²

alad \al-əd\ see ALID²

alam \äl-əm\ see OLUMN

alan \al-ən\ see ALLON

alance \al-əns\ balance, valance • imbalance, rebalance • counter-balance, overbalance, platform balance

alap \al-əp\ see ALLOP²

alar \ā-lər\ see AILER

alary \al-ə-rē\ calorie, gallery, salary, Valerie • rogues' gallery

alas \al-əs\ see ALIS²

alate \al-ət\ see ALLET²

ald \ȯld\ bald, scald, walled • so-called • Archibald, Buchenwald, coveralled
—also -ed *forms of verbs listed at* ALL[1]

ald² \ȯlt\ see ALT

alder \ȯl-dər\ alder, balder

ale¹ \ā-lē\ see AILY

ale² \āl\ see AIL

ale³ \äl\ see AL¹

ale⁴ \al\ see AL⁴

ale⁵ \äl-ē\ see OLLY¹

ale⁶ \al-ē\ see ALLY⁴

alea \ā-lē-ə\ see ALIA

aleck¹ \el-ik\ see ELIC

aleck² \al-ik\ see ALLIC

aled \āld\ see AILED

aleigh¹ \äl-ē\ see OLLY¹

aleigh² \ȯl-ē\ see AWLY

alement \āl-mənt\ see AILMENT

alen \ā-lən\ see OLLEN⁵

alent \al-ənt\ see ALLANT

alep \al-əp\ see ALLOP²

aler¹ \ā-lər\ see AILER

aler² \äl-ər\ see OLLAR

alerie \al-ə-rē\ see ALARY

ales¹ \ālz\ sales, Wales • entrails
• New South Wales, Prince of
Wales • cat-o'-nine-tails
—*also -s, -'s, and -s' forms of
nouns and -s forms of verbs listed
at* AIL

ales² \äl-əs\ see OLIS

alet \al-ət\ see ALLET²

alette \al-ət\ see ALLET²

aley \ā-lē\ see AILY

alf \af\ see APH

alfa \al-fə\ see ALPHA

algia \al-jə\ neuralgia, nostalgia

ali¹ \äl-ē\ see OLLY¹

ali² \al-ē\ see ALLY⁴

ali³ \ȯ-lē\ see AWLY

ali⁴ \ā-lē\ see AILY

alia \ā-lē-ə\ Australia, azalea, re-
galia • bacchanalia • parapherna-
lia

alian¹ \ā-lē-ən\ alien • Australian,
mammalian • bacchanalian
• Episcopalian

alian² \al-yən\ see ALLION

alic \al-ik\ see ALLIC

alice \al-əs\ see ALIS²

alid¹ \äl-əd\ see OLID

alid² \al-əd\ ballad, pallid, salad,
valid • invalid • Caesar salad,
Waldorf salad

alien \ā-lē-ən\ see ALIAN¹

aling \ā-liŋ\ see AILING

alinist \äl-ə-nəst\ see OLONIST

alinn \al-ən\ see ALLON

alion¹ \ā-lē-ən\ see ALIAN¹

alion² \al-yən\ see ALLION

aliph \ā-ləf\ see AILIFF

alis¹ \ā-ləs\ see AYLESS

alis² \al-əs\ Alice, callous, callus,
chalice, Dallas, malice, palace
• aurora borealis

alist \al-əst\ ballast, callused

ality¹ \äl-ət-ē\ jollity, quality
• equality, frivolity • coequality,
inequality

ality² \al-ət-ē\ brutality, fatality,
finality, formality, frugality, legal-
ity, locality, mentality, morality,
mortality, neutrality, rascality,
reality, totality, vitality • abnor-
mality, actuality, amorality, cor-
diality, factuality, functionality,
generality, geniality, hospitality,
illegality, immorality, immortal-
ity, informality, joviality, logical-
ity, musicality, nationality,
personality, practicality, punctu-
ality, rationality, sensuality, sexu-
ality, technicality, triviality,
unreality • congeniality, eventual-
ity, impartiality, impracticality,
irrationality, municipality, origi-
nality, sentimentality, spirituality,
split personality, theatricality,
universality • artificiality, confi-
dentiality, constitutionality, indi-
viduality, unconventionality,
virtual reality

alk \ȯk\ balk, caulk, chalk, gawk,
hawk, squawk, stalk, talk, walk
• back talk, Black Hawk, board-
walk, cakewalk, catwalk, corn-
stalk, crosswalk, eyestalk, fish

hawk, jaywalk, leafstalk, marsh hawk, Mohawk, moonwalk, nighthawk, Norfolk, outtalk, pep talk, racewalk, ropewalk, shoptalk, sidewalk, sleepwalk, small talk, space walk, sweet-talk, trash talk • baby talk, double-talk, Kitty Hawk, pillow talk, power walk, sparrow hawk, toma-hawk

alker \ȯ-kər\ gawker, hawker, squawker, stalker, walker • jay-walker, sleepwalker, spacewalker • double-talker

alkie \ȯ-kē\ balky, chalky, gawky, gnocchi, stalky, talky • Milwau-kee • walkie-talkie

alking \ȯ-kiŋ\ caulking, walking • racewalking, spacewalking —*also* -ing *forms of verbs listed at* ALK

alkland \ȯk-lənd\ see AUCKLAND

alky \ȯ-kē\ see ALKIE

all¹ \ȯl\ all, awl, ball, bawl, brawl, call, crawl, doll, drawl, fall, gall, hall, haul, mall, maul, pall, Paul, Gaul, scrawl, shawl, small, sprawl, squall, stall, tall, trawl, wall, y'all, yawl • and all, appall, air ball, at all, atoll, AWOL, baseball, Baikal, beach ball, beanball, befall, bird-call, blackball, brick wall, catcall, cell wall, close call, cornball, cure-all, curveball, de Gaulle, dodgeball, downfall, drywall, duck call, eight ball, enthrall, eyeball, fair ball, fastball, fireball, fire wall, foosball, football, fore-stall, foul ball, free-fall, game ball, golf ball, goofball, googol, hair ball, handball, hardball, holdall, house call, install, John Paul, jump ball, landfall, meat-ball, menthol, mess hall, moth-ball, Nepal, nightfall, oddball, paintball, pinball, pitfall, pratfall, prayer shawl, puffball, rainfall, rainsquall, recall, roll call, Saint Paul, screwball, seawall, short-haul, shortfall, sidewall, sleaze-ball, slimeball, snowball, snowfall, softball, sour ball, spitball, stick-ball, stonewall, stone wall, strip mall, tell-all, toll call, town hall, U-Haul, windfall, withdrawal, you-all • above all, aerosol, after all, alcohol, all in all, basketball, borough hall, butterball, cannon-ball, carryall, caterwaul, city hall, climbing wall, conference call, coverall, crystal ball, curtain call, Donegal, ethanol, free-for-all, gasohol, judgment call, know-it-all, knuckleball, methanol, music hall, Montreal, off-the-wall, over-all, overhaul, paddleball, parasol, protocol, racquetball, reinstall, Senegal, shopping mall, study hall, superball, tetherball, unin-stall, urban sprawl, volleyball, wake-up call, wall-to-wall, warts-and-all, waterfall, wherewithal • cholesterol, hole-in-the-wall, medicine ball, Neanderthal, total recall

all² \äl\ see AL¹

all³ \al\ see AL⁴

alla¹ \äl-ə\ see ALA²

alla² \al-ə\ see ALLOW⁴

allace \äl-əs\ see OLIS

allad \al-əd\ see ALID²

allage \al-ə-jē\ see ALOGY²

allah¹ \äl-ä\ see ALA¹

allah² \äl-ə\ see ALA²

allah³ \al-ə\ see ALLOW⁴

allan \al-ən\ see ALLON

allant \al-ənt\ gallant, talent

allas \al-əs\ see ALIS²

allast \al-əst\ see ALIST

alle¹ \al\ see AL⁴

alle² \al-ē\ see ALLY⁴

alle³ \äl-ē\ see OLLY¹

alled \ȯld\ see ALD¹

allee \al-ē\ see ALLY⁴

allen \al-ən\ see ALLON
aller[1] \ȯ-lər\ bawler, brawler, caller, crawler, drawler, hauler, mauler, scrawler, smaller, squaller, taller, trawler • installer, night crawler • melon baller
aller[2] \al-ər\ pallor, valor
alles \ī-əs\ see IAS[1]
allet[1] \äl-ət\ see OLLET
allet[2] \al-ət\ ballot, mallet, palate, palette, pallet, valet • secret ballot
alley \al-ē\ see ALLY[4]
alli \al-ē\ see ALLY[4]
allic \al-ik\ Gaelic, italic • metallic, smart aleck • nonmetallic
allid \al-əd\ see ALID[2]
allie \al-ē\ see ALLY[4]
alling \ȯ-liŋ\ calling, drawling, falling, galling, hauling, mauling, Pauling, stalling • appalling, name-calling
—also -ing forms of verbs listed at ALL[1]
allion \al-yən\ scallion, stallion • battalion, Italian, medallion, rapscallion
allis[1] \al-əs\ see ALIS[2]
allis[2] \al-ē\ see ALLY[4]
allis[3] \äl-əs\ see OLIS
allish \ȯ-lish\ smallish, tallish
allit \ä-lət\ see OLLET
allith[1] \äl-əs\ see OLIS
allith[2] \äl-ət\ see OLLET
allo \äl-ō\ see OLLOW[1]
allon \al-ən\ Alan, Allen, gallon, talon
allop[1] \äl-əp\ see OLLOP
allop[2] \al-əp\ gallop, scallop • bay scallop, sea scallop
allor \al-ər\ see ALLER[2]
allory \al-ə-rē\ see ALARY
allot \al-ət\ see ALLET[2]
allous \al-əs\ see ALIS[2]
allow[1] \el-ō\ see ELLO
allow[2] \äl-ə\ see ALA[2]
allow[3] \äl-ō\ see OLLOW[1]
allow[4] \al-ō\ callow, fallow, hallow, shallow, tallow • marshmallow
allows \al-ōz\ gallows
—also -s, -'s, and -s' forms of nouns listed at ALLOW[4]
alls \ȯlz\ Angel Falls • Niagara Falls, Yellowstone Falls • Victoria Falls, Yosemite Falls
—also -s, -'s, and -s' forms of nouns and -s forms of verbs listed at ALL[1]
allused \al-əst\ see ALIST
ally[1] \ā-lē\ see AILY
ally[2] \äl-ē\ see OLLY[1]
ally[3] \ȯ-lē\ see AWLY
ally[4] \al-ē\ alley, dally, galley, rally, Sally, tally, valley • blind alley, Death Valley, finale, Nepali • Central Valley, dillydally, Great Rift Valley, Mexicali, shilly-shally, Tin Pan Alley • lily of the valley, Yosemite Valley
allyn \al-ən\ see ALLON
alm \äm\ see OM[1]
almar \äm-ər\ see OMBER[1]
almer \äm-ər\ see OMBER[1]
almily \äm-ə-lē\ see OMALY
almish \äm-ish\ see AMISH[1]
almist \äm-ist\ psalmist • Islamist
almon \am-ən\ see AMMON
alms \ämz\ alms, Brahms, Psalms
—also -s, -'s, and -s' forms of nouns and -s forms of verbs listed at OM[1]
almy \äm-ē\ see AMI[1]
alo \äl-ō\ see OLLOW[1]
aloe \al-ō\ see ALLOW[4]
alogist \äl-ə-jəst\ see OLOGIST
alogy[1] \äl-ə-jē\ see OLOGY
alogy[2] \al-ə-jē\ analogy • mineralogy
alom \äl-əm\ see OLUMN
alon \al-ən\ see ALLON
alop \al-əp\ see ALLOP[2]
alor[1] \äl-ər\ see OLLAR
alor[2] \al-ər\ see ALLER[2]
alorie \al-ə-rē\ see ALARY
alory \al-ə-rē\ see ALARY

alp \alp\ alp, scalp
alpha \al-fə\ alpha • alfalfa
alque \ȯk\ see ALK
alsa \ȯl-sə\ balsa, salsa
alse \ȯls\ false, waltz
alt \ȯlt\ fault, halt, malt, salt, vault, volt, Walt • asphalt, assault, basalt, cobalt, default, exalt, no-fault, pole vault, rock salt • garlic salt, somersault, table salt • San Andreas Fault
alta \äl-tə\ Malta, Yalta
altar \ȯl-tər\ see ALTER
alter \ȯl-tər\ altar, alter, falter, halter, vaulter, Walter • Gibraltar, pole-vaulter
alti \ȯl-tē\ see ALTY
alting \ȯl-tiŋ\ halting, salting, vaulting
—also -ing forms of verbs listed at ALT
altless \ȯlt-ləs\ faultless, saltless
alto \al-tō\ alto • contralto • Palo Alto
alty \ȯl-tē\ faulty, salty
altz \ȯls\ see ALSE
alus¹ \ä-ləs\ see AYLESS
alus² \al-əs\ see ALIS²
alve¹ \äv\ see OLVE²
alve² \alv\ salve, valve • bivalve • safety valve, univalve
alve³ \av\ calve, halve, have, salve
alvin \al-vən\ Alvin, Calvin
aly \al-ē\ see ALLY⁴
alysis \al-ə-səs\ analysis, dialysis, paralysis
am¹ \äm\ see OM¹
am² \am\ am, clam, cram, dam, damn, damned, Graham, gram, ham, jam, jamb, lam, lamb, ma'am, Pam, ram, Sam, scam, scram, sham, slam, spam, swam, yam • exam, grand slam, imam, logjam, madame, Mailgram, program, webcam • Abraham, Amsterdam, Boulder Dam, cablegram, centigram, cryptogram, diagram, diaphragm, epigram, giant clam, hard-shell clam, hexagram, hologram, Hoover Dam, kilogram, milligram, Minicam, monogram, pentagram, pictogram, reprogram, Rotterdam, self-exam, soft-shell clam, Suriname, telegram, Uncle Sam • Grand Coulee Dam, ideogram, Virginia ham • parallelogram
ama¹ \äm-ə\ Brahma, comma, drama, lama, llama, mama, momma • pajama • Dalai Lama, diorama, docudrama, Fujiyama, melodrama, panorama, Suriname, Yokohama
ama² \am-ə\ Brahma, drama, gamma, mamma • da Gama, Miami, pajama • Alabama, diorama, docudrama, melodrama, panorama
amable \ā-mə-bəl\ blamable, claimable, framable, nameable, tamable
aman¹ \ā-mən\ see AMEN¹
aman² \äm-ən\ see OMMON
amant \ā-mənt\ see AYMENT
amash \äm-ish\ see AMISH¹
amateur \am-ət-ər\ see AMETER
amba \äm-bə\ mamba, samba
ambar¹ \äm-bər\ see OMBER²
ambar² \am-bər\ amber, Amber, clamber, timbre
amber¹ \am-bər\ see AMBAR²
amber² \am-ər\ see AMMER
ambia \am-bē-ə\ Gambia, Zambia
amble¹ \äm-bəl\ see EMBLE
amble² \am-bəl\ amble, bramble, gamble, ramble, scramble • unscramble
ambler \am-blər\ gambler, rambler, scrambler • unscrambler
ambol \am-bəl\ see AMBLE²
ame¹ \ām\ aim, blame, came, claim, dame, fame, flame, frame, game, lame, maim, name, same, shame, tame • A-frame, acclaim,

aflame, airframe, ball game, became, big game, big-name, board game, brand name, code name, declaim, defame, disclaim, exclaim, first name, inflame, last name, mainframe, mind game, misname, nickname, no-name, pen name, place-name, postgame, pregame, proclaim, reclaim, reframe, rename, selfsame, surname, time frame, trade name, war game • all the same, arcade game, counterclaim, domain name, family name, given name, Hall of Fame, just the same, maiden name, overcame, singing game, waiting game • baptismal name, name of the game, video game

ame² \äm\ see OM¹

ame³ \am\ see AM²

ame⁴ \äm-ə\ see AMA¹

ameable \ā-mə-bəl\ see AMABLE

amed \āmd\ named • ashamed • unashamed
—*also* -ed *forms of verbs listed at* AME¹

amel \am-əl\ see AMMEL

ameless \ām-ləs\ aimless, blameless, nameless, shameless

amely \ām-lē\ gamely, lamely, namely, tamely

amen¹ \ā-mən\ caiman, Cayman, Haman, layman, shaman, stamen, Yemen • Grand Cayman, highwayman

amen² \äm-ən\ see OMMON

ameness \ām-nəs\ lameness, sameness, tameness • selfsameness

ament \ā-mənt\ see AYMENT

amer \ā-mər\ see AIMER

ames \āmz\ James • fun and games • Olympic Games
—*also* -s, -'s, *and* -s' *forms of nouns and* -s *forms of verbs listed at* AME¹

ameter \am-ət-ər\ amateur • diam-

eter, hexameter, parameter, pentameter, tetrameter

amfer \am-pər\ see AMPER²

ami¹ \äm-ē\ balmy, mommy, palmy, swami, Tommy • pastrami, salami, tsunami • origami

ami² \am-ə\ see AMA²

ami³ \am-ē\ see AMMY

amic¹ \ō-mik\ see OMIC²

amic² \am-ik\ ceramic, dynamic • panoramic, undynamic • aerodynamic, thermodynamic

amics \äm-iks\ see OMICS

amie¹ \ā-mē\ Amy, Jamie, Mamie • cockamamy

amie² \am-ē\ see AMMY

amil¹ \äm-əl\ see OMMEL¹

amil² \am-əl\ see AMMEL

amin \am-ən\ see AMMON

amine \am-ən\ see AMMON

aming \ā-miŋ\ flaming, framing, gaming
—*also* -ing *forms of verbs listed at* AME¹

amish¹ \äm-ish\ Amish • schoolmarmish

amish² \am-ish\ Amish, famish

amist \äm-əst\ see ALMIST

amity \am-ət-ē\ amity • calamity

amma \am-ə\ see AMA²

ammable \am-ə-bəl\ flammable • inflammable, nonflammable, programmable • diagrammable

ammal \am-əl\ see AMMEL

ammar \am-ər\ see AMMER

amme \am\ see AM²

ammel \am-əl\ camel, mammal • enamel

ammer \am-ər\ clamber, clamor, crammer, glamour, grammar, hammer, jammer, scammer, slammer, spammer, stammer, yammer • clawhammer, enamor, jackhammer, programmer, sledgehammer • ball-peen hammer, yellowhammer

ammes \äm-əs\ see OMISE

ammie \am-ē\ see AMMY

amming \am-iŋ\ damning • programming
—*also* -ing *forms of verbs listed at* AM²

ammon \am-ən\ famine, salmon • backgammon, examine • crossexamine

ammy \am-ē\ chamois, clammy, Grammy, jammy, mammy, Sammy, whammy • Miami • double whammy

amn \am\ see AM²

amned \am\ see AM²

amning \am-iŋ\ see AMMING

amois \am-ē\ see AMMY

amon¹ \ā-mən\ see AMEN¹

amon² \äm-ən\ see OMMON

amor \am-ər\ see AMMER

amorous \am-rəs\ amorous, clamorous, glamorous

amos \ā-məs\ see AMOUS

amour \am-ər\ see AMMER

amous \ā-məs\ Amos, famous • ignoramus, Nostradamus

amp¹ \ämp\ see OMP¹

amp² \a\ see ANT¹

amp³ \amp\ amp, camp, champ, clamp, cramp, damp, lamp, ramp, scamp, stamp, tamp, tramp, vamp • arc lamp, boot camp, break camp, C-clamp, death camp, floor lamp, food stamp, off-ramp, onramp, revamp, sunlamp, tax stamp, time-stamp, unclamp • labor camp, postage stamp, rubber-stamp, writer's cramp

amper¹ \äm-pər\ see OMPER

amper² \am-pər\ camper, damper, hamper, pamper, scamper, tamper • happy camper

amphor \am-fər\ see AMFER

ampi¹ \äm-pē\ see OMPY

ampi² \am-pē\ see AMPY

ample \am-pəl\ ample, sample, trample • example • for example

ampy \am-pē\ crampy, scampi

amus¹ \ā-məs\ see AMOUS

amus² \äm-əs\ see OMISE

amy \ā-mē\ see AMIE¹

an¹ \äⁿ\ see ANT¹

an² \än\ see ON¹

an³ \ən\ see UN¹

an⁴ \aŋ\ see ANG²

an⁵ \an\ an, Ann, ban, bran, can, clan, Dan, fan, Jan, man, Nan, pan, plan, ran, scan, span, Stan, tan, van, Van • adman, afghan, Afghan, ape-man, Batman, bedpan, began, best man, Bhutan, birdman, boss man, caftan, caiman, CAT scan, caveman, Cayman, Cèzanne, chessman, Cheyenne, Chopin, deadpan, Diane, dishpan, divan, doorman, dustpan, flight plan, frogman, game plan, G-man, Greenspan, headman, he-man, Iran, Japan, jazzman, Joanne, Koran, life span, Luanne, madman, mailman, Milan, milkman, newsman, oilcan, oilman, oil pan, old man, oneman, outran, pecan, plowman, point man, postman, Queen Anne, Qur'an, rattan, Roseanne, routeman, Roxanne, Ruthann, Saipan, sandman, saucepan, sedan, snowman, spaceman, Spokane, spray can, straight man, strongman, stuntman, Sudan, suntan, Suzanne, Tarzan, tin can, toucan, trainman, trashman, vegan, Walkman, wingspan, wise man, yes-man • also-ran, anchorman, bogeyman, boogeyman, businessman, cameraman, caravan, cattleman, countryman, defenseman, family man, frying pan, garageman, garbageman, handyman, Julianne, Kazakhstan, Ku Klux Klan, Kurdistan, Kyrgyzstan, leading man, man-to-man, Marianne, master plan, middleman, minivan, minuteman, mountain man, muscleman, ombudsman, overran, Pakistan, Parmesan, partisan, Peter Pan, plainclothesman, Ramadan, rather than, repairman, selectman, serviceman, spick-and-span, superman, Superman, Teheran, Turkistan, weatherman, workingman, Yucatan • Afghanistan, attention span, bipartisan, catamaran, cavalryman, committeeman, deliveryman, medicine man, newspaperman, orangutan, radioman, Raggedy Ann, Tajikistan, Turkmenistan, Uzbekistan, watering can

an⁶ \äng\ see ONG¹

an⁷ \änt\ see ANT²

ana¹ \än-ə\ Anna, Donna, fauna, Ghana, Lana • Botswana, iguana, Madonna, mañana, nirvana, piranha, Tijuana • French Guiana, prima donna, Rosh Hashanah • Americana

ana² \ā-nə\ Dana, Lana

ana³ \an-ə\ Anna, Ghana, Hannah, Lana • banana, bandanna, cabana, Diana, Guiana, Guyana, gymkhana, Havana, hosanna, Joanna, Montana, savanna, Susanna • French Guiana, Indiana, Juliana, Mariana, poinciana, Pollyanna, Santa Ana • Americana, Louisiana

anacle \an-i-kəl\ see ANICAL

anagh \an-ə\ see ANA³

anah¹ \ō-nə\ see ONA¹

anah² \än-ə\ see ANA¹

analyst \an-ᵊl-ist\ analyst, panelist • psychoanalyst

anan \an-ən\ see ANNON

anary \an-rē\ see ANNERY

anate \an-ət\ see ANNET

anc¹ \aⁿ\ see ANT¹

anc² \aŋ\ see ANG²

anc³ \aŋk\ see ANK

anca \aŋ-kə\ Sanka • Casablanca

ance¹ \äⁿs\ nuance, Provence, séance • diligence, renaissance • insouciance • pièce de résistance
—*also -s, -'s and -s'forms of nouns and -s forms of verbs listed at* ANT¹

ance² \äns\ Hans • nuance, response, séance • nonchalance, renaissance

ance³ \ans\ chance, dance, France, glance, lance, Lance, prance, stance, trance • advance, askance, barn dance, break-dance, by chance, enhance, entrance, expanse, finance, freelance, line dance, outdance, romance, sideglance, snake dance, square dance, sun dance, sweatpants, tap dance, war dance • at first glance, ballroom dance, belly dance, circumstance, fighting chance, game of chance, happenstance, in advance, Port-au-Prince, refinance, smarty-pants, song and dance, underpants
—*also -s, -'s, and -s' forms of nouns and -s forms of verbs listed at* ANT⁵

ancement \an-smənt\ advancement, enhancement • self-advancement

ancer \an-sər\ answer, cancer, dancer • break-dancer, freelancer, line dancer, lung cancer, nondancer, square dancer, tap dancer • anticancer, ballroom dancer, belly dancer • Tropic of Cancer

ances \an(t)-səs\ see ANCIS

anch¹ \änch\ see AUNCH¹

anch² \ȯnch\ see AUNCH²

anch³ \anch\ blanch, Blanche, branch, ranch, stanch • dude ranch • avalanche, olive branch

anche¹ \anch\ see ANCH³

anche² \an-chē\ see ANCHY

anchi \an-chē\ see ANCHY

anchion \an-chən\ see ANSION

anchor \aŋ-kər\ see ANKER

anchy \an-chē\ branchy
• Comanche
ancial \an-chəl\ see ANTIAL
ancis \an(t)-səs\ Frances, Francis
• Aransas
—*also -s, -'s, and -s' forms of nouns and -s forms of verbs listed at* ANCE[3]
anck \änk\ see ONK[1]
anco \äŋ-kō\ see ONCO
ancor \aŋ-kər\ see ANKER
ancre \aŋ-kər\ see ANKER
anct \aŋt\ see ANKED
ancy \an-sē\ chancy, fancy, Nancy
and[1] \ä^n\ see ANT[1]
and[2] \änd\ see OND[1]
and[3] \and\ and, band, bland, brand, canned, gland, grand, hand, land, manned, sand, stand, strand • armband, at hand, backhand, badland, bandstand, brass band, broadband, brushland, cabstand, coastland, command, cowhand, crash-land, cropland, deckhand, demand, disband, dockhand, dreamland, expand, farmhand, farmland, field hand, firebrand, firsthand, foreland, freehand, gangland, grandstand, grassland, handstand, hatband, headband, headstand, heartland, homeland, hour hand, Iceland, inland, kickstand, Lapland, lefthand, longhand, mainland, marshland, newsstand, nightstand, offhand, oil gland, old hand, on hand, parkland, playland, quicksand, rangeland, right-hand, shorthand, stagehand, swampland, sweatband, sweat gland, Thailand, thirdhand, waistband, washstand, wasteland, watchband, wetland, withstand, wristband
• baby grand, beforehand, bellyland, borderland, contraband, countermand, Dixieland, fairyland, fatherland, Ferdinand, forestland, garage band, hand in hand, helping hand, high command, Holy Land, meadowland, minute hand, motherland, narrowband, no-man's-land, on demand, one-man band, out of hand, overhand, pastureland, promised land, public land, reprimand, Rio Grande, rubber band, Samarkand, secondhand, sleight of hand, taxi stand, timberland, try one's hand, understand, wonderland • misunderstand, multiplicand, to beat the band, vacationland • never-never land
• Alice-in-Wonderland
—*also -ed forms of verbs listed at* AN[5]
and[4] \än\ see ON[1]
and[5] \änt\ see ANT[2]
anda[1] \an-də\ panda • Amanda, Miranda, Uganda, veranda • giant panda, memoranda, propaganda
anda[2] \än-də\ see ONDA
andable \an-də-bəl\ expandable
• understandable
andaed \an-dəd\ see ANDED
andal \an-d°l\ see ANDLE
andaled \an-d°ld\ handled • wellhandled
—*also -ed forms of verbs listed at* ANDLE
andall \an-d°l\ see ANDLE
andam \an-dəm\ see ANDUM
andar \ənd-ər\ see UNDER
ande[1] \ən\ see UN[1]
ande[2] \an\ see AN[5]
ande[3] \an-dē\ see ANDY
ande[4] \and\ see AND[3]
ande[5] \än-də\ see ONDA
anded \an-dəd\ banded, branded, candid, handed, landed, stranded
• backhanded, bare-handed, highhanded, left-handed, one-handed, red-handed, right-handed, shorthanded, two-handed • emptyhanded, evenhanded,

heavy-handed, singlehanded, underhanded

—*also* -ed *forms of verbs listed at* AND³

andel \an-dᵊl\ see ANDLE

andem \an-dəm\ see ANDUM

ander¹ \en-dər\ see ENDER

ander² \än-dər\ see ONDER¹

ander³ \an-dər\ blander, brander, candor, gander, grander, grandeur, pander, sander, slander • bystander, commander, demander, left-hander, meander, right-hander • Alexander, coriander, salamander, wing commander

anders \an-dərz\ Flanders

—*also* -s, -'s, *and* -s' *forms of nouns and* -s *forms of verbs listed at* ANDER³

andes \an-dēz\ Andes

—*also* -s, -'s, *and* -s' *forms of nouns and* -s *forms of verbs listed at* ANDY

andeur \an-dər\ see ANDER³

andhi \an-dē\ see ANDY

andi \an-dē\ see ANDY

andible \an-də-bəl\ see ANDABLE

andid \an-dəd\ see ANDED

anding \an-diŋ\ branding, standing • commanding, crash landing, freestanding, long-standing, outstanding, upstanding • belly landing, mind-expanding, notwithstanding, pancake landing, understanding • instrument landing, misunderstanding

—*also* -ing *forms of verbs listed at* AND³

andish \an-dish\ blandish, brandish • outlandish

andist \an-dəst\ blandest, grandest • propagandist

andle \an-dᵊl\ candle, Handel, handle, Randall, sandal, scandal, vandal • manhandle, mishandle, panhandle • Roman candle, votive candle

andled \an-dᵊl\ see ANDALED

andly \an-lē\ see ANLY

ando \an-dō\ Brando • commando, Fernando, Orlando • San Fernando

andom \an-dəm\ see ANDUM

andor \an-dər\ see ANDER³

andra \an-drə\ Sandra • Cassandra • Alexandra

andrea \an-drē-ə\ see ANDRIA

andres \an-dərz\ see ANDERS

andria \an-drē-ə\ Andrea, Alexandria

andsome \an-səm\ see ANSOM

andum \an-dəm\ random, tandem • memorandum

andy \an-dē\ Andy, bandy, brandy, Brandy, candy, dandy, handy, Randy, sandy, Sandy • ear candy, eye candy, hard candy, jim-dandy, rock candy, unhandy • cotton candy, Rio Grande

ane¹ \ān\ bane, brain, Cain, cane, chain, crane, Crane, Dane, deign, drain, Duane, feign, gain, grain, Jane, lane, main, Maine, mane, pain, pane, plain, plane, rain, reign, rein, sane, Seine, skein, slain, Spain, sprain, stain, strain, train, vain, vane, vein, wane, Wayne, Zane • abstain, again, air lane, airplane, attain, Bahrain, biplane, birdbrain, bloodstain, brain drain, campaign, champagne, Champlain, choke chain, chow mein, cocaine, complain, constrain, contain, detain, disdain, domain, Elaine, explain, eyestrain, fast lane, floodplain, food chain, germane, Great Dane, Helene, humane, Hussein, inane, ingrain, insane, lamebrain, left brain, lo mein, Lorraine, maintain, membrane, methane, midbrain, migraine, mundane, New Spain, obtain, octane, ordain, pertain, plain-Jane, profane,

propane, ptomaine, raise Cain,
refrain, remain, restrain, retain,
retrain, right brain, sea-lane,
seaplane, sustain, tearstain, ter-
rain, Ukraine, unchain, urbane,
warplane • acid rain, aeroplane,
aquaplane, Aquitaine, ascertain,
bullet train, cell membrane, cello-
phane, Charlemagne, down the
drain, entertain, featherbrain, free
throw lane, high-octane, hurri-
cane, inclined plane, inhumane,
Mary Jane, memory lane, mono-
plane, multigrain, multilane,
Novocain, novocaine, overtrain,
pollen grain, preordain, reattain,
sandhill crane, scatterbrain, Spanish Main, sugarcane, Tamerlane,
toilet train, wagon train, water
main, weather vane, whooping
crane, windowpane • Serengeti
Plain

ane² \an\ see AN⁵
ane³ \än-ə\ see ANA¹
ane⁴ \än\ see ON¹
anea \ä-nē-ə\ see ANIA
anean \ä-nē-ən\ see ANIAN
aned \änd\ see AINED
anee \an-ē\ see ANNY
aneful \ān-fəl\ see AINFUL
anel \an-ᵊl\ see ANNEL
anelist \an-ᵊl-əst\ see ANALYST
aneous \ä-nē-əs\ extraneous, spon-
taneous • instantaneous, miscella-
neous, simultaneous
• contemporaneous, extempora-
neous
aner¹ \ā-nər\ see AINER
aner² \än-ər\ see ONOR¹
anet \an-ət\ see ANNET
aneum \ā-nē-əm\ see ANIUM
aney \ȯ-nē\ see AWNY¹
ang¹ \äŋ\ see ONG¹
ang² \aŋ\ bang, clang, dang, fang,
gang, hang, rang, sang, slang,
sprang, tang, twang • bang-bang,
big bang, chain gang, ginseng,

harangue, meringue, mustang,
shebang, slam-bang • antigang,
boomerang, give a hang, inter-
gang, overhang • orangutan
ang³ \ȯŋ\ see ONG²
anga \äŋ-gə\ see ONGA
angar \aŋ-ər\ see ANGER²
ange \ānj\ change, mange, range,
strange • arrange, chump change,
derange, estrange, exchange, free-
range, long-range, short-range,
shortchange, small change • Cascade Range, disarrange, driving
range, interchange, post
exchange, prearrange, rearrange,
stock exchange, Teton Range,
Wasatch Range • Alaska Range,
Aleutian Range
angel \aŋ-gəl\ see ANGLE
angell \aŋ-gəl\ see ANGLE
angement \ānj-mənt\ arrangement,
derangement, estrangement • pre-
arrangement, rearrangement
anger¹ \ān-jər\ changer, danger,
manger, ranger, stranger
• arranger, endanger, exchanger,
lone ranger, shortchanger • forest
ranger, money changer, Texas
Ranger • dog in the manger
anger² \aŋ-ər\ hangar, hanger
• cliff-hanger, coat hanger, head-
banger • paperhanger
anger³ \aŋ-gər\ anger, clangor
angi \aŋ-ē\ see ANGY²
angie \aŋ-ē\ see ANGY²
anging¹ \ān-jiŋ\ unchanging, wide-
ranging
—also -ing *forms of verbs listed at*
ANGE
anging² \aŋ-iŋ\ hanging • paper-
hanging
—also -ing *forms of verbs listed at*
ANG²
angle \aŋ-gəl\ angle, bangle, dan-
gle, jangle, mangle, spangle, stran-
gle, tangle, wangle, wrangle
• entangle, quadrangle, rectangle,

right angle, triangle, untangle, wide-angle • disentangle • Bermuda Triangle

angled \aŋ-gəld\ angled, tangled • newfangled, right-angled, star-spangled
—*also* -ed *forms of verbs listed at* ANGLE

angler \aŋ-glər\ angler, strangler, wrangler

angling \aŋ-gliŋ\ angling, gangling
—*also* -ing *forms of verbs listed at* ANGLE

angly \aŋ-glē\ gangly, jangly

ango \aŋ-gō\ mango, tango • fandango

angor¹ \aŋ-ər\ see ANGER²

angor² \aŋ-gər\ see ANGER³

angour \aŋ-ər\ see ANGER²

angster \aŋ-stər\ gangster, prankster

angue \aŋ\ see ANG²

anguer \aŋ-ər\ see ANGER²

anguish \aŋ-gwish\ anguish, languish

anguor \aŋ-ər\ see ANGER²

angy¹ \ān-jē\ mangy, rangy

angy² \aŋ-ē\ tangy, twangy

anha \än-ə\ see ANA¹

ani¹ \än-ē\ Bonnie, bonny, Connie, Donnie, Ronnie, tawny • afghani, Irani • Modigliani, Pakistani • mulligatawny

ani² \an-ē\ see ANNY

ania \ā-nē-ə\ mania • Tasmania • egomania, kleptomania, Lithuania, Mauritania, Oceania, Pennsylvania, pyromania, Transylvania • megalomania

anian \ā-nē-ən\ Albanian, Iranian, Jordanian, Romanian, Ukrainian • Lithuanian, Pennsylvanian, subterranean • Mediterranean

aniard \an-yərd\ lanyard, Spaniard

anic \an-ik\ manic, panic • Germanic, Hispanic, mechanic, organic, satanic, titanic, volcanic

• aldermanic, inorganic, messianic, oceanic, pre-Hispanic • transoceanic

anical \an-i-kəl\ manacle • botanical, mechanical, tyrannical • puritanical

anice \an-əs\ see ANISE

anicle \an-i-kəl\ see ANICAL

anics \an-iks\ annex, panics • mechanics

aniel¹ \an-ᵊl\ see ANNEL

aniel² \an-yəl\ see ANUAL¹

anion \an-yən\ banyan, canyon • Bryce Canyon, companion, Grand Canyon, Hells Canyon

anis \an-əs\ see ANISE

anise \an-əs\ anise, Janice, Janis • Johnannes • Scipio Africanus

anish \an-ish\ banish, clannish, mannish, Spanish, tannish, vanish

anister \an-ə-stər\ banister, canister

anite \an-ət\ see ANNET

anity \an-ət-ē\ sanity, vanity • humanity, insanity, profanity • Christianity, inhumanity

anium \ā-nē-əm\ cranium • geranium, titanium, uranium

ank \aŋk\ bank, blank, clank, crank, dank, drank, flank, franc, frank, Frank, hank, lank, plank, prank, rank, sank, shank, shrank, spank, stank, swank, tank, thank, yank, Yank • gangplank, outflank, outrank, point-blank, sandbank, snowbank, state bank, think tank, West Bank • antitank, data bank, draw a blank, Georges Bank, national bank, piggy bank, riverbank, walk the plank • clinkety-clank

anka \aŋ-kə\ see ANCA

anked \aŋt\ tanked • sacrosanct
—*also* -ed *forms of verbs listed at* ANK

ankee \aŋ-kē\ see ANKY

anker \aŋ-kər\ anchor, banker,

canker, flanker, hanker, rancor,
tanker, thanker • supertanker
—also -er *forms of adjectives listed at* ANK
ankh \äŋk\ see ONK[1]
ankie \aŋ-kē\ see ANKY
ankish \aŋ-kish\ crankish, prank-
ish
ankle \aŋ-kəl\ ankle, rankle
ankly \aŋ-klē\ blankly, frankly
anks \aŋs\ see ANX
ankster \aŋ-stər\ see ANGSTER
anky \aŋ-kē\ cranky, hankie,
lanky, skanky, swanky, Yankee
• hanky-panky
anley \an-lē\ see ANLY
anli \an-lē\ see ANLY
anly \an-lē\ blandly, grandly,
manly, Stanley • unmanly
ann[1] \an\ see AN[5]
ann[2] \än\ see ON[1]
anna[1] \än-ə\ see ANA[1]
anna[2] \an-ə\ see ANA[3]
annah \an-ə\ see ANA[3]
annalist \an-ᵊl-əst\ see ANALYST
annan \an-ən\ see ANNON
anne \an\ see AN[5]
anned \and\ see AND[1]
annel \an-ᵊl\ channel, Daniel,
flannel, panel • impanel • English
Channel
anner \an-ər\ banner, canner,
manner, manor, planner, scanner,
tanner • city planner
annery \an-rē\ cannery, granary,
tannery
annes \an-əs\ see ANISE
annet \an-ət\ granite, Janet, planet
• pomegranate
annexe \an-iks\ see ANICS
annibal \an-ə-bəl\ cannibal, Hanni-
bal
annic \an-ik\ see ANIC
annie \an-ē\ see ANNY
annin \an-ən\ see ANNON
annish \an-ish\ see ANISH
annon \an-ən\ cannon • Buchanan

annous \an-əs\ see ANISE
anns \anz\ see ANS[4]
annual \an-yəl\ see ANUAL[1]
anny \an-ē\ Annie, canny, cranny,
Danny, fanny, granny, Lanny,
nanny • afghani, uncanny • Hin-
dustani, hootenanny
ano[1] \än-ō\ guano • Chicano, piano, soprano • grand piano
• mezzo-soprano, player piano,
upright piano
ano[2] \an-ō\ piano, soprano
• mezzo-soprano
anon \an-ən\ see ANNON
anor \an-ər\ see ANNER
anous \an-əs\ see ANISE
anqui \aŋ-kē\ see ONKY
ans[1] \äns\ see ANCE[2]
ans[2] \änz\ see ONZE
ans[3] \ans\ see ANCE[3]
ans[4] \anz\ Hans
—also -s, -'s, *and* -s' *forms of
nouns and* -s *forms of verbs listed at* AN[5]
ans[5] \aⁿ\ see ANT[1]
ansard \an-sərd\ see ANSWERED
ansas \an(t)-səs\ see ANCIS
anse \ans\ see ANCE[3]
anser \an-sər\ see ANCER
ansion \an-chən\ mansion • expan-
sion
ansom \an-səm\ handsome, ransom • king's ransom
answer \an-sər\ see ANCER
answered \an-sərd\ answered,
mansard • unanswered
ansy \an-zē\ pansy, tansy • chimpanzee
ant[1] \äⁿ\ croissant, Mont Blanc,
Rouen, savant • aide-de-camp,
denouement
ant[2] \änt\ aunt, can't, flaunt, font,
fount, gaunt, taunt, want • gallant, grandaunt, piedmont, savant, Vermont • commandant,
confidant, debutante, dilettante,
nonchalant, restaurant

ant³ \ənt\ see ONT¹

ant⁴ \ȯnt\ see AUNT¹

ant⁵ \ant\ ant, aunt, can't, chant, grant, Grant, pant, plant, rant, scant, shan't, slant • eggplant, enchant, extant, fire ant, gallant, grandaunt, houseplant, implant, jade plant, land grant, recant, replant, savant, seed plant, supplant, transplant, white ant • adamant, commandant, confidant, confidante, cormorant, covenant, dilettante, gallivant, pitcher plant, power plant, rubber plant, spider plant, sycophant • flowering plant

anta \ant-ə\ Fanta, manta, Santa • Atlanta

antal \änt-ᵊl\ see ONTAL¹

antam \ant-əm\ bantam, phantom

antar \ant-ər\ see ANTER²

ante¹ \än-tā\ Brontë, Dante • andante

ante² \änt\ see ANT²

ante³ \ant\ see ANT⁵

ante⁴ \änt-ē\ see ANTI¹

ante⁵ \ant-ē\ ante, chantey, pantie, scanty, shanty • andante • vigilante

anted \an-təd\ disenchanted
—also -ed forms of verbs listed at ANT⁵

anter¹ \änt-ər\ see AUNTER¹

anter² \ant-ər\ banter, canter, granter, grantor, planter • decanter, enchanter, implanter • tam-o'-shanter

antes \an-tēz\ antes • Cervantes

antey \ant-ē\ see ANTE⁵

anther \an-thər\ anther, panther • Black Panther

anti¹ \änt-ē\ Brontë, jaunty • andante

anti² \ant-ē\ see ANTE⁵

antial \an-chəl\ substantial • circumstantial, insubstantial, nonfinancial, unsubstantial

antic \ant-ik\ antic, frantic • Atlantic, gigantic, pedantic, romantic • North Atlantic, transatlantic, unromantic

antie \ant-ē\ see ANTE⁵

anting¹ \ant-iŋ\ planting • enchanting
—also -ing forms of verbs listed at ANT⁵

anting² \ənt-iŋ\ see UNTING

antis \ant-əs\ mantis • Atlantis

anto \än-tō\ Squanto • Toronto

antom \ant-əm\ see ANTAM

antor \ant-ər\ see ANTER²

antos \an-təs\ see ANTIS

antre \ant-ər\ see ANTER²

ants \ans\ see ANCE³

antus \ant-əs\ see ANTIS

anty \ant-ē\ see ANTE⁵

anual¹ \an-yəl\ annual, Daniel, spaniel • biannual, field spaniel, Nathaniel • cocker spaniel, semiannual, springer spaniel, water spaniel

anual² \an-yə-wəl\ annual, manual, Manuel • biannual, Emmanuel, Immanuel • semiannual • Victor Emmanuel

anuel \an-yəl\ see ANUAL²

anus¹ \ā-nəs\ see AYNESS

anus² \an-əs\ see ANISE

anx \aŋs\ thanks • Fairbanks, Grand Banks, phalanx • Outer Banks
—also -s, -'s, and -s' forms of nouns and -s forms of verbs listed at ANK

any¹ \ā-nē\ see AINY

any² \en-ē\ see ENNY

anyan \an-yən\ see ANION

anyard \an-yərd\ see ANIARD

anyon \an-yən\ see ANION

anz \ans\ see ANCE³

anza \an-zə\ stanza • bonanza • Sancho Panza • extravaganza

anzee \an-zē\ see ANSY

ao¹ \ā-ō\ see EO¹

ao² \ō\ see OW¹
ao³ \aů\ see OW²
aoighis \äsh\ see ECHE¹
aole \aů-lē\ see OWLY²
aône \ōn\ see ONE¹
aori \aůr-ē\ see OWERY
aos¹ \aůs\ see OUSE²
aos² \ā-äs\ chaos, Laos
aotian \ō-shən\ see OTION
aow \aů\ see OW²
ap¹ \äp\ see OP¹
ap² \əp\ see UP
ap³ \ap\ cap, chap, clap, flap, gap,
  gape, hap, lap, Lapp, map, nap,
  nape, pap, rap, sap, scrap, slap,
  snap, strap, tap, trap, wrap, yap,
  zap • bootstrap, burlap, catnap,
  cell sap, claptrap, death cap,
  death trap, dunce cap, dewlap,
  dognap, earflap, entrap, enwrap,
  firetrap, gift wrap, hubcap, ice
  cap, jockstrap, kidnap, kneecap,
  madcap, mishap, mousetrap, mud
  flap, nightcap, on tap, pace lap,
  recap, remap, road map, sand
  trap, shrink-wrap, skullcap, sky-
  cap, snowcap, speed trap, stop-
  gap, unsnap, unstrap, unwrap,
  whitecap, wiretap • baseball cap,
  beat the rap, blasting cap, booby
  trap, gangsta rap, giddyap, ginger-
  snap, handicap, leghold trap, on
  the map, overlap, photomap,
  rattletrap, relief map, shoulder
  strap, stocking cap, thinking cap,
  thunderclap, tourist trap, weather
  map • Venus flytrap
apable \ā-pə-bəl\ capable • es-
  capable, incapable • inescapable
apal \ā-pəl\ see APLE
apboard \ab-ərd\ see ABARD
ape¹ \āp\ ape, cape, crape, crepe,
  drape, gape, grape, nape, scrape,
  shape, tape • agape, cloudscape,
  duct tape, escape, great ape,
  landscape, man ape, misshape,
  moonscape, North Cape, red tape,

reshape, Scotch tape, sea grape,
seascape, shipshape, snowscape,
take shape, townscape, undrape
• Barbary ape, cityscape, fire
escape, masking tape, ticker tape,
waterscape • audiotape, adhesive
tape, anthropoid ape, bent out of
shape, magnetic tape, videotape
ape² \ap\ see AP³
ape³ \äp-ē\ see OPPY
ape⁴ \ap-ē\ see APPY
apel \ap-əl\ see APPLE
apelin \ap-lən\ see APLAIN
apen \ā-pən\ capon • misshapen
aper \ā-pər\ caper, draper, gaper,
  paper, scraper, shaper, taper,
  tapir, vapor • crepe paper, flypa-
  per, graph paper, landscaper,
  newspaper, notepaper, reshaper,
  sandpaper, skyscraper, tar paper,
  term paper, wallpaper, wastepa-
  per, waxed paper • butcher paper,
  carbon paper, funny paper, tissue
  paper, toilet paper, tracing paper,
  writing paper
apery \ā-prē\ drapery, papery,
  vapory
apes \āps\ trapse
—also -s, -'s, and -s' forms of
nouns and -s forms of verbs listed
at APE¹
aph \af\ calf, chaff, gaffe, graph,
  half, laugh, staff, staph • bar
  graph, behalf, carafe, Falstaff,
  flagstaff, giraffe, half-staff, horse-
  laugh, line graph, riffraff • auto-
  graph, bathyscaphe, circle graph,
  epigraph, epitaph, half-and-half,
  lithograph, paragraph, phono-
  graph, photograph, polygraph,
  seismograph, telegraph, under-
  staff • choreograph
aphe¹ \äf\ see AFE¹
aphe² \af\ see APH
apher \af-ər\ see AFFER²
aphic \af-ik\ graphic, traffic • auto-
  graphic, biographic, demographic,

geographic, lithographic, phono-
graphic, photographic, seismo-
graphic, telegraphic, typographic
• choreographic

api \äp-ē\ see OPPY

apid \ap-əd\ rapid, vapid

apir \ā-pər\ see APER

apist \ā-pist\ rapist • escapist,
landscapist

aplain \ap-lən\ chaplain, Chaplin,
sapling

aple \ā-pəl\ maple, papal, staple
• red maple, rock maple • antipa-
pal, sugar maple

aples \ā-pəlz\ Naples, staples

apless \ap-ləs\ hapless, strapless

aplin \ap-lə-n\ see APLAIN

aply \ap-lē\ see APTLY

apo \äp-ō\ capo • da capo, gestapo

apon \ā-pən\ see APEN

apor \ā-pər\ see APER

apory \ā-prē\ see APERY

apour \ā-pər\ see APER

app \ap\ see AP³

appable \ap-ə-bəl\ mappable • re-
cappable, unflappable

appalli \äp-ə-lē\ see OPOLY

appe \ap\ see AP³

apped \apt\ see APT

apper¹ \äp-ər\ see OPPER

apper² \ap-ər\ clapper, dapper,
flapper, mapper, rapper, snapper,
tapper, trapper, wrapper, yapper,
zapper • backslapper, catnapper,
dognapper, dust wrapper, kidnap-
per, knee-slapper, red snapper,
thigh slapper, wiretapper
• gangsta rapper, whippersnapper

apphic \af-ik\ see APHIC

appie \äp-ē\ see OPPY

appily \ap-ə-lē\ happily, snappily
• unhappily

appiness \ap-ē-nəs\ happiness,
sappiness, snappiness • unhappi-
ness

apping \ap-iŋ\ capping, mapping,
strapping, trapping, wrapping

—*also* -ing *forms of verbs listed at*
AP³

apple \ap-əl\ apple, chapel, dapple,
grapple, scrapple • crab apple,
mayapple, pineapple, thorn apple
• Adam's apple

apps \aps\ see APSE

appy \ap-ē\ gappy, happy, sappy,
scrappy, snappy • serape,
slaphappy, unhappy • trigger-
happy

aps \aps\ see APSE

apse \aps\ chaps, lapse, taps, traps
• collapse, elapse, perhaps, re-
lapse, time-lapse
—*also* -s, -'s, *and* -s' *forms of*
nouns and -s *forms of verbs listed*
at AP³

apt \apt\ apt, rapt • adapt, snow-
capped, untapped
—*also* -ed *forms of verbs listed at*
AP³

apter \ap-tər\ captor, chapter,
raptor • adapter • oviraptor • ve-
lociraptor

aption \ap-shən\ caption • adap-
tion, contraption, miscaption

aptive \ap-tiv\ captive • adaptive

aptly \ap-lē\ aptly, raptly

aptor \ap-tər\ see APTER

apture \ap-chər\ rapture • enrap-
ture, recapture

apy \ap-ē\ see APPY

aq¹ \äk\ see OCK¹

aq² \ak\ see ACK²

aqi \äk-ē\ see OCKY

aque¹ \āk\ see AKE¹

aque² \ak\ see ACK²

aqui \äk-ē\ see OCKY

ar¹ \er\ see ARE⁴

ar² \òr\ see OR¹

ar³ \är\ are, bar, car, char, czar, far,
gar, jar, mar, noir, our, par, R,
scar, spar, star, tar, tsar, tzar • afar,
ajar, all-star, bazaar, bizarre,
boudoir, boxcar, Bronze Star, cash
bar, cigar, costar, cougar, crossbar,

crowbar, disbar, Dog Star, feldspar, film noir, five-star, fixed star, flatcar, four-star, guitar, Gunnar, Hagar, handcar, horsecar, hussar, Ishtar, jaguar, Jaguar, Kevlar, leaf scar, lounge car, lumbar, Lamar, lodestar, Magyar, memoir, Mylar, NASCAR, North Star, pace car, pine tar, polestar, prowl car, pulsar, Qatar, quasar, radar, railcar, raw bar, rebar, Renoir, roll bar, sandbar, scout car, shofar, sidecar, slot car, snack bar, solar, sonar, sports bar, sports car, stock car, streetcar, tank car, T-bar, toolbar, town car, unbar • air guitar, arctic char, au revoir, avatar, blazing star, Bolívar, bumper car, cable car, caviar, coffee bar, color bar, command car, commissar, dining car, double star, evening star, exemplar, falling star, giant star, handlebar, Indy car, insofar, isobar, jaguar, Jaguar, Kandahar, Leyden jar, mason jar, megastar, millibar, minibar, minicar, Miramar, morning star, motorcar, mudtdcar, muu'ilr nnr, Myanmar, neutron star, open bar, registrar, rent-a-car, repertoire, reservoir, rising star, salad bar, samovar, scimitar, seminar, shooting star, Silver Star, sleeping car, steel guitar, superstar, touring car, turbocar, VCR, Zanzibar • anti-roll bar, Doppler radar, Madagascar, Mount Palomar, radio car, radio star • Hawaiian guitar, horizontal bar

ara[1] \är-ə\ Laura • Guevara, Gomorrah, saguaro, tiara • capybara, sayonara • Guadalajara

ara[2] \er-ə\ see ERA[1]

ara[3] \ar-ə\ see ARROW[1]

ara[4] \ȯr-ə\ see ORA

arab \ar-əb\ Arab, Carib, carob, scarab • pan-Arab • anti-Arab

arable \ar-ə-bəl\ arable, bearable, parable, shareable, wearable • declarable, nonarable, unbearable

aracen \ar-ə-sən\ see ARISON

aracin \ar-ə-sən\ see ARISON

arage \ar-ij\ see ARRIAGE

aragon \ar-ə-gən\ paragon, tarragon

arah[1] \er-ə\ see ERA[1]

arah[2] \ar-ə\ see ARROW[1]

aral[1] \ar-əl\ see ARREL[2]

aral[2] \ȯr-əl\ see ERRAL

aralee \er-ə-lē\ see ARILY

aran[1] \er-ən\ see ARON[1]

aran[2] \ar-ən\ see ARON[2]

arant[1] \er-ənt\ see ARENT[1]

arant[2] \ar-ənt\ see ARENT[2]

araoh[1] \er-ō\ see ERO[2]

araoh[2] \ar-ō\ see ARROW[2]

aras \är-əs\ see ORRIS[1]

arass \ar-əs\ see ARIS[2]

arat \ar-ət\ carat, caret, carrot, karat, parrot • disparate

arate \ar-ət\ see ARAT

arative[1] \er-ət-iv\ declarative, imperative

arative[2] \ar-ət-iv\ narrative • comparative, declarative

arb \ärb\ barb, carb, garb • rhubarb

arbel \är-bəl\ see ARBLE

arber \är-bər\ see ARBOR

arble \är-bəl\ barbel, garble, marble

arboard \är-bərd\ barbered, larboard, starboard

arbor \är-bər\ arbor, barber, harbor • Ann Arbor, Pearl Harbor

arc[1] \äk\ see OCK[1]

arc[2] \ärk\ see ARK[1]

arce \ärs\ see ARSE[1]

arch \ärch\ arch, larch, march, March, parch, starch • cornstarch, dead march • Gothic arch, horseshoe arch, on the march, wedding march

archal \är-kəl\ sparkle • monar-
chal, outsparkle • hierarchal,
matriarchal, patriarchal
arche \ärsh\ see ARSH
arched \ärcht\ arched, parched
—*also* -ed *forms of verbs listed at*
ARCH
archer \är-chər\ archer, marcher
• departure
archic \är-kik\ anarchic, monar-
chic • hierarchic, oligarchic
archical \är-ki-kəl\ monarchical
• oligarchical
archon \är-kən\ see ARKEN
archy \är-kē\ snarky • anarchy,
malarkey, monarchy • hierarchy,
matriarchy, patriarchy, oligarchy
arck \ärk\ see ARK[1]
arct \ärkt\ see ARKED
arctic \ärt-ik\ see ARTIC
ard[1] \ärd\ bard, barred, card,
chard, guard, hard, lard, shard,
yard • Asgard, backyard,
bankcard, barnyard, Bernard,
blackguard, blowhard, boatyard,
bombard, brickyard, charge card,
churchyard, coast guard, court-
yard, die-hard, diehard, discard,
dockyard, dooryard, face card,
farmyard, flash card, Gerard,
graveyard, green card, ill-starred,
junkyard, lifeguard, mudguard,
noseguard, off guard, old guard,
on guard, phone card, placard,
point guard, postcard, punch
card, rear guard, rearguard, re-
gard, retard, safeguard, scorecard,
shipyard, smart card, sound card,
steelyard, stockyard, switchyard,
time card, unbarred, vanguard,
wild card • Abelard, avant-garde,
bodyguard, boulevard, business
card, calling card, Christmas card,
color guard, credit card, debit
card, disregard, greeting card,
honor guard, ID card, leotard,
lumberyard, MasterCard, national

guard, navy yard, no-holds-
barred, playing card, postal card,
report card, Saint Bernard, Scot-
land Yard, self-regard, union
card, unitard • picture-postcard,
video card • identity card
—*also* -ed *forms of verbs listed at*
AR[3]
ard[2] \är\ see AR[3]
ard[3] \ȯrd\ see OARD
ardant \ärd-ᵊnt\ ardent • flame-
retardant
arde \ärd\ see ARD[1]
arded[1] \ärd-əd\ guarded • retarded,
unguarded
—*also* -ed *forms of verbs listed at*
ARD[1]
arded[2] \ȯrd-əd\ corded, sordid
—*also* -ed *forms of verbs listed at*
OARD
arden[1] \ärd-ᵊn\ garden, harden,
pardon • rock garden, roof garden, tea garden • kitchen garden,
water garden
arden[2] \ȯrd-ᵊn\ cordon, Gordon,
Jordan, warden • churchwarden
ardener \ärd-nər\ gardener, pard-
ner, partner • landscape gardener
ardent \ärd-ᵊnt\ see ARDANT
arder[1] \ärd-ər\ ardor, guarder,
larder
arder[2] \ȯrd-ər\ see ORDER
ardi \ärd-ē\ see ARDY
ardian[1] \ärd-ē-ən\ guardian • Ed-
wardian
ardian[2] \ȯrd-ē-ən\ see ORDION
ardine \ärd-ⁿ\ see ARDEN[1]
arding \ȯrd-iŋ\ see ORDING[1]
ardom \ärd-əm\ czardom, stardom
• megastardom, superstardom
ardon \ärd-ᵊn\ see ARDEN[1]
ardoner \ärd-nər\ see ARDENER
ardor \ärd-ər\ see ARDER[1]
ardy \ärd-ē\ hardy, tardy • Bacardi,
foolhardy
are[1] \er-ē\ see ARY[1]
are[2] \är\ see AR[3]

are³ \är-ē\ see ARI¹
are⁴ \er\ air, bare, bear, Blair,
blare, care, chair, Claire, dare,
e'er, ere, err, fair, fare, flair, flare,
glare, hair, hare, Herr, heir, lair,
mare, ne'er, pair, pare, pear,
prayer, rare, rear, scare, share,
snare, spare, square, stair, stare,
swear, tear, their, there, they're,
ware, wear, where • affair, aglare,
airfare, antbear, armchair, aware,
bakeware, barware, beachwear,
beware, big hair, black bear,
bricklayer, brown bear, bugbear,
carfare, cave bear, clayware,
cochair, coheir, compare, cook-
ware, courseware, day-care, deck
chair, declare, despair, éclair,
elsewhere, ensnare, eyewear,
fanfare, flatware, footwear, for-
bear, forebear, forswear,
foursquare, freeware, giftware,
glassware, Great Bear, groupware,
hardware, health care, hectare,
high chair, horsehair, hot air,
impair, knitwear, life-care, long-
hair, loungewear, menswear,
midair, mohair, neckwear, night-
mare, no fair, nonglare, outstare,
out-there, outwear, playwear,
plowshare, Poor Clare, premiere,
prepare, rainwear, repair, self-
care, shareware, shorthair, Sin-
clair, skiwear, sleepwear, sloth
bear, software, somewhere,
sportswear, stemware, stoneware,
sun bear, swimwear, threadbare,
tinware, unfair, Voltaire, warfare,
welfare, wheelchair • aftercare,
air-to-air, antiglare, anywhere,
arctic hare, Asian pear, billion-
aire, bill of fare, boutonniere,
camel hair, Camembert,
chinaware, compressed air,
county fair, debonair, Delaware,
derriere, dinnerware, disrepair,
doctrinaire, earthenware, easy

chair, étagère, everywhere, germ
warfare, get somewhere, grizzly
bear, here and there, hide or hair,
in one's hair, in the air, ironware,
kitchenware, laissez-faire, legion-
naire, lion's share, Little Bear,
love affair, managed care, market
share, Medicare, metalware,
millionaire, on the square, open-
air, outerwear, overbear, perfect
square, plasticware, polar bear,
potty-chair, prickly pear, ques-
tionnaire, rocking chair, savoir
faire, science fair, self-aware, self-
despair, silverware, snowshoe
hare, solar flare, solitaire, swivel
chair, tableware, tear one's hair,
teddy bear, then and there,
thoroughfare, trench warfare,
Tupperware, unaware, under-
wear, vaporware, wash-and-wear,
wear and tear, woodenware,
world premiere, zillionaire
• breath of fresh air, concession-
aire, devil-may-care, director's
chair, electric chair, enamelware,
hyperaware, intensive care, Kodiak bear, lighter-than-air, out of
one's hair, primary care, ready to
wear, social welfare, spectacled
bear, surface-to-air, up in the air
• castle in the air, middle of
nowhere
area \er-ē-ə\ see ARIA
areable¹ \er-ə-bəl\ see EARABLE¹
areable² \ar-ə-bəl\ see ARABLE
areal \er-ē-əl\ see ARIAL
arean¹ \er-ē-ən\ see ARIAN¹
arean² \ar-ē-ən\ see ARIAN²
ared \erd\ see AIRED
aredness \ar-əd-nəs\ see ARIDNESS
arel \ar-əl\ see ARREL²
arely¹ \er-lē\ see AIRLY
arely² \är-lē\ see ARLIE
arem \er-əm\ see ARUM
arence¹ \er-əns\ Clarence, Terence
• forbearance

arence² \ar-ən(ts)\ see ARENTS

arent¹ \er-ənt\ daren't, errant, parent • aberrant, apparent, godparent, grandparent, house parent, knight-errant, nonparent, stepparent, transparent • heir apparent

arent² \ar-ənt\ daren't, parent • apparent, godparent, grandparent, stepparent, transparent • heir apparent

aren't¹ \er-ənt\ see ARENT¹

aren't² \ar-ənt\ see ARENT²

arents \ar-ən(t)s\ Clarence —also -s, -'s, and -s' forms of nouns listed at ARENT²

arer \er-ər\ see EARER¹

ares¹ \erz\ see AIRS

ares² \ar-ēz\ Buenos Aires —also -s, -'s, and -s' forms of nouns and -s forms of verbs listed at ARRY³

ares³ \är-əs\ see ORRIS¹

aret \ar-ət\ see ARAT

arey¹ \ar-ē\ see ARRY³

arey² \er-ē\ see ARY¹

arez \är-əs\ see ORRIS¹

arf¹ \ärf\ barf, scarf

arf² \órf\ see ORPH

argain \är-gən\ bargain, jargon • outbargain, plea-bargain • in the bargain

arge \ärj\ barge, charge, large, Marge, sarge • at-large, depth charge, discharge, enlarge, recharge, surcharge, take-charge • by and large, countercharge, cover charge, overcharge, service charge, undercharge • carrying charge

arger \är-jər\ charger • enlarger, recharger • turbocharger

arget \är-gət\ argot, target • off target, on target

argo \är-gō\ argot, cargo, Fargo, largo, Margot • embargo, Key Largo • supercargo

argon \är-gən\ see ARGAIN

argot¹ \är-gət\ see ARGET

argot² \är-gō\ see ARGO

arh \är\ see AR³

ari¹ \är-ē\ quarry, sari, scarry, sorry, starry • curare, safari • calamari, Kalahari, Stradivari

ari² \er-ē\ see ARY¹

ari³ \ar-ē\ see ARRY³

aria \er-ē-ə\ area • Bavaria, Bulgaria, hysteria, malaria, planaria, Samaria

arial \er-ē-əl\ aerial, burial • malarial • adversarial, secretarial

arian¹ \er-ē-ən\ Marian, Marion • agrarian, Aquarian, barbarian, Bavarian, Bulgarian, Cancerian, cesarean, grammarian, Hungarian, librarian, Maid Marian, ovarian, Rotarian, sectarian, Sumerian • antiquarian, centenarian, libertarian, nonsectarian, Presbyterian, proletarian, Rastafarian, Sagittarian, seminarian, Unitarian, vegetarian • Austro-Hungarian, authoritarian, disciplinarian, egalitarian, humanitarian, octogenarian, parliamentarian, totalitarian, utilitarian, veterinarian

arian² \ar-ē-ən\ carrion, clarion, Marian, Marion, agrarian, Aquarian, barbarian, Bavarian, Bulgarian, cesarean, Hungarian, ovarian, Rastafarian, Austro-Hungarian

ariat¹ \er-ē-ət\ lariat • commissariat, proletariat, secretariat

ariat² \ar-ē-ət\ chariot, lariat • commissariat, proletariat • Judas Iscariot

ariate \er-ē-ət\ see ARIAT¹

arib \ar-əb\ see ARAB

arice \ar-əs\ see ARIS²

aridness \ar-əd-nəs\ aridness • preparedness

aried¹ \er-ēd\ see ERRIED

aried² \ar-ēd\ see ARRIED

ariel \er-ē-əl\ see ARIAL

arier[1] \er-ē-ər\ see ERRIER
arier[2] \ar-ē-ər\ see ARRIER[2]
aries \ar-ēz\ see ARES[2]
arilee[1] \ar-ə-lē\ see ARALEE
arilee[2] \er-ə-lē\ see ARILY
arily \er-ə-lē\ merrily, scarily, war-
ily • primarily • arbitrarily, cus-
tomarily, legendarily, militarily,
momentarily, monetarily, neces-
sarily, ordinarily, secondarily,
temporarily, voluntarily • extraor-
dinarily, involuntarily, unneces-
sarily
arin \är-ən\ foreign, Lauren, Orin,
warren, Warren
arinate \ar-ə-nət\ see ARONET
arinet \ar-ə-nət\ see ARONET
aring[1] \er-iŋ\ airing, bearing,
Bering, daring, fairing, flaring,
glaring, herring, paring, raring,
sparing, tearing, wearing • ball
bearing, childbearing, seafaring,
time-sharing, unerring, unsparing,
wayfaring • overbearing, profit
sharing
—also -ing forms of verbs listed at
ARE[4]
aring[2] \er-ən\ see ARON[1]
ario \er-ē-ō\ stereo • Ontario
arion[1] \ar-ē-ən\ see ARIAN[2]
arion[2] \er-ē-ən\ see ARIAN[1]
ariot \ar-ē-ət\ see ARIAT[2]
arious \er-ē-əs\ Darius, various
• Aquarius, gregarious, hilarious,
nefarious, precarious, vicarious
• Stradivarius, Sagittarius
aris[1] \är-əs\ see ORRIS[1]
aris[2] \ar-əs\ Clarice, harass, Harris,
Paris • coheiress, embarrass,
Polaris • plaster of paris
arish[1] \er-ish\ bearish, cherish,
garish, perish, squarish • night-
marish
arish[2] \ar-ish\ garish, parish • vine-
garish
arison \ar-ə-sən\ garrison, Garrison,
Harrison, Saracen • comparison

arist \er-əst\ scenarist
—also -est forms of adjectives
listed at ARE[4]
aritan \er-ət-ᵊn\ see ERATIN
arity[1] \er-ət-ē\ see ERITY
arity[2] \ar-ət-ē\ charity, clarity,
parity, rarity • barbarity, dispar-
ity, hilarity, polarity, vulgarity
• angularity, circularity, familiar-
ity, muscularity, peculiarity,
popularity, regularity, similarity,
singularity, solidarity • dissimilar-
ity, irregularity, unfamiliarity,
unpopularity
arium \er-ē-əm\ aquarium, herbar-
ium, solarium, terrarium, vivar-
ium • honorarium, oceanarium,
planetarium, sanitarium
arius \er-ē-əs\ see ARIOUS
ark[1] \ärk\ arc, ark, bark, Clark,
dark, hark, lark, Marc, mark,
Mark, narc, nark, park, quark,
shark, spark, stark • aardvark,
airpark, ballpark, benchmark,
birchbark, birthmark, Bismarck,
blue shark, bookmark, check
mark, debark, Denmark, ear-
mark, embark, hallmark, hash
mark, landmark, monarch,
Ozark, pitch-dark, pockmark,
postmark, remark, shagbark,
skylark, theme park, tidemark,
trademark, whale shark • basking
shark, disembark, double-park,
Estes Park, great white shark,
Joan of Arc, make one's mark,
mako shark, matriarch, mead-
owlark, oligarch, patriarch, question mark, thresher shark, tiger
shark, toe the mark, watermark,
water park • amusement park,
high-water mark, in the ballpark,
shot in the dark, vest-pocket park
• whistle in the dark
ark[2] \órk\ see ORK[2]
ark[3] \ərk\ see ORK[1]
arke \ärk\ see ARK[1]

arked \ärkt\ marked • ripple-
marked
—*also* -ed *forms of verbs listed at*
ARK[1]
arken \är-kən\ darken, hearken
arker \är-kər\ barker, darker,
marker, Parker, starker • book-
marker, Ozarker, skylarker
• Magic Marker, nosey parker
arkey \är-kē\ see ARCHY
arkic \är-kik\ see ARCHIC
arking \är-kiŋ\ barking, marking,
parking • loan-sharking • valet
parking
—*also* -ing *forms of verbs listed at*
ARK[1]
arkle \är-kəl\ see ARCHAL
arks \ärks\ Marx • Ozarks
—*also* -s, -'s, *and* -s' *forms of*
nouns and -s *forms of verbs listed*
at ARK[1]
arky \är-kē\ see ARCHY
arl \ärl\ Carl, gnarl, Karl, quarrel,
snarl • ensnarl, unsnarl
arla \är-lə\ Carla, Darla, Marla
arlan \ä-lən\ see ARLINE
arlay \är-lē\ see ARLIE
arle \ärl\ see ARL
arlen \är-lən\ see ARLINE
arler \är-lər\ see ARLOR
arless \är-ləs\ Carlos, starless
arlet \är-lət\ Charlotte, harlot,
scarlet, starlet, varlet
arley \är-lē\ see ARLIE
arlie \är-lē\ barley, Charlie, gnarly,
Harley, parlay, parley, snarly
• bizarrely
arlin \är-lən\ see ARLINE
arline \är-lən\ Harlan, marlin,
Marlin • blue marlin, white marlin
arling \är-liŋ\ darling, starling
—*also* -ing *forms of verbs listed at*
ARL
arlor \är-lər\ parlor, quarreler
arlos \är-ləs\ see ARLESS
arlot \är-lət\ see ARLET

arlotte \är-lət\ see ARLET
arlous \är-ləs\ see ARLESS
arly \är-lē\ see ARLIE
arlyn \ä-lən\ see ARLINE
arm[1] \ärm\ arm, charm, farm,
harm • alarm, disarm, firearm,
fish farm, forearm, nonfarm,
rearm, schoolmarm, sidearm,
strong-arm, tree farm, unarm,
wind farm • arm in arm, buy the
farm, false alarm, overarm, twist
one's arm, underarm • collective
farm, shot in the arm
arm[2] \äm\ see OM[1]
arm[3] \òrm\ see ORM[2]
arma[1] \är-mə\ karma, Parma
arma[2] \ər-mə\ see ERMA
armed \ärmd\ armed, charmed
• unarmed
—*also* -ed *forms of verbs listed at*
ARM[1]
arment \är-mənt\ garment, varmint
• disbarment • undergarment,
overgarment
armer[1] \är-mər\ armor, charmer,
farmer • snake charmer • tenant
farmer
armer[2] \òr-mər\ see ORMER
armic \ər-mik\ see ERMIC
arming[1] \är-miŋ\ charming, farm-
ing • alarming, disarming, Prince
Charming
—*also* -ing *forms of verbs listed at*
ARM[1]
arming[2] \òr-miŋ\ see ORMING
armint \är-mənt\ see ARMENT
armless \ärm-ləs\ armless, charm-
less, harmless
armoir \är-mər\ see ARMER[1]
army \är-mē\ army, smarmy
• standing army • Salvation Army
arn[1] \ärn\ barn, darn, yarn
arn[2] \òrn\ see ORN[1]
arna \ər-nə\ see ERNA
arnate \är-nət\ garnet • incarnate
arne[1] \ärn\ see ARN[1]
arne[2] \är-nē\ see ARNY

arner \ȯr-nər\ see ORNER
arness \är-nəs\ harness
• bizarreness
arnet \är-nət\ see ARNATE
arney \är-nē\ see ARNY
arning \ȯr-niŋ\ see ORNING
arnish \är-nish\ garnish, tarnish,
varnish
arny \är-nē\ Barney, blarney, carny
• Killarney • chili con carne
aro[1] \er-ō\ see ERO[2]
aro[2] \ar-ō\ see ARROW[2]
aro[3] \är-ə\ see ARA[1]
aro[4] \är-ō\ see ORROW[1]
arob \ar-əb\ see ARAB
aroe[1] \ar-ō\ see ARROW[2]
aroe[2] \er-ō\ see ERO[2]
arol \ar-əl\ see ARREL[2]
arold \er-əld\ see ERALD
arole \ar-əl\ see ARREL[2]
arom \er-əm\ see ARUM
aron[1] \er-ən\ Aaron, baron,
Charon, Erin, heron, raring,
Sharon • sub-Saharan
aron[2] \ar-ən\ Aaron, baron, barren,
Charon, Sharon • sub-Saharan
aronet \ar-ə-nət\ baronet, clarinet
arous[1] \er-əs\ see ERROUS
arous[2] \ar-əs\ see ARIS[2]
arp[1] \ärp\ carp, harp, sharp, tarp
• Jew's harp • Autoharp, super-
sharp
arp[2] \ȯrp\ see ORP
arpen \är-pən\ sharpen, tarpon
arper \är-pər\ carper, sharper
arpie \är-pē\ see ARPY
arpon \är-pən\ see ARPEN
arpy \är-pē\ harpy, sharpie
arque \ärk\ see ARK[1]
arqui \är-kē\ see ARCHY
arrable \ar-ə-bəl\ see ARABLE
arrage \är-ij\ see [1]orage
arragon \ar-ə-gən\ see ARAGON
arrant[1] \ar-ənt\ see ARENT[2]
arrant[2] \ȯr-ənt\ see ORRENT
arras \ar-əs\ see ARIS[2]
arrass \ar-əs\ see ARIS[2]

arrative \ar-ət-iv\ see ARATIVE[2]
arre \är\ see AR[3]
arred \ärd\ see ARD[1]
arrel[1] \ȯr-əl\ see ORAL
arrel[2] \ar-əl\ Aral, barrel, carol,
Carol, Darryl • apparel • cracker-
barrel
arreler \är-lər\ see ARLOR
arrell \ar-əl\ see ARREL[2]
arrely \är-lē\ see ARLIE
arren[1] \ar-ən\ see ARON[2]
arren[2] \ȯr-ən\ see ORIN[1]
arren[3] \är-ən\ see ARIN
arrener \ȯr-ə-nər\ see ORONER
arreness \är-nəs\ see ARNESS
arret \ar-ət\ see ARAT
arrett \ar-ət\ see ARAT
arrh \är\ see AR[3]
arriage \ar-ij\ carriage, marriage
• disparage, miscarriage, mixed
marriage • baby carriage, horse-
less carriage, intermarriage, un-
dercarriage
arrie \ar-ē\ see ARRY[3]
arried \ar-ēd\ harried, married,
varied • unmarried
arrier[1] \ȯr-ē-ər\ see ARRIOR
arrier[2] \ar-ē-ər\ barrier, carrier
• ballcarrier, mail carrier, noncar-
rier, sound barrier, spear-carrier
• aircraft carrier, letter carrier
arrion \ar-ē-ən\ see ARIAN[2]
arrior \ȯr-ē-ər\ sorrier, warrior
• weekend warrior
arris \ar-əs\ see ARIS[2]
arrison \ar-ə-sən\ see ARISON
arro \är-ō\ see ORROW[1]
arroll \ar-əl\ see ARREL[2]
arron \ar-ən\ see ARON[2]
arrot \ar-ət\ see ARAT
arroty \ar-ət-ē\ see ARITY[2]
arrow[1] \ar-ə\ Clara, Kara, Sarah,
Tara • mascara, Sahara, tiara
• capybara, marinara, Santa Clara
arrow[2] \ar-ō\ arrow, barrow, har-
row, marrow, narrow, pharaoh,
sparrow, taro, tarot, yarrow

• bone marrow, house sparrow, Point Barrow, song sparrow, straight-arrow, tree sparrow, wheelbarrow • straight and narrow • Kilimanjaro

arry[1] \är-ē\ see ARI[1]

arry[2] \ȯr-ē\ see ORY

arry[3] \ar-ē\ Barry, Carrie, carry, Cary, chary, Gary, Harry, Larry, marry, nary, parry, Shari, tarry • miscarry, safari • cash-and-carry, hari-kari, intermarry, Stradivari • Tom, Dick, and Harry

arryl \ar-əl\ see ARREL[2]

ars \ärz\ Lars, Mars, ours • behind bars, Stars and Bars
—*also* -s, -'s, *and* -s' *forms of nouns and* -s *forms of verbs listed at* AR[3]

arse[1] \ärs\ farce, sparse

arse[2] \ärz\ see ARS

arsh \ärsh\ harsh, marsh • salt marsh

arshal \är-shəl\ see ARTIAL

arshall \är-shəl\ see ARTIAL

arsle \äs-əl\ see OSSAL

arson \ärs-ᵊn\ arson, Carson, parson

art[1] \ärt\ art, Art, Bart, cart, chart, Chartres, dart, hart, heart, kart, mart, part, smart, start, tart • apart, at heart, bar chart, Bogart, by heart, clip art, depart, dogcart, Earhart, eye chart, false start, fine art, folk art, go-cart, golf cart, handcart, head start, Hobart, impart, in part, jumpstart, kick-start, mouthpart, Mozart, outsmart, oxcart, pie chart, pop art, pushcart, rampart, restart, street-smart, Stuttgart, sweetheart, take heart, take part, upstart, voice part • à la carte, applecart, bleeding heart, Bonaparte, change of heart, counterpart, fall apart, flying start, for one's part, heart-to-heart, martial

art, mini-mart, multipart, on one's part, open-heart, poles apart, Purple Heart, running start, set apart, take apart, underpart • for the most part, performance art, state-of-the-art

art[2] \ȯrt\ see ORT[1]

arta \är-tə\ Marta, Sparta • Jakarta • Magna Carta

artan \ärt-ᵊn\ see ARTEN

artar \ärt-ər\ see ARTER[1]

arte[1] \ärt-ē\ see ARTY[1]

arte[2] \ärt\ see ART[1]

arted[1] \ärt-əd\ see EARTED

arted[2] \ȯrt-əd\ see ORTED

arten \ärt-ᵊn\ carton, hearten, Martin, smarten, Spartan, tartan • dishearten, Saint Martin • kindergarten

arter[1] \ärt-ər\ barter, Carter, charter, garter, martyr, starter, tartar • nonstarter, self-starter, snail darter
—*also* -er *forms of adjectives listed at* ART[1]

arter[2] \ȯt-ər\ see ATER[1]

arter[3] \ȯrt-ər\ see ORTER

artes \ärt\ see ART[1]

arth \ärth\ Garth, hearth • openhearth

arti \ärt-ē\ see ARTY[1]

artial \är-shəl\ marshal, Marshal, Marshall, martial, partial • courtmartial, earl marshal, field marshal, grand marshal, impartial, sky marshal

artic \ärt-ik\ arctic, Arctic • antarctic, Antarctic, cathartic

article \ärt-i-kəl\ article, particle • alpha particle, beta particle, microparticle

artile \ȯrt-ᵊl\ see ORTAL

artily \ärt-ᵊl-ē\ artily, heartily

artin \ärt-ᵊn\ see ARTEN

arting \ärt-iŋ\ carting, charting, karting, parting, starting • selfstarting

—*also* -ing *forms of verbs listed at*
ART[1]

artisan \ärt-ə-zən\ artisan, partisan
• bipartisan, nonpartisan

artizan \ärt-ə-zən\ see ARTISAN

artless \ärt-ləs\ artless, heartless

artly[1] \ärt-lē\ partly, smartly, tartly

artly[2] \ort-lē\ see ORTLY

artner \ärt-nər\ partner • kinder-
gartner, secret partner

arton \ärt-ᵊn\ see ARTEN

artre \ärt\ see ART[1]

artres \ärt\ see ART[1]

artridge \är-trij\ cartridge, par-
tridge

arts[1] \är\ see AR[3]

arts[2] \ärts\ street smarts • private
parts • master of arts, principal
parts
—*also* -s, -'s, *and* -s' *forms of nouns
and* -s *forms of verbs listed at* ART[1]

arture \är-chər\ see ARCHER

arty[1] \ärt-ē\ arty, hearty, party,
smarty • block party, Havarti, tea
party, war party • cocktail party,
slumber party

arty[2] \ort-ē\ see ORTY

artyr \ärt-ər\ see ARTER[1]

artz[1] \orts\ see ORTS

artz[2] \ärts\ see ARTS[2]

arum \er-əm\ harem • harum-
scarum

arus \ar-əs\ see ARIS[2]

arval \är-vəl\ see ARVEL

arve \ärv\ carve, starve

arvel \är-vəl\ larval, marvel

ary[1] \er-ē\ aerie, airy, berry, bury,
Carey, Cary, Cherie, cherry,
Cherry, dairy, Derry, fairy, ferry,
Gary, Gerry, hairy, Jerry, Kerry,
Mary, marry, merry, Merry, nary,
Perry, prairie, query, scary, Shari,
sherry, terry, Terry, vary, very,
wary • barberry, bayberry, bear-
berry, bing cherry, blackberry,
black cherry, blueberry, canary,
chokeberry, chokecherry, con-

trary, cranberry, dewberry, goose-
berry, hackberry, Hail Mary,
library, mulberry, nondairy,
primary, raspberry, rosemary,
Rosemary, soapberry, strawberry,
summary, tooth fairy, unwary
• actuary, adversary, antiquary,
apiary, arbitrary, aviary, beriberi,
black raspberry, boysenberry,
budgetary, Canterbury, capillary,
cautionary, cemetery, centenary,
chinaberry, commentary, com-
missary, corollary, coronary,
culinary, customary, dictionary,
dietary, dignitary, dromedary,
dysentery, elderberry, emissary,
estuary, February, fragmentary,
functionary, honorary, huckle-
berry, intermarry, January, lec-
tionary, legendary, legionary,
lingonberry, literary, loganberry,
luminary, mercenary, military,
millinery, missionary, momen-
tary, monastery, monetary, mor-
tuary, necessary, ordinary,
partridgeberry, planetary, pul-
monary, red mulberry, reliquary,
salivary, salmonberry, salutary,
sanctuary, sanitary, secondary,
secretary, sedentary, seminary,
serviceberry, solitary, sugar
cherry, stationary, stationery,
statuary, Stradivari, temporary,
Tipperary, Tom and Jerry, tribu-
tary, Typhoid Mary, unitary,
urinary, Virgin Mary, visionary,
voluntary, winterberry • bicentenary, confectionery, contempo-
rary, deflationary, disciplinary,
discretionary, extemporary, ex-
traordinary, hereditary, illusion-
ary, imaginary, incendiary,
inflationary, insanitary, interli-
brary, involuntary, itinerary,
judiciary, lending library, nonmil-
itary, obituary, on the contrary,
pituitary, precautionary, prelimi-

nary, probationary, reactionary, subsidiary, uncustomary, unnecessary, unsanitary, veterinary, vocabulary • beneficiary, evolutionary, intermediary, interplanetary, paramilitary, penitentiary, revolutionary

ary² \ar-ē\ see ARRY³

ary³ \är-ē\ see ARI¹

aryan¹ \er-ē-ən\ see ARIAN¹

aryan² \ar-ē-ən\ see ARIAN²

aryl \ar-əl\ see ARREL²

as¹ \ash\ see ASH³

as² \as\ see ASS³

as³ \az\ see AZZ

as⁴ \ä\ see A¹

as⁵ \äsh\ see ASH¹

as⁶ \äz\ see OISE¹

as⁷ \əz\ see EUSE¹

as⁸ \äs\ see OS¹

as⁹ \ȯ\ see AW¹

asa¹ \äs-ə\ Lhasa, Ossa • kielbasa

asa² \äz-ə\ see AZA¹

asable \ā-sə-bəl\ see ACEABLE

asal \ā-zəl\ Basil, hazel, Hazel, nasal, phrasal • appraisal, witch hazel

asally \āz-lē\ see AISLEY

asca \as-kə\ see ASKA

ascal \as-kəl\ paschal, rascal

ascar \as-kər\ see ASKER

ascent \ās-ᵊnt\ see ACENT

asch¹ \ask\ see ASK

asch² \äsh\ see ASH¹

asch³ \ȯsh\ see ASH²

aschal \as-kəl\ see ASCAL

ascia \ā-shə\ see ACIA

ascible \as-ə-bəl\ see ASSABLE

ascicle \as-i-kəl\ see ASSICAL

asco¹ \äs-kō\ see OSCOE

asco² \as-kō\ fiasco, Tabasco

ascot \as-kət\ see ASKET

ascus \as-kəs\ Damascus, Velázquez

ase¹ \ās\ see ACE¹

ase² \āz\ see AZE¹

ase³ \äz\ see OISE¹

asel \äz-əl\ see OZZLE

ased \āst\ see ACED

aseless \ā-sləs\ see ACELESS

aseman \ā-smən\ see ACEMAN

asement \ās-mənt\ basement, casement • abasement, debasement • bargain-basement, self-abasement

aser¹ \ā-sər\ see ACER¹

aser² \ā-zər\ see AZER

asey \ā-sē\ see ACY

ash¹ \äsh\ gosh, josh, mosh, nosh, posh, quash, slosh, squash, swash, wash • awash, backwash, eyewash, galosh, goulash, kibosh, mishmash, mouthwash, whitewash • acorn squash, hubbard squash, mackintosh, summer squash, winter squash

ash² \ȯsh\ gosh, quash, slosh, squash, swash, wash • awash, backwash, brainwash, car wash, eyewash, hogwash, mouthwash, prewash, whitewash • acorn squash, hubbard squash, summer squash, winter squash

ash³ \ash\ ash, bash, brash, cache, cash, clash, crash, dash, flash, gash, gnash, hash, lash, mash, rash, sash, slash, smash, splash, stash, thrash, thresh, trash • abash, backlash, backslash, cold cash, eyelash, gate-crash, goulash, green flash, heat rash, hot flash, mishmash, moustache, mustache, potash, rehash, slapdash, tongue-lash, unlash, Wabash, whiplash, white ash • balderdash, calabash, diaper rash, mountain ash, nettle rash, petty cash, prickly rash, succotash • settle one's hash

ashan \ash-ən\ see ASSION

ashed¹ \ȯsht\ sloshed • stonewashed, unwashed • acid-washed

—*also* -ed *forms of verbs listed at* ASH²

ashed[2] \asht\ dashed, smashed
• unabashed
—*also* -ed *forms of verbs listed at* ASH[3]

ashen \ash-ən\ see ASSION

asher[1] \äsh-ər\ josher, mosher, nosher, squasher, washer • dishwasher

asher[2] \òsh-ər\ washer • brainwasher, dishwasher, whitewasher

asher[3] \ash-ər\ basher, crasher, rasher, slasher, smasher • gatecrasher • atom-smasher, haberdasher

ashi[1] \äsh-ē\ see ASHY[1]

ashi[2] \ash-ē\ see ASHY[2]

ashing \ash-iŋ\ crashing, dashing, flashing, mashing, slashing, smashing • tongue-lashing
—*also* -ing *forms of verbs listed at* ASH[3]

ashion \ash-ən\ see ASSION

asht \asht\ see ASHED[2]

ashy[1] \äsh-ē\ squashy • wishy-washy

ashy[2] \ash-ē\ ashy, flashy, splashy, trashy

asi[1] \äs-ē\ see OSSY[1]

asi[2] \äz-ē\ see AZI[1]

asi[3] \äsh-ē\ see ASHY[1]

asia \ā-zhə\ Asia • Caucasia, Eurasia, fantasia, Malaysia • Anastasia, Australasia, euthanasia

asian[1] \ā-shən\ see ATION[1]

asian[2] \ā-zhən\ see ASION

asic \ā-zik\ phasic • euthanasic, multiphasic

asid \as-əd\ see ACID

asie \ā-sē\ see ACY

asil[1] \as-əl\ see ASSEL[2]

asil[2] \az-əl\ see AZZLE

asil[3] \āz-əl\ see ASAL

asil[4] \äz-əl\ see OZZLE

asin \ās-ᵊn\ see ASON[1]

asing[1] \ā-siŋ\ see ACING

asing[2] \ā-ziŋ\ see AISING

asion \ā-zhən\ Asian • abrasion, Caucasian, dissuasion, equation, Eurasian, evasion, invasion, occasion, persuasion • Amerasian, anti-Asian, Australasian, on occasion

asis \ā-səs\ basis • oasis • homeostasis

asive \ā-siv\ abrasive, evasive, invasive, persuasive, pervasive

ask \ask\ ask, bask, Basque, cask, flask, mask, task • death mask, face mask, gas mask, ski mask, unmask • multitask, take to task, vacuum flask • oxygen mask

aska \as-kə\ Alaska, Nebraska

asked \ast\ see AST[2]

asker \as-kər\ masker • Madagascar

asket \as-kət\ ascot, basket, casket, gasket • breadbasket, handbasket, wastebasket • blow a gasket

asking \as-kiŋ\ multitasking
—*also* -ing *forms of verbs listed at* ASK

asm \az-əm\ chasm, plasm, spasm • phantasm, sarcasm • ectoplasm, protoplasm • enthusiasm

asma \az-mə\ asthma, plasma • miasma

asn't \əz-ᵊnt\ doesn't, wasn't

aso[1] \as-ō\ see ASSO[1]

aso[2] \äs-ō\ see ASSO[2]

ason[1] \ās-ᵊn\ basin, caisson, chasten, hasten, Jason, mason, Mason • Freemason, Great Basin, stonemason, washbasin

ason[2] \āz-ᵊn\ see AZON

asp \asp\ asp, clasp, gasp, grasp, hasp, rasp • handclasp, last-gasp, unclasp

asque \ask\ see ASK

asquer \as-kər\ see ASKER

ass[1] \ās\ see ACE[1]

ass[2] \äs\ see OS[1]

ass[3] \as\ ass, bass, brass, class, crass, gas, glass, grass, has, lass, mass, pass, sass • air mass, alas,

Alsace, amass, art glass, beach grass, bear grass, bent grass, black bass, Black Mass, bluegrass, bunchgrass, bypass, crabgrass, crevasse, cuirass, cut glass, degas, eelgrass, en masse, eyeglass, first-class, folk mass, ground glass, harass, high-class, high mass, hourglass, impasse, jackass, jump pass, landmass, Madras, milk glass, morass, oat grass, outclass, plate glass, quack grass, rock bass, ryegrass, salt grass, sandglass, saw grass, screen pass, sea bass, sheet glass, shortgrass, smart-ass, spun glass, spyglass, stained glass, striped bass, subclass, sung mass, surpass, sweetgrass, switchgrass, sword grass, tallgrass, teargas, third-class, trespass, turfgrass, wheatgrass, white bass, wineglass, wire grass, wiseass, witchgrass, world-class, yard grass • bottled gas, Brenner Pass, Cajon Pass, channel bass, cocktail glass, come to pass, demitasse, Donner Pass, fiberglass, forward pass, Khyber Pass, largemouth bass, laughing gas, lemongrass, looking glass, lowerclass, middle-class, opera glass, overpass, Plexiglas, safety glass, sassafras, second-class, Simplon Pass, smallmouth bass, solemn mass, tourist class, underclass, underpass, upper-class, water glass, working-class • atomic mass, critical mass, laughing jackass, snake in the grass
assable \as-ə-bəl\ passable • impassable, irascible • unsurpassable
assail \äs-əl\ see OSSAL
assal \as-əl\ see ASSEL[2]
assar \as-ər\ see ASSER
asse[1] \as\ see ASS[3]
asse[2] \äs\ see OS[1]
assed \ast\ see AST[2]

assee \as-ē\ see ASSY
assel[1] \äs-əl\ see OSSAL
assel[2] \as-əl\ Basil, castle, facile, hassle, passel, tassel, vassal, wrestle • forecastle
asser \as-ər\ crasser, gasser • amasser, harasser • antimacassar
asset \as-ət\ see ACET
assian \ash-ən\ see ASSION
assible \as-ə-bəl\ see ASSABLE
assic \as-ik\ classic • Jurassic, Triassic • neoclassic, semiclassic
assical \as-i-kəl\ classical, fascicle • semiclassical
assid \as-əd\ see ACID
assie[1] \as-ē\ see ASSY
assie[2] \äs-ē\ see OSSY[1]
assim \äs-əm\ see OSSUM
assin \as-ᵊn\ see ASTEN[2]
assion \ash-ən\ ashen, fashion, passion, ration • compassion, high fashion, impassion, refashion • after a fashion
assis \as-ē\ see ASSY
assist \ā-sist\ bassist, racist • contrabassist, double bassist
assive \as-iv\ massive, passive • impassive
assle \as-əl\ see ASSEL[2]
assness \as-nəs\ see ASTNESS
asso[1] \as-ō\ basso, lasso • El Paso, Picasso, sargasso
asso[2] \äs-ō\ Picasso • Burkina Faso
assock \as-ək\ cassock, hassock
assus \as-əs\ see ASSIS
assy \as-ē\ brassy, chassis, classy, gassy, glassy, grassy, lassie, sassy • Tallahassee • Haile Selassie
ast[1] \əst\ see UST[1]
ast[2] \ast\ blast, cast, caste, fast, hast, last, mast, past, vast • aghast, at last, avast, Belfast, bombast, broadcast, contrast, downcast, forecast, foremast, full blast, gymnast, half-caste, halfmast, mainmast, miscast, newscast, offcast, outcast, repast,

sandblast, sportscast, steadfast, topmast, typecast, unasked, webcast, windblast • acid-fast, at long last, colorcast, colorfast, counterblast, flabbergast, hard-and-fast, mizzenmast, overcast, plaster cast, simulcast, telecast, weathercast • enthusiast, iconoclast
—*also* -ed *forms of verbs listed at* ASS[3]

asta \as-tə\ canasta • Mount Shasta
astable \at-ə-bəl\ *see* ATIBLE
astard \as-tərd\ bastard, dastard, plastered
aste[1] \āst\ *see* ACED
aste[2] \ast\ *see* AST[2]
asted \as-təd\ blasted, masted
—*also* -ed *forms of verbs listed at* AST[2]
asteful \āst-fəl\ tasteful, wasteful • distasteful
asten[1] \ās-ᵊn\ *see* ASON[1]
asten[2] \as-ᵊn\ fasten • assassin, unfasten
aster[1] \ā-stər\ baster, taster • wine taster
aster[2] \as-tər\ aster, Astor, blaster, caster, castor, faster, master, pastor, plaster • bandmaster, brewmaster, broadcaster, choirmaster, disaster, dockmaster, drillmaster, grand master, headmaster, newscaster, past master, paymaster, postmaster, quizmaster, remaster, ringmaster, sandblaster, schoolmaster, scoutmaster, sportscaster, spymaster, surf caster, taskmaster, toastmaster, webcaster • alabaster, burgomaster, China aster, concertmaster, ghetto blaster, harbormaster, quartermaster, stationmaster, telecaster, wagon master, weathercaster
astered \as-tərd\ *see* ASTARD
astering \as-tə-riŋ\ plastering • overmastering

—*also* -ing *forms of verbs listed at* ASTER[2]
astes \as-tēz\ Ecclesiastes
—*also* -s, -'s, *and* -s' *forms of nouns listed at* ASTY[2]
asthma \az-mə\ *see* ASMA
astic \as-tik\ drastic, plastic, spastic • bombastic, dynastic, elastic, fantastic, gymnastic, monastic, sarcastic, scholastic • ecclesiastic, enthusiastic, iconoclastic, interscholastic
astics \as-tiks\ gymnastics, slimnastics
astid \as-təd\ *see* ASTED
astie \as-tē\ *see* ASTY[2]
astiness \ā-stē-nəs\ hastiness, tastiness
asting[1] \ā-stiŋ\ basting, wasting
—*also* -ing *forms of verbs listed at* ACED
asting[2] \as-tiŋ\ casting, lasting • fly casting, linecasting, surf casting, typecasting • central casting, everlasting
—*also* -ing *forms of verbs listed at* AST[2]
astle \as-əl\ *see* ASSEL[2]
astly \ast-lē\ ghastly, lastly, vastly • steadfastly
astness \as-nəs\ crassness • steadfastness • colorfastness
astor \as-tər\ *see* ASTER[2]
astoral \as-trəl\ *see* ASTRAL
astral \as-trəl\ astral, pastoral
astre \as-tər\ *see* ASTER[2]
asty[1] \ā-stē\ hasty, pasty, tasty
asty[2] \as-tē\ nasty • capacity, contrasty • angioplasty, overcapacity
asuble \as-ə-bəl\ *see* ASSABLE
asure[1] \ā-shər\ glacier • erasure
asure[2] \ā-zhər\ *see* AZIER
asy \as-ē\ *see* ASSY
at[1] \ä\ *see* A[1]
at[2] \ät\ *see* OT[1]
at[3] \ət\ *see* UT[1]
at[4] \ȯt\ *see* OUGHT[1]

at⁵ \at\ bat, brat, cat, chat, drat, fat, flat, frat, gat, gnat, hat, mat, Matt, matte, pat, Pat, phat, plait, plat, rat, sat, scat, slat, spat, splat, stat, that, vat • all that, at bat, at that, bath mat, begat, bobcat, brickbat, brown rat, Cassatt, chitchat, combat, comsat, coon cat, cowpat, cravat, Croat, defat, dingbat, doormat, fat cat, fiat, fly at, format, fruit bat, get at, go at, hard hat, have at, hellcat, high-hat, house cat, keep at, look at, Manx cat, meerkat, milk fat, mole rat, mudflat, muskrat, nonfat, old hat, pack rat, pick at, place mat, polecat, rug rat, salt flat, silk hat, sneeze at, snowcat, stand pat, tomcat, top hat, trans fat, whereat, white hat, wildcat, wombat • acrobat, alley cat, Ararat, arrive at, autocrat, bell the cat, bureaucrat, butterfat, Cheshire cat, chew the fat, copycat, cowboy hat, democrat, diplomat, habitat, hang one's hat, jungle cat, Laundromat, leopard cat, Norway rat, off the bat, Persian cat, photostat, pit-a-pat, plutocrat, poke fun at, pussycat, rat-a-tat, reformat, scaredy-cat, smell a rat, take aim at, technocrat, thermostat, tiger cat, tit for tat, vampire bat, water rat, welcome mat, where it's at • Angora cat, aristocrat, go to the mat, Jehoshaphat, kangaroo rat, Siamese cat, single combat, talk through one's hat, ten-gallon hat, throw money at, under one's hat • proletariat, secretariat

at⁶ \a\ see AH³

ata¹ \ät-ə\ cantata, Carlotta, pinata, regatta, ricotta, sonata • terracotta • persona non grata, Rio de la Plata

ata² \āt-ə\ beta, data, eta, strata, theta, zeta • peseta, potato, substrata, tomato

ata³ \at-ə\ data • regatta • persona non grata

atable¹ \āt-ə-bəl\ debatable, inflatable, locatable, relatable, rotatable, translatable • cultivatable, untranslatable

atable² \at-ə-bəl\ see ATIBLE

atal \āt-ᵊl\ fatal, natal • nonfatal, postnatal, prenatal

atalie \at-ᵊl-ē\ see ATTILY

atally \āt-ᵊl-ē\ fatally, natally • postnatally, prenatally

atalyst \at-ᵊl-əst\ catalyst • philatelist

atan¹ \āt-ən\ see ATEN¹

atan² \at-ᵊn\ see ATIN²

atant¹ \āt-ᵊnt\ blatant, latent, patent

atant² \at-ᵊnt\ patent • combatant • noncombatant

atar \ät-ər\ see OTTER

atary \ät-ə-rē\ see OTTERY

atch¹ \ech\ see ETCH

atch² \äch\ see OTCH

atch³ \ach\ batch, catch, hatch, latch, match, natch, patch, scratch, snatch, thatch • attach, crosshatch, detach, dispatch, fair catch, from scratch, mismatch, night latch, nuthatch, outmatch, rematch, Sasquatch, unlatch, Wasatch • booby hatch, coffee klatch, escape hatch, safety match, shoulder patch

atcher¹ \äch-ər\ watcher • birdwatcher, clock-watcher, topnotcher

atcher² \ach-ər\ batcher, catcher, stature • cowcatcher, dispatcher, dogcatcher, eye-catcher, flycatcher, head-scratcher • body snatcher, train dispatcher

atchet \ach-ət\ hatchet, ratchet • bury the hatchet

atchily \ach-ə-lē\ patchily,
scratchily

atching \ach-iŋ\ catching • back-
scratching, cross-hatching, eye-
catching, head-scratching,
nonmatching
—*also* -ing *forms of verbs listed at*
ATCH³

atchman \äch-mən\ see OTCHMAN

atchment \ach-mənt\ catchment
• attachment, detachment

atchouli \ach-ə-lē\ see ATCHILY

atchy \ach-ē\ catchy, patchy,
scratchy • Apache

ate¹ \āt\ ate, bait, Cate, crate, date,
eight, fate, freight, gait, gate,
grate, great, hate, Kate, late,
mate, pate, plait, plate, rate, sate,
skate, slate, spate, state, straight,
strait, trait, wait, weight • abate,
aerate, age-mate, airfreight, await,
bandmate, baseplate, Bass Strait,
berate, birthrate, blank slate,
blind date, bookplate, breastplate,
cheapskate, checkmate, citrate,
classmate, collate, create, cre-
mate, curate, cut-rate,
deadweight, death rate, debate,
deflate, dictate, dilate, donate,
elate, equate, estate, filtrate, first-
rate, fixate, floodgate, flyweight,
frustrate, gestate, gyrate, help-
mate, home plate, hot plate,
housemate, hydrate, ice-skate,
inflate, ingrate, inmate, innate,
instate, irate, khanate, Kuwait,
lactate, legate, lightweight, locate,
magnate, mandate, messmate,
migrate, misstate, mutate, name-
plate, narrate, negate, nitrate,
notate, of late, orate, ornate,
outwait, placate, playdate, play-
mate, portrait, postdate, predate,
primate, prime rate, probate,
prorate, prostrate, pulsate, rain
date, rebate, relate, restate, room-
mate, rotate, schoolmate, seat-

mate, sedate, shipmate, soul mate,
spectate, stagnate, stalemate,
substrate, tailgate, teammate,
tenth-rate, third-rate, tinplate, to
date, tollgate, translate, tristate,
truncate, update, upstate, V-8,
vacate, vibrate, workmate • abdi-
cate, acclimate, activate, advo-
cate, aggravate, aggregate, agitate,
allocate, alternate, amputate,
animate, annotate, apartheid,
apostate, arbitrate, automate,
bantamweight, Bering Strait,
cabinmate, Cabot Strait, calcu-
late, calibrate, caliphate, candi-
date, captivate, carbonate,
carbon-date, castigate, celebrate,
chief of state, chlorinate, circu-
late, city-state, cogitate, collocate,
compensate, complicate, concen-
trate, condensate, confiscate,
conjugate, consecrate, constipate,
consummate, contemplate, cop-
perplate, correlate, corrugate,
counterweight, culminate, culti-
vate, Davis Strait, decimate, deco-
rate, dedicate, dehydrate,
delegate, demarcate, demonstrate,
denigrate, Denmark Strait, deviate, deprecate, desecrate, desig-
nate, desolate, detonate,
devastate, deviate, dislocate,
dissipate, distillate, dominate,
double date, duplicate, educate,
elevate, elongate, emanate, emi-
grate, emirate, emulate, escalate,
estimate, excavate, exchange rate,
exculpate, explicate, expurgate,
extirpate, extricate, fabricate,
fascinate, fashion plate, feather-
weight, federate, flagellate, fluctu-
ate, formulate, fulminate,
fumigate, generate, germinate,
Golden Gate, graduate, granulate,
gravitate, heavyweight, hesitate,
hibernate, Hudson Strait, hyphen-
ate, illustrate, imitate, immigrate,

immolate, implicate, incarnate, incubate, inculcate, indicate, infiltrate, in-line skate, innovate, instigate, insulate, interstate, intimate, inundate, irrigate, irritate, isolate, iterate, lacerate, laminate, laureate, legislate, levitate, liberate, license plate, liquidate, litigate, lubricate, magistrate, marinate, masticate, mediate, medicate, meditate, middleweight, militate, mitigate, moderate, modulate, mortgage rate, motivate, multistate, mutilate, nation-state, nauseate, navigate, nominate, obfuscate, obligate, obviate, on a plate, operate, orchestrate, oscillate, out-of-date, overstate, overweight, paperweight, penetrate, percolate, perforate, permeate, perpetrate, police state, pollinate, populate, potentate, predicate, profligate, promulgate, propagate, punctuate, radiate, real estate, recreate, re-create, regulate, reinstate, relegate, relocate, renovate, replicate, reprobate, resonate, roller-skate, ruminate, running mate, salivate, saturate, scintillate, second-rate, segregate, self-portrait, separate, ship of state, silver plate, simulate, situate, speculate, stablemate, starting gate, steady state, stimulate, stipulate, subjugate, sublimate, suffocate, sultanate, supplicate, surrogate, syncopate, syndicate, tablemate, tabulate, target date, terminate, tête-à-tête, titillate, tolerate, triplicate, underrate, understate, underweight, vaccinate, vacillate, validate, vegetate, venerate, ventilate, vertebrate, vindicate, violate, vitiate, Watergate, welfare state, welterweight • abbreviate, accel-

erate, accentuate, accommodate, accumulate, adjudicate, adulterate, affiliate, agglomerate, alienate, alleviate, amalgamate, ameliorate, annihilate, anticipate, appreciate, appropriate, approximate, articulate, asphyxiate, assassinate, assimilate, associate, at any rate, attenuate, authenticate, barbiturate, bicarbonate, capitulate, certificate, coagulate, collaborate, commemorate, commiserate, communicate, compassionate, confederate, conglomerate, congratulate, consolidate, contaminate, cooperate, coordinate, corroborate, deactivate, decapitate, decelerate, deescalate, defoliate, degenerate, deliberate, delineate, depopulate, depreciate, desegregate, devaluate, discriminate, disintegrate, disseminate, dissociate, domesticate, elaborate, electroplate, eliminate, elucidate, emaciate, emancipate, emasculate, encapsulate, enumerate, enunciate, equivocate, eradicate, evacuate, evaluate, evaporate, exaggerate, exasperate, exfoliate, exhilarate, exonerate, expropriate, extenuate, exterminate, facilitate, fish or cut bait, gesticulate, hallucinate, humiliate, illuminate, impersonate, inactivate, inaugurate, incarcerate, incinerate, incorporate, incriminate, indoctrinate, inebriate, infatuate, infuriate, ingratiate, initiate, inoculate, insinuate, interpolate, interrelate, interrogate, intimidate, intoxicate, invalidate, investigate, invigorate, irradiate, Italianate, Korea Strait, legitimate, manipulate, necessitate, negotiate, noncandidate, obliterate, officiate, Orange Free State, orientate, originate, oxygenate, participate, perpetuate, pontificate, precipitate, predominate, prefabricate, premeditate, prevaricate, procrastinate, prognosticate, proliferate, proportionate, quadruplicate, quintuplicate, reciprocate, recuperate, redecorate, reduplicate, reeducate, refrigerate, regenerate, regurgitate, reincarnate, reiterate, rejuvenate, repudiate, resuscitate, retaliate, reverberate, Singapore Strait, sophisticate, subordinate, substantiate, vanity plate • adjustable rate, circumnavigate, decontaminate, deteriorate, differentiate, discombobulate, disorientate, disproportionate, excommunicate, expiration date, hyperventilate, incapacitate, intermediate, misappropriate, overcompensate, overeducate, overestimate, overmedicate, overpopulate, overstimulate, recapitulate, rehabilitate, renegotiate, superannuate, underestimate

ate⁷ \ət\ see ɪT⁵

ate³ \ät\ see OT¹
ate⁴ \ät-ē\ see ATI¹
ate⁵ \ət\ see UT¹

ated \āt-əd\ dated, fated, gated, stated • belated, ill-fated, outdated, related, truncated • animated, antiquated, caffeinated, calculated, carbonated, complicated, corrugated, dedicated, educated, elevated, hyphenated, integrated, laminated, liberated, perforated, saturated, simulated, syncopated, understated • affiliated, articulated, coordinated, decaffeinated, domesticated, encapsulated, incorporated, inebriated, interrelated, intoxicated, opinionated, premeditated, sophisticated, uncalculated, uncomplicated, underinflated,

unmitigated, unsaturated • unadulterated, unanticipated, undereducated, underpopulated, unsophisticated • underappreciated
—*also* -ed *forms of verbs listed at* ATE¹

ateful \āt-fəl\ fateful, grateful, hateful • ungrateful
atel¹ \ət-ᵊl\ see OTTLE
atel² \ät-ᵊl\ see ATAL
ateless \āt-ləs\ dateless, weightless
atelist \at-ᵊl-əst\ see ATALYST
ately¹ \āt-lē\ greatly, lately, stately • innately • Johnny-come-lately
ately² \at-ᵊl-ē\ see ATTILY
atem \ät-əm\ see ATUM¹
atement \āt-mənt\ statement • abatement, misstatement, restatement • overstatement, reinstatement, understatement
aten¹ \āt-ᵊn\ Dayton, Satan, straighten
aten² \at-ᵊn\ see ATIN²
aten³ \ät-ᵊn\ see OTTEN
atent¹ \āt-ᵊnt\ see ATANT¹
atent² \at-ᵊnt\ see ATANT²
ater¹ \ot-ər\ daughter, slaughter, tauter, water • backwater, bathwater, breakwater, deepwater, dishwater, floodwater, forequarter, freshwater, goddaughter, Goldwater, granddaughter, groundwater, headwater, highwater, hindquarter, hold water, hot water, ice water, jerkwater, manslaughter, meltwater, rainwater, saltwater, seawater, selfslaughter, stepdaughter, still water, tap water, tidewater, tread water, wastewater, white-water • above water, holy water, in deep water, mineral water, overwater, running water, soda water, toilet water, underwater • dead in the water, fish out of water, hell or high water

ater² \āt-ər\ see ATOR
atering \ȯt-ə-riŋ\ slaughtering
• mouthwatering • overwatering
atery \āt-ə-rē\ see OTTERY
ates¹ \āts\ Yeats • Gulf States
• Levant States, Papal States,
Trucial States • Persian Gulf
States, United States • house of
delegates
—*also* -s, -'s, *and* -s' *forms of
nouns and* -s *forms of verbs listed
at* ATE¹
ates² \āt-ēz\ Euphrates
—*also* -s, -'s, *and* -s' *forms of
nouns listed at* ATY
atest \āt-əst\ latest • at the latest
—*also* -est *forms of adjectives
listed at* ATE¹
atey \āt-ē\ see ATY
ath¹ \äth\ see OTH¹
ath² \ȯth\ see OTH²
ath³ \ath\ bath, hath, lath, math,
path, wrath • birdbath, blood-
bath, flight path, footbath, foot-
path, glide path, half bath,
sunbath, towpath, warpath • af-
termath, bridle path, psychopath,
shower bath, take a bath,
telepath, whirlpool bath • so-
ciopath
atha \ät-ə\ see ATA¹
athe¹ \āth\ bathe, lathe, scathe,
swathe • sunbathe
athe² \ath\ see ATH³
ather¹ \äth-ər\ bother, father,
rather • forefather, godfather,
grandfather, Our Father, stepfa-
ther • city father, founding father,
Holy Father
ather² \əth-ər\ see OTHER¹
ather³ \ath-ər\ blather, Cather,
gather, lather, rather, slather
• woolgather
athering \ath-riŋ\ woolgathering
—*also* -ing *forms of verbs listed at*
ATHER³
athi \ät-ē\ see ATI¹

athlon \ath-lən\ decathlon, pentathlon, triathlon
ati¹ \ät-ē\ Dottie, dotty, knotty,
naughty, potty, Scotty, snotty,
spotty • karate, Scarlatti • glit-
terati, Gujarati, literati, manicotti,
Maserati • illuminati
ati² \atē\ see ATTY
ati³ \äts\ see OTS
ati⁴ \as\ see ASS³
atia \ā-shə\ see ACIA
atial \ā-shəl\ see ACIAL
atian \ā-shən\ see ATION¹
atians \ā-shənz\ see ATIONS
atible \at-ə-bəl\ compatible, getat-
able • incompatible
atic¹ \ät-ik\ see OTIC
atic² \at-ik\ attic, static • aquatic,
asthmatic, chromatic, climatic,
dogmatic, dramatic, ecstatic,
emphatic, erratic, fanatic, lym-
phatic, phlegmatic, pneumatic,
pragmatic, prismatic, quadratic,
rheumatic, schematic, Socratic,
thematic, traumatic • acrobatic,
Adriatic, aerobatic, antistatic,
aromatic, Asiatic, autocratic,
automatic, bureaucratic, charis-
matic, cinematic, democratic,
diplomatic, emblematic, enig-
matic, Hippocratic, nonemphatic,
operatic, photostatic, problem-
atic, programmatic, symptomatic,
systematic, technocratic, thermo-
static, undogmatic, undramatic
• aristocratic, axiomatic, diagram-
matic, electrostatic, idiomatic,
melodramatic, overdramatic,
overemphatic, psychosomatic,
uncinematic, undemocratic,
undiplomatic • semiautomatic
atica \at-i-kə\ hepatica, sciatica,
viatica
atical \at-i-kəl\ fanatical, grammat-
ical, sabbatical • mathematical,
ungrammatical
atics \at-iks\ dramatics • acro-

batics, mathematics
—*also* -s, -'s, *and* -s' *forms of nouns listed at* ATIC[2]
atie \āt-ē\ see ATY
atiens \ā-shənz\ see ATIONS
atik \at-ik\ see ATIC[2]
atile \at-ᵊl-ē\ see ATTILY
atim \āt-əm\ see ATUM[1]
atin[1] \āt-ᵊn\ see OTTEN
atin[2] \at-ᵊn\ batten, fatten, flatten, Latin, Patton, satin • Manhattan, Mountbatten, pig latin, Powhatan
atin[3] \āt-ᵊn\ see ATEN[1]
ating \āt-iŋ\ grating, plating, rating, skating • bearbaiting, bullbaiting, call-waiting, frustrating, race-baiting, self-hating, self-rating, speed skating • aggravating, calculating, carbon dating, fascinating, figure skating, in-line skating, maid-in-waiting, nauseating, operating, penetrating, suffocating, titillating • accommodating, discriminating, humiliating, lady-in-waiting, self-deprecating, self-operating, self-regulating, self-replicating, subordinating, undeviating, unhesitating • self perpetuating
—*also* -ing *forms of verbs listed at* ATE[1]
atinous \at-nəs\ see ATNESS
ation[1] \ā-shən\ Asian, Haitian, nation, ration, station, Thracian • aeration, Alsatian, carnation, causation, cessation, cetacean, citation, Claymation, conflation, C ration, creation, cremation, Croatian, crustacean, dalmatian, damnation, deflation, dictation, dilation, donation, duration, elation, equation, Eurasian, filtration, fixation, flirtation, flotation, formation, foundation, frustration, gas station, gestation, gradation, gyration, hydration, inflation, K ration, lactation,

legation, libation, location, migration, mutation, narration, negation, notation, oration, ovation, plantation, privation, probation, prostration, pulsation, quotation, relation, rotation, salvation, sedation, sensation, space station, stagnation, starvation, substation, summation, taxation, temptation, translation, truncation, vacation, vibration, vocation, way station, workstation • abdication, aberration, acclamation, accusation, activation, adaptation, admiration, adoration, adulation, affectation, affirmation, aggravation, aggregation, agitation, allegation, allocation, amputation, alteration, altercation, alternation, Amerasian, animation, annexation, annotation, Appalachian, application, approbation, arbitration, aspiration, attestation, augmentation, automation, aviation, avocation, calculation, calibration, cancellation, carbonation, celebration, chlorination, circulation, coloration, combination, commendation, commutation, compensation, compilation, complication, computation, concentration, condemnation, condensation, confirmation, confiscation, conflagration, confrontation, congregation, conjugation, connotation, consecration, conservation, consolation, constellation, consternation, constipation, consultation, contemplation, conversation, convocation, coronation, corporation, correlation, corrugation, crop rotation, culmination, cultivation, cumulation, declamation, declaration, decoration, dedication, defamation, defecation, deformation, degradation, dehydration, delegation, demonstration, denigration, deportation, deprivation, derivation, desecration, designation, desolation, desperation, destination, detonation, devastation, deviation, dislocation, dissertation, divination, domination, duplication, education, elevation, emigration, emulation, escalation, estimation, evocation, exaltation, excavation, exclamation, expectation, expiration, explanation, exploitation, exploration, exportation, exultation, fabrication, fascination, federation, fermentation, filling station, fire station, flagellation, fluoridation, fluctuation, forestation, formulation, fragmentation, fumigation, gene mutation, generation, germination, graduation, habitation, heat prostration, hesitation, hibernation, hyphenation, illustration, imitation, immigration, implantation, implication, importation, incantation, incarnation, inclination, incubation, indentation, indication, indignation, infestation, infiltration, inflammation, information, innovation, inspiration, installation, instigation, insulation, integration, intonation, invitation, invocation, irrigation, irritation, isolation, jubilation, laceration, lamentation, legislation, levitation, liberation, limitation, liquidation, litigation, lubrication, medication, meditation, misquotation, mistranslation, moderation, modulation, molestation, motivation, multination, mutilation, navigation, nomination, obfuscation, obligation, observation, occupation, operation, orchestration, ordination, oscillation, ostentation, penetration, percolation,

perforation, perspiration, pigmentation, police station, pollination, population, power station, preparation, presentation, preservation, proclamation, procreation, prolongation, propagation, protestation, provocation, publication, punctuation, radiation, recitation, re-creation, recreation, reformation, refutation, registration, regulation, rehydration, relaxation, relocation, renovation, replication, reputation, reservation, resignation, respiration, restoration, retardation, revelation, revocation, ruination, sanitation, saturation, segmentation, segregation, separation, service station, simulation, situation, speculation, stimulation, stipulation, stylization, suffocation, syncopation, syndication, tabulation, termination, T formation, titillation, toleration, transformation, transmigration, transportation, trepidation, tribulation, usurpation, vaccination, valuation, variation, vegetation, veneration, ventilation, vindication, violation, weather station • abbreviation, abomination, acceleration, accommodation, accreditation, accumulation, adjudication, administration, affiliation, alienation, amplification, annihilation, anticipation, appreciation, appropriation, approximation, argumentation, articulation, asphyxiation, assassination, assimilation, association, authentication, authorization, beautification, centralization, certification, civilization, clarification, classification, coeducation, cohabitation, collaboration, colonization, commemoration, communication, confederation, configuration, congratulation, consideration, consolidation, contamination, continuation, cooperation, coordination, cross-pollination, crystallization, de-escalation, deforestation, degeneration, deification, deliberation, demonization, denomination, denunciation, depreciation, deregulation, desegregation, determination, devaluation, digitization, discoloration, discrimination, disinclination, disintegration, dissemination, documentation, dramatization, echolocation, elaboration, elimination, elucidation, emancipation, enumeration, equalization, eradication, evacuation, evaluation, evaporation, exaggeration, examination, exasperation, exhilaration, extermination, falsification, feminization, fertilization, fortification, globalization, glorification, gratification, hallucination, harmonization, humiliation, hyperinflation, illumination, imagination, immunization, impersonation, implementation, improvisation, inauguration, incarceration, incineration, incorporation, incrimination, indoctrination, infatuation, initiation, inoculation, instrumentation, interpretation, interrelation, interrogation, intimidation, intoxication, invalidation, investigation, itemization, justification, legalization, liberalization, magnetization, magnification, manifestation, manipulation, mechanization, memorization, misapplication, miscalculation, misinformation, mobilization, modernization, modification, multiplication, mystification, nationalization, naturalization, negotiation, normalization, notifi-

cation, obliteration, organization, origination, orientation, ornamentation, overinflation, oxygenation, participation, pasteurization, perpetuation, polarization, postgraduation, post-Reformation, precipitation, predestination, preoccupation, prepublication, preregistration, prettification, procrastination, proliferation, pronunciation, purification, qualification, ratification, reaffirmation, realization, recommendation, recuperation, redecoration, rededication, reduplication, reforestation, reformulation, refrigeration, regeneration, regimentation, reincarnation, reiteration, rejuvenation, remuneration, renunciation, representation, retaliation, reverberation, sedimentation, Serbo-Croatian, signification, simplification, socialization, solicitation, sophistication, specialization, specification, stabilization, standardization, sterilization, subordination, supplementation, transfiguration, uglification, unification, unionization, urbanization, verification, victimization, vocalization, vulgarization, westernization, x-radiation • characterization, circumnavigation, commercialization, criminalization, cross-examination, decentralization, decontamination, deterioration, differentiation, disorientation, disorganization, disqualification, diversification, electrification, excommunication, experimentation, generalization, homogenization, hospitalization, hyperventilation, idealization, identification, insubordination, intensification, megacorporation, militarization, miniaturization, misappropriation, miscommunication, misinterpretation, mispronunciation, misrepresentation, monopolization, overcompensation, overpopulation, personification, popularization, reconciliation, reconsideration, rehabilitation, reorganization, revitalization, solidification, underestimation, visualization

ation² \ā-zhən\ see ASION

ation³ \ash-ən\ see ASSION

ational¹ \ā-shnəl\ sensational • confrontational, congregational, conversational, educational, generational, gravitational, inspirational, motivational, recreational • coeducational, improvisational, organizational

ational² \ash-nəl\ national, rational • irrational • international, multinational

ationist \ā-shnəst\ conservationist, isolationist, preservationist, segregationist

ations \ā-shənz\ Galatians, relations • Lamentations, League of Nations, Revelations • United Nations

atious \ā-shəs\ see ACIOUS

atis \at-əs\ see ATUS²

atist \āt-əst\ see ATEST

atitude \at-ə-tüd\ see ATTITUDE

atius \ā-shəs\ see ACIOUS

ative \āt-iv\ dative, native • creative, nonnative • contemplative, cumulative, decorative, imitative, innovative, irritative, legislative, meditative, operative, penetrative, qualitative, quantitative, speculative, vegetative • administrative, appreciative, authoritative, collaborative, commemorative, communicative, cooperative, degenerative, deliberative, investigative, postoperative • uncommunicative

atl \ät-ᵊl\ see OTTLE

atlas \at-ləs\ atlas, Atlas, fatless, hatless

atless \at-ləs\ see ATLAS

atli \ät-lē\ see OTLY

atling \at-liŋ\ rattling • saber rattling
   —*also* -ing *forms of verbs listed at* ATTLE

atly \at-lē\ flatly, rattly

atness \at-nəs\ fatness, flatness • gelatinous

ato¹ \ät-ō\ auto, blotto, grotto, lotto, motto, Otto • legato, staccato, tomato, vibrato • moderato, pizzicato

ato² \āt-ō\ Cato, Plato • potato, tomato • couch potato, hot potato, plum tomato, sweet potato • cherry tomato

atom \at-əm\ see ATUM²

aton \at-ᵊn\ see ATIN²

ator \āt-ər\ crater, dater, freighter, gator, grater, hater, later, satyr, skater, traitor, waiter • creator, curator, debater, dictator, donator, dumbwaiter, equator, firstrater, headwaiter, ice-skater, locator, Mercator, migrator, narrator, pond skater, rotator, spectator, speed skater, tailgater, theater, third-rater, translator • abdicator, activator, agitator, alligator, alternator, animator, arbitrator, aviator, calculator, carburetor, circulator, commentator, cultivator, decorator, demonstrator, educator, elevator, escalator, estimator, excavator, figure skater, fumigator, generator, gladiator, illustrator, imitator, incubator, indicator, in-line skater, innovator, inspirator, instigator, insulator, liberator, mediator, moderator, motivator, navigator, numerator, operator, orchestrator, percolator, perpe-

trator, pollinator, radiator, regu-
lator, renovator, respirator, roller
skater, second-rater, separator,
simulator, Sunset Crater, termina-
tor, valuator, ventilator, violator
• accelerator, administrator,
annihilator, collaborator, concil-
iator, coordinator, denominator,
emancipator, enumerator, evalua-
tor, exterminator, facilitator,
grain elevator, impersonator,
incinerator, interrogator, investi-
gator, negotiator, perambulator,
procrastinator, refrigerator,
sooner or later
　—*also* -er *forms of adjectives listed
at* ATE[1]
atre \at\ see AT[5]
atric \a-trik\ Patrick • theatric
• geriatric, pediatric, psychiatric
atrick \a-trik\ see ATRIC
atrics \a-triks\ theatrics • pedi-
atrics
atrix \ā-triks\ matrix • Beatrix
atron \ā-trən\ matron, patron
ats[1] \äts\ see OTS
ats[2] \ats\ bats, rats • Bonneville
Salt Flats
　—*also* -s, -'s, *and* -s' *forms of
nouns and* -s *forms of verbs listed
at* AT[5]
atsa \ät-sə\ see ATZO[1]
atsch \ach\ see ATCH[3]
atsu \ät-sü\ Matsu • shiatsu
atsy \at-sē\ see AZI[3]
att[1] \at\ see AT[5]
att[2] \ät\ see OT[1]
atta \ät-ə\ see ATA[1]
attage \ät-ij\ see OTTAGE
attan \at-ᵊn\ see ATIN[2]
atte \at\ see AT[5]
attel \at-ᵊl\ see ATTLE
atten \at-ᵊn\ see ATIN[2]
atter \at-ər\ batter, chatter, clatter,
fatter, flatter, hatter, latter, matter, patter, platter, satyr, scatter,
shatter, spatter, splatter, tatter

• dark matter, gray matter, no
matter, standpatter, the matter
• antimatter, for that matter,
pitter-patter, printed matter,
subject matter
attering \at-ə-riŋ\ scattering, smat-
tering • earth-shattering, unflat-
tering
　—*also* -ing *forms of verbs listed at*
ATTER
attern \at-ərn\ pattern, Saturn,
slattern • test pattern • holding
pattern
attery \at-ə-rē\ battery, flattery
atti[1] \ät-ē\ see ATI[1]
atti[2] \at-ē\ see ATTY
attic \at-ik\ see ATIC[2]
attica \at-i-kə\ see ATICA
attice[1] \at-əs\ see ATUS[2]
attice[2] \at-ish\ see ATTISH
attie \at-ē\ see ATTY
attily \at-ᵊl-ē\ cattily, chattily,
Natalie, nattily, rattly • philately
atting \at-iŋ\ batting, matting,
tatting
　—*also* -ing *forms of verbs listed at*
AT[5]
attish \at-ish\ brattish, rattish,
flattish
attitude \at-ə-tüd\ attitude, gratitude, latitude, platitude • beatitude, ingratitude, midlatitude
attle \at-ᵊl\ battle, cattle, prattle,
rattle, tattle • beef cattle, death
rattle, embattle, pitched battle,
Seattle • dairy cattle, tittle-tattle
attling \at-liŋ\ see ATLING
attly[1] \at-ᵊl-ē\ see ATTILY
attly[2] \at-lē\ see ATLY
atto[1] \at-ə\ see ATA[3]
atto[2] \ät-ō\ see ATO[1]
atton \at-ᵊn\ see ATIN[2]
atty \at-ē\ batty, bratty, catty,
chatty, fatty, Hattie, natty, patty,
Patty, ratty • nonfatty • Cincinnati
atum[1] \ät-əm\ substratum, verba-
tim • ultimatum

atum[2] \at-əm\ atom • substratum
atur \āt-ər\ see ATOR
ature[1] \ā-chər\ nature • 4-H'er
• force of nature, freak of nature,
human nature, Mother Nature,
nomenclature, second nature
ature[2] \ach-ər\ see ATCHER[2]
aturn \at-ərn\ see ATTERN
atus[1] \āt-əs\ gratis, status, stratus
• hiatus • altostratus, apparatus,
cirrostratus, nimbostratus
atus[2] \at-əs\ gratis, lattice, status,
stratus • clematis • altostratus,
apparatus, cirrostratus, nimbostratus
atute \ach-ət\ see ATCHET
aty \āt-ē\ eighty, Haiti, Katie,
Leyte, matey, weighty, yeti • Pa-
peete
atyr \āt-ər\ see ATOR
atz[1] \ats\ see ATS[2]
atz[2] \äts\ see OTS
atzo[1] \ät-sə\ matzo • piazza
atzo[2] \ät-sō\ see AZZO
atzu \ät-sü\ see ATSU
au[1] \ō\ see OW[1]
au[2] \ü\ see EW[1]
au[3] \au̇\ see OW[2]
au[4] \o̅\ see AW[1]
aub \äb\ see OB[1]
aube \ōb\ see OBE[1]
auber \ȯb-ər\ Micawber, mud
dauber
auble \äb-əl\ see ABBLE[1]
auce \ȯs\ see OSS[1]
aucer \ȯ-sər\ see OSSER
auch \äch\ see OTCH
auche \ōsh\ see OCHE[2]
auckland \ȯk-lənd\ Auckland,
Falkland
aucous \ȯ-kəs\ caucus, raucous
aucus \ȯ-kəs\ see AUCOUS
aud[1] \ȯd\ awed, broad, Claude,
clawed, flawed, fraud, god, jawed,
laud, Maude • abroad, applaud,
defraud, maraud • antifraud, wire
fraud

—also -ed *forms of verbs listed at*
AW[1]
aud[2] \äd\ see OD[1]
audable \ȯd-ə-bəl\ audible, laud-
able • applaudable, inaudible
aude[1] \au̇d-ē\ see OWDY
aude[2] \ȯd-ē\ see AWDY
aude[3] \ȯd\ see AUD[1]
audible \ȯd-ə-bəl\ see AUDABLE
audit \ȯd-ət\ audit, plaudit
audy[1] \äd-ē\ see ODY[1]
audy[2] \ȯd-ē\ see AWDY
auer \au̇r\ see OWER[2]
auffeur \ō-fər\ see OFER
auge \āj\ see AGE[3]
auged \ājd\ see AGED
auger[1] \o̅-gər\ see OGGER[2]
auger[2] \ā-jər\ see AGER[1]
augh[1] \af\ see APH
augh[2] \ä\ see A[1]
augh[3] \äk̲\ see ACH[1]
augh[4] \o̅\ see AW[1]
aughable \af-ə-bəl\ see AFFABLE
augham \o̅m\ see AUM[1]
aughn[1] \än\ see ON[1]
aughn[2] \ȯn\ see ON[3]
aught[1] \ät\ see OT[1]
aught[2] \ȯt\ see OUGHT[1]
aughter[1] \af-tər\ see AFTER
aughter[2] \ȯt-ər\ see ATER[1]
aughty[1] \ȯt-ē\ haughty, naughty
• Buonarroti
aughty[2] \ät-ē\ see ATI[1]
augre \o̅g-ər\ see OGGER[2]
augur \o̅g-ər\ see OGGER[2]
aui \au̇-ē\ see OWIE
auk \ȯk\ see ALK
aukee \ȯ-kē\ see ALKIE
aul \ȯl\ see ALL[1]
aulay \ȯ-lē\ see AWLY
auld[1] \ȯl\ see ALL[1]
auld[2] \ō\ see OW[1]
auled \ȯld\ see ALD[1]
auler \ȯ-lər\ see ALLER[1]
aulin \ȯ-lən\ see ALLEN
auling \ȯ-liŋ\ see ALLING
aulish \ȯ-lish\ see ALLISH

aulk \ȯk\ see ALK
aulker \ȯ-kər\ see ALKER
aulking \ȯ-kiŋ\ see ALKING
aulle \ȯl\ see ALL[1]
aulm \ȯm\ see AUM[1]
ault[1] \ȯlt\ see ALT
ault[2] \ō\ see OW[1]
aulter \ȯl-tər\ see ALTER
aulting \ȯl-tiŋ\ see ALTING
aultless \ȯlt-ləs\ see ALTLESS
aulty \ȯl-tē\ see ALTY
aum[1] \ȯm\ qualm • meerschaum
aum[2] \äm\ see OM[1]
aun[1] \än\ see ON[1]
aun[2] \ən\ see UN[1]
aun[3] \ȯn\ see ON[3]
aun[4] \aůn\ see OWN[2]
auna[1] \än-ə\ see ANA[1]
auna[2] \ȯn-ə\ see ONNA[1]
aunch[1] \änch\ conch, paunch,
  stanch
aunch[2] \ȯnch\ haunch, launch,
  paunch, stanch, staunch
aunchy \ȯn-chē\ paunchy, raunchy
aunder[1] \ȯn-dər\ launder, maunder
aunder[2] \än-dər\ see ONDER[1]
aunish \än-ish\ see ONISH
aunt[1] \ȯnt\ daunt, flaunt, gaunt,
  haunt, jaunt, taunt, want • avaunt
aunt[2] \ant\ see ANT[5]
aunt[3] \änt\ see ANT[2]
aunted \ȯnt-əd\ see ONTED
aunter[1] \änt-ər\ saunter, taunter
aunter[2] \ȯnt-ər\ haunter, saunter,
  taunter
aunty[1] \ȯnt-ē\ flaunty, jaunty
aunty[2] \änt-ē\ see ANTI[1]
aunus \än-əs\ see ONUS[1]
aupe \ōp\ see OPE
auphin \ȯ-fən\ see OFFIN
aur[1] \aůr\ see OWER[2]
aur[2] \ȯr\ see OR[1]
aura[1] \ȯr-ə\ see ORA
aura[2] \är-ə\ see ARA[1]
aural \ȯr-əl\ see ORAL
aure \ȯr\ see OR[1]
aurea \ȯr-ē-ə\ see ORIA

aurean \ȯr-ē-ən\ see ORIAN
aurel \ȯr-əl\ see ORAL
auren[1] \är-ən\ see ARIN
auren[2] \ȯr-ən\ see ORIN[1]
aurence \ȯr-ən(t)s\ see AWRENCE
aureus \ȯr-ē-əs\ see ORIOUS
auri \aůr-ē\ see OWERY
aurian \ȯr-ē-ən\ see ORIAN
auric \ȯr-ik\ see ORIC
aurice[1] \är-əs\ see ORRIS[1]
aurice[2] \ȯr-əs\ see AURUS
auricle \ȯr-i-kəl\ see ORICAL
aurie[1] \ȯr-ē\ see ORY
aurie[2] \är-ē\ see ARI[1]
aurous \ȯr-əs\ see AURUS
aurus \ȯr-əs\ Boris, chorus, Doris,
  Horace, Maurice, morris, Morris,
  Norris, porous, Taurus • Centau-
  rus, decorous, Dolores, phospho-
  rous, sonorous, thesaurus
  • allosaurus, brontosaurus,
  stegosaurus • apatosaurus, tyran-
  nosaurus
aury \ȯr-ē\ see ORY
aus[1] \aůs\ see OUSE[2]
aus[2] \ȯz\ see AUSE[1]
ausal \ȯ-zəl\ causal • menopausal
ause[1] \ȯz\ cauuse, claws, clause,
  gauze, pause, yaws • applause,
  because • grasp at straws,
  menopause, Santa Claus
  — also -s, -'s, and -s' forms of
  nouns and -s forms of verbs listed
  at AW[1]
ause[2] \əz\ see EUSE[1]
auseous \ȯ-shəs\ see AUTIOUS
auss \aůs\ see OUSE[1]
aussie[1] \äs-ē\ see OSSY[1]
aussie[2] \ȯ-sē\ see OSSY[2]
aust[1] \aůst\ see OUST[1]
aust[2] \ȯst\ see OST[3]
austen \ȯs-tən\ see OSTON
austin \ȯs-tən\ see OSTON
austless \ȯst-ləs\ costless • ex-
  haustless
aut[1] \ō\ see OW[1]
aut[2] \aůt\ see OUT[3]

aut[3] \ät\ see OT[1]
aut[4] \ȯt\ see OUGHT[1]
aute \ōt\ see OAT
autics \ät-iks\ see OTICS
autious \ȯ-shəs\ cautious, nauseous • incautious • overcautious
auto[1] \ȯt-ō\ auto, Giotto • risotto
auto[2] \ät-ō\ see ATO[1]
auve \ōv\ see OVE[2]
auze \ȯz\ see AUSE[1]
auzer \au̇-zər\ see OUSER
av[1] \äv\ see OLVE[2]
av[2] \av\ see ALVE[2]
ava[1] \äv-ə\ fava, guava, java, Java, lava • cassava • balaclava, Bratislava, Costa Brava
ava[2] \av-ə\ java • balaclava
avage \av-ij\ ravage, savage
avan \ā-vən\ see AVEN[1]
avant \av-ənt\ haven't, savant
avarice \av-rəs\ see AVEROUS
ave[1] \äv-ā\ clave, grave, Jahveh
ave[2] \āv\ brave, cave, crave, Dave, fave, gave, grave, knave, lave, nave, pave, rave, save, shave, slave, stave, they've, waivė, wave, Wave • airwave, behave, brain wave, close shave, cold wave, concave, conclave, deprave, enclave, engrave, enslave, forgave, Great Slave, heat wave, octave, repave, shock wave, shortwave, sine wave, sound wave, wage slave • after-shave, Fingal's Cave, Mammoth Cave, microwave, misbehave, tidal wave • permanent wave, radio wave
ave[3] \av\ see ALVE[3]
ave[4] \äv\ see OLVE[2]
aved \āvd\ waved • depraved, unsaved
—also -ed forms of verbs listed at AVE[2]
avel \av-əl\ cavil, gavel, gravel, ravel, travel • unravel • gavel-to-gavel
aveling \av-liŋ\ traveling

—also -ing forms of verbs listed at AVEL
avement \āv-mənt\ pavement • enslavement
aven[1] \ā-vən\ Avon, craven, graven, haven, maven, raven, shaven • New Haven, night raven • riboflavin, Winter Haven • Stratford-upon-Avon
aven[2] \av-ən\ see AVIN
aven't \av-ənt\ see AVANT
aver[1] \äv-ər\ slaver • palaver
aver[2] \ā-vər\ braver, caver, favor, flavor, graver, quaver, raver, savor, shaver, slaver, waiver, waver • disfavor, engraver, facesaver, flag-waver, lifesaver, screen saver, time-saver
aver[3] \av-ər\ slaver • cadaver, palaver
avern \av-ərn\ cavern, tavern
averous \av-rəs\ avarice • cadaverous
avery \āv-rē\ Avery, bravery, knavery, quavery, savory, slavery • unsavory, white slavery • antislavery
avey[2] \ā-vē\ see AVY
avia \ā-vē-ə\ Belgravia, Moldavia, Moravia • Scandinavia
avian \ā-vē-ən\ avian • Moravian • Scandinavian
avid \av-əd\ avid, gravid
avie \ā-vē\ see AVY
avil \av-əl\ see AVEL
avin \av-ən\ Avon, raven
aving \ā-viŋ\ caving, craving, paving, raving, saving, shaving • engraving, face-saving, flagwaving, lifesaving, time-saving • laborsaving
—also -ing forms of verbs listed at AVE[2]
avis \ā-vəs\ Davis, Mavis
avish[1] \ā-vish\ knavish, slavish
avish[2] \av-ish\ lavish, ravish
avity \av-ət-ē\ cavity, gravity • de-

pravity • antigravity, body cavity,
zero gravity • center of gravity
avl \äv-əl\ see OVEL[1]
avo \äv-ō\ bravo • centavo • Rio
Bravo
avon[1] \ā-vən\ see AVEN[1]
avon[2] \a-vən\ see AVIN
avor \ā-vər\ see AVER[2]
avored \ā-vərd\ favored, flavored
• ill-favored
—*also* -ed *forms of verbs listed at*
AVER[2]
avory \āv-rē\ see AVERY
avus \ā-vəs\ see AVIS
avvy \av-ē\ navvy, savvy
avy \ā-vē\ Davy, gravy, navy,
slavey, wavy
aw[1] \ȯ\ aw, awe, caw, claw, craw,
draw, flaw, gnaw, haw, jaw, la,
law, maw, pa, paw, pshaw, Ra,
rah, raw, saw, shah, slaw, spa,
squaw, straw, thaw, yaw • band
saw, bedstraw, blue law, bucksaw,
buzz saw, bylaw, chain saw,
Choctaw, coleslaw, Corn Law,
Danelaw, declaw, dewclaw, Esau,
forepaw, geegaw, grandma,
grandpa, guffaw, hacksaw, hand-
saw, hee-haw, hurrah, in-law,
jackdaw, jigsaw, last straw, leash
law, lockjaw, macaw, Moose Jaw,
Nassau, outdraw, outlaw, pasha,
pawpaw, rickshaw, ripsaw,
scofflaw, scrimshaw, seesaw,
southpaw, Utah, Warsaw, whip-
saw, withdraw • Arkansas, Chick-
asaw, Chippewa, civil law,
common-law, court of law, crosscut saw, foofaraw, higher law,
homestead law, in the raw, keyhole saw, Kiowa, lemon law,
mackinaw, Murphy's Law,
Omaha, Ottawa, oversaw, panama,
private law, public law, roman
law, Saginaw, son-in-law, tragic
flaw, Wichita, williwaw • brother-
in-law, circular saw, criminal law,

daughter-in-law, father-in-law,
mother-in-law, sister-in-law, stick
in one's craw, unwritten law
aw[2] \äv\ see OLVE[2]
aw[3] \ȯf\ see OFF[2]
aw[4] \äf\ see OFF[1]
awa[1] \ä-wə\ Chihuahua, Tarawa
• Okinawa, Tokugawa
awa[2] \ä-və\ see AVA[1]
awar \au̇r\ see OWER[2]
awber[1] \äb-ər\ see OBBER
awber[2] \ȯb-ər\ see AUBER
awd \ȯd\ see AUD[1]
awddle \äd-ᵊl\ see ODDLE
awdry \ȯ-drē\ Audrey, tawdry
awdy \ȯd-ē\ bawdy, gaudy
awe \ȯ\ see AW[1]
awed \ȯd\ see AUD[1]
aweless \ȯ-ləs\ see AWLESS
awer \ȯr\ see OR[1]
awers \ȯrz\ see OORS
awful \ȯ-fəl\ awful, lawful, offal
• unlawful
awfully \ȯf-ə-lē\ awfully, lawfully
• unlawfully
awing \ȯiŋ\ cloying, drawing • line
drawing
—*also* -ing *forms of verbs listed at*
AW[1]
awk \ȯk\ see ALK
awker \ȯ-kər\ see ALKER
awkish \ȯ-kish\ hawkish, mawkish
awky \ȯ-kē\ see ALKIE
awl \ȯl\ see ALL[1]
awler \ȯ-lər\ see ALLER[1]
awless \ȯ-ləs\ flawless, lawless
awling \ȯ-liŋ\ see ALLING
awly \ȯ-lē\ brawly, crawly, dolly,
drawly, Raleigh, scrawly, squally
• Bengali
awm \ȯm\ see AUM[1]
awn[1] \än\ see ON[1]
awn[2] \ȯn\ see ON[3]
awner[1] \ȯn-ər\ fawner, goner
awner[2] \än-ər\ see ONOR[1]
awney \ȯ-nē\ see AWNY[1]
awning \än-iŋ\ see ONING[1]

awny[1] \ȯ-nē\ brawny, scrawny, tawny • mulligatawny

awny[2] \än-ē\ see ANI[1]

awrence \ȯr-ən(t)s\ Florence, Lawrence, warrants • abhorrence, Saint Lawrence

awry \ȯr-ē\ see ORY

aws \ȯz\ see AUSE[1]

awse \ȯz\ see AUSE[1]

awy \ȯi\ see OY

awyer \ȯ-yər\ lawyer, sawyer • trial lawyer • criminal lawyer

ax[1] \äks\ see OX

ax[2] \aks\ ax, fax, flax, lax, max, Max, sax, tax, wax • Ajax, anthrax, beeswax, borax, broadax, climax, earwax, Fairfax, IMAX, meat-ax, pickax, poll tax, pretax, relax, sales tax, surtax, syntax, thorax • aftertax, ball of wax, battle-ax, Halifax, hidden tax, income tax, overtax, sealing wax, to the max, Turtle Wax • anticlimax

—*also* -s, -'s, *and* -s' *forms of nouns and* -s *forms of verbs listed at* ACK[2]

axant \ak-sənt\ see ACCENT

axen \ak-sən\ see AXON

axi \ak-sē\ see AXY

axon \ak-sən\ flaxen, Jackson, Saxon, waxen • Anglo-Saxon

axy \ak-sē\ maxi, taxi, waxy • air taxi • water taxi

ay[1] \ā\ a, ae, bay, bray, clay, day, eh, Faye, fey, flay, fray, gay, gray, hay, hey, Hue, j, jay, Jay, k, Kay, lay, lei, may, May, nay, née, neigh, pay, play, pray, prey, quay, Rae, ray, Ray, re, say, slay, sleigh, spay, splay, spray, stay, stray, sway, they, tray, way, weigh, whey, yea • airplay, airway, aisleway, all-day, allay, archway, array, ashtray, assay, astray, at bay, away, aweigh, ballet, base pay, belay, beltway, beret, betray,

bikeway, birthday, Biscay, Bizet, blasé, Bombay, bouquet, breezeway, Broadway, buffet, byway, café, Cape May, Cartier, Cathay, causeway, chalet, child's play, cliché, convey, Coos Bay, crawlway, crochet, croquet, DA, daresay, D-day, death ray, decay, deejay, defray, delay, dismay, display, DJ, doomsday, doorway, dossier, downplay, driveway, duvet, Earl Grey, entrée, essay, fair play, fairway, field day, filet, fillet, fishway, Flag Day, flight pay, flyway, foray, forte, foul play, foyer, frappé, freeway, Friday, Galway, gangway, Gaspé, gateway, give way, gourmet, Green Bay, gunplay, hair spray, halfway, hallway, harm's way, hatchway, headway, hearsay, heyday, highway, hold sway, hooray, horseplay, in play, inlay, Jolliet, leeway, Lord's day, maguey, mainstay, make hay, Malay, Manet, Marseilles, match play, May Day, Mayday, melee, midday, midway, Midway, Millay, mislay, misplay, Monday, Monet, moray, noonday, Norway, no way, obey, OK, olé, one-way, osprey, outlay, outplay, outstay, outweigh, PA, parfait, parkway, parlay, parquet, partway, passé, pathway, payday, pearl gray, Pele, per se, Pompeii, portray, prepay, puree, purvey, raceway, Rahway, railway, relay, Rene, Renee, repay, replay, risqué, roadway, Roget, role-play, runway, sachet, saint's day, sashay, sauté, screenplay, seaway, Shark Bay, shar-pei, shipway, sick bay, sick day, sick pay, slideway, soiree, someday, soufflé, speedway, spillway, squeeze play, stairway, Steinway, stingray, straightway, stroke play, subway, Sunday, survey, swordplay, Taipei, tea tray, three-way, thruway, Thursday, today, tollway, touché, toupee, trackway, Tuesday, Twelfth Day, two-way, valet, V-day, veejay, walkway, waylay, Wednesday, weekday, wordplay, workday, X ray • Agnus Dei, A-OK, alleyway, All Fools' Day, All Saints' Day, All Souls' Day, all the way, antigay, anyway, appliqué, Arbor Day, attaché, back away, Baffin Bay, bang away, Bastille Day, beta ray, bird of prey, Biscayne Bay, blow away, Boxing Day, breakaway, break away, Bristol Bay, Buzzards Bay, by the way, cabaret, cableway, Cam Ranh Bay, canapé, Cape Cod Bay, caraway, carriageway, Cartier, castaway, cathode ray, china clay, Chippewa, cog railway, consommé, cosmic ray, croupier, cutaway, day-to-day, déclassé, devotee, Dingle Bay, disarray, disobey, divorcé, divorcée, DNA, dollar day, double play, dress-down day, eagle ray, ember day, émigré, Empire Day, entranceway, entryway, everyday, exposé, expressway, fall away, Faraday, faraway, Fathers Day, feet of clay, fiancé, fiancée, fire away, foldaway, gal Friday, gamma ray, getaway, girl Friday, giveaway, give away, Glacier Bay, Groundhog Day, Guy Fawkes Day, hell to pay, Hemingway, hideaway, hit the hay, holiday, holy day, Hudson Bay, Hugh Capet, Humboldt Bay, in a way, interplay, IRA, Joliet, judgment day, keep-away, Labor Day, layaway, lay away, lingerie, macramé, Mandalay, manta ray, matinee, meet halfway, MIA, Milky Way, Monterrey, Mother's

Day, motorway, multiday, mystery play, negligee, New Year's Day, New York Bay, night and day, off Broadway, Ojibwa, on the way, out of play, overlay, overpay, overplay, overstay, overweigh, Paraguay, passageway, pass away, passion play, pepper spray, photoplay, play-by-play, plug-and-play, power play, present-day, protégé, Prudhoe Bay, pull away, put away, Rabelais, rainy-day, reconvey, repartee, résumé, ricochet, right away, right-of-way, RNA, runaway, run away, salt away, San Jose, Santa Fe, São Tomé, Saturday, severance pay, sock away, square away, stowaway, straightaway, street railway, Table Bay, takeaway, taxiway, thataway, throwaway, throw away, Thunder Bay, triple play, turn away, Turtle Bay, underlay, underpay, underway, Uruguay, vertebra, waterway, Whitsunday, workaday, working day, Zuider Zee • Appian Way, April Fool's Day, Ascension Day, Australia Day, Bay of Biscay, Botany Bay, carry away, Chesapeake Bay, Columbus Day, communiqué, corps de ballet, Delaware Bay, devil to pay, Dominion Day, Election Day, electric ray, far and away, fiddle away, Frobisher Bay, Giant's Causeway, High Holiday, instant replay, Jamaica Bay, Korea Bay, medley relay, Midsummer Day, miracle play, Montego Bay, Morgan le Fay, off-off-Broadway, out-of-the-way, papier-mâché, Patriots' Day, photo-essay, preholiday, Presidents' Day, Rogation Day, Saginaw Bay, Saint Patrick's Day, superhighway, Thanksgiving Day, Valentine's

Day, Veterans Day • Independence Day, Memorial Day, morality play • cinema verité

ay² \ē\ see EE[1]

ay³ \ī\ see Y[1]

aya¹ \ī-ə\ see IAH[1]

aya² \ā-ə\ see AIA[1]

ayable \ā-ə-bəl\ payable, playable, sayable • displayable, unplayable, unsayable

ayah \ī-ə\ see IAH[1]

ayal \āl\ see AIL

ayan¹ \ā-ən\ crayon • Chilean, Malayan, Pompeian • Galilean, Himalayan

ayan² \ī-ən\ see ION[1]

aybe¹ \ā-bē\ see ABY

aybe² \eb-ē\ see EBBY

ayday \ā-dā\ Mayday, May Day

aye¹ \ā\ see AY[1]

aye² \ī\ see Y[1]

ayed \ād\ see ADE[1]

ayer \ā-ər\ layer, mayor, payer, player, prayer, slayer, sprayer, stayer • ballplayer, betrayer, bricklayer, cardplayer, conveyor, doomsayer, manslayer, naysayer, purveyor, soothsayer, surveyor, taxpayer
—*also -er forms of adjectives listed at* AY[1]

ayered \erd\ see AIRED

ayest \ā-əst\ mayest, sayest • essayist
—*also -est forms of adjectives listed at* AY[1]

ayin¹ \ī-ən\ see ION[1]

ayin² \īn\ see INE[1]

aying \ā-iŋ\ fraying, playing, saying • bricklaying, doomsaying, long-playing, nay-saying, soothsaying, surveying, taxpaying
—*also -ing forms of verbs listed at* AY[1]

ayish \ā-ish\ clayish, grayish

ayist \ā-əst\ see AYEST

ayle \āl\ see AIL

ayless \ā-ləs\ rayless, talus, wayless • aurora australis

ayling \ā-liŋ\ see AILING

aylor \ā-lər\ see AILER

ayman \ā-mən\ see AMEN[1]

ayment \ā-mənt\ claimant, payment, raiment • co-payment, down payment, nonpayment, prepayment, stop payment

ayne \ān\ see ANE[1]

ayness \ā-nəs\ grayness, heinous, Janus • Uranus • everydayness

ayo¹ \ā-ō\ see EO[1]

ayo² \ī-ō\ see IO[1]

ayon \ā-ən\ see AYAN[1]

ayor \ā-ər\ see AYER

ayou¹ \ī-ə\ see IAH[1]

ayou² \ī-ō\ see IO[1]

ayr \er\ see ARE[4]

ays¹ \ez\ fez, Fez, prez, says • Chávez, Cortés, Inez, Suez, unsays • Mayagüez

ays² \āz\ see AZE[1]

aysia \ā-zhə\ see ASIA

ay-so \ā-sō\ see ESO

ayyid¹ \ī-əd\ see YAD

ayyid² \ēd-ē\ see EEDY

az¹ \az\ see AZZ

az² \äz\ see OISE[1]

az³ \äts\ see OTS

aza¹ \äz-ə\ Gaza, plaza • piazza

aza² \az-ə\ plaza • piazza

aze¹ \āz\ blaze, braise, chaise, craze, days, daze, faze, gaze, glaze, graze, haze, laze, maize, Mays, maze, phase, phrase, praise, raise, raze, vase, ways • ablaze, amaze, appraise, crossways, dog days, edgeways, endways, leastways, lengthways, malaise, pj's, rephrase, Roget's, sideways, slantways, stargaze, weekdays • anyways, holidays, hollandaise, mayonnaise, multiphase, nowadays, out of phase, overgraze, overpraise, paraphrase • parting of the ways

—also -s, -'s, *and* -s' *forms of nouns and* -s *forms of verbs listed at* AY[1]

aze[2] \äz\ see OISE[1]

aze[3] \äz-ē\ see AZI[1]

azed \āzd\ unfazed
—also -ed *forms of verbs listed at* AZE[1]

azen \āz-ᵊn\ see AZON

azer \ā-zǝr\ blazer, glazer, laser, razor, Taser • appraiser, fund-raiser, hair-raiser, hell-raiser, stargazer, trailblazer • crystal-gazer, curtain-raiser

azi[1] \äz-ē\ quasi, Swazi • Benghazi • Anasazi, Ashkenazi, kamikaze

azi[2] \az-ē\ see AZZY

azi[3] \at-sē\ Nazi, patsy, Patsy • neo-Nazi

azier \ā-zhǝr\ brazier, Frasier, leisure, measure, pleasure, treasure

azing \ā-ziŋ\ see AISING

azon \āz-ᵊn\ blazon, brazen, raisin • emblazon

azor \ā-zǝr\ see AZER

azquez \as-kǝs\ see ASCUS

azy \ā-zē\ crazy, daisy, Daisy, hazy, lazy, mazy • like crazy, stir-crazy • Shasta daisy

azz \az\ as, has, jazz, razz • free jazz, Hejaz, La Paz, pizzazz, topaz, whereas • razzmatazz

azza[1] \az-ǝ\ see AZA[2]

azza[2] \äz-ǝ\ see AZA[1]

azza[3] \ät-sǝ\ see ATZO[1]

azzle \az-ǝl\ basil, Basil, dazzle, frazzle • bedazzle, sweet basil • razzle-dazzle

azzo \ät-sō\ matzo • palazzo • paparazzo

azzy \az-ē\ jazzy, snazzy • pizzazzy • Ashkenazi

E

e[1] \ā\ see AY[1]

e[2] \ē\ see EE[1]

é \ā\ see AY[1]

ea[1] \ā\ see AY[1]

ea[2] \ā-ǝ\ see AIA[1]

ea[3] \ē\ see EE[1]

ea[4] \ē-ǝ\ see IA[1]

eabee \ē-bē\ see EBE[1]

eace \ēs\ see IECE

eaceable \ē-sǝ-bǝl\ see EASABLE[1]

each \ēch\ beach, beech, bleach, breach, each, leach, leech, peach, preach, reach, screech, speech, teach • beseech, free speech, impeach, Long Beach, outreach, Palm Beach, unteach • copper beech, Myrtle Beach, Newport Beach,

overreach, part of speech, practice-teach • Daytona Beach, figure of speech, Huntington Beach, Miami Beach, Omaha Beach, Redondo Beach, Virginia Beach

eachable \ē-chǝ-bǝl\ bleachable, reachable, teachable • impeachable, unreachable, unteachable • unimpeachable

eacher \ē-chǝr\ bleacher, creature, feature, preacher, reacher, screecher, teacher • schoolteacher • double feature, overreacher, practice teacher, student teacher

eaching \ē-chiŋ\ see EECHING

eachy \ē-chē\ beachy, chichi, Nietzsche, peachy, preachy, screechy

eacly \ē-klē\ *see* EEKLY
eacon \ē-kən\ beacon, deacon, sleeken, weaken • archdeacon, Mohican, subdeacon • Nuyorican, radar beacon • radio beacon
ead¹ \ed\ bed, bled, bread, bred, dead, dread, ed, Ed, fed, fled, Fred, head, Jed, lead, led, med, Ned, pled, read, red, Red, said, shed, shred, sled, sped, spread, stead, Ted, thread, tread, wed • abed, ahead, airhead, baldhead, beachhead, bedspread, bedstead, behead, biped, blackhead, blockhead, bloodred, bloodshed, bobsled, bonehead, brain-dead, break bread, brown bread, bulkhead, bullhead, coed, corn bread, cornfed, cowshed, crossbred, daybed, deadhead, death's-head, deathbed, dogsled, drop-dead, egghead, embed, farmstead, fathead, flatbed, forehead, French bread, fry bread, gearhead, godhead, highbred, hogshead, homebred, homestead, hotbed, hothead, illbred, inbred, instead, jarhead, knock dead, lowbred, lunkhead, masthead, meathead, misled, misread, moped, outsped, outspread, phys ed, pinhead, point spread, premed, purebred, quick bread, redhead, red lead, retread, roadbed, roadstead, saphead, scarehead, screw thread, seabed, seedbed, sheepshead, shortbread, sickbed, skinhead, sorehead, spearhead, spoon bread, streambed, subhead, sweetbread, toolshed, towhead, trailhead, unbred, undead, unread, unsaid, unthread, warhead, well-bred, well-read, white-bread, whitehead, white lead, widespread, wingspread, woodshed • aforesaid, arrowhead, bubblehead, chowderhead, chucklehead, cop-

perhead, Diamond Head, dunderhead, featherbed, featherhead, fiddlehead, figurehead, fountainhead, get ahead, gingerbread, go-ahead, hammerhead, head-to-head, infrared, interbred, knucklehead, letterhead, Lizard Head, loggerhead, Marblehead, metalhead, newlywed, overhead, overspread, pinniped, quadruped, riverbed, Samoyed, scratch one's head, showerhead, sleepyhead, slugabed, soda bread, standardbred, straight-ahead, talking head, thoroughbred, thunderhead, turn one's head, underbred, underfed, watershed • cylinder head, fire-engine red, go to one's head, over one's head
ead² \ēd\ *see* EED
ead³ \əd\ *see* UD¹
eadable \ed-ə-bəl\ *see* EDIBLE
eaded \ed-əd\ bedded, headed • bareheaded, bullheaded, clearheaded, coolheaded, embedded, hardheaded, hotheaded, lightheaded, pigheaded, unleaded, wrongheaded • empty-headed, hydra-headed, levelheaded, muddleheaded
—also -ed *forms of verbs listed at* EAD¹
eaden \ed-ᵊn\ deaden, leaden, redden • Armageddon
eader¹ \ēd-ər\ beader, bleeder, breeder, cedar, feeder, kneader, leader, pleader, reader, seeder, speeder, weeder • bandleader, cheerleader, floor leader, lay reader, lip-reader, loss leader, mind reader, nonreader, proofreader, ringleader, sight reader, stockbreeder • bottom-feeder
eader² \ed-ər\ cheddar, header, shredder, sledder, spreader, threader, treader • homesteader • doubleheader, triple-header

eadily \ed-ᵊl-ē\ headily, readily,
steadily • unsteadily

eading[1] \ed-iŋ\ bedding, heading,
Reading, sledding, wedding • bob-
sledding, farmsteading, subhead-
ing • featherbedding
—*also* -ing *forms of verbs listed at*
EAD[1]

eading[2] \ed-ᵊn\ see EADEN

eading[3] \ēd-ᵊn\ see EDON

eading[4] \ēd-iŋ\ see EEDING[1]

eadle[1] \ed-ᵊl\ see EDAL[1]

eadle[2] \ēd-ᵊl\ see EEDLE

eadly \ed-lē\ see EDLEY

eady[1] \ed-ē\ Eddie, eddy, Freddie,
heady, ready, steady, Teddy • al-
ready, go steady, unsteady • at the
ready, rough-and-ready

eady[2] \ēd-ē\ see EEDY

eaf[1] \ef\ see EF[1]

eaf[2] \ēf\ see IEF[1]

eafy \ē-fē\ see EEFY

eag \ēg\ see IGUE

eagan \ā-gən\ see AGIN

eager \ē-gər\ eager, meager • be-
leaguer, big leaguer, bush leaguer,
intriguer • Ivy Leaguer, Little
Leaguer, major leaguer, overeager

eagh \ā\ see AY[1]

eagle \ē-gəl\ see EGAL

eague \ēg\ see IGUE

eaguer \ē-gər\ see EAGER

eah \ē-ə\ see IA[1]

eak[1] \ēk\ beak, bleak, cheek, chic,
clique, creak, creek, Creek, eke,
freak, geek, Greek, leak, leek,
meek, peak, peek, pique, reek,
seek, sheikh, shriek, Sikh, sleek,
sneak, speak, squeak, streak,
teak, tweak, weak, week, wreak
• antique, batik, Belgique, be-
speak, blue streak, boutique,
Cloud Peak, critique, debeak,
Grays Peak, grosbeak, hairstreak,
midweek, misspeak, muzhik,
mystique, nonpeak, oblique, off-
peak, physique, Pikes Peak, pip-

squeak, technique, Tajik, unique,
workweek • Battle Creek, Boundary Peak, Chesapeake, control
freak, doublespeak, ecofreak,
Granite Peak, hide-and-seek, Holy
Week, Lassen Peak, Lenin Peak,
Martinique, Mozambique, Passion
Week, tongue-in-cheek, up the
creek, Wheeler Peak, widow's
peak • microtechnique, quarterback sneak, semi-antique • Communism Peak, opéra comique,
turn the other cheek

eak[2] \āk\ see AKE[1]

eak[3] \ek\ see ECK

eakable \ā-kə-bəl\ see AKABLE

eake \ēk\ see EAK[1]

eaked[1] \ē-kəd\ peaked, streaked

eaked[2] \ēkt\ beaked, freaked,
peaked, streaked
—*also* -ed *forms of verbs listed at*
EAK[1]

eaken \ē-kən\ see EACON

eaker[1] \ē-kər\ beaker, leaker,
phreaker, seeker, sneaker,
speaker, squeaker • loudspeaker,
self-seeker, sunseeker • keynote
speaker
—*also* -er *forms of adjectives listed
at* EAK[1]

eaker[2] \ā-kər\ see AKER[1]

eaking \ē-kiŋ\ freaking, phreaking,
sneaking, speaking, streaking
• heat-seeking, self-seeking • public speaking
—*also* -ing *forms of verbs listed at*
EAK[1]

eakish \ē-kish\ cliquish, freakish,
weakish

eakly \ē-klē\ see EEKLY

eaky \ē-kē\ cheeky, cliquey,
creaky, freaky, geeky, leaky,
sneaky, squeaky, streaky, tiki
• boutiquey, dashiki

eal[1] \ē-əl\ laryngeal, marmoreal,
pharyngeal

eal[2] \ēl\ creel, deal, eel, feel, heal,

heel, he'll, keel, kneel, meal, Neil, peal, peel, real, reel, seal, she'll, spiel, squeal, steal, steel, teal, veal, we'll, wheel, zeal • all-wheel, anneal, appeal, Bastille, big deal, big wheel, bonemeal, Camille, cam wheel, Castile, cartwheel, Cecile, chenille, cogwheel, conceal, congeal, cornmeal, done deal, eared seal, fifth wheel, fish meal, flywheel, for real, fourwheel, freewheel, fur seal, genteel, get real, good deal, great seal, handwheel, harp seal, ideal, Lucille, mill wheel, misdeal, mobile, Mobile, monk seal, mouthfeel, New Deal, newsreel, nosewheel, oatmeal, ordeal, piecemeal, pinwheel, prayer wheel, raw deal, repeal, reveal, schlemiel, spike heel, surreal, Tar Heel, unreal, unreel, unseal • bearded seal, bloodmobile, bookmobile, carbon steel, chamomile, cockatiel, color wheel, commonweal, conger eel, cut a deal, dishabille, down-at-heel, Ferris wheel, glockenspiel, goldenseal, Guayaquil, harbor seal, lamprey eel, leopard seal, megadeal, mercantile, moray eel, orange peel, package deal, paddle wheel, pedal steel, potter's wheel, reel-to-reel, skimobile, snob appeal, snowmobile, spinning reel, stainless steel, thunderpeal, waterwheel • automobile, electric eel, elephant seal, Solomon's seal, stiletto heel

eal³ \āl\ see AIL

eal⁴ \il\ see ILL

ealable \ē-lə-bəl\ peelable, reelable, stealable • appealable, concealable, resealable

ealand \ē-lənd\ see ELAND

eald \ēld\ see IELD

ealed \ēld\ see IELD

ealer \ē-lər\ dealer, feeler, healer, peeler, sealer • concealer, faith healer, four-wheeler, freewheeler, New Dealer, newsdealer, scenestealer, side-wheeler, sternwheeler, three-wheeler, two-wheeler, ward heeler • double-dealer, eighteen-wheeler, 18-wheeler, paddle wheeler, snowmobiler, wheeler-dealer

ealie \ē-lē\ see EELY

ealing \ē-liŋ\ see EELING

eally¹ \il-ē\ see ILLY

eally² \ē-lē\ see EELY

ealm \elm\ see ELM

ealot \el-ət\ see ELLATE

ealotry \el-ə-trē\ see ELOTRY

ealous \el-əs\ Ellis, jealous, trellis, zealous • Marcellus

ealousy \el-ə-sē\ see ELACY

ealth \elth\ health, stealth, wealth • bill of health, commonwealth, public health

ealthy \el-thē\ healthy, stealthy, wealthy • heart-healthy, unhealthy

ealty \ēl-tē\ fealty, realty

eam¹ \ēm\ beam, cream, crèeme, deem, dream, gleam, meme, Nîmes, ream, scheme, scream, seam, seem, steam, stream, team, teem, theme • agleam, airstream, bireme, blaspheme, bloodstream, centime, coal seam, cold cream, crossbeam, daydream, downstream, dream team, esteem, extreme, Gulf Stream, high beam, hornbeam, I beam, ice cream, inseam, jet stream, low beam, mainstream, midstream, millstream, moonbeam, pipe dream, redeem, regime, rhyme scheme, slipstream, sour cream, sunbeam, supreme, tag team, trireme, upstream • academe, balance beam, blow off steam, double-team, head of steam, heavy cream, on the beam, Ponzi scheme, self-esteem • ancien régime, in the extreme, vanishing cream • American dream, Bavarian cream

eam² \im\ see IM¹

eaman \ē-mən\ see EMON¹

eamed¹ \emt\ see EMPT

eamed² \emd\ steamed
—*also* -ed *forms of verbs listed at* EAM¹

eamer \ē-mər\ creamer, dreamer, femur, lemur, reamer, screamer, steamer, streamer • blasphemer, daydreamer, redeemer

eaming \ē-miŋ\ see EEMING

eamish \ē-mish\ beamish, squeamish

eamless \ēm-ləs\ dreamless, seamless

eamon \ē-mən\ see EMON¹

eamster \ēm-stər\ seamster, teamster

eamy \ē-mē\ creamy, dreamy, gleamy, preemie, seamy, steamy

ean¹ \ē-ən\ eon, Ian, Leon, paean, peon • Aegean, Chilean, Crimean, Fijian, Judaean, Korean, plebeian • Caribbean, cyclopean, empyrean, European, Galilean, Herculean, Jacobean, Manichaean, Sisyphean, Tennessean • epicurean, Ponce de Leon, Pythagorean, un-European • Indo-European

ean² \ēn\ see INE³

ean³ \ón\ see ON³

ean⁴ \ā-ən\ see AYAN¹

eane \ēn\ see INE³

eaner \ē-nər\ cleaner, gleaner, screener, wiener • demeanor, dry cleaner, pipe cleaner • misdemeanor, submariner, trampoliner, vacuum cleaner
—*also* -er *forms of adjectives listed at* INE³

eanery \ēn-rē\ beanery, greenery, scenery • machinery

eanie \ē-nē\ see INI¹

eaning \ē-niŋ\ leaning, meaning, screening • dry cleaning, housecleaning, spring-cleaning, well-meaning • overweening
—*also* -ing *forms of verbs listed at* INE³

eanist \ē-nəst\ see INIST²

eanliness \en-lē-nəs\ see ENDLINESS

eanly¹ \ēn-lē\ cleanly, keenly, meanly, queenly • routinely

eanly² \en-lē\ see ENDLY

eanne \ēn\ see INE³

eanness \ēn-nəs\ cleanness, greenness, keenness, meanness • uncleanness

eannie \ē-nē\ see INI¹

eano \ē-nō\ see INO²

eanor \ē-nər\ see EANER

eanse \enz\ see ENS¹

eant \ent\ see ENT¹

eany \ē-nē\ see INI¹

eap \ēp\ see EEP

eapen \ē-pən\ see EEPEN

eaper \ē-pər\ see EEPER

eapie \ē-pē\ see EEPY

eapo \ē-pō\ see EPOT

ear¹ \er\ see ARE⁴

ear² \ir\ see EER²

earable¹ \er-ə-bəl\ bearable, shareable, spareable, tearable, terrible, wearable • unbearable, unwearable

earable² \ar-ə-bəl\ see ARABLE

earage \ir-ij\ see EERAGE

earance¹ \ir-əns\ see ERENCE¹

earance² \er-əns\ see ARENCE¹

earch \ərch\ see URCH

eard¹ \ird\ beard, eared, tiered, weird • bat-eared, crop-eared, dog-eared, graybeard, jug-eared, lop-eared, spade beard, whitebeard • chandeliered, engineered, multitiered • pre-engineered
—*also* -ed *forms of verbs listed at* EER²

eard² \ərd\ see IRD

eare \ir\ see EER²

earean \ir-ē-ən\ see ERIAN[1]

eared[1] \erd\ see AIRED

eared[2] \ird\ see EARD[1]

earer[1] \er-ər\ bearer, error, sharer, terror, wearer • cupbearer, pallbearer, seafarer, talebearer, torchbearer, wayfarer • standard-bearer, stretcherbearer
—*also* -er *forms of adjectives listed at* ARE[4]

earer[2] \ir-ər\ mirror • sheepshearer • rearview mirror
—*also* -er *forms of adjectives listed at* EER[2]

earful \ir-fəl\ cheerful, earful, fearful, tearful

earies \ir-ēz\ see ERIES

earing[1] \ir-iŋ\ clearing, earring, gearing, searing • God-fearing, sheepshearing • engineering, hard-of-hearing, mountaineering, power steering • orienteering • bioengineering, social engineering
—*also* -ing *forms of verbs listed at* EER[2]

earing[2] \er-iŋ\ see ARING[1]

earish \er-ish\ see ARISH[1]

earl \ərl\ see IRL

earler \ər-lər\ see IRLER

earless \ir-ləs\ cheerless, fearless, peerless, tearless

earling \ər-lən\ see ERLIN

early[1] \ir-lē\ clearly, dearly, merely, nearly, queerly, sheerly, yearly • austerely, biyearly, severely, sincerely • cavalierly, insincerely, semiyearly

early[2] \ər-lē\ see URLY

earn \ərn\ see URN

earned \ərnd\ see URNED

earner \ər-nər\ see URNER

earnist \ər-nəst\ see ERNIST

earnt \ərnt\ burnt, learnt, weren't

earring \ir-iŋ\ see EARING[1]

earsal \ər-səl\ see ERSAL

earse \ərs\ see ERSE

earst \ərst\ see URST

eart \ärt\ see ART[1]

earted \ärt-əd\ parted • bighearted, coldhearted, departed, downhearted, fainthearted, goodhearted, greathearted, halfhearted, hard-hearted, kindhearted, largehearted, lighthearted, softhearted, stouthearted, truehearted, uncharted, warmhearted, wholehearted • brokenhearted, chickenhearted, openhearted, tenderhearted
—*also* -ed *forms of verbs listed at* ART[1]

earth[1] \ärth\ see ARTH

earth[2] \ərth\ see IRTH

eartha \ər-thə\ see ERTHA

earthy \ər-thē\ see ORTHY

eartily \ärt-ᵊl-ē\ see ARTILY

eartless \ärt-ləs\ see ARTLESS

earty \ärt-ē\ see ARTY[1]

eary \ir-ē\ aerie, beery, bleary, cheery, dreary, eerie, Erie, leery, Peary, query, teary, veery, weary • Fort Erie, Kashmiri, Lake Erie, Valkyrie, world-weary • hara-kiri

eas \ē-əs\ see EUS[1]

easable[1] \ē-sə-bəl\ leasable, peaceable

easable[2] \ē-zə-bəl\ see EASIBLE

easand \iz-ᵊn\ see ISON[2]

ease[1] \ēs\ see IECE

ease[2] \ēz\ see EZE

eased[1] \ēzd\ diseased, self-pleased
—*also* -ed *forms of verbs listed at* EZE

eased[2] \ēst\ see EAST[1]

easel \ē-zəl\ bezel, diesel, easel, teasel, weasel

easeless \ē-sləs\ ceaseless, creaseless, greaseless

easelly \ē-zlē\ see EASLY

easer[1] \ē-sər\ greaser, piecer

easer[2] \ē-zər\ Caesar, freezer, geezer, greaser, pleaser, squeezer,

teaser, tweezer • appeaser, brain-
teaser, crowd-pleaser

eash \ēsh\ see ICHE[2]

easible \ē-zə-bəl\ feasible, squeez-
able

easil \ē-zəl\ see EASEL

easily \ēz-lē\ see EASLY

easing[1] \ē-siŋ\ leasing • unceasing
—also -ing forms of verbs listed at
IECE

easing[2] \ē-ziŋ\ freezing, pleasing
• subfreezing
—also -ing forms of verbs listed at
EZE

easingly \ē-siŋ-lē\ decreasingly,
increasingly, unceasingly

easle \ē-zəl\ see EASEL

easly \ēz-ə-lē\ easily, measly,
weaselly

eason \ēz-³n\ reason, season, treason • high treason, in season, off-
season, postseason, preseason,
with reason • age of reason,
diocesan, open season, out of
season, rhyme or reason, silly
season, within reason

easonable \ēz-nə-bəl\ reasonable,
seasonable, treasonable • unrea-
sonable, unseasonable

easoning \ēz-niŋ\ reasoning, sea-
soning • unreasoning

easor \ē-zər\ see EASER[2]

east[1] \ēst\ beast, east, East, feast,
fleeced, least, priest, yeast • arch-
priest, artiste, at least, batiste,
deceased, Far East, Near East,
northeast, southeast • baker's
yeast, hartebeest, Middle East,
north-northeast, pointillist, wilde-
beest
—also -ed forms of verbs listed at
IECE

east[2] \est\ see EST

easted \es-təd\ see ESTED

easter \ē-stər\ Easter, feaster,
keister • northeaster

eastly \ēst-lē\ beastly, priestly

easurable \ezh-rə-bəl\ pleasurable,
treasurable • immeasurable

easure[1] \ezh-ər\ leisure, measure,
pleasure, treasure • displeasure,
dry measure, square measure,
tape measure • countermeasure,
cubic measure, for good measure,
liquid measure

easure[2] \ā-zhər\ see AZIER

easurer \ezh-ər-ər\ measurer,
treasurer

easy[1] \ē-zē\ breezy, cheesy, easy,
greasy, queasy, sleazy, sneezy,
wheezy • breathe easy, go easy,
Parcheesi, speakeasy, uneasy,
Zambezi • free and easy, over
easy

easy[2] \ē-sē\ see EECY

eat[1] \ēt\ beat, beet, bleat, cheat,
cleat, Crete, deet, eat, feat, fleet,
greet, heat, meat, meet, mete,
neat, peat, Pete, pleat, seat, sheet,
skeet, sleet, street, suite, sweet,
teat, treat, tweet, wheat • aes-
thete, athlete, backbeat, backseat,
backstreet, bedsheet, box seat,
browbeat, buckwheat, car seat,
cheat sheet, cold feet, compete,
complete, conceit, concrete,
crabmeat, crib sheet, deadbeat,
dead heat, dead meat, deceit,
defeat, delete, deplete, discreet,
discrete, downbeat, drumbeat,
dutch treat, effete, elite, entreat,
esthete, excrete, gamete, ground-
sheet, hard wheat, heartbeat,
helpmeet, hoofbeat, hot seat, ice
sheet, ill-treat, jump seat, love
seat, Main Street, maltreat,
mesquite, mincemeat, mistreat,
offbeat, petite, preheat, rap sheet,
receipt, red heat, red meat, re-
heat, repeat, replete, retreat,
secrete, side street, soft wheat,
spreadsheet, swap meet, through
street, unseat, upbeat, Wall Street,
white heat • balance sheet, bitter-

sweet, booster seat, bucket seat, cellulite, cookie sheet, county seat, decathlete, drag one's feet, driver's seat, durum wheat, easy street, incomplete, indiscreet, lorikeet, make ends meet, Marguerite, meet and greet, miss a beat, nonathlete, obsolete, on one's feet, overeat, overheat, Paraclete, parakeet, pentathlete, prickly heat, rumble seat, saddle seat, scandal sheet, semisweet, shredded wheat, spirochete, to one's feet, triathlete, trick or treat, two-way street, window seat • beat a retreat, ejection seat, man in the street, radiant heat, take a back seat, vote with one's feet

eat² \āt\ see ATE¹

eat³ \et\ see ET¹

eat⁴ \it\ see IT¹

eatable \ēt-ə-bəl\ beatable, eatable, heatable, treatable • defeatable, repeatable, unbeatable

eated¹ \ēt-əd\ heated, pleated • conceited, deep-seated, repeated • overheated, superheated
—*also* -ed *forms of verbs listed at* EAT¹

eated² \et-əd\ see ETID

eated³ \it-əd\ see ITTED

eaten¹ \ēt-ᵊn\ eaten, beaten, Cretan, cretin, Eton, neaten, sweeten, wheaten • browbeaten, Grand Teton, moth-eaten, unbeaten, worm-eaten • overeaten, weatherbeaten

eaten² \āt-ᵊn\ see ATEN¹

eater¹ \ēt-ər\ beater, cheater, eater, greeter, heater, liter, meter, Peter, teeter, tweeter • ammeter, anteater, beefeater, Demeter, eggbeater, fire-eater, flowmeter, light meter, man-eater, ohmmeter, repeater, space heater, voltmeter, Wall Streeter, wattmeter, world-beater • altimeter, cen-

tiliter, centimeter, deciliter, decimeter, dekaliter, dekameter, hectoliter, lotus-eater, milliliter, millimeter, overeater, parking meter, postage meter, taximeter, trick-or-treater, water heater, water meter
—*also* -er *forms of adjectives listed at* EAT¹

eater² \et-ər\ see ETTER

eath¹ \ēth\ heath, Keith, sheath, wreath • beneath, bequeath • underneath

eath² \ēth\ see EATHE

eathe \ēth\ breathe, seethe, sheathe, teethe, wreathe • bequeath, unsheathe

eather¹ \eth-ər\ see ETHER¹

eather² \ē-thər\ see EITHER

eathery \eth-rē\ feathery, leathery

eathing \ē-thiŋ\ breathing, sheathing, teething • air-breathing, firebreathing
—*also* -ing *forms of verbs listed at* EATHE

eathless \eth-ləs\ breathless, deathless

eating \ēt-iŋ\ beating, eating, fleeting, greeting, meeting, seating, sheeting • breast-beating, camp meeting, drumbeating, fire-eating, man-eating, prayer meeting, space heating, town meeting
—*also* -ing *forms of verbs listed at* EAT¹

eatise \ēt-əs\ see ETUS

eatly¹ \āt-lē\ see ATELY¹

eatly² \ēt-lē\ see EETLY

eaton \ēt-ᵊn\ see EATEN¹

eats¹ \ēts\ Keats
—*also* -s, -'s, *and* -s' *forms of nouns and* -s *forms of verbs listed at* EAT¹

eats² \āts\ see ATES¹

eature \ē-chər\ see EACHER

eaty \ēt-ē\ meaty, peaty, sleety, sweetie, treaty, ziti • entreaty, graffiti, Tahiti • spermaceti

eau \ō\ see OW[1]

eaucracy \äk-rə-sē\ see OCRACY

eauteous \üt-ē-əs\ see UTEOUS

eautiful \üt-i-fəl\ see UTIFUL

eauty \üt-ē\ see OOTY[1]

eaux \ō\ see OW[1]

eavable \ē-və-bəl\ see EIVABLE

eaval \ē-vəl\ see IEVAL

eave[1] \ēv\ eve, Eve, grieve, heave, leave, peeve, sheave, sleeve, Steve, thieve, weave, we've • achieve, aggrieve, believe, bereave, conceive, deceive, frost heave, Maldive, motive, naive, perceive, pet peeve, receive, relieve, reprieve, retrieve, shirtsleeve, shore leave, sick leave, unweave • basket weave, disbelieve, Genevieve, interleave, interweave, makebelieve, misconceive, on one's sleeve, preconceive, Tel Aviv, up one's sleeve • overachieve, Saint Agnes' Eve, underachieve • absent without leave

eave[2] \iv\ see IVE[2]

eaved \ēvd\ leaved, sleeved • aggrieved, bereaved, broad leaved, relieved
—also -ed forms of verbs listed at EAVE[1]

eavement \ēv-mənt\ see EVEMENT

eaven \ev-ən\ Devon, Evan, heaven, Kevin, leaven, seven • eleven, hog heaven • seventh heaven

eaver \ē-vər\ see IEVER

eaward \ē-wərd\ see EEWARD

eaze[1] \ēz\ see EZE

eaze[2] \āz\ see AZE[1]

eazo \ē-zō\ see IZO

eazy \ē-zē\ see EASY[1]

eb \eb\ deb, ebb, reb, web • celeb, cobweb, Horeb, subdeb, Zagreb • cause célèbre, Johnny Reb, spiderweb, World Wide Web

eba \ē-bə\ Reba, Sheba • amoeba, Beersheba

ebate \ab-ət\ see ABIT

ebb \eb\ see EB

ebbie \eb-ē\ see EBBY

ebble \eb-əl\ pebble, rebel, treble

ebby \eb-ē\ Debbie, webby • cobwebby

ebe[1] \ē-bē\ BB, freebie, Phoebe, Seabee

ebe[2] \ēb\ plebe • sahib

ebel \eb-əl\ see EBBLE

eber \ā-bər\ see ABOR

ebes \ēbz\ Thebes
—also -s, -'s, and -s' forms of nouns listed at EBE[2]

eble \eb-əl\ see EBBLE

ebo \ē-bō\ see IBO

ebral \ē-brəl\ cerebral, vertebral

ebs \eps\ see EPS

ebt \et\ see ET[1]

ebted \et-əd\ see ETID

ebtor \et-ər\ see ETTER

ec[1] \ek\ see ECK

ec[2] \ets\ see ETS

eca \ē-kə\ see IKA[1]

ecan \ek-ən\ see ECKON

ecca \ek-ə\ Decca, mecca, Mecca • Rebecca

eccable \ek-ə-bəl\ see ECKABLE

eccan \ek-ən\ see ECKON

ecce \ek-ē\ see ECKY

ecco \ek-ō\ see ECHO

ecency \ēs-ᵊn-sē\ decency, recency • indecency

ecent \ēs-ᵊnt\ decent, recent • indecent

ech[1] \ek\ see ECK

ech[2] \ək\ see UCK[1]

ech[3] \esh\ see ESH[1]

eche[1] \āsh\ crèche • Andhra Pradesh, Madhya Pradesh, Uttar Pradesh

eche[2] \esh\ see ESH[1]

eche[3] \ē-chē\ see EACHY

êche \esh\ see ESH[1]

èche \esh\ see ESH[1]

eched \echt\ see ETCHED

echie \ek-ē\ see ECKY

echin \ek-ən\ see ECKON
echo \ek-ō\ echo, gecko • art deco, El Greco, reecho
echt \ekt\ see ECT
ecia \ē-shə\ see ESIA¹
ecially \esh-lē\ see ESHLY
ecian \ē-shən\ see ETION¹
ecibel \es-ə-bəl\ see ESSIBLE
ecie¹ \ē-sē\ see EECY
ecie² \ē-shē\ see ISHI
ecies \ē-sēz\ species, theses • prostheses, subspecies
ecil¹ \ē-səl\ Cecil, diesel
ecil² \es-əl\ see ESTLE¹
ecile \es-əl\ see ESTLE¹
eciman \es-mən\ see ESSMAN
ecious \ē-shəs\ specious • capricious, facetious, Lucretius
eck \ek\ beck, check, Czech, deck, dreck, fleck, heck, Lech, neck, pec, peck, sec, spec, speck, trek, wreak, wreck • Aztec, bed check, bedeck, Bishkek, blank check, breakneck, bull neck, crew neck, cross-check, exec, fact-check, flight deck, flyspeck, gooseneck, gut check, hatcheck, henpeck, high tech, in check, kopeck, low-tech, Lubeck, on deck, OPEC, parsec, paycheck, poop deck, Quebec, rain check, roughneck, shipwreck, spell-check, spot-check, Steinbeck, sundeck, tape deck, Toltec, Uzbek, V-neck, vo-tech • biotech, bottleneck, cashier's check, Chiang Kai-shek, countercheck, discotheque, double-check, double-deck, hunt-and-peck, leatherneck, neck and neck, quarterdeck, rubber check, rubberneck, turtleneck, weather deck, Yucatec, Zapotec • breathe down one's neck, cinematheque, Melchizedek, mock turtleneck, promenade deck, Toulouse-Lautrec, traveler's check • reality check

eckable \ek-ə-bəl\ checkable • impeccable
ecked \ekt\ see ECT
ecker \ek-ər\ checker, decker, pecker, trekker, wrecker • fact-checker, Quebecer, spell-checker, three-decker, woodpecker • double-decker, rubbernecker, triple-decker
ecking \ek-iŋ\ necking
—*also* -ing *forms of verbs listed at* ECK
ecklace \ek-ləs\ see ECKLESS
eckle \ek-əl\ freckle, heckle, shekel, speckle
eckless \ek-ləs\ feckless, necklace, reckless
ecko \ek-ō\ see ECHO
eckon \ek-ən\ beckon, reckon • Aztecan, misreckon, Toltecan • Yucatecan
ecks, eks see EX
ecky \ek-ē\ Becky, techie
econ \ek-ən\ see ECKON
econd \ek-ənd\ see ECUND
ecque \ek\ see ECK
ecs \eks\ see EX
ect \ekt\ Brecht, necked, sect, specked • abject, affect, aspect, bisect, bullnecked, collect, connect, correct, cowl-necked, defect, deflect, deject, detect, direct, dissect, Dordrecht, effect, eject, elect, erect, expect, goosenecked, infect, inflect, inject, insect, inspect, neglect, object, perfect, project, prospect, protect, reflect, reject, respect, roll-necked, select, stiff-necked, subject, suspect, transect, trisect, Utrecht, V-necked • architect, birth defect, circumspect, deselect, dialect, disconnect, disinfect, disrespect, double-decked, genuflect, incorrect, indirect, in effect, intellect, interject, intersect, misdirect, preselect, recollect, reconnect,

redirect, reelect, resurrect, retrospect, self-respect, side effect, turtlenecked • aftereffect, Doppler effect, idiolect, interconnect, ripple effect • domino effect, landscape architect, placebo effect • politically correct
—*also* -ed *forms of verbs listed at* ECK

ectable \ek-tə-bəl\ collectible, connectable, correctable, delectable, detectable, electable, expectable, injectable, perfectible, respectable, selectable • undetectable

ectacle \ek-ti-kəl\ see ECTICAL

ectal \ek-t³l\ see ECTILE

ectant \ek-tənt\ expectant • disinfectant

ectar \ek-tər\ see ECTOR

ected \ek-təd\ affected, collected, connected, dejected, directed, dissected • disaffected, disconnected, fuel-injected, self-selected, unaffected, undirected, unexpected, unprotected, unselected • inner-directed, interconnected, other-directed
—*also* -ed *forms of verbs listed at* ECT

ecter \ek-tər\ see ECTOR

ectible \ek-tə-bəl\ see ECTABLE

ectic \ek-tik\ hectic • eclectic • anorectic, apoplectic, dialectic

ectical \ek-ti-kəl\ spectacle • dialectical

ectile \ek-t³l\ projectile • dialectal

ecting \ek-tiŋ\ affecting, respecting • self-correcting, self-respecting
—*also* -ing *forms of verbs listed at* ECT

ection \ek-shən\ flexion, section • affection, collection, complexion, confection, connection, convection, correction, cross section, C-section, defection, deflection, dejection, detection, direction,

ejection, election, infection, inflection, injection, inspection, midsection, objection, perfection, projection, protection, reflection, rejection, selection, subjection, subsection, trisection • circumspection, conic section, disaffection, disinfection, fuel injection, golden section, imperfection, indirection, insurrection, interjection, intersection, introspection, misdirection, predilection, recollection, reconnection, redirection, reelection, reinfection, resurrection, self-direction, self-protection, self-selection, stage direction, vivisection • equal protection, general election, house of correction, interconnection • cesarean section

ectional \ek-shnəl\ sectional • correctional, cross-sectional, directional • omnidirectional, unidirectional

ectionist \ek-shə-nəst\ perfectionist, projectionist, protectionist • insurrectionist

ective \ek-tiv\ affective, collective, connective, corrective, defective, detective, directive, effective, elective, invective, objective, perspective, prospective, protective, reflective, respective, selective, subjective • cost-effective, house detective, ineffective, introspective, nonobjective, retrospective, self-reflective • private detective

ectless \ek-ləs\ see ECKLESS

ectly \ekt-lē\ abjectly, correctly, directly, erectly • circumspectly, incorrectly, indirectly

ectomy \ek-tə-mē\ mastectomy, vasectomy • appendectomy, hysterectomy, laryngectomy, tonsillectomy

ector \ek-tər\ hector, Hector, lector, nectar, rector, sector, specter, vector • collector, connector, defector, detector, director, ejector, elector, erector, injector, inspector, objector, projector, prospector, protector, reflector, selector, subsector • lie detector, smoke detector, stage director • casting director, funeral director, program director, solar collector

ectoral \ek-trəl\ pectoral, spectral • electoral

ectorate \ek-tə-rət\ directorate, electorate, protectorate

ectory \ek-tə-rē\ rectory • directory, trajectory

ectral \ek-trəl\ see ECTORAL

ectrum \ek-trəm\ plectrum, spectrum • broad-spectrum

ectual \ek-chə-wəl\ effectual • ineffectual, intellectual • anti-intellectual

ectually \ek-chə-lē\ effectually • ineffectually, intellectually

ectural¹ \ek-chə-rəl\ conjectural • architectural

ectural² \ek-shrəl\ conjectural • architectural

ecture \ek-chər\ lecture • conjecture • architecture

ecular \ek-yə-lər\ secular • molecular

ecund \ek-ənd\ fecund, second • split-second • microsecond, millisecond, nanosecond
—*also* -ed *forms of verbs listed at* ECKON

ed \ed\ see EAD¹

e'd \ēd\ see EED

eda¹ \ēd-ə\ Frieda, Leda • Alameda

eda² \ād-ə\ see ADA²

edal¹ \ed-ᵊl\ medal, meddle, pedal, peddle • Air Medal, backpedal, soft-pedal • service medal

edal² \ēd-ᵊl\ see EEDLE

edance \ēd-ᵊns\ see EDENCE

edar¹ \ed-ər\ see EADER²

edar² \ēd-ər\ see EADER¹

edator \ed-ət-ər\ see EDITOR

edd \ed\ see EAD¹

eddar \ed-ər\ see EADER²

edded \ed-əd\ see EADED

edden \ed-ᵊn\ see EADEN

edder \ed-ər\ see EADER²

eddie \ed-ē\ see EADY¹

edding \ed-iŋ\ see EADING¹

eddle \ed-ᵊl\ see EDAL¹

eddler \ed-lər\ meddler, peddler • intermeddler

eddon \ed-ᵊn\ see EADEN

eddy \ed-ē\ see EADY¹

ede¹ \ād\ see ADE¹

ede² \ēd\ see EED

ede³ \ā-dā\ see AYDAY

edel \ād-əl\ see ADLE

eden \ēd-ᵊn\ Eden, Sweden • Garden of Eden

edence \ēd-ᵊns\ credence • impedance, precedence

edent \ēd-ᵊnt\ needn't • decedent, precedent • antecedent

eder¹ \ād-ər\ see ADER

eder² \ēd-ər\ see EADER¹

edge \ej\ dredge, edge, fledge, hedge, ledge, pledge, sedge, sledge, veg, wedge • allege, gilt-edge, knife-edge, on edge, straightedge • cutting edge, flying wedge, leading edge, trailing edge

edged \ejd\ edged, wedged • alleged, full-fledged, gilt-edged, hard-edged, rough-edged, unfledged • double-edged
—*also* -ed *forms of verbs listed at* EDGE

edger \ej-ər\ dredger, hedger, ledger, pledger

edgie \ej-ē\ see EDGY

edgy \ej-ē\ edgy, Reggie, veggie, wedgie

edi \ād-ē\ see ADY

edia \ēd-ē-ə\ media • mixed media • multimedia • encyclopedia

edian \ēd-ē-ən\ median • comedian, tragedian

ediant \ēd-ē-ənt\ see EDIENT

edible \ed-ə-bəl\ credible, edible, spreadable • incredible, inedible

edic \ed-ik\ comedic • orthopedic • encyclopedic

edience \ēd-ē-əns\ expedience, obedience • disobedience
—*also -s, -'s, and -s' forms of nouns listed at* EDIENT

edient \ēd-ē-ənt\ expedient, ingredient, obedient • disobedient, inexpedient

ediment \ed-ə-mənt\ pediment, sediment • impediment

edin \ēd-³n\ see EDEN

eding \ēd-iŋ\ see EEDING[1]

edious \ē-jəs\ see EGIS

edit \ed-ət\ credit, edit • accredit, discredit • copyedit, line of credit

editor \ed-ət-ər\ creditor, editor, predator • chief editor, coeditor • city editor, copy editor

edium \ēd-ē-əm\ medium, tedium • mass medium

edlar \ed-lər\ see EDDLER

edley \ed-lē\ deadly, medley

edly \ed-lē\ see EDLEY

edo[1] \ēd-ō\ credo, speedo • aikido, libido, Toledo, torpedo, tuxedo

edo[2] \äd-ō\ see ADO[2]

edo[3] \ēd-ə\ see EDA[1]

edo[4] \e-dō\ Edo, meadow

edom \ēd-əm\ see EDUM

edon \ēd-³n\ Eden • cotyledon

edouin \ed-wən\ see EDWIN

edulous \ej-ə-ləs\ credulous, sedulous • incredulous

edum \ēd-əm\ Edam, freedom • Medal of Freedom

edure \ē-jər\ besieger, procedure

edwin \ed-wən\ Edwin • bedouin

ee[1] \ē\ b, be, bee, Brie, c, cay, cee, Cree, d, Dee, e, fee, flea, flee, free, g, gee, glee, he, key, knee, lea, lee, Lee, Leigh, me, mi, p, pea, pee, plea, quay, re, sea, see, she, si, ski, spree, t, tea, tee, the, thee, three, ti, tree, v, vee, we, wee, whee, ye, z, zee • agree, at sea, bailee, banshee, bee tree, Belgae, big tree, Black Sea, bootee, break free, bungee, Capri, carefree, CB, CD, Chablis, chickpea, chili, cowpea, curie, Curie, Dead Sea, debris, decree, deepsea, degree, draftee, Dundee, emcee, ennui, esprit, flame tree, foresee, for free, germfree, goatee, grandee, grand prix, grantee, greens fee, green tea, he/she, high tea, home free, hot key, Humvee, IV, Jaycee, jayvee, KP, latchkey, look-see, low-key, LP, lychee, Marie, marquee, MC, métis, ming tree, must-see, Nancy, North Sea, OD, off-key, Parsi, passkey, Pawnee, payee, PC, peewee, pewee, PG, puree, qt, rani, Red Sea, Ross Sea, rupee, RV, scot-free, settee, shade tree, Shawnee, s/he, shift key, shoe tree, sightsee, signee, sirree, smoke tree, snap pea, snow pea, spondee, squeegee, standee, state tree, strophe, suttee, TB, tepee, testee, 3-D, to-be, toll-free, to sea, trainee, trochee, trustee, turnkey, tutee, Tutsi, TV, White Sea, whoopee, would-be, Yangtze • abductee, absentee, addressee, adoptee, advisee, amputee, apogee, appointee, Aral Sea, assignee, attendee, awardee, Beaufort Sea, Bering Sea, bourgeoisie, bumblebee, camphor tree, Cherokee, chickadee, chimpanzee, China Sea, Christmas tree, coati, conferee, cop a plea, Coral Sea, counselee, cruelty-free, DDT, Debussy, deportee, detainee, devotee, disagree, divorcé, divorcée, dungaree, duty-free, employee, enlistee, enrollee, escapee, ESP, evictee, family tree, fancy-free, fantasy, filigree, franchisee, fricassee, function key, Galilee, Gemini, Greenland Sea, guarantee, Hawaii, HIV, Holy See, honeybee, honoree, housemaid's knee, inductee, Inland Sea, invitee, Irish Sea, jamboree, Java Sea, Joshua tree, jubilee, Judas tree, killer bee, LCD, LED, licensee, LSD, maître d', Malay Sea, master key, Medici, Model T, nominee, oversea, oversee, parolee, pedigree, peppertree, pharisee, planer tree, potpourri, referee, refugee, repartee, retiree, Rosemarie, rubber tree, Sadducee, Salton Sea, selectee, shivaree, spelling bee, Tappan Zee, Tennessee, third degree, TNT, to a tee, transferee, tulip tree, undersea, user fee, VIP, vis-à-vis, wannabe, warrantee, Wounded Knee • advanced degree, Aegean Sea, Amundsen Sea, carpenter bee, Caspian Sea, Celebes Sea, East China Sea, evacuee, fortunately, Galilei, interviewee, Labrador Sea, omega-3, Sargasso Sea, Sault Sainte Marie, Simon Legree, skeleton key, South China Sea, to a degree, umbrella tree • Adriatic Sea, Africanized bee, Arabian Sea, bark up the wrong tree, Caribbean Sea, Ionian Sea, Sea of Galilee • Tweedledum and Tweedledee

ee² \ā\ see AY¹
ée \ā\ see AY¹
eeable \ē-ə-bəl\ seeable, skiable • agreeable, foreseeable • disagreeable, unforeseeable
eebie \ē-bē\ see EBE¹
eece \ēs\ see IECE
eeced \ēst\ see EAST¹
eech \ēch\ see EACH

eecher \ē-chər\ see EACHER
eeches \ich-əz\ see ITCHES
eeching \ē-chiŋ\ screeching, teaching • far-reaching • practice teaching, student teaching
—*also* -ing *forms of verbs listed at* EACH
eechy \ē-chē\ see EACHY
eecy \ē-sē\ fleecy, greasy • Tbilisi, AC/DC
eed \ēd\ bead, bleed, breed, cede, creed, deed, feed, greed, he'd, heed, keyed, knead, kneed, lead, mead, need, plead, read, reed, Reed, Reid, screed, seed, she'd, speed, steed, Swede, treed, tweed, Tweed, we'd, weed • accede, airspeed, bindweed, birdseed, blueweed, breast-feed, cheerlead, chickweed, concede, crossbreed, duckweed, exceed, fireweed, flaxseed, force-feed, Godspeed, ground speed, gulfweed, half-breed, hand-feed, hawkweed, hayseed, high-speed, horseweed, impede, inbreed, indeed, ironweed, knapweed, knotweed, Lake Mead, linseed, lip-read, milkweed, misdeed, mislead, misread, moonseed, nosebleed, oilseed, pigweed, pinweed, pokeweed, pondweed, precede, proceed, proofread, ragweed, rapeseed, recede, reseed, rockweed, seaweed, secede, Siegfried, sight-read, smartweed, sneezeweed, speed-read, spoon-feed, stall-feed, stampede, stinkweed, succeed, ten-speed, warp speed, weak-kneed, witchweed, wormseed • aniseed, beggarweed, bottle-feed, bugleweed, centipede, chicken feed, cottonseed, crazyweed, double reed, Ganymede, go to seed, interbreed, intercede, jewelweed, jimsonweed, locoweed, millipede, Nicene Creed, overfeed, pedi-

greed, poppy seed, Port Said,
pumpkinseed, Runnymede, super-
sede, thimbleweed, title deed,
tumbleweed, underfeed, up to
speed, waterweed • Apostles'
Creed, canary seed, caraway seed
—*also* -ed *forms of verbs listed at*
EE[1]

eedal \ēd-ᵊl\ see EEDLE

eeder \ēd-ər\ see EADER[1]

eedful \ēd-fəl\ heedful, needful

eeding[1] \ēd-iŋ\ bleeding, breeding,
leading, reading • inbreeding,
lipreading, preceding, proceeding
• care and feeding
—*also* -ing *forms of verbs listed at*
EED

eeding[2] \ēd-ᵊn\ see EDON

eedle \ēd-ᵊl\ needle, wheedle
• darning needle

eedless \ēd-ləs\ heedless, needless,
seedless

eedn't \ēd-ᵊnt\ see EDENT

eedo \ēd-ō\ see EDO[1]

eedom \ēd-əm\ see EDUM

eeds \ēdz\ Leeds, needs • love
beads, prayer beads, proceeds
• special needs, worry beads
—*also* -s, -'s, *and* -s' *forms of nouns
and* -s *forms of verbs listed at* EED

eedy \ēd-ē\ beady, greedy, needy,
reedy, seedy, speedy, tweedy,
weedy

eef \ēf\ see IEF[1]

eefe \ēf\ see IEF[1]

eefy \ē-fē\ beefy, leafy

eegee \ē-jē\ see IJI

eeing \ē-iŋ\ being, seeing, skiing
• farseeing, sightseeing, well-being
• waterskiing
—*also* -ing *forms of verbs listed at*
EE[1]

eek[1] \ik\ see ICK

eek[2] \ēk\ see EAK[1]

eeked \ēkt\ see EAKED[2]

eeken \ē-kən\ see EACON

eeker \ē-kər\ see EAKER[1]

eekie \ē-kē\ see EAKY

eeking \ē-kiŋ\ see EAKING

eekly \ē-klē\ bleakly, meekly,
sleekly, weakly, weekly, treacly
• biweekly, midweekly,
newsweekly

eeky \ē-kē\ see EAKY

eel \ēl\ see EAL[2]

eelable \ē-lə-bəl\ see EALABLE

eele \ēl\ see EAL[2]

eeled \ēld\ see IELD

eeler \ē-lər\ see EALER

eeley \ē-lē\ see EELY

eelie \ē-lē\ see EELY

eeling \ē-liŋ\ ceiling, dealing, feel-
ing, peeling • appealing, Darjeel-
ing, faith healing, freewheeling,
glass ceiling, revealing, self-seal-
ing, unfeeling • double-dealing,
hit the ceiling, snowmobiling,
unappealing
—*also* -ing *forms of verbs listed at*
EAL[2]

eely \ē-lē\ eely, freely, mealy,
really, steelie, steely, stele,
wheelie • Swahili • Isle of Ely,
touchy-feely

eem \ēm\ see EAM[1]

eeman \ē-mən\ see EMON[1]

eemer \ē-mər\ see EAMER

eemle \ē-mē\ see EAMY

eeming \ē-miŋ\ scheming, scream-
ing, seeming, streaming
—*also* -ing *forms of verbs listed at*
EAM[1]

eemly \ēm-lē\ seemly • extremely,
supremely, unseemly

een[1] \in\ see IN[1]

een[2] \ēn\ see INE[3]

e'en \ēn\ see INE[3]

eena \ē-nə\ see INA[2]

eene \ēn\ see INE[3]

eener \ē-nər\ see EANER

eenery \ēn-rē\ see EANERY

eening \ē-niŋ\ see EANING

eenly \ēn-lē\ see EANLY[1]

eenness \ēn-nəs\ see EANNESS

eens \ēnz\ Queens, teens • by all means, by no means, Grenadines, New Orleans, Philippines, refried beans, smithereens, ways and means

eenwich \in-ich\ see INACH

eeny \ē-nē\ see INI[1]

eep \ēp\ beep, bleep, cheap, cheep, creep, deep, heap, Jeep, keep, leap, peep, reap, seep, sheep, sleep, steep, sweep, veep, weep • asleep, barkeep, black sheep, bopeep, dirt cheap, housekeep, knee-deep, scrap heap, skin-deep, upkeep, upsweep • bighorn sheep, chimney sweep, mountain sheep, on the cheap, overleap, oversleep, quantum leap • Louis Philippe

eepage \ē-pij\ creepage, seepage

eepen \ē-pən\ cheapen, deepen, steepen

eepence \əp-əns\ see UPPANCE

eeper \ē-pər\ beeper, creeper, Dnieper, keeper, leaper, peeper, reaper, sleeper, sweeper, weeper • barkeeper, beekeeper, bookkeeper, doorkeeper, gamekeeper, gatekeeper, goalkeeper, grim reaper, groundskeeper, housekeeper, innkeeper, minesweeper, peacekeeper, scorekeeper, shopkeeper, spring peeper, storekeeper, timekeeper, zookeeper • chimney sweeper
—also -er forms of adjectives listed at EEP

eepie \ē-pē\ see EEPY

eeping \ē-piŋ\ creeping, keeping, weeping • beekeeping, bookkeeping, gatekeeping, housekeeping, minesweeping, peacekeeping, safekeeping, timekeeping
—also -ing forms of verbs listed at EEP

eeple \ē-pəl\ see EOPLE

eepy \ē-pē\ cheapie, creepy, seepy, sleepy, tepee, weepy

eer[1] \ē-ər\ seer, skier, we're • sightseer • overseer, water-skier

eer[2] \ir\ beer, bier, blear, cheer, clear, dear, deer, ear, fear, gear, hear, here, jeer, Lear, leer, mere, near, peer, pier, Pierre, queer, rear, sear, seer, shear, sheer, smear, sneer, spear, sphere, steer, tear, tier, veer, weir, we're, year • adhere, all clear, ampere, appear, austere, besmear, brassiere, Bronx cheer, by ear, Cape Fear, career, cashier, cashmere, Cheshire, clavier, cohere, dog-ear, endear, footgear, frontier, headgear, inhere, Kashmir, killdeer, leap year, light-year, man-year, midyear, mishear, monsieur, mule deer, musk deer, nadir, New Year, off year, premier, premiere, red deer, rehear, reindeer, revere, Revere, roe deer, root beer, severe, Shakespeare, Shropshire, sincere, steer clear, Tangier, tapir, tin ear, veneer, Vermeer, vizier, wind shear, worm gear, Yorkshire, Zaire • atmosphere, auctioneer, balladeer, bandolier, belvedere, biosphere, black-tailed deer, bombardier, boutonniere, brigadier, buccaneer, budgeteer, cannoneer, canyoneer, cavalier, chandelier, chanticleer, chocolatier, commandeer, crystal clear, disappear, domineer, ecosphere, engineer, fallow deer, financier, fiscal year, gadgeteer, gazetteer, ginger beer, Gloucestershire, gondolier, grenadier, Guinevere, hemisphere, Herefordshire, Hertfordshire, Holy Year, inner ear, insincere, interfere, in the clear, Lancashire, landing gear, marketeer, middle ear, mountaineer, Mount Rainier, muleteer, multiyear, musketeer, mutineer, outer ear, overhear, overseer, Oxford-

shire, pamphleteer, persevere,
pioneer, privateer, profiteer,
puppeteer, racketeer, rocketeer,
sloganeer, sonneteer, souvenir,
Staffordshire, steering gear, strat-
osphere, summiteer, swimmer's
ear, troposphere, vintage year,
Vladimir, volunteer, Warwick-
shire, white-tailed deer, Worcestershire, yesteryear • black
marketeer, charioteer, conven-
tioneer, electioneer, ionosphere,
Nottinghamshire, orienteer • academic year, bioengineer, cauliflower ear, civil engineer, Jammu
and Kashmir

e'er \er\ see ARE⁴
eerage \ir-ij\ peerage, steerage
eered \ird\ see EARD¹
eerer \ir-ər\ see EARER²
eeress \ir-əs\ see EROUS
eerful \ir-fəl\ see EARFUL
eerie \ir-ē\ see EARY
eering \ir-iŋ\ see EARING¹
eerist \ir-əst\ see ERIST¹
eerless \ir-ləs\ see EARLESS
eerly \ir-lē\ see EARLY¹
eersman \irz-mən\ steersman
• frontiersman
eerut \ir-ət\ see IRIT
eery \ir-ē\ see EARY
ees \ēz\ see EZE
eese \ēz\ see EZE
eesh \ēsh\ see ICHE²
eesi \ē-zē\ see EASY¹
eesia \ē-zhə\ see ESIA²
eest¹ \āst\ see ACED
eest² \ēst\ see EAST¹
eesy \ē-zē\ see EASY¹
eet \ēt\ see EAT¹
eetah \ēt-ə\ see ITA
eete \āt-ē\ see ATY
eeten \ēt-ᵊn\ see EATEN¹
eeter \ēt-ər\ see EATER¹
eethe \ēth\ see EATHE
eether \ē-thər\ see EITHER
eething \ē-thiŋ\ see EATHING

eetie \ēt-ē\ see EATY
eeting \ēt-iŋ\ see EATING
eetle \ēt-ᵊl\ see ETAL¹
eetly \ēt-lē\ fleetly, neatly, sweetly
• completely, concretely, dis-
creetly • bittersweetly, incom-
pletely, indiscreetly
eety \ēt-ē\ see EATY
ee-um \ē-əm\ see EUM¹
eeve \ēv\ see EAVE¹
eeved \ēvd\ see EAVED
eevil \ē-vəl\ see IEVAL
eevish \ē-vish\ peevish, thievish
eeward \ē-wərd\ leeward, seaward
eewee \ē-wē\ kiwi, peewee, pewee
eewit \ü-ət\ see UET
eez \ēz\ see EZE
eezable \ē-zə-bəl\ see EASIBLE
eeze \ēz\ see EZE
eezer \ē-zər\ see EASER²
eezing \ē-ziŋ\ see EASING²
eezy \ē-zē\ see EASY¹
ef¹ \ef\ chef, clef, deaf, ef, f, ref
• bass clef, Brezhnev, C clef, Kiev,
stone-deaf, tone-deaf • emf, Gorbachev, treble clef, UNICEF
• Prokofiev
ef² \ēf\ see EAF¹
ef³ \ēf\ see IEF¹
efanie \ef-ə-nē\ see EPHONY
efany \ef-ə-nē\ see EPHONY
eferable \ef-rə-bəl\ preferable,
referable
eference \ef-rəns\ deference, pref-
erence, reference • cross-refer-
ence • frame of reference
eferent \ef-rənt\ deferent, referent
eff \ef\ see EF¹
effer \ef-ər\ see EPHOR
eficence \ef-ə-səns\ beneficence,
maleficence
eft \eft\ cleft, deft, eft, heft, left,
theft • bereft, grand theft, stage
left • ultraleft • identity theft
efty \ef-tē\ hefty, lefty
eg¹ \āg\ Craig, plague, vague • The
Hague • bubonic plague

eg² \eg\ beg, Craig, egg, Greg, keg, leg, peg, reg • bootleg, bowleg, foreleg, JPEG, MPEG, nutmeg, peg leg, renege • break a leg, powder keg, pull one's leg, Winnipeg • mumblety-peg

eg³ \ej\ see EDGE

ega¹ \eg-ə\ mega • omega • Lake Onega, rutabaga

ega² \ā-gə\ see AGA²

ega³ \ē-gə\ see IGA

egal \ē-gəl\ beagle, eagle, legal, regal • bald eagle, illegal, sea eagle, spread-eagle • golden eagle

egan \ē-gən\ Megan, vegan • Mohegan, Monhegan, Waukegan

ege¹ \ezh\ cortege, Liège

ege² \eg\ see EG²

ege³ \ej\ see EDGE

ege⁴ \ēg\ see IGUE

ege⁵ \ig\ see IG

eged \ejd\ see EDGED

egel \āgəl\ see AGEL

eger \ej-ər\ see EDGER

egg \eg\ see EG²

eggar \eg-ər\ see EGGER

eggary \eg-ə-rē\ beggary, Gregory

egger \eg-ər\ beggar • bootlegger • thousand-legger, Winnipegger

eggie \ej-ē\ see EDGY

eggs \egz\ see EGS

eggy \eg-ē\ leggy, Peggy, plaguey • Carnegie

egia \ē-jə\ Ouija • paraplegia, quadriplegia

egian \ē-jən\ see EGION

egic \ē-jik\ strategic • paraplegic, quadriplegic

egie \eg-ē\ see EGGY

egion \ē-jən\ legion, region • collegian, Norwegian, subregion

egious \ē-jəs\ see EGIS

egis \ē-jəs\ aegis, Regis, tedious • egregious

egm \em\ see EM¹

egn \ān\ see ANE¹

egnant \eg-nənt\ pregnant, regnant

egnly \ān-lē\ see AINLY

ego¹ \ē-gō\ ego • amigo • alter ego, impetigo

ego² \ā-gō\ see AGO²

egory \eg-ə-rē\ see EGGARY

egs \egz\ yellowlegs • daddy longlegs

—*also* -s, -'s, *and* -s' *forms of nouns and* -s *forms of verbs listed at* EG²

eh¹ \ā\ see AY¹

eh² \a\ see AH³

ehen \ān\ see ANE¹

ehner \ā-nər\ see AINER

ei¹ \ā\ see AY¹

ei² \ī\ see Y¹

eia¹ \ē-ə\ see IA¹

eia² \ī-ə\ see IAH¹

eial \ē-əl\ see EAL¹

eian¹ \ē-ən\ see EAN¹

eian² \ā-ən\ see AYAN¹

eiche \āsh\ see ECHE¹

eickel \ī-kəl\ see YCLE¹

eid¹ \āt\ see ATE¹

eid² \īt\ see ITE¹

eid³ \ēd\ see EED

eidel¹ \ād-əl\ see ADLE

eidel² \īd-ᵊl\ see IDAL

eidi \īd-ē\ see IDAY

eidon \īd-ᵊn\ see IDEN

eier \īr\ see IRE¹

eifer \ef-ər\ see EPHOR

eige \āzh\ beige • Mount Neige

eiger \ī-gər\ see IGER

eigh¹ \ā\ see AY¹

eigh² \ē\ see EE¹

eighbor \ā-bər\ see ABOR

eight¹ \āt\ see ATE¹

eight² \īt\ see ITE¹

eighter \āt-ər\ see ATOR

eightless \āt-ləs\ see ATELESS

eights \īts\ see IGHTS

eighty \āt-ē\ see ATY

eign \ān\ see ANE¹

eigner \ā-nər\ see AINER

eii \ā\ see AY¹

eiian \ā-ən\ see AYAN¹

eiji \ā-jē\ see AGY

eik \ēk\ see EAK[1]

eikh \ēk\ see EAK[1]

eil[1] \āl\ see AIL

eil[2] \el\ see EL[1]

eil[3] \ēl\ see EAL[2]

eil[4] \īl\ see ILE[1]

eila \ē-lə\ see ELA[1]

eiled \āld\ see AILED

eiler \ī-lər\ see ILAR

eiling[1] \ā-liŋ\ see AILING

eiling[2] \ē-liŋ\ see EELING

eill \ēl\ see EAL[2]

eilles[1] \ā\ see AY[1]

eilles[2] \ālz\ see ALES[1]

eilly \ā-lē\ see AILY

eim[1] \ām\ see AME[1]

eim[2] \īm\ see IME[1]

eimer \ī-mər\ see IMER[1]

eims[1] \ä\ⁿs\ see ANCE[1]

eims[2] \ēmz\ Rheims
—also -s, -'s, and -s' forms of
nouns and -s forms of verbs listed
at EAM[1]

ein[1] \ān\ see ANE[1]

ein[2] \ē-ən\ see EAN[1]

ein[3] \ūn\ see INE[3]

ein[4] \īn\ see INE[1]

eine[1] \ān\ see ANE[1]

eine[2] \ēn\ see INE[3]

eine[3] \ī-nə\ see INA[1]

eine[4] \en\ see EN[1]

eined \ānd\ see AINED

einer[1] \ā-nər\ see AINER

einer[2] \ē-nər\ see EANER

eing \ē-iŋ\ see EEING

einie \ī-nē\ see INY[1]

eining \ā-niŋ\ see AINING

einous \ā-nəs\ see AYNESS

eins \ānz\ see AINS

eint \ānt\ see AINT

einte \ant\ see ANT[5]

einy \ā-nē\ see AINY

eipt \ēt\ see EAT[1]

eir \er\ see ARE[4]

eira \ir-ə\ see ERA[2]

eird \ird\ see EARD[1]

eiress \ar-əs\ see ARIS[2]

eiric \ī-rik\ see YRIC

eiro \er-ō\ see ERO[2]

eirs \erz\ see AIRS

eis[1] \ās\ see ACE[1]

eis[2] \ē-əs\ see EUS[1]

eis[3] \īs\ see ICE[1]

eisant \ēs-ⁿnt\ see ECENT

eise \ēz\ see EZE

eisel \ī-zəl\ see ISAL[2]

eisen \īz-ⁿn\ see IZEN[1]

eiser \ī-zər\ see IZER

eisha[1] \ā-shə\ see ACIA

eisha[2] \ē-shə\ see ESIA[1]

eisin \ēz-ⁿn\ see EASON

eiss \īs\ see ICE[1]

eissen \īs-ⁿn\ see ISON[1]

eist[1] \ā-əst\ see AYEST

eist[2] \īst\ see IST[1]

eister[1] \ī-stər\ keister, shyster
• spinmeister • concertmeister

eister[2] \ē-stər\ see EASTER

eisure \ē-zhər\ see EIZURE

eit[1] \ē-ət\ fiat • albeit

eit[2] \it\ see IT[1]

eit[3] \ēt\ see EAT[1]

eit[4] \īt\ see ITE[1]

eited \ēt-əd\ see EATED[1]

eiter[1] \it-ər\ see ITTER

eiter[2] \ī-tər\ see ITER[1]

eith \ēth\ see EATH[1]

either \ē-thər\ breather, either,
neither • fire-breather

eitus \īt-əs\ see ITIS

eity \ē-ət-ē\ deity • spontaneity
• homogeneity, simultaneity

eivable \ē-və-bəl\ achievable, be-
lievable, conceivable, perceivable,
receivable, retrievable • incon-
ceivable, irretrievable, unbeliev-
able

eive \ēv\ see EAVE[1]

eiver \ē-vər\ see IEVER

eix \āsh\ see ECHE[1]

eize[1] \āz\ see AZE[1]

eize[2] \ēz\ see EZE

eizure \ē-zhər\ leisure, seizure

eji \ej-ē\ see EDGY
ejo \ā-ō\ see EO[1]
ek \ek\ see ECK
eka[1] \ek-ə\ see ECCA
eka[2] \ē-kə\ see IKA[1]
ekah \ek-ə\ see ECCA
eke \ēk\ see EAK[1]
ekel \ek-əl\ see ECKLE
ekh \ek\ see ECK
eki \ek-ē\ see ECKY
ekker \ek-ər\ see ECKER
ekoe \ē-kō\ see ICOT
el[1] \el\ bell, Bell, belle, cell, dell, dwell, el, Elle, fell, gel, hell, jell, knell, l, quell, sell, shell, smell, spell, swell, tell, they'll, well, yell • Adele, band shell, barbell, befell, bluebell, bombshell, Boswell, cartel, Chanel, clamshell, compel, Cornell, corral, cowbell, Cromwell, Danielle, dispel, doorbell, dry cell, dumbbell, eggshell, Estelle, excel, expel, farewell, fat cell, foretell, fuel cell, gazelle, germ cell, Giselle, groundswell, half shell, handbell, hard sell, hotel, impel, inkwell, lapel, Maxwell, Michelle, misspell, Moselle, motel, nerve cell, Nobel, noel, nutshell, oil well, Orwell, outsell, pastel, pell-mell, pixel, propel, rappel, Ravel, rebel, repel, respell, retell, Roswell, scalpel, seashell, sequel, Seychelles, sleigh bell, soft sell, soft-shell, stairwell, star shell, stem cell, tooth shell, unwell, wind-bell • Annabelle, Appenzell, asphodel, bagatelle, Cape Farewell, caramel, caravel, carousel, chanterelle, chaparral, citadel, clientele, cockleshell, Cozumel, decibel, diving bell, fare-thee-well, Isabel, Jezebel, killer cell, kiss-and-tell, ne'er-do-well, New Rochelle, nonpareil, oversell, parallel, personnel, Philomel, pimpernel, Raphael, rebel yell, red blood cell, Sanctus bell, San Rafael, São Miguel, show-and-tell, sickle cell, solar cell, tortoiseshell, undersell, white blood cell, William Tell, zinfandel • Aix-la-Chapelle, artesian well, au naturel, crème caramel, mademoiselle, maître d'hôtel, matériel, Mont-Saint-Michel • antipersonnel • AWOL
el[2] \āl\ see AIL
ela[1] \ē-lə\ chela, Leila, Sheila • tequila • Philomela
ela[2] \ā-lə\ see ALA[3]
ela[3] \el-ə\ see ELLA
elable \el-ə-bəl\ see ELLABLE
elacy \el-ə-sē\ jealousy, prelacy
elagh \ā-lē\ see AILY
elah \ē-lə\ see ELA[1]
eland \ē-lənd\ eland, Zeeland • New Zealand
elanie \el-ə-nē\ see ELONY
elar \ē-lər\ see EALER
elate \el-ət\ see ELLATE
elatin \el-ət-ᵊn\ see ELETON
elba \el-bə\ Elba, Elbe, Melba
elbe \el-bə\ see ELBA
elbert \el-bərt\ Delbert, Elbert • Mount Elbert
elch \elch\ belch, squelch, welch
eld[1] \eld\ geld, held, meld, shelled, weld • beheld, handheld, hardshelled, upheld, withheld • jet-propelled, self-propelled • unparalleled
—*also* -ed *forms of verbs listed at* EL[1]
eld[2] \elt\ see ELT
elder \el-dər\ elder, welder
eldt \elt\ see ELT
ele[1] \ā-lē\ see AILY
ele[2] \el\ see EL[1]
ele[3] \el-ē\ see ELLY
ele[4] \ē-lē\ see EELY
eled[1] \eld\ see ELD[1]
eled[2] \ēld\ see IELD
elen \el-ən\ see ELON

eleon \ēl-yən\ see ELIAN[2]

eleton \el-ət-³n\ gelatin, skeleton

eleus \ē-lē-əs\ see ELIOUS

elf \elf\ elf, pelf, self, shelf • bookshelf, herself, himself, itself, myself, oneself, ourself, top-shelf, thyself, yourself • mantelshelf, off-the-shelf, Ross Ice Shelf • do-it-yourself • continental shelf

elfish \el-fish\ elfish, selfish • unselfish

elhi \el-ē\ see ELLY

eli \el-ē\ see ELLY

elia[1] \ēl-yə\ Delia, Lelia, Sheila • Amelia, camellia, Camellia, Cecilia, Cornelia, Karelia, lobelia, Ophelia • psychedelia

elia[2] \il-ē-ə\ see ILIA[1]

elian[1] \ē-lē-ən\ Pelion • Mendelian

elian[2] \ēl-yən\ Aurelian, chameleon, Mendelian, parhelion • perihelion • Aristotelian, Mephistophelian

elian[3] \el-ē-ən\ see ELLIAN

elible \el-ə-bəl\ see ELLABLE

elic \el-ik\ relic • angelic, smart aleck • archangelic, philatelic, psychedelic

elion[1] \el-ē-ən\ see ELLIAN

elion[2] \ēl-yən\ see ELIAN[2]

elion[3] \ēl-ē-ən\ see ELIAN[1]

elios \ē-lē-əs\ see ELIOUS

elious \ē-lē-əs\ Helios • Cornelius

elish \el-ish\ see ELLISH

elist \el-əst\ cellist, trellised • Nobelist, pastelist

elius \ē-lē-əs\ see ELIOUS

elix \ē-liks\ Felix, helix • double helix

elk[1] \elk\ elk, whelk

elk[2] \ilk\ see ILK

ell \el\ see EL[1]

e'll \ēl\ see EAL[2]

ella \el-ə\ Della, Ella, fella, fellah, Stella • Estella, Gisela, Luella, Marcella, Mandela, novella, patella, rubella, umbrella, vanilla • a cappella, Cinderella, citronella, Isabella, mozzarella, salmonella, sarsaparilla, tarantella

ellable \el-ə-bəl\ sellable • compellable, indelible

ellah \el-ə\ see ELLA

ellan \el-ən\ see ELON

ellant \el-ənt\ appellant, flagellant, propellant, repellent • water-repellent

ellar \el-ər\ see ELLER

ellas \el-əs\ see EALOUS

ellate \el-ət\ pellet, prelate, zealot • appellate

elle[1] \el\ see EL[1]

elle[2] \el-ə\ see ELLA

ellean \el-ē-ən\ see ELLIAN

elled \eld\ see ELD[1]

ellen \el-ən\ see ELON

ellent \el-ənt\ see ELLANT

eller \el-ər\ cellar, dweller, seller, sheller, speller, stellar, teller, yeller • best seller, bookseller, foreteller, propeller, tale-teller • fortune-teller, interstellar, Rockefeller, storyteller

elles[1] \el\ see EL[1]

elles[2] \elz\ see ELLS

ellet \el-ət\ see ELLATE

elley \el-ē\ see ELLY

elli \el-ē\ see ELLY

ellia \ēl-yə\ see ELIA[1]

ellian \el-ē-ən\ Orwellian • Machiavellian

ellie \el-ē\ see ELLY

elline \el-ən\ see ELON

elling \el-iŋ\ dwelling, selling, spelling, swelling, telling • best-selling, bookselling, cliff-dwelling, compelling, lake dwelling, misspelling, tale-telling, upwelling • fortune-telling, self-propelling, storytelling
—also -ing *forms of verbs listed at* EL[1]

ellington \el-iŋ-tən\ Ellington, Wellington • beef Wellington

ellion \el-yən\ hellion • rebellion

ellis \el-əs\ see EALOUS

ellised \el-əst\ see ELIST

ellish \el-ish\ hellish, relish • embellish

ellist \el-əst\ see ELIST

ello \el-ō\ bellow, cello, fellow, Jell-O, mellow, yellow • bedfellow, bordello, Longfellow, marshmallow, Odd Fellow, Othello, playfellow, schoolfellow • Pirandello • Robin Goodfellow, violoncello

ell-o \el-ō\ see ELLO

ellous \el-əs\ see EALOUS

ellow¹ \el-ə\ see ELLA

ellow² \el-ō\ see ELLO

ells \elz\ Seychelles • Dardanelles —*also -s, -'s, and -s' forms of nouns and -s forms of verbs listed at* EL¹

ellum \el-əm\ vellum • clitellum, flagellum, postbellum • antebellum, cerebellum

ellus \el-əs\ see EALOUS

elly \el-ē\ belly, Delhi, deli, jelly, Kelly, Nellie, Shelley, smelly, telly • New Delhi, pork belly, potbelly, sowbelly • Botticelli, Delhi belly, nervous Nellie, royal jelly, underbelly, vermicelli • Machiavelli

ellyn \el-ən\ see ELON

elm \elm\ elm, helm, realm • overwhelm

elma \el-mə\ Selma, Velma

elmar \el-mər\ see ELMER

elmer \el-mər\ Delmar, Elmer

elmet \el-mət\ helmet, Helmut • crash helmet, pith helmet

elmut \el-mət\ see ELMET

elo \ē-lō\ see ILO²

elon \el-ən\ Ellen, felon, Helen, melon • Magellan, muskmelon • watermelon • Strait of Magellan

elony \el-ə-nē\ felony, Melanie

elop \el-əp\ develop, envelop • overdevelop

elos \ā-ləs\ see AYLESS

elot \el-ət\ see ELLATE

elotry \el-ə-trē\ helotry, zealotry

elp \elp\ help, kelp, whelp, yelp • self-help

elsea \el-sē\ see ELSIE

elsie \el-sē\ Chelsea, Elsie

elt \elt\ belt, Celt, dealt, dwelt, felt, melt, pelt, smelt, spelt, svelte, veld, welt • black belt, Frostbelt, greenbelt, heartfelt, lap belt, rust belt, seat belt, snowbelt, snowmelt, Sunbelt, web belt • Bible Belt, cartridge belt, Roosevelt, safety belt, shoulder belt • asteroid belt, below the belt

elte \elt\ see ELT

elted \el-təd\ belted, melted, pelted

elter \el-tər\ shelter, smelter, swelter, welter • tax shelter • helterskelter

eltered \el-tərd\ tax-sheltered —*also -ed forms of verbs listed at* ELTER

elting \el-tiŋ\ belting, felting, melting —*also -ing forms of verbs listed at* ELT

elve \elv\ delve, shelve, twelve

elves \elvz\ elves • ourselves, themselves, yourselves —*also -s, -'s, and -s' forms of nouns and -s forms of verbs listed at* ELVE

elvin \el-vən\ Elvin, Kelvin, Melvin

elvyn \el-vən\ see ELVIN

ely \ē-lē\ see EELY

em¹ \em\ Clem, crème, em, gem, hem, m, phlegm, REM, stem, them • ahem, AM, brain stem, condemn, FM, item, mayhem, modem, poem, problem, pro tem • ABM, Bethlehem, diadem, stratagem • ad hominem, cable modem, carpe diem, crème de la crème, ICBM • collector's item, post meridiem

em² \əm\ see UM[1]

ema \ē-mə\ Lima • eczema, edema • emphysema, Hiroshima, Iwo Jima

emacist \em-ə-səst\ see EMICIST

eman¹ \em-ən\ see EMON[2]

eman² \ē-mən\ see EMON[1]

emane \em-ə-nē\ see EMONY

ember \em-bər\ ember, member • December, dismember, nonmember, November, remember, September • charter member

emble \em-bəl\ tremble • assemble, dissemble, resemble • disassemble

embler \em-blər\ temblor • assembler, dissembler

emblor \em-blər\ see EMBLER

embly \em-blē\ trembly • assembly • disassembly, subassembly

eme¹ \em\ see EM[1]

eme² \ēm\ see EAM[1]

emely \ēm-lē\ see EEMLY

emen¹ \ē-mən\ see EMON[1]

emen² \em-ən\ see EMON[2]

emen³ \ā-mən\ see AMEN[1]

emer \ē-mər\ see EAMER

emery \em-rē\ emery, Emory, memory

emi \em-ō\ see EMMY

emia \ē-mē-ə\ anemia, bohemia, Bohemia, leukemia, toxemia, uremia • academia

emic¹ \ē-mik\ anemic, uremic • emphysemic

emic² \em-ik\ endemic, pandemic, polemic, systemic, totemic • academic, epidemic

emical \em-i-kəl\ chemical • alchemical, polemical • biochemical, petrochemical

emicist \em-ə-səst\ polemicist, supremacist • white supremacist

eming \em-iŋ\ Fleming, lemming —also -ing forms of verbs listed at EM[1]

eminge \em-iŋ\ see EMING

emini \em-ə-nē\ see EMONY

eminy \em-ə-nē\ see EMONY

emis \ē-məs\ see EMUS

emish \em-ish\ blemish, Flemish

emlin \em-lən\ gremlin, Kremlin

emma \em-ə\ Emma • dilemma

emme \em\ see EM[1]

emmer \em-ər\ hemmer, tremor

emming \em-iŋ\ see EMING

emmy \em-ē\ Emmy, phlegmy, semi, stemmy

emn \em\ see EM[1]

emner \em-ər\ see EMMER

emnity \em-nət-ē\ indemnity, solemnity

emo \em-ō\ demo, memo

emon¹ \ē-mən\ demon, freeman, seaman • Lake Leman, Philemon

emon² \em-ən\ Bremen, lemon, Yemen

emone \em-ə-nē\ see EMONY

emony \em-ə-nē\ Gemini, lemony • anemone, Gethsemane, hegemony

emor \em-ər\ see EMMER

emory \em-rē\ see EMERY

emous \ē-məs\ see EMUS

emp \emp\ hemp, temp

emplar \em-plər\ exemplar, Knight Templar

emption \em-shən\ see ANT[1]

empt \emt\ dreamt, tempt • attempt, contempt, exempt, preempt, undreamed, unkempt • tax-exempt

emption \em-shən\ exemption, preemption, redemption

emptive \em-tiv\ preemptive, redemptive

emur \ē-mər\ see EAMER

emus \ē-məs\ Remus • in extremis, Polyphemus

emy \ē-mē\ see EAMY

en¹ \en\ Ben, den, en, glen, Glen, Gwen, hen, Ken, Len, men, n, pen, Penn, Seine, Sten, ten, then, when, wren, yen, Zen • again, amen, Ardennes, Big Ben, bull pen, Cayenne, Cheyenne, Estienne, game hen, hang ten, light pen, marsh hen, moorhen, peahen, pigpen, Phnom Penh, playpen, RN • Adrienne, bornagain, cactus wren, five-and-ten, fountain pen, guinea hen, lion's den, LPN, mother hen, Sun Yatsen, water hen • carcinogen, comedienne, equestrienne, time and again • again and again

en² \ēn\ see INE³

en³ \aⁿ\ see IN⁴

en⁴ \ən\ see UN¹

en⁵ \äⁿ\ see ANT¹

ena¹ \ā-nə\ see ANA²

ena² \ē-nə\ see INA²

enable \en-ə-bəl\ tenable • amenable, untenable

enace \en-əs\ see ENIS

enae \e-nē\ see INI¹

enal \ēn-ᵊl\ penal, renal, venal • adrenal, vaccinal

enant \en-ənt\ pennant, tenant • lieutenant, subtenant • sublieutenant

enary \en-ə-rē\ hennery, plenary • centenary, millenary • bicentenary

enas \ē-nəs\ see ENUS¹

enate \en-ət\ see ENNET

enator \en-ət-ər\ see ENITOR

ençal \en-səl\ see ENCIL

ence¹ \ens\ see ENSE

ence² \äⁿs\ see ANCE¹

ence³ \äns\ see ANCE²

encel \en-səl\ see ENCIL

enceless \en-sləs\ see ENSELESS

encer \en-sər\ see ENSOR

ench \ench\ bench, clench, drench, French, mensch, quench, stench, trench, wench, wrench • entrench, pipe wrench, retrench, unclench, workbench • Allen wrench, monkey wrench, socket wrench • Mariana Trench

enchant \en-chənt\ see ENTIENT

encher \en-chər\ see ENTURE

enchman \ench-mən\ Frenchman, henchman

encia \en-chə\ see ENTIA

encil \en-səl\ pencil, stencil, tensile • grease pencil, lead pencil, prehensile, utensil • eyebrow pencil

end \end\ bend, blend, end, fend, friend, lend, mend, rend, send, spend, tend, trend, vend, wend • amend, append, ascend, attend, bartend, befriend, Big Bend, bookend, boyfriend, commend, contend, dead end, dead-end, defend, depend, descend, distend, downtrend, emend, expend, extend, front-end, girlfriend, godsend, high-end, impend, intend, Land's End, loose end, low-end, misspend, no end, offend, on end, outspend, portend, pretend, rearend, resend, South Bend, split end, stipend, suspend, tag end, tail end, tight end, transcend, unbend, upend, uptrend, weekend, year-end • apprehend, bitter end, business end, comprehend, condescend, dividend, in the end, on the mend, overspend, recommend • at one's wit's end, hyperextend, misapprehend, overextend, stock dividend, superintend • go off the deep end —*also* -ed *forms of verbs listed at* EN¹

enda \en-də\ Brenda, Glenda • agenda • hacienda • hidden agenda

endable \en-də-bəl\ lendable, mendable, spendable • commendable, defendable, dependable, expendable, extendable, unbendable • recommendable, undependable

endal \en-dᵊl\ Grendel, Kendall, Mendel, Wendell

endall \en-dᵊl\ see ENDAL

endance \en-dəns\ see ENDENCE
endancy \en-dən-sē\ see ENDENCY
endant \en-dənt\ see ENDENT
ende[1] \end\ see END
ende[2] \en-dē\ see ENDI
ended \en-dəd\ ended, splendid • extended, intended, pretended, unfriended • open-ended
—*also* -ed *forms of verbs listed at* END
endel \en-dᵊl\ see ENDAL
endell \en-dᵊl\ see ENDAL
endence \en-dəns\ ascendance, attendance, dependence, transcendence • independence, Independence
—*also* -s, -'s, *and* -s' *forms of nouns listed at* ENDENT
endency \en-dən-sē\ tendency • ascendancy, dependency • codependency
endent \en-dənt\ pendant • ascendant, attendant, defendant, dependent, descendant, intendant, transcendent • codependent, independent • overdependent, superintendent
ender \en-dər\ bender, blender, fender, gender, lender, render, sender, slender, spender, splendor, tender, vendor • bartender, commender, contender, defender, engender, extender, fork-tender, goaltender, hellbender, offender, pretender, surrender, suspender, transgender, weekender • moneylender
endi \en-dē\ trendy, Wendy • modus vivendi
endible \en-də-bəl\ see ENDABLE
endid \en-dəd\ see ENDED
ending \en-diŋ\ ending, pending, sending • ascending, attending, fence-mending, goaltending, heartrending, mind-bending, nerve ending, unbending, unending • condescending, gender-

bending • uncomprehending
—*also* -ing *forms of verbs listed at* END
endless \end-ləs\ endless, friendless
endliness \en-lē-nəs\ cleanliness, friendliness • uncleanliness, unfriendliness
endly \en-lē\ friendly • uncleanly, unfriendly • user-friendly
endo \en-dō\ kendo • crescendo • innuendo
endor \en-dər\ see ENDER
endous \en-dəs\ horrendous, stupendous, tremendous
ends \enz\ see ENS[1]
endum \en-dəm\ addendum • referendum
endy \en-dē\ see ENDI
ene[1] \en\ see EN[1]
ene[2] \en-ē\ see ENNY
ene[3] \ē-nē\ see INI[1]
ene[4] \ēn\ see INE[3]
ene[5] \än\ see ANE[1]
enel \en-ᵊl\ see ENNEL
ener \ē-nər\ see EANER
enery[1] \en-ə-rē\ see ENARY
enery[2] \ēn-rē\ see EANERY
enet \en-ət\ see ENNET
eng[1] \aŋ\ see ANG[2]
eng[2] \əŋ\ see UNG[1]
enge \enj\ avenge, revenge, Stonehenge
ength[1] \eŋth\ length, strength • arm's-length, at length, floor-length, full-length, half-length, wavelength • industrial-strength
ength[2] \enth\ see ENTH
engthen \eŋ-thən\ lengthen, strengthen
enh \en\ see EN[1]
enia[1] \ē-nē-ə\ Armenia, Slovenia • schizophrenia
enia[2] \ē-nyə\ Armenia, Eugenia, gardenia
enial \ē-nē-əl\ genial, menial, venial • congenial

enian \ē-nē-ən\ Armenian, Athenian, Cyrenian, Slovenian, Turkmenian

enic¹ \ēn-ik\ scenic • hygienic

enic² \en-ik\ arsenic, Edenic, Hellenic, hygienic • allergenic, calisthenic, cryogenic, hygienic, photogenic, schizophrenic, telegenic • carcinogenic • hallucinogenic, hypoallergenic

enice \en-əs\ see ENIS

enics \en-iks\ calisthenics, cryogenics

—also -s, -'s, and -s' forms of nouns listed at ENIC²

enie¹ \en-ē\ see ENNY

enie² \ē-nē\ see INI¹

enience \ē-nyəns\ lenience • convenience • inconvenience

enient \ēn-yənt\ lenient • convenient • inconvenient

enim \en-əm\ see ENOM

enin \en-ən\ see ENNON

enis \en-əs\ Dennis, genus, menace, tennis, Venice • lawn tennis • table tennis

enison¹ \en-ə-sən\ Tennyson, venison

enison² \en-ə-zən\ denizen, venison

enitor \en-ət-ər\ senator • progenitor

enity \en-ət-ē\ see ENTITY

enizen \en-ə-zən\ see ENISON²

enn \en\ see EN¹

enna \en-ə\ Glenna, henna • antenna, sienna, Vienna • whip antenna

ennae \en-ē\ see ENNY

ennant \en-ənt\ see ENANT

enne¹ \en\ see EN¹

enne² \en-ē\ see ENNY

enne³ \an\ see AN⁵

ennec \en-ik\ see ENIC²

enned \end\ see END

ennel \en-ᵊl\ fennel, kennel

ennery \en-ə-rē\ see ENARY

ennes \en\ see EN¹

ennet \en-ət\ senate, tenet

ennett \en-ət\ see ENNET

enney \en-ē\ see ENNY

enni \en-ē\ see ENNY

ennial \en-ē-əl\ biennial, centennial, decennial, millennial, perennial, quadrennial, triennial • bicentennial

ennig \en-ik\ see ENIC²

ennin \en-ən\ see ENNON

ennis \en-əs\ see ENIS

ennit \en-ət\ see ENNET

ennium \en-ē-əm\ biennium, millennium

ennon \en-ən\ Lenin, Lennon • antivenin

enny \en-ē\ any, benny, Benny, Denny, genie, Jenny, Kenny, many, penny, Penny • antennae, halfpenny, sixpenny, so many, tenpenny, threepenny, twopenny • spinning jenny

ennyson \en-ə-sən\ see ENISON¹

eno \ā-nō\ see ANO²

enom \en-əm\ denim, venom

enon \en-ən\ see ENNON

enous \ē-nəs\ see ENUS¹

ens¹ \enz\ cleanse, lens • amends, hand lens, weekends, zoom lens • odds and ends • Homo sapiens
—also -s, -'s, and -s' forms of nouns and -s forms of verbs listed at EN¹

ens² \ens\ see ENSE

ensable \en-sə-bəl\ see ENSIBLE

ensal \en-səl\ see ENCIL

ensary \ens-rē\ see ENSORY

ensch \ench\ see ENCH

ense \ens\ dense, fence, hence, pence, sense, tense, thence, whence • commence, condense, defense, dispense, expense, horse sense, immense, incense, intense, nonsense, offense, past tense, pretense, sequence, sixpence, sixth sense, suspense, twopence • common sense, confidence,

consequence, diffidence, evidence, frankincense, no-nonsense, present tense, providence, Providence, recompense, residence, self-defense, zone defense • coincidence, inconsequence, nonresidence, self-confidence
—*also* -s, -'s, *and* -s' *forms of nouns listed at* ENT[1]

enseful \ens-fəl\ senseful • suspenseful

enseless \en-sləs\ fenceless, senseless • defenseless, offenseless

enser \en-sər\ see ENSOR

ensian \en-chən\ see ENSION

ensible \en-sə-bəl\ sensible • defensible, dispensable, extensible, insensible, ostensible • commonsensible, comprehensible, indefensible, indispensable, reprehensible • incomprehensible

ensil \en-səl\ see ENCIL

ensile \en-səl\ see ENCIL

ension \en-shən\ mention, pension, tension • abstention, ascension, attention, contention, convention, declension, detention, dimension, dissension, extension, high-tension, indention, intention, invention, pretension, prevention, retention, suspension • apprehension, circumvention, comprehension, condescension, contravention, fourth dimension, hypertension, hypotension, inattention, reinvention, third dimension • hyperextension, incomprehension, misapprehension, nonintervention, overextension • Geneva convention, honorable mention

ensional \ench-nəl\ conventional, dimensional, intentional • four-dimensional, one-dimensional, three-dimensional, two-dimensional, unconventional, unintentional

ensis \en-səs\ see ENSUS

ensity \en-sət-ē\ density • immensity, intensity, propensity

ensive \en-siv\ pensive • defensive, expensive, extensive, intensive, offensive • apprehensive, comprehensive, inexpensive, inoffensive • counteroffensive, labor-intensive

ensor \en-sər\ censor, fencer, sensor, Spencer, tensor • condenser, dispenser, extensor, sequencer
—*also* -er *forms of adjectives listed at* ENSE

ensory \ens-rē\ sensory • dispensary • extrasensory, multisensory

ensual[1] \en-chəl\ see ENTIAL

ensual[2] \ench-wəl\ see ENTUAL[1]

ensure \en-chər\ see ENTURE

ensus \en-səs\ census • consensus • amanuensis

ent[1] \ent\ bent, Brent, cent, dent, gent, Ghent, Kent, lent, Lent, meant, pent, rent, scent, sent, spent, tent, Trent, vent, went • absent, accent, Advent, ascent, assent, augment, cement, comment, consent, content, convent, descent, dissent, event, extent, ferment, foment, fragment, frequent, hell-bent, indent, intent, invent, lament, low-rent, outspent, percent, pigment, portent, present, prevent, pup tent, relent, repent, resent, segment, Tashkent, torment, well-meant • accident, argument, circumvent, compartment, complement, compliment, confident, diffident, discontent, document, evident, heaven-sent, implement, incident, instrument, malcontent, nonevent, ornament, orient, president, provident, regiment, reinvent, represent, resident, sediment, Stoke-on-Trent, subsequent, supplement, underwent • age of consent, disorient, experiment, glove compartment,

misrepresent, nonresident, oxygen tent, portland cement, rubber cement, self-confident, self-evident, vice president • in any event, media event
ent² \änt\ see ANT²
ent³ \äⁿ\ see ANT¹
enta \ent-ə\ magenta, placenta, polenta
entable \ent-ə-bəl\ rentable • lamentable, presentable, preventable • documentable, representable
entacle \ent-i-kəl\ see ENTICAL
entage \ent-ij\ tentage • percentage
ental \ent-ᵊl\ dental, gentle, lentil, mental, rental • judgmental, parental • accidental, apartmental, compartmental, continental, departmental, detrimental, elemental, fundamental, governmental, grandparental, incidental, incremental, instrumental, monumental, nonjudgmental, occidental, oriental, ornamental, regimental, sacramental, sentimental, supplemental, temperamental, transcendental • coincidental, developmental, environmental, experimental, transcontinental • intercontinental, interdepartmental
entalist \ent-ᵊl-əst\ fundamentalist, instrumentalist, orientalist, sentimentalist, transcendentalist • environmentalist
entance \ent-ᵊns\ see ENTENCE
entary \en-trē\ entry, gentry, sentry • reentry, subentry • alimentary, complementary, complimentary, documentary, elementary, mockumentary, parliamentary, port of entry, sedimentary, supplementary • uncomplimentary
entative \ent-ət-iv\ tentative • preventative • argumentative, representative

ente¹ \ent-ē\ see ENTY
ente² \änt\ see ANT²
ented \ent-əd\ contented, demented, lamented, segmented • discontented, malcontented, oriented, self-contented • unprecedented • overrepresented, underrepresented
—*also* -ed *forms of verbs listed at* ENT¹
enten \ent-ᵊn\ dentin, Lenten, Quentin, Trenton
entence \ent-ᵊns\ sentence • death sentence, repentance
enter \ent-ər\ center, enter, mentor, renter • dissenter, frequenter, inventor, nerve center, presenter, reenter, tormentor • epicenter, front and center, shopping center, trauma center • experimenter
entered \en-tərd\ centered • self-centered
—*also* -ed *forms of verbs listed at* ENTER
enterie \en-trē\ see ENTARY
entful \ent-fəl\ eventful, resentful • uneventful
enth \enth\ nth, strength, tenth • crème de menthe • industrial-strength
enthe \enth\ see ENTH
enti \ent-ē\ see ENTY
entia \en-shə\ dementia, Valencia • in absentia
ential \en-shəl\ consensual, credential, essential, eventual, potential, prudential, sequential, tangential, torrential • confidential, consequential, deferential, differential, existential, exponential, inessential, influential, nonessential, penitential, pestilential, preferential, presidential, providential, quintessential, residential, reverential, unessential • inconsequential, vice presidential
entian \en-shən\ see ENSION

entiary \ensh-rē\ century • penitentiary • plenipotentiary

entical \ent-i-kəl\ tentacle • identical

entice \ent-əs\ see ENTOUS

enticle \ent-i-kəl\ see ENTICAL

entient \en-chənt\ penchant, sentient, trenchant

entil \ent-ᵊl\ see ENTAL

entin \ent-ᵊn\ see ENTEN

enting \ent-iŋ\ dissenting • unrelenting
—*also* -ing *forms of verbs listed at* ENT¹

ention \en-shən\ see ENSION

entional \ensh- nəl\ see ENSIONAL

entioned \en-shənd\ mentioned • aforementioned, well-intentioned

entious \en-chəs\ contentious, licentious, pretentious, sententious, tendentious • conscientious, unpretentious

entis \ent-əs\ see ENTOUS

entity \en-ət-ē\ entity • amenity, identity, nonentity, obscenity, ⬛⬛⬛⬛⬛

entive \ent-iv\ attentive, incentive, inventive, preventive, retentive • inattentive

entle \ent-ᵊl\ see ENTAL

entment \ent-mənt\ contentment, resentment • discontentment

ento \en-tō\ lento • memento, pimiento, Sorrento • Sacramento • divertimento, risorgimento • pronunciamento

enton \ent-ᵊn\ see ENTEN

entor \ent-ər\ see ENTER

entous \ent-əs\ apprentice, momentous, portentous • compos mentis • non compos mentis

entry \en-trē\ see ENTARY

ents \ents\ two cents • at all events, dollars-and-cents
—*also* -s, -'s, *and* -s' *forms of nouns and* -s *forms of verbs listed at* ENT¹

entual¹ \en-shə-wəl\ sensual • accentual, consensual, eventual

entual² \en-chəl\ see ENTIAL

enture \en-chər\ censure, denture, quencher, venture • adventure, backbencher, debenture, indenture • misadventure

entury \ench-rē\ see ENTIARY

enty \ent-ē\ plenty, twenty • aplenty • horn of plenty, twenty-twenty

enuis \en-yə-wəs\ see ENUOUS

enum \en-əm\ see ENOM

enuous \en-yə-wəs\ strenuous, tenuous • ingenuous • disingenuous

enus¹ \ē-nəs\ genus, venous, Venus • Maecenas • intravenous

enus² \en-əs\ see ENIS

eny \ā-nē\ see AINY

enys \en-əs\ see ENIS

enza \en-zə\ cadenza, credenza • influenza

eo¹ \ā-ō\ kayo, mayo • cacao, rodeo • Galileo, San Mateo • Montevideo

eo² \ē-ō\ see IO²

eoff¹ ⬛⬛⬛ see ⬛⬛

eoff² \ēf\ see IEF¹

eoffor \ef-ər\ see EPHOR

eoman \ō-mən\ see OMAN

eon¹ \ē-ən\ see EAN¹

eon² \ē-än\ eon, Freon, neon, prion

eopard \ep-ərd\ leopard, peppered, shepherd • snow leopard • German shepherd

eopardess \ep-ərd-əs\ leopardess, shepherdess

eople \ē-pəl\ people, steeple • craftspeople, laypeople, salespeople, townspeople, tradespeople • businesspeople, little people • beautiful people

eorem \ir-əm\ see ERUM

eorge \órj\ see ORGE

eorist \ir-əst\ see ERIST¹

eoul \ōl\ see OLE¹

eous \ē-əs\ see EUS[1]

ep \ep\ pep, prep, rep, schlepp, step, steppe, strep, yep • doorstep, footstep, goose-step, half step, instep, in step, lockstep, misstep, sidestep, twelve-step, whole step • in lockstep, out of step, overstep, step-by-step

eparable \ep-rə-bəl\ reparable, separable • inseparable, irreparable

epard \ep-ərd\ see EOPARD

epe \āp\ see APE[1]

epee \ē-pē\ see EEPY

eper \ep-ər\ see EPPER

eperous \ep-rəs\ leprous • obstreperous

eph \ef\ see EF[1]

ephen \ē-vən\ see EVEN

epherd \ep-ərd\ see EOPARD

epherdess \ep-ərd-əs\ see EOPARDESS

ephone \ef-ə-nē\ see EPHONY

ephony \ef-ə-nē\ Stephanie • Persephone, telephony

ephor \ef-ər\ heifer, zephyr

epht \eft\ see EFT

ephyr \ef-ər\ see EPHOR

epid \ep-əd\ tepid • intrepid

epo \ēp-ō\ see EPOT

epot \ēp-ō\ depot • el cheapo

epp \ep\ see EP

eppe \ep\ see EP

epped \ept\ see EPT

epper \ep-ər\ leper, pepper • bell pepper, green pepper, hot pepper, red pepper, sidestepper, sweet pepper • chili pepper

eppy \ep-ē\ peppy, preppy

eprous \ep-rəs\ see EPEROUS

eps \eps\ biceps, forceps, triceps • quadriceps
—*also* -s, -'s, *and* -s' *forms of nouns and* -s *forms of verbs listed at* EP

ept \ept\ crept, kept, slept, stepped, swept, wept • accept, adept, backswept, concept, except, inept, precept, upswept, windswept • intercept, overslept
—*also* -ed *forms of verbs listed at* EP

eptable \ep-tə-bəl\ see EPTIBLE

eptacle \ep-ti-kəl\ skeptical • receptacle

eptible \ep-tə-bəl\ acceptable, perceptible, susceptible • imperceptible, unacceptable

eptic \ep-tik\ peptic, septic, skeptic • dyspeptic • antiseptic, epileptic, narcoleptic

eptical \ep-ti-kəl\ see EPTACLE

eption \ep-shən\ conception, deception, exception, inception, perception, reception • interception, misconception, preconception, take exception

epy \ep-ē\ see EPPY

epys \ēps\ for keeps
—*also* -s, -'s, *and* -s' *forms of nouns and* -s *forms of verbs listed at* EEP

equal \ē-kwəl\ equal, sequel • coequal, unequal

eque \ek\ see ECK

equel \ē-kwəl\ see EQUAL

equer \ek-ər\ see ECKER

er[1] \ā\ see AY[1]

er[2] \er\ see ARE[4]

er[3] \ər\ see EUR[1]

er[4] \ir\ see EER[2]

era[1] \er-ə\ Berra, era, Hera, Sarah • mascara, Rivera, Sahara, sierra, tiara • aloe vera, Common Era, habanera, riviera, Riviera, Santa Clara • Islamic Era, Spanish Sahara, Western Sahara

era[2] \ir-ə\ era, Hera, lira, Vera • chimera, Madeira, mbira • Common Era • Islamic Era

erah \ir-ə\ see ERA[2]

eral[1] \ir-əl\ Cyril, feral, virile

eral[2] \er-əl\ see ERIL

eral[3] \ər-əl\ see ERRAL

erald \er-əld\ Gerald, Harold, herald

eraph \er-əf\ see ERIF

eratin \er-ət-ᵊn\ keratin, Sheraton • Samaritan

erative \er-ət-iv\ see ARATIVE[1]

eraton \er-ət-ᵊn\ see ERATIN

erb \ərb\ blurb, curb, herb, Serb, verb • adverb, disturb, exurb, perturb, proverb, reverb, suburb, superb

erbal \ər-bəl\ burble, gerbil, herbal, verbal • nonverbal

erbally \ər-bə-lē\ verbally • hyperbole, nonverbally

erber \ər-bər\ see URBER

erbia \ər-bē-ə\ see URBIA

erbil \ər-bəl\ see ERBAL

erbole \ər-bə-lē\ see ERBALLY

erby \ər-bē\ derby, herby, Kirby • Roller Derby • demolition derby

erce \ərs\ see ERSE

ercery \ərs-rē\ see URSARY

erch \ərch\ see URCH

ercial \ər-shəl\ Herschel • commercial • controversial, infomercial, uncommercial

ercian \ər-shən\ see ERTIAN

ercible \ər-sə-bəl\ see ERSIBLE

ercion \ər-zhən\ see ERSION[1]

ercive \ər-siv\ see ERSIVE

ercular \ər-kyə-lər\ see IRCULAR

ercy \ər-sē\ Circe, mercy, Percy • controversy

erd \ərd\ see IRD

erde[1] \erd\ see AIRED

erde[2] \ərd\ see IRD

erde[3] \ərd-ē\ see URDY

erder \ərd-ər\ birder, girder, herder, murder • sheepherder

erdi \ər-dē\ see URDY

erding \ərd-iŋ\ wording • sheepherding

—also -ing forms of verbs listed at IRD

erdure \ər-jər\ see ERGER

ere[1] \er\ see ARE[4]

ere[2] \er-ē\ see ARY[1]

ere[3] \ir\ see EER[2]

ere[4] \ir-ē\ see EARY

ere[5] \ər\ see EUR[1]

e're \ē-ər\ see EER[1]

ère \er\ see ARE[4]

ereal \ir-ē-əl\ see ERIAL

ereid \ir-ē-əd\ see ERIOD

erek \erik\ see ERIC[1]

erely \ir-lē\ see EARLY[1]

erence[1] \ir-əns\ clearance • adherence, appearance, coherence • disappearance, incoherence, interference, perseverance • run interference

erence[2] \ər-əns\ see URRENCE

erence[3] \er-əns\ see ARENCE[1]

erent \er-ənt\ see ARENT[1]

eren't[1] \ərnt\ see EARNT

eren't[2] \ər-ənt\ see URRENT

ereo \er-ē-ō\ see ARIO

ereous \ir-ē-əs\ see ERIOUS

erer \ir-ər\ see EARER[2]

eres[1] \erz\ see AIRS

eres[2] \ir-ēz\ see ERIES

eres[3] \ərs\ see ERS[1]

ereth \er-ət\ see ERIT

ereus \ir-ē-əs\ see ERIOUS

erf \ərf\ see URF

erge \ərj\ see URGE

ergence \ər-jəns\ convergence, divergence, emergence, resurgence

—also -s, -'s, and -s' forms of nouns listed at URGENT

ergency \ər-jən-sē\ urgency • emergency, insurgency • counterinsurgency

ergent \ər-jənt\ see URGENT

ergeon \ər-jin\ see URGEON

erger \ər-jər\ merger, perjure, verdure

ergic \ər-jik\ allergic • dramaturgic

ergne[1] \ərn\ see URN

ergne[2] \ern\ see ERN[1]

ergy \ər-jē\ see URGY

eri[1] \er-ē\ see ARY[1]

eri² \ir-ē\ see EARY
eria¹ \ir-ē-ə\ Syria • Algeria, Assyria, bacteria, criteria, diphtheria, Elyria, Iberia, Illyria, Liberia, Nigeria, Siberia, wisteria • cafeteria
eria² \er-ē-ə\ see ARIA
erial \ir-ē-əl\ aerial, cereal, serial • arterial, bacterial, ethereal, funereal, imperial, material, venereal • immaterial, magisterial, managerial, ministerial, raw material • antibacterial
erian¹ \ir-ē-ən\ Algerian, Assyrian, Chaucerian, criterion, Faulknerian, Hitlerian, Iberian, Liberian, Nigerian, Shakespearean, Siberian, Sumerian, valerian, Wagnerian • Presbyterian
erian² \er-ē-ən\ see ARIAN¹
eric¹ \er-ik\ cleric, Derek, derrick, Eric • generic, Homeric, numeric • atmospheric, esoteric, hemispheric, stratospheric • alphanumeric, ionospheric
eric² \ir-ik\ lyric, Pyrrhic, spheric • satiric, vampiric • atmospheric, hemispheric, panegyric, stratospheric
erica \er-i-kə\ Erica • America • North America, South America • Central America, Latin America, Middle America
erical¹ \er-i-kəl\ clerical, spherical • hysterical, numerical • anticlerical
erical² \ir-i-kəl\ lyrical, miracle, spherical • empirical • hemispherical
erich \erik\ see ERIC¹
erics \er-iks\ hysterics
—also -s, -'s, and -s' forms of nouns listed at ERIC¹
eried \ir-ē-əd\ see ERIOD
eries \ir-ēz\ Ceres, queries, series • in series, World Series • miniseries

—also -s, -'s, and -s' forms of nouns listed at EARY
erif \er-əf\ seraph, sheriff
eriff \er-əf\ see ERIF
erik \erik\ see ERIC¹
erika \er-i-kə\ see ERICA
eril \er-əl\ beryl, Beryl, Cheryl, Errol, feral, peril, Sheryl, sterile • imperil
erile \er-əl\ see ERIL
erilous \er-ə-ləs\ perilous, querulous
erin \er-ən\ see ARON¹
ering \ar-iŋ\ see ARING¹
eriod \ir-ē-əd\ myriad, period • grace period
erion \ir-ē-ən\ see ERIAN¹
erior \ir-ē-ər\ anterior, exterior, inferior, interior, posterior, superior, ulterior • Lake Superior
—also -er forms of adjectives listed at EARY
eriot \er-ē-ət\ see ARIAT¹
erious \ir-ē-əs\ serious, Sirius • delirious, imperious, mysterious, Tiberius • deleterious
eris¹ \ir-əs\ see EROUS
eris² \er-əs\ see ERROUS
erist¹ \ir-əst\ theorist
—also -est forms of adjectives listed at EER²
erist² \er-əst\ see ARIST
erit \er-ət\ ferret, merit • demerit, inherit • disinherit
eritable \er-ət-ə-bəl\ veritable • inheritable
eritor \er-ət-ər\ ferreter • inheritor
erity \er-ət-ē\ rarity, verity • asperity, austerity, dexterity, posterity, prosperity, severity, sincerity, temerity • insincerity
erium \ir-ē-əm\ Miriam • bacterium, delirium
erius¹ \er-ē-əs\ see ARIOUS
erius² \ir-ē-əs\ see ERIOUS
erjure \ər-jər\ see ERGER
erjury \ərj-rē\ perjury, surgery

• tree surgery • microsurgery, neurosurgery, plastic surgery, psychosurgery

erk \ərk\ see ORK[1]

erker \ər-kər\ see ORKER[1]

erkin \ər-kən\ see IRKIN

erking \ər-kiŋ\ see ORKING

erky \ər-kē\ jerky, murky, perky, smirky, turkey, Turkey • talk turkey • Albuquerque, herky-jerky

erle \ərl\ see IRL

erlie \er-lē\ see AIRLY

erlin \er-lən\ merlin, Merlin, yearling

erling \ər-liŋ\ see URLING

erlon \ər-lən\ see ERLIN

erlyn \ər-lən\ see ERLIN

erm \ərm\ see ORM[1]

erma \ər-mə\ dharma, Irma • terra firma

ermal \ər-məl\ dermal, thermal • epidermal

erman \ər-mən\ ermine, German, Herman, merman, sermon, Sherman, vermin • determine, Mount Hermon • predetermine

ermanent \ərm-nənt\ permanent • determinant, impermanent • semipermanent

ermann \ər-mən\ see ERMAN

erment \ər-mənt\ deferment, interment, preferment • disinterment

ermi \ər-mē\ see ERMY

ermic \ər-mik\ karmic • geothermic, hypodermic, taxidermic

ermin \ər-mən\ see ERMAN

erminal \ərm-nəl\ germinal, terminal

erminant \ərm-nənt\ see ERMANENT

ermine \ər-mən\ see ERMAN

ermined \ər-mənd\ ermined • determined • self-determined • overdetermined

erminous \ər-mə-nəs\ terminus, verminous

erminus \ər-mə-nəs\ see ERMINOUS

ermis \ər-məs\ dermis, thermos • epidermis

ermit \ər-mət\ hermit, Kermit

ermon \ər-mən\ see ERMAN

ermos \ər-məs\ see ERMIS

ermy \ər-mē\ germy, squirmy, wormy • taxidermy

ern[1] \ern\ bairn, cairn

ern[2] \ərn\ see URN

erna \ər-nə\ Myrna, Verna

ernal \ərn-ᵊl\ colonel, journal, kernel, vernal • eternal, external, fraternal, infernal, internal, maternal, nocturnal, paternal

erne[1] \ern\ see ERN[1]

erne[2] \ərn\ see URN

erned \ərnd\ see URNED

ernel \ərn-ᵊl\ see ERNAL

erner \ər-nər\ see URNER

ernes[1] \ern\ see ERN[1]

ernes[2] \ərn\ see URN

ernest \ər-nəst\ see ERNIST

ernia \ər-ne-ə\ hernia • Hibernia

ernian \ər-nē-ən\ Hibernian, Saturnian

ernible \ər-nə-bəl\ see URNABLE

ernie \ər-nē\ see OURNEY[1]

ernion \ər-nē-ən\ see ERNIAN

ernist \ər-nəst\ earnest, Ernest • internist

ernity \ər-nət-ē\ eternity, fraternity, maternity, modernity, paternity

ernment \ərn-mənt\ adjournment, discernment, internment

erny \ər-nē\ see OURNEY[1]

ero[1] \ē-rō\ gyro, hero, Nero, zero • ground zero, subzero • superhero

ero[2] \er-ō\ pharaoh, taro, tarot • bolero, sombrero, torero, vaquero • caballero, pistolero • Rio de Janeiro

ero[3] \ir-ō\ gyro, hero, zero • ground zero, subzero

erold \er-əld\ see ERALD

eron \er-ən\ see ARON[1]

erous \ir-əs\ cirrus, Eris, peeress, Pyrrhus, seeress
erp \ərp\ see URP
erpe \ər-pē\ see IRPY
erque \ər-kē\ see ERKY
err¹ \er\ see ARE⁴
err² \ər\ see EUR¹
erra \er-ə\ see ERA¹
errace \er-əs\ see ERROUS
erral \ər-əl\ squirrel • conferral, deferral, referral, transferal
errance \er-əns\ see ARENCE¹
errand \er-ənd\ errand, gerund
errant \er-ənt\ see ARENT¹
erre \er\ see ARE⁴
errell \er-əl\ see ERIL
errence¹ \ər-əns\ see URRENCE
errence² \er-əns\ see ARENCE¹
erret \er-ət\ see ERIT
erreter \er-ət-ər\ see ERITOR
erria \er-ē-ə\ see ARIA
errible \er-ə-bəl\ see EARABLE¹
erric \er-ik\ see ERIC¹
errick \er-ik\ see ERIC¹
errie \er-ē\ see ARY¹
erried \er-ēd\ berried, serried, varied
  —also -ed forms of verbs listed at ARY¹
errier \er-ē-ər\ terrier • bull terrier, fox terrier, Welsh terrier
  —also -er forms of adjectives listed at ARY¹
errill \er-əl\ see ERIL
errily \er-ə-lē\ see ARILY
erring¹ \ar-iŋ\ see ARING¹
erring² \ər-iŋ\ see URRING
erris \er-əs\ see ERROUS
errol \er-əl\ see ERIL
errold \er-əld\ see ERALD
erron \er-ən\ see ARON¹
error \er-ər\ see EARER¹
errous \er-əs\ Eris, terrace • millionairess
errule \er-əl\ see ERIL
erry \er-ē\ see ARY¹

ers¹ \ərz\ hers • somewheres
  —also -s, -'s, and -s' forms of nouns and -s forms of verbs listed at EUR¹
ers² \ā\ see AY¹
ersable \ər-sə-bəl\ see ERSIBLE
ersal \ər-səl\ dispersal, rehearsal, reversal, traversal • dress rehearsal, universal
ersary \ərs-rē\ see URSARY
erse \ərs\ curse, hearse, nurse, purse, terse, verse, worse • adverse, averse, coerce, commerce, converse, Converse, disburse, disperse, diverse, free verse, immerse, inverse, Nez Percé, obverse, perverse, rehearse, reverse, scrub nurse, submerse, transverse, traverse, wet nurse • e-commerce, in reverse, intersperse, nonsense verse, reimburse, universe • chapter and verse, practical nurse, registered nurse, visiting nurse • chamber of commerce
ersed \ərst\ see URST
ersey \ər-zē\ jersey, Jersey, Mersey • New Jersey
erschel \ər-shəl\ see ERCIAL
ershel \ər-shəl\ see ERCIAL
ersial \ər-shəl\ see ERCIAL
ersian \ər-zhən\ see ERSION¹
ersible \ər-sə-bəl\ conversable, immersible, reversible, submersible • irreversible
ersion¹ \ər-zhən\ Persian, version • aversion, coercion, conversion, dispersion, diversion, excursion, immersion, incursion, inversion, perversion, reversion, submersion, subversion • extroversion, introversion, King James Version, reconversion
ersion² \ər-shən\ see ERTIAN
ersive \ər-siv\ cursive • coercive, discursive, subversive
erson \ərs-ᵊn\ person, worsen

• chairperson, craftsperson, first person, in person, layperson, MacPherson, newsperson, salesperson, spokesperson, third person • anchorperson, businessperson, second person, weatherperson

erst \ərst\ see URST

ersy \ər-sē\ see ERCY

ert[1] \ərt\ Bert, blurt, curt, Curt, dirt, flirt, hurt, pert, shirt, skirt, spurt, squirt • advert, alert, assert, avert, concert, convert, covert, desert, dessert, divert, dress shirt, exert, expert, frankfurt, hair shirt, hoopskirt, inert, insert, invert, nightshirt, overt, pay dirt, pervert, revert, Schubert, seagirt, sea squirt, stuffed shirt, subvert, sweatshirt, T-shirt • disconcert, extrovert, in concert, inexpert, introvert, miniskirt, overskirt, polo shirt, reconvert, red alert, undershirt, underskirt • Hawaiian shirt

ert[2] \er\ see ARE[4]

ert[3] \at\ see AT[5]

erta \ərt-ə\ Gerta • Alberta, Roberta

ertain \ərt-[3]n\ Burton, certain, curtain • for certain, uncertain

erted \ərt-əd\ concerted, perverted, T-shirted • extroverted, miniskirted, undershirted
—*also* -ed *forms of verbs listed at* ERT[1]

erter \ərt-ər\ curter, squirter • converter, deserter, frankfurter, Frankfurter

erth \ərth\ see IRTH

ertha \ər-thə\ Bertha, Eartha

ertial \ər-shəl\ see ERCIAL

ertian \ər-shən\ assertion, Cistercian, desertion, exertion, insertion • self-assertion

ertile \ərt-[3]l\ fertile, hurtle, myrtle, Myrtle, turtle • crape myrtle,

infertile, sea turtle, turn turtle, wax myrtle • snapping turtle

erting \ərt-iŋ\ shirting, skirting • disconcerting
—*also* -ing *forms of verbs listed at* ERT[1]

ertion \ər-shən\ see ERTIAN

ertive \ərt-iv\ furtive • assertive • self-assertive, unassertive

erton \ərt-n\ see ERTAIN

ertor \ərt-ər\ see ERTER

erts \ərts\ hertz • gigahertz, kilohertz, megahertz
—*also* -s, -'s, *and* -s' *forms of nouns and* -s *forms of verbs listed at* ERT[1]

erty \ər-tē\ see IRTY

ertz \ərts\ see ERTS

erule \er-əl\ see ERIL

erulous \er-ə-ləs\ see ERILOUS

erum \ir-əm\ theorem, serum • blood serum, truth serum

erund \er-ənd\ see ERRAND

erunt \er-ənt\ see ARENT[1]

erval \ər-vəl\ see ERVIL

ervancy \ər-vən-sē\ see ERVENCY

ervant \ər-vənt\ fervent, servant • bond servant, maidservant, manservant, observant • civil servant, inobservant, public servant

ervative \ər-vət-iv\ conservative, preservative • ultraconservative

erve \ərv\ curve, MIRV, nerve, serve, swerve, verve • conserve, deserve, hors d'oeuvre, observe, preserve, reserve, self-serve, sine curve, unnerve • facial nerve, in reserve, learning curve, optic nerve, spinal nerve, vagus nerve • cranial nerve, sciatic nerve

erved \ərvd\ nerved • deserved, reserved • unreserved
—*also* -ed *forms of verbs listed at* ERVE

ervency \ər-vən-sē\ fervency • conservancy

ervent \ər-vənt\ see ERVANT
erver \ər-vər\ fervor, server • con-
server, observer, timeserver • altar server, life preserver
ervice \ər-vəs\ nervous, service
• curb service, disservice, full-
service, lip service, room service,
self-service, wire service • civil
service, divine service, foreign
service, public service, secret
service, social service
ervil \ər-vəl\ chervil, servile
ervile \ər-vəl\ see ERVIL
erving \ər-viŋ\ Erving, Irving,
serving • deserving, self-serving,
timeserving, unswerving
—*also* -ing *forms of verbs listed at*
ERVE
ervor \ər-vər\ see ERVER
ervous \ər-vəs\ see ERVICE
ervy \ər-vē\ see URVY
erwick \er-ik\ see ERIC¹
erwin \ər-wən\ Irwin, Sherwin
ery¹ \er-ē\ see ARY¹
ery² \ir-ē\ see EARY
eryl \er-əl\ see ERIL
es¹ \ā\ see AY¹
es² \ās\ see ACE¹
es³ \āz\ see AZE¹
es⁴ \es\ see ESS
es⁵ \ēz\ see EZE
e's \ēz\ see EZE
esa \ā-sə\ mesa • Theresa
esage \es-ij\ see ESSAGE
esan¹ \āz-ᵊn\ see AZON
esan² \ēz-ᵊn\ see EASON
esant \ez-ᵊnt\ peasant, pheasant,
pleasant, present • at present,
unpleasant, omnipresent
esce \es\ see ESS
escence \es-ᵊns\ essence • excres-
cence, florescence, fluorescence,
pubescence, quintessence, senes-
cence • acquiescence, adoles-
cence, convalescence,
effervescence, efflorescence,
evanescence, incandescence,

iridescence, luminescence, obso-
lescence, phosphorescence
—*also* -s, -'s, *and* -s' *forms of*
nouns listed at ESCENT
escent \es-ᵊnt\ crescent • depres-
sant, fluorescent, incessant, pu-
bescent, quiescent, senescent,
suppressant • acquiescent, adoles-
cent, convalescent, effervescent,
efflorescent, evanescent, Fertile
Crescent, incandescent, irides-
cent, luminescent, obsolescent,
phosphorescent • antidepressant,
preadolescent
escible \es-ə-bəl\ see ESSIBLE
escive \es-iv\ see ESSIVE
esco \es-kō\ fresco • alfresco,
UNESCO • Ionesco
escue \es-kyü\ fescue, rescue
ese¹ \ēs\ see IECE
ese² \ēz\ see EZE
ese³ \ā-sē\ see ACY
eseus \ē-sē-əs\ Theseus • Tiresias
esh¹ \esh\ crèche, flesh, fresh,
mesh, thresh • afresh, enmesh,
gooseflesh, refresh • Bangladesh,
Gilgamesh, intermesh, in the
flesh, Marrakech, press the flesh
• Uttar Pradesh
esh² \āsh\ see ECHE¹
esh³ \ash\ see ASH³
eshed \esht\ fleshed, meshed
—*also* -ed *forms of verbs listed at*
ESH¹
eshen \esh-ən\ see ESSION
esher \esh-ər\ see ESSURE
eshly \esh-lē\ fleshly, freshly, spe-
cially • especially
esi¹ \ā-zē\ see AZY
esi² \ā-sē\ see ACY
esia¹ \ē-shə\ Letitia, Lucretia,
Phoenicia
esia² \ē-zhə\ amnesia, Rhodesia,
Silesia, Tunisia • analgesia, anes-
thesia, Indonesia, kinesthesia,
Melanesia, Micronesia, Polynesia,
synesthesia • milk of magnesia

esian[1] \ē-zhən\ lesion • adhesion, Cartesian, cohesion, Rhodesian • Indonesian, Melanesian, Micronesian, Polynesian • Peloponnesian

esian[2] \ē-shən\ see ETION[1]

esias \ē-sē-əs\ see ESEUS

esidency \ez-əd-ən-sē\ presidency, residency • vice presidency

esident \ez-əd-ənt\ president, resident • nonresident, vice president

esion \ē-zhən\ see ESIAN[1]

esis \ē-səs\ Croesus, thesis • prosthesis • Dionysus, exegesis • Peloponnesus, telekinesis • amniocentesis

esium \ē-zē-əm\ see EZIUM

esk \esk\ see ESQUE

esley \es-lē\ see ESSLY

eslie \es-lē\ see ESSLY

esne \ēn\ see INE[3]

eso \ā-sō\ peso, say-so

espite \es-pət\ see ESPOT

espot \es-pət\ despot, respite

esque \esk\ desk • burlesque, grotesque • arabesque, copydesk, gigantesque, picaresque, picturesque, statuesque

ess \es\ bless, chess, dress, ess, fess, guess, less, mess, press, s, stress, tress, yes • abscess, access, address, assess, bench-press, caress, clothespress, compress, confess, cross-dress, depress, destress, digress, distress, drill press, duress, excess, express, finesse, full-dress, headdress, housedress, impress, largess, Loch Ness, much less, nightdress, no less, obsess, oppress, outguess, possess, princess, process, profess, progress, recess, regress, repress, shirtdress, SS, success, sundress, suppress, transgress, undress, unless, winepress • ABS, acquiesce, baroness, bitter cress, coa-

lesce, convalesce, crown princess, decompress, deliquesce, dispossess, effervesce, evanesce, full-court press, granny dress, in-process, less and less, letterpress, minidress, more or less, nonetheless, overdress, politesse, repossess, reprocess, retrogress, second-guess, SOS, underdress, watercress, word process • keynote address, nevertheless, random-access • limited-access

essa \es-ə\ see ESSE[3]

essable \es-ə-bəl\ see ESSIBLE

essage \es-ij\ message, presage

essamine \es-mən\ see ESSMAN

essan \es-ᵊn\ see ESSEN

essant \es-ᵊnt\ see ESCENT

esse[1] \es\ see ESS

esse[2] \es-ē\ see ESSY

esse[3] \es-ə\ Hesse • Odessa, Vanessa

essed \est\ see EST

essedly \es-əd-lē\ blessedly • confessedly, professedly

essel \es-əl\ see ESTLE[1]

essen \es-ᵊn\ Essen, lessen, lesson • object lesson • delicatessen

essence \es-ᵊns\ see ESCENCE

esser \es-ər\ see ESSOR

essex \es-iks\ Essex, Wessex

essful \es-fəl\ stressful • distressful, successful • unsuccessful

essian \esh-ən\ see ESSION

essible \es-ə-bəl\ decibel, guessable • accessible, assessable, compressible, expressible • inaccessible, inexpressible, irrepressible

essie \es-ē\ see ESSY

essile \es-əl\ see ESTLE[1]

ession \esh-ən\ freshen, session • accession, aggression, bull session, compression, concession, confession, depression, digression, discretion, expression, impression, jam session, obsession, oppression, possession, procession, profession, progression, recession, regression, repression, secession, skull session, succession, suppression, transgression • decompression, indiscretion, intercession, misimpression, nonaggression, repossession, self-confession, self-expression

essional \esh-nəl\ congressional, obsessional, processional, professional, recessional • unprofessional

essionist \esh-nəst\ expressionist, impressionist, secessionist

essity \es-tē\ see ESTY

essive \es-iv\ aggressive, depressive, digressive, excessive, expressive, impressive, obsessive, oppressive, possessive, progressive, successive, transgressive • inexpressive, unexpressive • manic-depressive, passive-aggressive

essly \es-lē\ Leslie, Wesley • expressly

essman \es-mən\ chessman, pressman • specimen

essment \es-mənt\ see ESTMENT

esson \es-ᵊn\ see ESSEN

essor \es-ər\ dresser, lesser, stressor • addresser, aggressor, assessor, compressor, confessor, cross-dresser, hairdresser, oppressor, processor, professor, successor, transgressor • food processor, predecessor, word processor

essure \esh-ər\ fresher, pressure • blood pressure, high-pressure, low-pressure, refresher • acupressure

essy \es-ē\ Bessie, dressy, Jesse, Jessie, messy

est \est\ best, breast, Brest, chest, crest, guest, jest, lest, nest, pest, quest, rest, test, vest, west, West, wrest, zest • abreast, abscessed,

armrest, arrest, at best, at rest, attest, backrest, bed rest, behest, bequest, blood test, Celeste, compressed, conquest, contest, crow's nest, depressed, detest, digest, distressed, divest, field-test, flight-test, footrest, gabfest, hard-pressed, headrest, high-test, hope chest, houseguest, incest, infest, ingest, inquest, interest, invest, Key West, lovefest, love nest, low-test, Midwest, molest, northwest, pretest, professed, protest, repressed, request, road test, scratch test, screen test, sea chest, skin test, slugfest, southwest, stress test, suggest, unblessed, undressed, unrest, unstressed, war chest, Wild West • acid test, anapest, Bucharest, Budapest, decongest, disinvest, empty-nest, false arrest, hornet's nest, house arrest, manifest, north-northwest, placement test, predigest, reinvest, second-best, self-addressed, self-confessed, self-interest, self-possessed, sweatervest, true-false test, vision quest • aptitude test, beauty contest, compound interest, feather one's nest, robin redbreast, simple interest, under arrest, vested interest • citizen's arrest

—*also* -ed *forms of verbs listed at* ESS

esta \es-tə\ Vesta • celesta, fiesta, siesta

estable \es-tə-bəl\ see ESTIBLE

estae \es-tē\ see ESTY

estan \es-tən\ see ESTINE

estant \es-tənt\ contestant, protestant • decongestant

este \est\ see EST

ested \es-təd\ crested, tested, vested • time-tested • barrel-chested, double-breasted, hairy-chested, single-breasted

—*also* -ed *forms of verbs listed at*
EST
ester \es-tər\ Chester, Esther, fester,
Hester, jester, Leicester, Lester,
nester, pester, quester, tester • an-
cestor, arrester, investor, Man-
chester, molester, northwester,
Rochester, semester, sequester,
southwester, sou'wester, Sylvester,
trimester, Winchester • empty
nester, polyester
esti \es-tē\ see ESTY
estible \es-tə-bəl\ testable • co-
mestible, detestable, digestible,
suggestible • incontestable, indi-
gestible
estic \es-tik\ domestic, majestic
• anapestic
estimate \es-tə-mət\ estimate,
guesstimate • underestimate
estine \es-tən\ destine • clandestine, intestine, predestine • large
intestine, small intestine
esting \es-tiŋ\ resting • arresting
• interesting
—*also* ing *forms of verbs listed at*
EST
estion \es-chən\ question • conges-
tion, cross-question, digestion,
ingestion, self-question, sugges-
tion • call in question, decongestion,
essay question, indigestion,
pop the question • autosuggestion
estive \es-tiv\ festive, restive • congestive, digestive, suggestive • de-
congestive
estle[1] \es-əl\ Cecil, nestle, pestle,
trestle, vessel, wrestle • blood
vessel • Indian-wrestle
estle[2] \as-əl\ see ASSEL[2]
estle[3] \əs-əl\ see USTLE
estment \es-mənt\ vestment • as-
sessment, divestment, investment
• reinvestment
esto \es-tō\ pesto, presto
• Modesto • manifesto

eston \es-tən\ see ESTINE
estor \es-tər\ see ESTER
estra \es-trə\ orchestra
• Clytemnestra
estral \es-trəl\ kestrel • ancestral,
orchestral
estrel \es-trəl\ see ESTRAL
estrian \es-trē-ən\ equestrian,
pedestrian
estry \es-trē\ vestry • ancestry
esty \es-tē\ chesty, pesty, testy,
zesty • necessity
esus \ē-səs\ see ESIS
et[1] \et\ bet, Bret, Chet, debt, fête,
fret, get, jet, let, Lett, met, net,
pet, set, sweat, Tet, threat, vet,
wet, whet, yet • abet, all wet,
Annette, asset, Babette, baguette,
banquette, barrette, beget, beset,
briquette, brochette, brunet,
cadet, cassette, Claudette, Colette,
coquette, cornet, corvette, cro-
quette, dinette, dip net, diskette,
dragnet, duet, egret, fan-jet, fish-
net, forget, gazette, Georgette,
Gillette, gillnet, gill net, handset,
headset, ink-jet, inlet, inset,
Jeanette, jet set, Juliet, kismet,
layette, life net, Lynette, Mar-
quette, mind-set, moonset, motet,
Nanette, nerve net, nonet, octet,
offset, onset, outlet, outset,
pipette, preset, quartet, quintet,
ramjet, regret, reset, rocket,
rosette, roulette, septet, sestet,
sextet, soubrette, spinet, sublet,
subset, sunset, tea set, thickset,
Tibet, toilette, typeset, upset,
vignette, well-set, Yvette • alphabet, Antoinette, avocet, bassinet,
bayonet, Bernadette, calumet,
castanet, cigarette, clarinet, coro-
net, crepe suzette, epaulet, epi-
thet, Ethernet, etiquette,
featurette, flannelette, heavyset,
Joliet, Juliet, kitchenette,
Lafayette, launderette,

leatherette, luncheonette, majorette, marmoset, martinet, minaret, minuet, netiquette, novelette, Olivet, parapet, pirouette, safety net, silhouette, sobriquet, soviet, space cadet, statuette, suffragette, superjet, teacher's pet, towelette, triple threat, usherette, vinaigrette • bachelorette, drum majorette, marionette, microcassette, mosquito net, Russian roulette, snowy egret • audiocassette, Marie Antoinette, videocassette

et² \ā\ see AY[1]

et³ \āt\ see ATE[1]

et⁴ \es\ see ESS

eta¹ \āt-ə\ see ATA[2]

eta² \et-ə\ see ETTA

eta³ \ēt-ə\ see ITA

etable¹ \et-ə-bəl\ see ETTABLE

etable² \ēt-ə-bəl\ see EATABLE

etal¹ \ēt-ᵊl\ beetle, fetal

etal² \et-ᵊl\ see ETTLE

etan¹ \et-ᵊn\ Breton, threaten • Cape Breton, Tibetan

etan² \ēt-ᵊn\ see EATEN[1]

etch \ech\ catch, etch, fetch, ketch, kvetch, retch, sketch, stretch, vetch, wretch • backstretch, homestretch, outstretch

etched \echt\ teched • far-fetched
—also -ed forms of verbs listed at ETCH

etcher \ech-ər\ etcher, catcher, fetcher, Fletcher, lecher, sketcher, stretcher • cowcatcher, dogcatcher, dream catcher, eyecatcher, flycatcher

etching \ech-iŋ\ etching, fetching
—also -ing forms of verbs listed at ETCH

etchy \ech-ē\ sketchy, stretchy, tetchy

ete¹ \āt\ see ATE[1]

ete² \et\ see ET[1]

ete³ \ēt\ see EAT[1]

ete⁴ \āt-ē\ see ATY

ête \āt\ see ATE[1]

eted \ād\ see ADE[1]

etel \ēt-ᵊl\ see ETAL[1]

etely \ēt-lē\ see EETLY

eteor \ēt-ē-ər\ meteor
—also -er forms of adjectives listed at EATY

eter \ēt-ər\ see EATER[1]

etera \e-trə\ see ETRA

etes \ēt-əs\ see ETUS

eth¹ \eth\ Beth, breath, breadth, death, saith, Seth • black death, brain death, crib death, handbreadth, hairbreadth, Macbeth • baby's breath, hold one's breath, in one breath, kiss of death, life-and-death, living death, morning breath, out of breath, shibboleth, sudden death, waste one's breath • Elizabeth, under one's breath

eth² \ās\ see ACE[1]

eth³ \āt\ see ATE[1]

eth⁴ \et\ see ET[1]

etha \ē-thə\ Aretha, Ibiza

ethane \e-thān\ ethane, methane

ether¹ \eth-ər\ feather, heather, Heather, leather, nether, tether, weather, whether • bellwether, buff leather, fair-weather, glove leather, kid leather, pinfeather, shoe-leather, together, untether • altogether, get-together, hang together, hell-for-leather, knock together, patent leather, pull together, put together, saddle leather, tar and feather, throw together • under the weather

ether² \əth-ər\ see OTHER[1]

ethyl \eth-əl\ Bethel, Ethel, ethyl, methyl

eti¹ \ēt-ē\ see EATY

eti² \āt-ē\ see ATY

etia \ē-shə\ see ESIA[1]

etian \ē-shən\ see ETION[1]

etic \et-ik\ aesthetic, ascetic, athletic, balletic, bathetic, cosmetic, eidetic, frenetic, gametic, genetic, hermetic, kinetic, magnetic, pathetic, phonetic, poetic, prophetic, prosthetic, synthetic • alphabetic, anesthetic, apathetic, arithmetic, copacetic, cybernetic, diabetic, dietetic, diuretic, empathetic, energetic, sympathetic, synesthetic • apologetic, geomagnetic, hyperkinetic, peripatetic, telekinetic, unsympathetic • electromagnetic, general anesthetic, unapologetic • onomatopoetic

etical \et-i-kəl\ heretical, poetical • antithetical, arithmetical, hypothetical, parenthetical, theoretical

etics \et-iks\ aesthetics, athletics, genetics, kinetics, phonetics, poetics, prosthetics • cybernetics, dietetics
—*also* -s, -'s, *and* -s' *forms of nouns listed at* ETIC

etid \et-əd\ fetid, fretted, sweated • indebted
—*also* -ed *forms of verbs listed at* ET[1]

etin \ēt-ᵊn\ see EATEN[1]

etion[1] \ē-shən\ Grecian • accretion, completion, deletion, depletion, excretion, Helvetian, Phoenician, secretion, Tahitian, Venetian • Diocletian, Melanesian, Polynesian

etion[2] \esh-ən\ see ESSION

etious \ē-shəs\ see ECIOUS

etis \ēt-əs\ see ETUS

etist \et-əst\ cornetist, librettist • clarinetist

etius \ē-shəs\ see ECIOUS

etl[1] \āt-ᵊl\ see ATAL

etl[2] \et-ᵊl\ see ETTLE

etland \et-lənd\ Shetland, wetland

eto[1] \āt-ō\ see ATO[2]

eto[2] \ēt-ō\ see ITO[1]

eton \ēt-ᵊn\ see EATEN[1]

etor[1] \et-ər\ see ETTER

etor[2] \ēt-ər\ see EATER[1]

etous \ēt-əs\ see ETUS

etra \e-trə\ Petra, tetra • etcetera

etric \e-trik\ metric • obstetric, symmetric • asymmetric, barometric, diametric, geometric, isometric

etrical \e-tri-kəl\ metrical • obstetrical, symmetrical • asymmetrical, diametrical, geometrical, unsymmetrical

etrics \e-triks\ metrics, obstetrics • isometrics

ets \ets\ let's
—*also* -s, -'s, *and* -s' *forms of nouns and* -s *forms of verbs listed at* ET[1]

ett \et\ see ET[1]

etta \et-ə\ Etta, feta, Greta • biretta, bruschetta, Loretta, poinsettia, Rosetta, vendetta • Henrietta, Marietta, operetta

ettable \et-ə-bəl\ forgettable, regrettable • unforgettable

ette \et\ see ET[1]

etter \et-ər\ better, bettor, debtor, fetter, letter, setter, sweater • abettor, air letter, bed wetter, begetter, block letter, bonesetter, chain letter, dead letter, fan letter, four-letter, go-getter, jetsetter, Ledbetter, newsletter, pacesetter, pinsetter, red-letter, trendsetter, typesetter, unfetter • English setter, go one better, Irish setter, open letter, scarlet letter

ettered \et-ərd\ lettered • unfettered, unlettered

ettes \ets\ see ETS

ettia \et-ə\ see ETTA

ettie \et-ē\ see ETTY[1]

ettier \it-ē-ər\ see ITTIER

ettiness \it-ē-nəs\ see ITTINESS

etting \et-iŋ\ netting, setting • bedwetting, bloodletting, jet-setting, pacesetting, place setting, trendsetting, typesetting

—*also* -ing *forms of verbs listed at*
ET[1]

ettish \et-ish\ fetish, Lettish, pettish, wettish • coquettish

ettle \et-ᵊl\ fettle, kettle, metal, mettle, nettle, petal, settle, shtetl • bimetal, nonmetal, teakettle, unsettle • Popocatépetl

etto \et-ō\ ghetto • falsetto, palmetto, stiletto • saw palmetto, Tintoretto

etty[1] \et-ē\ Betty, Getty, jetty, Nettie, netty, petty, sweaty, yeti • brown Betty, confetti, machete, Rossetti, spaghetti • Donizetti, Serengeti, spermaceti

etty[2] \it-ē\ see ITTY

etus \ēt-əs\ fetus, Thetis, treatise • diabetes

etzsche \ē-chē\ see EACHY

euben \ü-bən\ Cuban, Reuben, Steuben

euce \üs\ see USE[1]

eucey \ü-sē\ see UICY

euch \ük\ see UKE

eud[1] \üd\ see UDE[1]

eud[2] \öid\ see OID[1]

eudal \üd-ᵊl\ see OODLE

eudist \üd-əst\ see UDIST[1]

eudo \üd-ō\ see UDO

eue \ü\ see EW[1]

euer \ü-ər\ see EWER[1]

euil \āl\ see AIL

euille \ē\ see EE[1]

euk \ük\ see UKE

eul[1] \əl\ see ULL[1]

eul[2] \ərl\ see IRL

eulah \ü-lə\ see ULA

eulean \ü-lē-ən\ see ULEAN

eum[1] \ē-əm\ lyceum, museum, nosee-um, per diem • coliseum, colosseum, mausoleum, wax museum

eum[2] \ā-əm\ see AHUM

eum[3] \üm\ see OOM[1]

euma \ü-mə\ see UMA

eume \üm\ see OOM[1]

eumon \ü-mən\ see UMAN

eumy \ü-mē\ see OOMY

eunice \ü-nəs\ see EWNESS

eunuch \ü-nik\ see UNIC

eur[1] \ər\ blur, burr, Burr, cur, err, fir, for, fur, her, myrrh, per, purr, sir, slur, spur, stir, 'twere, were, whir, your, you're • as per, astir, aver, bestir, Big Sur, chauffeur, coiffeur, concur, confer, danseur, defer, demur, deter, hauteur, him/her, his/her, incur, infer, inter, jongleur, larkspur, liqueur, masseur, occur, Pasteur, poseur, prefer, recur, refer, sandbur, sandspur, transfer, voyeur, white fir • amateur, balsam fir, cocklebur, connoisseur, curvature, de rigueur, disinter, Douglas fir, Fraser fir, monseigneur, raconteur, saboteur, underfur, voyageur • carillonneur, entrepreneur, provocateur, restaurateur

eur[2] \ur\ see URE[1]

eure \ər\ see EUR[1]

eurish \ər-ish\ see OURISH

eurs \ərz\ see ERS

eury \ur-ē\ see URY[1]

eus[1] \ē-əs\ Aeneas, Linnaeus • Judas Maccabaeus

eus[2] \üs\ see USE[1]

euse[1] \əz\ buzz, 'cause, does, fuzz, 'twas, was • abuzz, because, outdoes, undoes

euse[2] \üs\ see USE[1]

euse[3] \üz\ see USE[2]

eut \üt\ see UTE

euter \üt-ər\ see UTER

euth \üth\ see OOTH[2]

eutian \ü-shən\ see UTION

eutical \üt-i-kəl\ see UTICAL

eutist \üt-əst\ see UTIST

euton \üt-ᵊn\ see UTAN

euve \əv\ see OVE[1]

euver \ü-vər\ see OVER[3]

eux \ü\ see EW[1]

ev[1] \ef\ see EF[1]

ev² \ȯf\ see OFF²

eva \ē-və\ see IVA²

eval \ē-vəl\ see IEVAL

evalent \ev-ə-lənt\ see EVOLENT

evan¹ \ē-vən\ see EVEN

evan² \ev-ən\ see EAVEN

eve¹ \ev\ rev • Kiev, Negev

eve² \ēv\ see EAVE¹

evel \ev-əl\ bevel, devil, level, Neville, revel • bedevil, daredevil, dishevel, dust devil, high-level, low-level, sea level, split-level • entry-level, on the level, water level

eveler \ev-lər\ leveler, reveler

evelly \ev-ə-lē\ heavily, reveille

evement \ēv-mənt\ achievement, bereavement • underachievement

even \ē-vən\ even, Stephen • break even, Genevan, get even, uneven

eventh \ev-ənth\ seventh • eleventh

ever¹ \ev-ər\ clever, ever, lever, never, sever, Trevor • endeavor, forever, however, whatever, whenever, wherever, whichever, whoever, whomever • whatsoever, whomsoever, whosoever

ever² \ē-vər\ see IEVER

everage \ev-rij\ beverage, leverage

everence \ev-rəns\ reverence, severance • irreverence

every \ev-rē\ every, reverie

evice \ev-əs\ crevice • Ben Nevis

evil \ē-vəl\ see IEVAL

eville \ev-əl\ see EVEL

evilry \ev-əl-rē\ devilry, revelry • daredevilry

evin \ev-ən\ see EAVEN

evious \ē-vē-əs\ devious, previous

evis¹ \ev-əs\ see EVICE

evis² \ē-vəs\ see EVUS

evity \ev-ət-ē\ brevity, levity • longevity

evocable \ev-ə-kə-bəl\ evocable, revocable • irrevocable

evolence \ev-ə-ləns\ prevalence • benevolence, malevolence

evolent \ev-ə-lənt\ prevalent • benevolent, malevolent

evor \ev-ər\ see EVER¹

evous \ē-vəs\ grievous • Saint Kitts-Nevis

evus \ē-vəs\ see EVOUS

evy \ev-ē\ bevy, heavy, levee, levy • top-heavy

ew¹ \ü\ blue, boo, brew, chew, clue, coo, coup, crew, cue, dew, do, Drew, due, ewe, few, flew, flu, flue, glue, gnu, goo, hew, hue, Hugh, Jew, knew, lieu, loo, Lou, mew, moo, new, ooh, pew, phew, pooh, q, queue, rue, screw, shoe, shoo, shrew, Sioux, skew, slew, slough, slue, spew, stew, strew, sue, Sue, threw, through, to, too, true, two, u, view, whew, who, woo, Wu, yew, you, zoo • accrue, achoo, adieu, ado, aircrew, anew, Anjou, askew, au jus, Baku, bamboo, bayou, bijou, boo-boo, brand-new, breakthrough, can-do, canoe, Cebu, construe, Corfu, corkscrew, coypu, cuckoo, curfew, debut, doo-doo, ensue, eschew, fondue, ground crew, gumshoe, guru, hairdo, hereto, Hindu, home brew, Honshu, horseshoe, how-to, HQ, Hutu, igloo, IQ, K2, kazoo, Khufu, kung fu, lean-to, long view, make-do, Matthew, me-too, mildew, milieu, miscue, muumuu, Nehru, one-two, on view, outdo, outgrew, Peru, preview, pursue, purview, ragout, redo, renew, review, revue, run-through, see-through, set-to, shampoo, sinew, skiddoo, snafu, snowshoe, subdue, taboo, tattoo, thank-you, thereto, thumbscrew, to-do, tree shrew, undo, undue, unglue, unscrew, untrue, venue, voodoo, wahoo, walk-through, whereto, who's who, withdrew, worldview, ya-

hoo, yoo-hoo • avenue, baby
blue, ballyhoo, barbecue, bird's-
eye view, black-and-blue,
Brunswick stew, buckaroo, buga-
boo, caribou, cobalt blue, cocka-
too, counterview, curlicue,
derring-do, follow-through, hith-
erto, honeydew, Iguaçu, ingenue,
interview, IOU, Irish stew,
Jiangsu, kangaroo, Kathmandu,
kinkajou, manitou, marabou,
microbrew, midnight blue, Mon-
tague, Montesquieu, Mountain
View, ormolu, overdo, overdue,
overflew, overgrew, overshoe,
overthrew, overview, parvenu,
pay-per-view, PDQ, peacock blue,
peekaboo, petting zoo, point of
view, rendezvous, residue, ret-
inue, revenue, Richelieu, Ryukyu,
seppuku, sneak preview,
switcheroo, talking-to, teleview,
thitherto, Timbuktu, w, waterloo,
well-to-do, what have you,
whoop-de-do, Xanadu • bolt from
the blue, Brian Boru, cardinal
virtue, cornflower blue, didgeri-
doo, downy mildew, hullabaloo,
in deep doo-doo, Kalamazoo,
mulligan stew, Ouagadougou, out
of the blue, Seattle Slew, Vanu-
atu, Wandering Jew
ew² \ō\ see OW¹
ewable¹ \ō-ə-bəl\ see OWABLE¹
ewable² \ü-ə-bəl\ see UABLE
ewal \ü-əl\ see UEL¹
ewar \ü-ər\ see EWER¹
eward¹ \ürd\ see URED¹
eward² \ü-ərd\ Seward, steward
• shop steward
ewd \üd\ see UDE¹
ewdness \üd-nəs\ see UDINOUS
ewe¹ \ō\ see OW¹
ewe² \ü\ see EW¹
ewed \üd\ see UDE¹
ewee \ē-wē\ see EEWEE
ewel \ü-əl\ see UEL¹

eweled \üld\ see OOLED
ewell \ü-əl\ see UEL¹
ewer¹ \ü-ər\ brewer, chewer, doer,
ewer, fewer, sewer, skewer,
viewer, you're • me-tooer, mis-
doer, reviewer, snowshoer,
wrongdoer • barbecuer, evildoer,
interviewer, microbrewer
—*also* -er *forms of adjectives listed
at* EW¹
ewer² \ür\ see URE¹
ewer³ \ō-ər\ see OER⁴
ewerage \ür-ij\ see OORAGE¹
ewery \ür-ē\ see URY¹
ewey \ü-ē\ see EWY
ewie \ü-ē\ see EWY
ewing¹ \ō-iŋ\ see OING¹
ewing² \ü-iŋ\ see OING²
ewish \ü-ish\ bluish, Jewish,
newish, shrewish
ewl \ül\ see OOL¹
ewless \ü-ləs\ clueless, crewless,
dewless, shoeless, viewless
ewly \ü-lē\ see ULY
ewman \ü-mən\ see UMAN
ewn \ün\ see OON¹
ewness \ü-nəs\ blueness, Eunice,
newness, Tunis
ewpie \ü-pē\ see OOPY
ews \üz\ see USE²
ewsman \üz-mən\ bluesman, newsman
ewsy \ü-zē\ see OOZY
ewt \üt\ see UTE
ewter \üt-ər\ see UTER
ewton \üt-ᵊn\ see UTAN
ewy \ü-ē\ bluey, buoy, chewy,
Dewey, dewy, gluey, gooey,
hooey, Louie, Louis, newie,
phooey, screwy • bell buoy, chop
suey, life buoy, mildewy • rata-
touille
ex \eks\ ex, flex, hex, sex, specs,
vex, x • annex, apex, codex, complex, convex, cortex, duplex,
funplex, ibex, index, Kleenex,
latex, narthex, perplex, Pyrex,

reflex, Rx, spandex, telex, Tex-Mex, triplex, unsex, vertex, vortex • belowdecks, circumflex, cross-index, gentle sex, haruspex, intersex, Malcolm X, megaplex, Middlesex, multiplex, Rolodex, thumb index, unisex • cerebral cortex, Oedipus complex
—*also* -s, -'s, *and* -s' *forms of nouns and* -s *forms of verbs listed at* ECK

exas \ek-səs\ see EXUS
exed \ekst\ see EXT
exia \ek-sē-ə\ dyslexia • anorexia
exion \ek-shən\ see ECTION
exis \ek-səs\ see EXUS
exity \ek-sət-ē\ complexity, convexity, perplexity
ext \ekst\ next, sexed, text, vexed • context, perplexed, pretext • hypertext
—*also* -ed *forms of verbs listed at* EX
extant \ek-stənt\ extant, sextant
exural \ek-shrəl\ see ECTURAL²
exus \ek-səs\ nexus, Texas • Alexis • solar plexus
exy \ek-sē\ sexy • apoplexy
ey¹ \ā\ see AY¹
ey² \ē\ see EE¹
ey³ \ī\ see Y¹
eya¹ \ā-ə\ see AIA¹
eya² \ē-ə\ see IA¹
eyance \ā-əns\ abeyance, conveyance, surveillance
ey'd \ād\ see ADE¹
eye \ī\ see Y¹
eyed¹ \ēd\ see EED
eyed² \īd\ see IDE¹
eyeless \ī-ləs\ see ILUS
eyelet \ī-lət\ see ILOT
eyen \īn\ see INE¹
eyer \īr\ see IRE¹
eyes \īz\ see IZE¹
eying \ā-iŋ\ see AYING
ey'll¹ \āl\ see AIL
ey'll² \el\ see EL¹

eyn \in\ see IN¹
eynes \ānz\ see AINS
eyness \ā-nəs\ see AYNESS
eyor \ā-ər\ see AYER
eyre \er\ see ARE⁴
ey're \er\ see ARE⁴
eyrie \ir-ē\ see IRY
eys \ēz\ see EZE
eyser \ī-zər\ see IZER
eyte \ā-tē\ see ATY
ey've \āv\ see AVE²
ez¹ \ez\ see AYS¹
ez² \ā\ see AY¹
ez³ \ās\ see ACE¹
eza \ē-zə\ Giza, Lisa, Pisa, visa, Visa
eze \ēz\ breeze, cheese, ease, freeze, frieze, he's, jeez, please, seize, she's, sleaze, sneeze, squeeze, tease, tweeze, wheeze • Andes, appease, Aries, at ease, Belize, big cheese, blue cheese, Burmese, chemise, Chinese, deep-freeze, Denise, disease, displease, d.t.'s, Elise, Ganges, Hermes, jack cheese, Kirghiz, Louise, Maltese, marquise, Pisces, quick-freeze, Ramses, reprise, sea breeze, striptease, strong breeze, Swiss cheese, Tabriz, trapeze, unease, unfreeze, Xerxes • antifreeze, Balinese, Bengalese, Bhutanese, Brooklynese, Cantonese, Cervantes, Ceylonese, cheddar cheese, Congolese, cottage cheese, Damocles, diocese, Eloise, expertise, Hebrides, Heracles, Hercules, ill at ease, Japanese, Javanese, journalese, Lake Louise, legalese, overseas, Pekingese, Pericles, Pyrenees, shoot the breeze, Siamese, Socrates, Sophocles, to one's knees • antipodes, archdiocese, bona fides, computerese, Diogenes, Dodecanese, Dutch elm disease, eminence grise, Euripides, Florida Keys, Great Pyrenees, Hippocrates, Indo-Chinese,

mad cow disease, Thucydides, Vietnamese • Aristophanes, foot-and-mouth disease, Legionnaires' disease, Lou Gehrig's disease, Mephistopheles, Parkinson's disease, sword of Damocles • Pillars of Hercules

—*also* -s, -'s, *and* -s' *forms of nouns and* -s *forms of verbs listed at* EE[1]

ezel \ē-zəl\ see EASEL
ezi \ē-zē\ see EASY[1]
ezium \ē-zē-əm\ cesium • magnesium, trapezium

I

i[1] \ē\ see EE[1]
i[2] \ī\ see Y[1]
i[3] \ā\ see AY[1]
ia[1] \ē-ə\ Gaea, Leah, Mia, rhea, Rhea, via • Crimea, idea, Judaea, Korea, mantilla, Maria, Medea, Nicaea, rupiah, sangria, Sophia, tortilla • bougainvillea, diarrhea, Eritrea, fantasia, Galatea, gonorrhea, Hialeah, Kampuchea, Nicosia, panacea, pizzeria, pyorrhea, Santeria, Tanzania • Andalusia, Ave Maria, Cassiopeia, Sacagawea • onomatopoeia
ia[2] \ī-ə\ see IAH[1]
ia[3] \ä\ see A[1]
iable[1] \ī-ə-bəl\ dryable, dyeable, flyable, friable, liable, pliable, viable • deniable, reliable • certifiable, classifiable, falsifiable, justifiable, quantifiable, undeniable, verifiable • identifiable
iable[2] \ē-ə-bəl\ see EEABLE
iacal \ī-ə-kəl\ maniacal, zodiacal • egomaniacal
iad \ī-əd\ see YAD
iah[1] \ī-ə\ Maya, via • Mariah, messiah, papaya, pariah, Thalia • Hezekiah, jambalaya, Jeremiah, Nehemiah, Obadiah, Zechariah, Zephaniah • Iphigenia
iah[2] \ē-ə\ see IA[1]

ial \īl\ see ILE[1]
ialer \ī-lər\ see ILAR
ially \ē-ə-lē\ see EALLY[1]
iam \ī-əm\ Priam • per diem • carpe diem
ian[1] \ē-ən\ see EAN[1]
ian[2] \ī-ən\ see ION[1]
iance \ī-əns\ science • alliance, appliance, compliance, defiance, nonscience, reliance • misalliance, noncompliance, self-reliance —*also* -s, -'s, *and* -s' *forms of nouns listed at* IANT
iant \ī-ənt\ Bryant, client, giant, pliant • compliant, defiant, reliant • self-reliant, sleeping giant, supergiant
iao \aú\ see OW[2]
iaour \aúr\ see OWER[2]
iaper \ī-pər\ see IPER
iar \īr\ see IRE[1]
iary[1] \ī-ə-rē\ diary, fiery, friary, priory
iary[2] \īr-ē\ see IRY
ias[1] \ī-əs\ bias, dais, pious, Pius • Elias, Tobias
ias[2] \ē-əs\ see EUS[1]
ias[3] \äsh\ see ASH[1]
iasis \ī-ə-səs\ diocese • archdiocese, psoriasis • elephantiasis, schistosomiasis
iat[1] \ē-ət\ see EIT[1]

iat² \ī-ət\ see IET
iate \ī-ət\ see IET
iath¹ \ī-əth\ Wyeth • Goliath
iath² \ē-ə\ see IA¹
iatry \ī-ə-trē\ podiatry, psychiatry
iaus \aùs\ see OUSE²
ib¹ \ib\ bib, crib, fib, glib, jib, nib, rib, sib, squib • ad-lib, corncrib, false rib, sahib • floating rib
ib² \ēb\ see EBE²
ib³ \ēv\ see EAVE¹
iba \ē-bə\ see EBA
ibable \ī-bə-bəl\ bribable • indescribable
ibal \ī-bəl\ bible, Bible, libel, scribal, tribal • family Bible
ibb \ib\ see IB¹
ibband \ib-ən\ see IBBON
ibbed \ibd\ rock-ribbed
—also -ed forms of verbs listed at IB¹
ibber \ib-ər\ cribber, fibber, gibber, ribber
ibbet \ib-ət\ exhibit, inhibit, prohibit • flibbertigibbet
ibble \ib-əl\ dribble, kibble, nibble, quibble, scribble, sibyl, Sibyl • double dribble
ibbler \ib-lər\ dribbler, nibbler, quibbler, scribbler
ibbon \ib-ən\ gibbon, ribbon • blue ribbon
ibby \ib-ē\ Libby, ribby
ibe¹ \īb\ bribe, jibe, scribe, tribe, vibe • ascribe, describe, imbibe, inscribe, prescribe, proscribe, subscribe, transcribe • circumscribe, diatribe • oversubscribe
ibe² \ē-bē\ see EBE¹
ibel \ī-bəl\ see IBAL
iber \ī-bər\ briber, fiber, Khyber, Tiber • subscriber
ibi \ē-bē\ see EBE¹
ibia \i-bē-ə\ Libya, tibia • Namibia
ibin \ib-ən\ see IBBON
ibit \ib-ət\ see IBBET
ibitor \ib-ət-ər\ exhibitor, inhibitor

ible \ī-bəl\ see IBAL
iblet \ib-lət\ driblet, giblet
ibo \ē-bō\ gazebo, placebo
ibs \ibz\ dibs • short ribs, spareribs
—also -s, -'s, and -s' forms of nouns and -s forms of verbs listed at IB¹
ibute¹ \ib-yət\ tribute • attribute, contribute, distribute • redistribute
ibute² \ib-ət\ see IBBET
ibutive \ib-yət-iv\ attributive, contributive, distributive
ibutor \ib-ət-ər\ see IBITOR
ibyl \ib-əl\ see IBBLE
ic¹ \ik\ see ICK
ic² \ēk\ see EAK¹
ica¹ \ī-kə\ mica, Micah, pica • Formica • balalaika
ica² \ē-kə\ see IKA¹
icable \ik-ə-bəl\ despicable, explicable, extricable • inexplicable, inextricable
icah \ī-kə\ see ICA¹
ical \ik-əl\ see ICKLE
ican \ē-kən\ see EACON
icar \ik-ər\ see ICKER¹
icative \ik-ət-iv\ applicative, indicative
iccative \ik-ət-iv\ see ICATIVE
ice¹ \īs\ Bryce, dice, Ice, lice, mice, nice, price, rice, slice, spice, splice, thrice, twice, vice, vise • advice, allspice, black ice, brown rice, concise, deice, device, dry ice, entice, excise, fried rice, list price, make nice, no dice, on ice, pack ice, precise, shelf ice, suffice, white rice, wild rice • asking price, break the ice, comma splice, imprecise, merchandise, on thin ice, overprice, paradise, roll the dice, sacrifice, Spanish rice, sticker price • basmati rice, self-sacrifice
ice² \ē-chā\ see ICHE¹
ice³ \ēs\ see IECE
ice⁴ \ī-sē\ see ICY

ice⁵ \īz\ see IZE¹

iceless \ī-sləs\ iceless, priceless, spiceless

icely \is-lē\ see ISTLY

iceous \ish-əs\ see ICIOUS¹

icey \ī-sē\ see ICY

ich¹ \ich\ see ITCH

ich² \ik\ see ICK

ichael \ī-kəl\ see YCLE¹

iche¹ \ēsh\ leash, niche, quiche, sheesh • pastiche, unleash • nouveau riche

iche² \ish\ see ISH¹

iche³ \ich\ see ITCH

iche⁴ \ē-chē\ see EACHY

icher \ich-ər\ see ITCHER

iches \ich-əz\ see ITCHES

ichi¹ \ē-chē\ see EACHY

ichi² \ē-shē\ see ISHI

ichment \ich-mənt\ see ITCHMENT

ichore \ik-rē\ see ICKERY

ichu \ish-ü\ see ISSUE¹

icia¹ \ish-ə\ see ITIA¹

icia² \ēsh-ə\ see ESIA¹

icial \ish-əl\ initial, judicial, official • artificial, beneficial, prejudicial, sacrificial, superficial, unofficial

ician \ē-shən\ see ETION¹

icient \ish-ənt\ deficient, efficient, omniscient, proficient, sufficient • coefficient, cost-efficient, inefficient, insufficient, self-sufficient

icing¹ \ī-siŋ\ icing • gene-splicing • self-sacrificing
—also -ing forms of verbs listed at ICE¹

icing² \ī-ziŋ\ see IZING

icious¹ \ish-əs\ vicious • ambitious, auspicious, capricious, delicious, fictitious, judicious, malicious, Mauritius, nutritious, officious, pernicious, propitious, seditious, suspicious • avaricious, expeditious, inauspicious, injudicious, meretricious, Red Delicious, repetitious, superstitious, surreptitious

icious² \ē-shəs\ see ECIOUS

icipal \is-ə-bəl\ see ISSIBLE

icit \is-ət\ complicit, elicit, explicit, illicit, implicit, solicit

icitor \is-tər\ see ISTER

icitous \is-ət-əs\ duplicitous, felicitous, solicitous • infelicitous

icity¹ \is-ət-ē\ centricity, complicity, duplicity, ethnicity, felicity, publicity, simplicity, toxicity, triplicity • authenticity, domesticity, eccentricity, elasticity, electricity, infelicity, multiplicity, specificity • ethnocentricity, inauthenticity, inelasticity, periodicity

icity² \is-tē\ Christie, misty, twisty, wristy • Corpus Christi

ick \ik\ brick, chick, click, crick, creek, Dick, flick, hick, kick, lick, nick, Nick, pic, pick, prick, quick, rick, sic, sick, slick, stick, thick, tic, tick, trick, wick • airsick, broomstick, carsick, Chap Stick, chick flick, chopstick, cowlick, deer tick, dipstick, dog tick, drop-kick, drumstick, ear pick, firebrick, fish stick, free kick, frog kick, goal kick, handpick, hat trick, hayrick, heartsick, homesick, ice pick, joystick, lipstick, lovesick, matchstick, nightstick, nitpick, nonstick, nutpick, oil slick, peacenik, pinprick, placekick, rubric, salt lick, seasick, self-stick, sidekick, slapstick, toothpick, unstick, uptick, wood tick, yardstick • bailiwick, biopic, Bolshevik, bone to pick, call in sick, candlestick, cattle tick, cherry-pick, corner kick, Dominic, do the trick, doublequick, flutter kick, heretic, lunatic, meterstick, pogo stick, point-and-click, politic, Reykjavik, rhythm stick, scissors kick, walking stick • arithmetic, carrotand-stick, impolitic, penalty kick

icka \ē-kə\ see IKA[1]
icked \ikt\ see ICT[1]
ickel \ik-əl\ see ICKLE
icken \ik-ən\ chicken, quicken, sicken, stricken, thicken • awestricken, spring chicken • panic-stricken, prairie chicken, rubber-chicken • poverty-stricken
ickens \ik-ənz\ dickens, Dickens, pickings
—*also* -s, -'s, *and* -s' *forms of nouns and* -s *forms of verbs listed at* ICKEN
icker[1] \ik-ər\ bicker, clicker, dicker, flicker, kicker, liquor, nicker, picker, pricker, slicker, snicker, sticker, ticker, vicar, wicker • dropkicker, nitpicker, placekicker, ragpicker • bumper sticker, cherry picker, city slicker, politicker
—*also* -er *forms of adjectives listed at* ICK
icker[2] \ek-ər\ see ECKER
ickery \ik-rē\ chicory, flickery, hickory, trickery • Terpsichore
icket \ik-ət\ cricket, picket, spigot, thicket, ticket, wicket • big-ticket, hot ticket, meal ticket • season ticket
ickett \ik-ət\ see ICKET
ickety \ik-ət-ē\ rickety, thickety • persnickety
ickey \ik-ē\ see ICKY
icki \ik-ē\ see ICKY
ickie \ik-ē\ see ICKY
icking \ik-iŋ\ flat-picking, high-sticking, nit-picking, rollicking • cotton-picking, fingerpicking
—*also* -ing *forms of verbs listed at* ICK
ickings \ik-ənz\ see ICKENS
ickish \ik-ish\ sickish, thickish
ickit \ik-ət\ see ICKET
ickle \ik-əl\ fickle, nickel, pickle, prickle, sickle, tickle, trickle • bicycle, dill pickle, icicle, obstacle, Popsicle, tricycle • pumpernickel • hammer and sickle
ickler \ik-lər\ stickler, tickler • bicycler, particular
ickly \ik-lē\ prickly, quickly, sickly, slickly, thickly
ickness \ik-nəs\ quickness, sickness, slickness, thickness • airsickness, car sickness, homesickness, lovesickness, seasickness • motion sickness, mountain sickness, sleeping sickness
icksy \ik-sē\ see IXIE
icky \ik-ē\ dickey, hickey, icky, Mickey, picky, quickie, sickie, sticky, tricky, Vicky • doohickey, slapsticky
icle \ik-əl\ see ICKLE
icly[1] \ik-lē\ see ICKLY
icly[2] \ē-klē\ see EEKLY
ico \ē-kō\ see ICOT
icory \ik-rē\ see ICKERY
icot \ē-kō\ tricot • Puerto Rico
ics \iks\ see IX[1]
ict[1] \ikt\ strict, ticked • addict, afflict, conflict, constrict, convict, depict, district, edict, evict, inflict, lipsticked, predict, restrict, verdict • Benedict, contradict, derelict, interdict, Lake District • eggs Benedict
—*also* -ed *forms of verbs listed at* ICK
ict[2] \īt\ see ITE[1]
ictable \īt-ə-bəl\ see ITABLE[1]
icted \ik-təd\ conflicted, restricted
—*also* -ed *forms of verbs listed at* ICT[1]
icter \ik-tər\ see ICTOR
ictim \ik-təm\ see ICTUM
iction \ik-shən\ diction, fiction, friction • addiction, affliction, constriction, conviction, depiction, eviction, infliction, nonfiction, prediction, restriction • benediction, contradiction, crucifixion, dereliction, interdiction, jurisdiction, science fiction

ictional \ik-shnəl\ fictional • non-
fictional • jurisdictional
ictive \ik-tiv\ fictive • addictive,
afflictive, constrictive, predictive,
restrictive, vindictive • nonrestric-
tive
ictment \īt-mənt\ see ITEMENT
ictor \ik-tər\ victor • constrictor,
depicter, inflicter • boa constrictor
ictory \ik-tə-rē\ victory • contra-
dictory, valedictory
ictual \it-ᵊl\ see ITTLE
ictum \ik-təm\ dictum, victim
icture \ik-chər\ picture, stricture
• big picture • motion picture
icular¹ \ik-yə-lər\ curricular, funic-
ular, particular, vehicular • in
particular, perpendicular • ex-
tracurricular
icular² \ik-lər\ see ICKLER
iculate \ik-yə-lət\ articulate, partic-
ulate • inarticulate
iculous \ik-yə-ləs\ meticulous,
ridiculous
icy \ī-sē\ dicey, icy, pricey, spicy
id¹ \id\ bid, did, grid, hid, id, kid,
Kidd, lid, mid, quid, rid, skid,
slid, squid • amid, backslid, El
Cid, eyelid, forbid, grandkid,
Madrid, nonskid, outdid,
schoolkid, undid • arachnid, giant
squid, katydid, pyramid, underbid
• Valladolid
id² \ēd\ see EED
I'd \īd\ see IDE¹
ida¹ \ēd-ə\ see EDA¹
ida² \ī-də\ Haida, Ida • Oneida
idal \īd-ᵊl\ bridal, bridle, idle, idol,
idyll, sidle, tidal • fratricidal,
fungicidal, genocidal, germicidal,
herbicidal, homicidal, pesticidal,
suicidal
idance \īd-ᵊns\ guidance • misguid-
ance
iday \īd-ē\ Friday, Heidi, tidy • girl
Friday, Good Friday, man Friday,
untidy • bona fide

idd \id\ see ID¹
idden \id-ᵊn\ bidden, hidden, rid-
den • bedridden, forbidden
• overridden
idder \id-ər\ bidder, kidder • con-
sider • reconsider
iddie \id-ē\ see IDDY
iddish \id-ish\ kiddish, Yiddish
iddity \id-ət-ē\ see IDITY
iddle \id-ᵊl\ fiddle, griddle, middle,
piddle, riddle, twiddle • bass
fiddle • play second fiddle
iddling \id-liŋ\ fiddling, middling,
piddling
iddly \id-le\ diddly, piddly, Ridley
iddock \id-ik\ see IDIC
iddur \id-ər\ see IDDER
iddy \id-ē\ biddy, giddy, kiddie
ide¹ \īd\ bide, bride, chide, Clyde,
eyed, fried, glide, guide, hide, I'd,
pied, plied, pride, ride, side, slide,
snide, stride, tide, tried, wide
• abide, allied, applied, aside,
astride, backside, backslide,
beachside, bedside, beside, be-
stride, betide, blue-eyed, broad-
side, bromide, bug-eyed,
clear-eyed, cockeyed, cold-eyed,
collide, confide, courtside,
cowhide, cross-eyed, curbside,
decide, deride, divide, dockside,
downside, downslide, dry-eyed,
ebb tide, elide, field guide, fire-
side, flip side, flood tide, fluoride,
four-eyed, free ride, freeze-dried,
Girl Guide, graveside, hang glide,
hawkeyed, hayride, high tide,
hillside, horsehide, inside, in
stride, joyride, lakeside, landslide,
low tide, lynx-eyed, misguide,
noontide, offside, onside, outride,
outside, poolside, pop-eyed, pre-
side, provide, rawhide, red tide,
reside, ringside, riptide, roadside,
seaside, sharp-eyed, shipside,
snowslide, springtide, squint-eyed,
stateside, statewide, storewide,

streamside, subside, tongue-tied, topside, untried, upside, vat-dyed, walleyed, wayside, wide-eyed, wild-eyed, worldwide, yuletide • alongside, bleary-eyed, bona fide, chicken-fried, Christmastide, citified, citywide, classified, coincide, countrified, countryside, countrywide, cut-and-dried, cyanide, dignified, dioxide, double-wide, eagle-eyed, Eastertide, eventide, far and wide, fratricide, fungicide, genocide, germicide, goggle-eyed, googly-eyed, harborside, herbicide, homicide, misty-eyed, monoxide, mountainside, nationwide, Naugahyde, on the side, open-eyed, override, Passiontide, pesticide, planetwide, qualified, rarefied, riverside, side by side, sissified, subdivide, suicide, underside, waterside, wintertide • by the wayside, dissatisfied, fit to be tied, formaldehyde, infanticide, insecticide, Jekyll and Hyde, preoccupied, self-satisfied • carbon dioxide, carbon monoxide, overqualified

—*also* -ed *forms of verbs listed at* Y[1]

ide[2] \ēd\ see EED

idean \id-ē-ən\ see IDIAN

ided \īd-əd\ sided • divided, lopsided, misguided, one-sided • many-sided

—*also* -ed *forms of verbs listed at* IDE[1]

iden \īd-ᵊn\ guidon, Haydn, Leiden, Sidon, widen • Poseidon

idence \īd-ᵊns\ see IDANCE

ident \īd-ᵊnt\ strident, trident

ideon \id-ē-ən\ see IDIAN

ideous \id-ē-əs\ see IDIOUS

ider[1] \īd-ər\ cider, glider, rider, snider, spider, wider • backslider, decider, divider, hang glider, insider, joyrider, lowrider, mis-guider, outrider, outsider, provider, sea spider, Top-Sider, wolf spider • paraglider, waterstrider

ider[2] \id-ər\ see IDDER

ides \īdz\ ides • besides

—*also* -s, -'s, *and* -s' *forms of nouns and* -s *forms of verbs listed at* IDE[1]

idge \ij\ bridge, fridge, midge, ridge • abridge, Blue Ridge, drawbridge, footbridge, Oak Ridge, truss bridge • biting midge, contract bridge, covered bridge • suspension bridge

idged \ijd\ unabridged

—*also* -ed *forms of verbs listed at* IDGE

idgen \ij-ən\ see YGIAN

idget \ij-ət\ Brigitte, digit, fidget, midget, widget • double-digit

idgin \ij-ən\ see YGIAN

idi \id-ē\ see IDDY

idia \i-dē-ə\ Lydia • Numidia

idian \id-ē-ən\ Gideon, Lydian, Midian • Floridian, meridian, obsidian, quotidian • prime meridian

idic \id-ik\ acidic, druidic, Hasidic

idical \id-i-kəl\ druidical, juridical • pyramidical

idiem \id-ē-əm\ idiom • iridium • post meridiem • ante meridiem

iding \īd-iŋ\ riding, siding, tiding • abiding, confiding, deciding, hang gliding, joyriding • law-abiding, paragliding

—*also* -ing *forms of verbs listed at* IDE[1]

idiom \id-ē-əm\ see IDIEM

idious \id-ē-əs\ hideous • fastidious, insidious, invidious, perfidious

idity \id-ət-ē\ acidity, aridity, avidity, cupidity, fluidity, frigidity, humidity, liquidity, lucidity, morbidity, rapidity, rigidity, solidity, stupidity, timidity, validity

idium \id-ē-əm\ ´see IDIEM
idle \īd-ᵊl\ see IDAL
idley \id-lē\ see IDDLY
idney \id-nē\ kidney, Sidney, Sydney
ido¹ \īd-ō\ Dido, fido • Hokkaido
ido² \ēd-ō\ see EDO¹
idol \īd-ᵊl\ see IDAL
ids¹ \idz\ rapids • Grand Rapids
—*also* -s, -'s, *and* -s' *forms of nouns and* -s *forms of verbs listed at* ID¹
ids² \ēdz\ see EEDS
idst \idst\ didst, midst • amidst
idual¹ \ij-wəl\ residual • individual
idual² \ij-əl\ see IGIL
idy \īd-ē\ see IDAY
idyll \īd-ᵊl\ see IDAL
ie¹ \ā\ see AY¹
ie² \ē\ see EE¹
ie³ \ī\ see Y¹
iece \ēs\ cease, crease, fleece, grease, Greece, lease, Nice, niece, peace, piece • apiece, at peace, Bernice, Burmese, caprice, chemise, Chinese, Clarice, Cochise, crosspiece, decease, decrease, Denise, Dumfries, earpiece, Elise, eyepiece, Felice, grandniece, hairpiece, headpiece, increase, Maltese, Matisse, Maurice, mouthpiece, nosepiece, obese, one-piece, police, release, showpiece, sublease, Therese, timepiece, three-piece, two-piece, valise • altarpiece, Balinese, Bengalese, Brooklynese, Cantonese, centerpiece, Ceylonese, chimneypiece, Congolese, diocese, expertise, frontispiece, Gabonese, Golden Fleece, Guyanese, hold one's peace, Japanese, Javanese, journalese, kiss of peace, Lebanese, legalese, manganese, mantelpiece, masterpiece, Nepalese, of a piece, Pekingese, Portuguese, predecease, rerelease,

Siamese, timed-release, Viennese • archdiocese, bureaucratese, computerese, Indo-Chinese, officialese, Peloponnese, secret police, Vietnamese • conversation piece, justice of the peace
iecer \ē-sər\ see EASER¹
ied¹ \ēd\ see EED
ied² \ēt\ see EAT¹
ied³ \īd\ see IDE¹
ieda \ēd-ə\ see EDA¹
ief¹ \ēf\ beef, brief, chief, fief, grief, leaf, reef, sheaf, thief • bay leaf, belief, chipped beef, crew chief, debrief, fig leaf, fire chief, gold leaf, in brief, kerchief, loose-leaf, motif, relief, sneak thief, Tallchief • bas-relief, cloverleaf, come to grief, disbelief, handkerchief, misbelief, neckerchief, unbelief • barrier reef, comic relief • commander in chief, editor in chief, Great Barrier Reef
ief² \ēv\ see EAVE¹
iefly \ē-flē\ briefly, chiefly
ieg¹ \ēg\ see IGUE
ieg² \ig\ see IG
iege¹ \ēj\ siege • besiege, prestige
iege² \ēzh\ see IGE¹
ieger \ē-jər\ see EDURE
iek \ēk\ see EAK¹
iel \ēl\ see EAL²
iela \el-ə\ see ELLA
ield \ēld\ field, shield, wheeled, wield, yield • afield, airfield, coalfield, cornfield, force field, four-wheeled, Garfield, goldfield, heat shield, ice field, infield, left field, midfield, minefield, oil field, outfield, right field, snowfield, Springfield, unsealed, well-heeled, windshield • Bakersfield, battlefield, center field, landing field, Mount Mansfield, playing field, track-and-field
—*also* -ed *forms of verbs listed at* EAL²

ielder \ēl-dər\ fielder, shielder
• infielder, left fielder, midfielder,
outfielder, right fielder • center
fielder

ields \ēldz\ elysian fields
—also -s, -'s, and -s' forms of
nouns and -s forms of verbs listed
at IELD

ieler \ē-lər\ see EALER

ieless \ī-ləs\ see ILUS

ieling \ē-lin̄\ see EELING

iem¹ \ē-əm\ see EUM¹

iem² \ī-əm\ see IAM

ien \ēn\ see INE³

ience \ī-əns\ see IANCE

iend \end\ see END

iendless \en-ləs\ see ENDLESS

iendliness \en-lē-nəs\ see ENDLINESS

iendly \en-lē\ see ENDLY

iene \ēn\ see INE³

iener¹ \ē-nər\ see EANER

iener² \ē-nē\ see INI¹

ienic \en-ik\ see ENIC²

ienics \en-iks\ see ENICS

ienie \ē-nē\ see INI¹

ienist \ē-nəst\ see INIST²

iennes \en\ see ENI¹

ient \ī-ənt\ see IANT

ieper \ē-pər\ see EEPER

ier¹ \ir\ see EER²

ier² \ē-ər\ see EER¹

ier³ \īr\ see IRE¹

ierate \ir-ət\ see IRIT

ierce \irs\ fierce, pierce

iere¹ \er\ see ARE⁴

iere² \ir\ see EER²

iered \ird\ see EARD¹

ieria \ir-ē-ə\ see ERIA¹

ierial \ir-ē-əl\ see ERIAL

ierian \ir-ē-ən\ see ERIAN¹

ierly \ir-lē\ see EARLY¹

ierre¹ \ir\ see EER²

ierre² \er\ see ARE⁴

iers \irz\ Sears • Algiers
—also -s, -'s, and -s' forms of
nouns and -s forms of verbs listed
at EER²

iersman \irz-mən\ see EERSMAN

iery \ī-ə-rē\ see IARY¹

ies¹ \ēz\ see EZE

ies² \ē\ see EE¹

ies³ \ēs\ see IECE

iesel¹ \ē-zəl\ see EASEL

iesel² \ē-səl\ see ECIL¹

iesian \ē-zhən\ see ESIAN¹

iesis \ī-ə-səs\ see IASIS

iest \ēst\ see EAST¹

iester \ē-stər\ see EASTER

iestley \ēst-lē\ see EASTLY

iestly \ēst-lē\ see EASTLY

iet \ī-ət\ diet, fiat, quiet, riot • dis-
quiet, race riot, run riot, unquiet

ietal \ī-ət-ᵊl\ parietal, societal,
varietal

ieter \ī-ət-ər\ dieter, rioter • propri-
etor

ietor \ī-ət-ər\ see IETER

iety \ī-ət-ē\ piety • anxiety, impiety,
propriety, sobriety, society, variety • impropriety, notoriety • garden variety, honor society, secret
society

ietzsche \ē-chē\ see EACHY

ieu \ü\ see EW¹

ieur \ir\ see EER²

iev \ef\ see EF¹

ievable \ē-və-bəl\ see EIVABLE

ieval \ē-vəl\ evil, weevil • boll
weevil, coeval, medieval,
primeval, retrieval, upheaval

ieve¹ \iv\ see IVE²

ieve² \ēv\ see EAVE¹

ieved \ēvd\ see EAVED

ievement \ēv-mənt\ see EVEMENT

iever \ē-vər\ beaver, cleaver, fever,
weaver • achiever, believer, con-
ceiver, deceiver, orb weaver,
receiver, reliever, retriever, trans-
ceiver • cantilever, disbeliever,
eager beaver, true believer, unbe-
liever, wide receiver • golden
retriever, overachiever, under-
achiever

ievish \ē-vish\ see EEVISH

ievous \ē-vəs\ see EVOUS
ieze \ēz\ see EZE
if¹ \if\ see IFF
if² \ēf\ see IEF¹
ife¹ \īf\ fife, Fife, knife, life, rife, strife, wife • good life, half-life, housewife, jackknife, lowlife, midlife, nightlife, penknife, real-life, shelf life, steak knife, still life, true-life, wildlife • afterlife, bowie knife, Duncan Phyfe, fact of life, get a life, nurse-midwife, palette knife, paring knife, pocketknife, putty knife, Yellowknife • utility knife
ife² \ēf\ see IEF¹
ifeless \ī-fləs\ lifeless, strifeless, wifeless
ifer \ī-fər\ see IPHER
iferous \if-ər-əs\ coniferous, pestiferous, splendiferous, vociferous • odoriferous
iff \if\ biff, cliff, diff, glyph, if, jiff, miff, riff, skiff, sniff, stiff, tiff, whiff • midriff, what-if • hieroglyph
iffany \if-ə-nē\ see IPHONY
iffe \if\ see IFF
iffed \ift\ see IFT
iffey \if-ē\ see IFFY
iffish \if-ish\ sniffish, stiffish
iffle \if-əl\ riffle, sniffle, Wiffle
iffness \if-nəs\ stiffness, swiftness
iffy \if-ē\ iffy, jiffy, Liffey, sniffy, spiffy
ific \if-ik\ horrific, pacific, Pacific, prolific, specific, terrific • beatific, hieroglyphic, honorific, scientific, soporific, South Pacific
ifle \ī-fəl\ rifle, stifle, trifle • air rifle, a trifle, squirrel rifle • assault rifle, Enfield rifle, M1 rifle, Springfield rifle
ifling \ī-fliŋ\ rifling, stifling, trifling
ift \ift\ drift, gift, lift, rift, shift, shrift, sift, swift, Swift, thrift • adrift, airlift, chairlift, down-

shift, face-lift, forklift, gearshift, makeshift, shape-shift, shoplift, ski lift, snowdrift, spendthrift, spindrift, split shift, stick shift, swing shift, uplift, upshift • chimney swift, graveyard shift • continental drift
—*also* -ed *forms of verbs listed at* IFF
ifter \if-tər\ drifter, sifter • scene-shifter, shape-shifter, shoplifter, weight lifter
ifth \ith\ see ITH²
iftness \if-nəs\ see IFFNESS
ifty \if-tē\ drifty, fifty, nifty, shifty, thrifty • fifty-fifty, LD₅₀
ig \ig\ big, brig, cig, dig, fig, gig, Grieg, jig, pig, prig, rig, sprig, swig, twig, Whig, wig, zig • bigwig, Danzig, earwig, Leipzig, renege, shindig • guinea pig, hit it big, jury-rig, whirligig, WYSIWYG • potbellied pig, thingamajig
iga \ē-gə\ Antigua, omega
igamous \ig-ə-məs\ bigamous • polygamous
igamy \ig-ə-mē\ bigamy • polygamy
igate \ig-ət\ see IGOT¹
ige¹ \ēzh\ siege • prestige
ige² \ēj\ see IEGE¹
igel \ij-əl\ see IGIL
igenous \ij-ə-nəs\ see IGINOUS
igeon \ij-ən\ see YGIAN
iger \ī-gər\ tiger • Bengal tiger, paper tiger • saber-toothed tiger • Siberian tiger, Tasmanian tiger
igerent \ij-rənt\ belligerent, refrigerant
iggard \ig-ərd\ triggered
—*also* -ed *forms of verbs listed at* IGGER
igged \igd\ twigged • jerry-rigged
—*also* -ed *forms of verbs listed at* IG
igger \ig-ər\ chigger, jigger, rigor, snigger, trigger, vigor • ditchdig-

ger, gold digger, hair trigger, outrigger • pull the trigger

iggered \ig-ərd\ see IGGARD

iggie \ig-ē\ see IGGY

iggish \ig-ish\ biggish, piggish, priggish

iggle \ig-əl\ giggle, jiggle, squiggle, wiggle, wriggle

iggler \ig-lər\ giggler, wiggler, wriggler

iggy \ig-ē\ biggie, piggy, twiggy

igh \ī\ see Y[1]

ighed \īd\ see IDE[1]

ighland \ī-lənd\ highland, island, Thailand • Long Island, Rhode Island, Wake Island • Christmas Island, Coney Island, Devil's Island, Easter Island, Ellis Island, Staten Island • Prince Edward Island, Vancouver Island

ighlander \ī-lən-dər\ highlander, islander

ighlands \ī-lənz\ Highlands • Aran Islands, Cayman Islands, Channel Islands, Falkland Islands, Gilbert Islands, Leeward Islands, Marshall Islands, Thousand Islands, Virgin Islands, Windward Islands • Aegean Islands, Aleutian Islands, Canary Islands, Hawaiian Islands, Philippine Islands
—also -s, -'s, and -s' forms of nouns listed at IGHLAND

ighly \ī-lē\ see YLY

ighness \ī-nəs\ see INUS[1]

ight \īt\ see ITE[1]

ightable \īt-ə-bəl\ see ITABLE[1]

ighted \īt-əd\ blighted, sighted • benighted, clear-sighted, far-sighted, foresighted, nearsighted, shortsighted, united
—also -ed forms of verbs listed at ITE[1]

ighten \īt-ᵊn\ brighten, chitin, frighten, heighten, lighten, tighten, titan, Titan, triton, whiten • enlighten

ightener \īt-nər\ brightener, lightener, tightener, whitener

ightening \īt-niŋ\ see IGHTNING

ighter \īt-ər\ see ITER[1]

ightful \īt-fəl\ frightful, rightful, spiteful • delightful, insightful

ightie \īt-ē\ see ITE[2]

ighting \īt-iŋ\ see ITING

ightless \īt-ləs\ flightless, lightless, nightless, sightless

ightly \īt-lē\ brightly, knightly, lightly, nightly, rightly, slightly, sprightly, tightly • contritely, finitely, forthrightly, politely, unsightly, uprightly • impolitely

ightment \īt-mənt\ see ITEMENT

ightning \īt-niŋ\ lightning, tightening • ball lightning, belt-tightening, heat lightning, sheet lightning
—also -ing forms of verbs listed at IGHTEN

ighton \īt-ən\ see IGHTEN

ights \īts\ lights, nights, tights • by rights, footlights, houselights, last rites, states' rights, weeknights • bill of rights, civil rights, Golan Heights, human rights, northern lights, Shaker Heights, southern lights • animal rights
—also -s, -'s, and -s' forms of nouns and -s forms of verbs listed at ITE[1]

ighty \īt-ē\ see ITE[2]

igian \ij-ən\ see YGIAN

igid \ij-əd\ Brigid, frigid, rigid

igil \ij-əl\ vigil • residual

iginous \ij-ə-nəs\ indigenous, vertiginous

igion \ij-ən\ see YGIAN

igious \ij-əs\ litigious, prestigious, prodigious, religious • irreligious

igit \ij-ət\ see IDGET

igitte \ij-ət\ see IDGET

igm[1] \im\ see IM[1]

igm[2] \īm\ see IME[1]

igma \ig-mə\ sigma, stigma • enigma

igment \ig-mənt\ figment, pigment
ign \īn\ see INE[1]
ignant \ig-nənt\ indignant, malignant
igned \īnd\ see IND[1]
igner \ī-nər\ see INER[1]
igning \ī-niŋ\ see INING
ignity \ig-nət-ē\ dignity • indignity
ignly \īn-lē\ see INELY[1]
ignment \īn-mənt\ alignment, assignment, confinement, refinement • realignment
ignon \in-yən\ see INION
igo \ē-gō\ see EGO[1]
igoe \ē-gō\ see EGO[1]
igor \ig-ər\ see IGGER
igorous \ig-rəs\ rigorous, vigorous
igot[1] \ig-ət\ bigot, frigate, spigot
igot[2] \ik-ət\ see ICKET
igour \ig-ər\ see IGGER
igue \ēg\ Grieg, league • big-league, blitzkrieg, bush-league, colleague, fatigue, intrigue • Ivy League, Little League, major-league, minor-league • battle fatigue, combat fatigue
iguer \ē-gər\ see EAGER
iguous \ig-yə-wəs\ ambiguous, contiguous • unambiguous
igured \ig-ərd\ see IGGARD
ii \ī\ see Y[1]
iing \ē-iŋ\ see EEING
ija \ē-jə\ see EGIA
iji \ē-jē\ Fiji, squeegee
ijia\ē-jə\ see EGIA
ijl \īl\ see ILE[1]
ijn \īn\ see INE[1]
ik[1] \ik\ see ICK
ik[2] \ēk\ see EAK[1]
ika[1] \ē-kə\ paprika, Topeka • Costa Rica, Dominica, Frederica, Tanganyika
ika[2] \ī-kə\ see ICA[1]
ike[1] \ī-kē\ crikey, Nike, Psyche, spiky
ike[2] \īk\ bike, dike, hike, like, mike, Mike, pike, psych, shrike, spike, strike, trike, tyke • alike, boatlike, childlike, Christlike, dirt bike, dislike, dreamlike, feel like, fishlike, flu-like, godlike, grasslike, hitchhike, Klondike, lifelike, rocklike, springlike, suchlike, trail bike, trancelike, turnpike, unlike, vicelike, warlike, wavelike, winglike • and the like, businesslike, down the pike, hunger strike, ladylike, leatherlike, look-alike, machinelike, minibike, motorbike, mountain bike, northern pike, open mike, soundalike, sportsmanlike, statesmanlike, take a hike, workmanlike • exercise bike, sympathy strike, unsportsmanlike
iked \īkt\ spiked
—*also* -ed *forms of verbs listed at* IKE[2]
iker \ī-kər\ biker, hiker, striker • hitchhiker • hunger striker, minibiker, mountain biker
ikey \ī-kē\ see IKE[1]
ikh \ēk\ see EAK[1]
iki[1] \ik-ē\ see ICKY
iki[2] \ē-kē\ see EAKY
iking \ī-kiŋ\ liking, striking, Viking
—*also* -ing *forms of verbs listed at* IKE[2]
ikker \ik-ər\ see ICKER[1]
iky \ī-kē\ see IKE[1]
il[1] \il\ see ILL
il[2] \ēl\ see EAL[2]
ila[1] \il-ə\ see ILLA[2]
ila[2] \ē-lə\ see ELA[1]
ilae \ī-le\ see YLY
ilage \ī-lij\ mileage, silage
ilar \ī-lər\ dialer, filer, miler, smiler, styler, tiler, Tyler • compiler, rottweiler, stockpiler
ilate \ī-lət\ see ILOT
ilbert \il-bərt\ filbert, Gilbert
ilch[1] \ilk\ see ILK
ilch[2] \ilch\ filch, zilch
ild[1] \īld\ child, mild, piled, wild,

Wilde • brainchild, godchild, grandchild, hog-wild, Rothschild, schoolchild, self-styled, stepchild, with child • flower child, latchkey child, poster child, self-exiled
—*also* -ed *forms of verbs listed at* ILE[1]
ild² \il\ see ILL
ild³ \ilt\ see ILT
ild⁴ \ild\ see ILLED
ilde \īld\ see ILD[1]
ilder¹ \il-dər\ builder • bewilder, boatbuilder, Mound Builder, shipbuilder • bodybuilder
ilder² \īl-dər\ Wilder
—*also* -er *forms of adjectives listed at* ILD[1]
ilding \il-diŋ\ building, gilding • boatbuilding, outbuilding, shipbuilding • bodybuilding
—*also* -ing *forms of verbs listed at* ILLED
ildish \īl-dish\ childish, wildish
ildly \īld-lē\ mildly, wildly
ile¹ \īl\ aisle, bile, dial, file, guile, I'll, isle, Kyle, Lyle, mile, Nile, pile, rile, smile, style, tile, trial, vial, vile, viol, while • agile, air mile, argyle, awhile, bass viol, beguile, Blue Nile, compile, defile, denial, docile, erstwhile, exile, febrile, field trial, fragile, freestyle, futile, gentile, hairstyle, high style, hostile, lifestyle, meanwhile, mistrial, mobile, nail file, nubile, on file, profile, puerile, quartile, redial, reptile, retrial, revile, sandpile, senile, servile, stockpile, sundial, tactile, tensile, textile, time trial, turnstile, unpile, virile, woodpile, worthwhile • chamomile, crocodile, domicile, family style, in denial, infantile, insectile, juvenile, low-profile, mercantile, percentile, prehensile, projectile, rank and file, reconcile, self-denial, single file, statute

mile, versatile • audiophile, circular file, Indian file, once in a while • cafeteria-style
ile² \il\ see ILL
ile³ \ē-lē\ see EELY
ile⁴ \ēl\ see EAL[2]
ile⁵ \il-ē\ see ILLY
ilead \il-ē-əd\ see ILIAD
ileage \ī-lij\ see ILAGE
ileal \il-ē-əl\ see ILIAL
iler¹ \ē-lər\ see EALER
iler² \ī-lər\ see ILAR
iles \īlz\ Giles, Miles • British Isles, Western Isles
—*also* -s, -'s, *and* -s' *forms of nouns and* -s *forms of verbs listed at* ILE[1]
iley \ī-lē\ see YLY
ili¹ \il-ē\ see ILLY
ili² \ē-lē\ see EELY
ilia¹ \il-ē-ə\ Celia, cilia • Cecilia • hemophilia • memorabilia
ilia² \il-yə\ Brasília • bougainvillea • memorabilia
ilia³ \ēl-yə\ see ELIA[1]
iliad \il-ē-əd\ Gilead, Iliad • balm of Gilead
ilial \il-ē-əl\ filial • familial
ilian¹ \il-ē-ən\ Gillian, Ilian, Lillian • reptilian • crocodilian
ilian² \il-yən\ see ILLION
ilias \il-ē-əs\ see ILIOUS[1]
ilic \il-ik\ acrylic, Cyrillic, dactylic, idyllic
ilience \il-yəns\ see ILLIANCE
iliency \il-yən-sē\ see ILLIANCY
ilient \il-yənt\ brilliant • resilient
iling¹ \ī-liŋ\ filing, piling, styling, tiling • hairstyling
—*also* -ing *forms of verbs listed at* ILE[1]
iling² \ē-liŋ\ see EELING
ilion¹ \il-yən\ see ILLION
ilion² \il-ē-ən\ see ILIAN[1]
ilious¹ \il-ē-əs\ punctilious • supercilious
ilious² \il-yəs\ bilious • supercilious

ility \il-ət-ē\ ability, agility, civility, debility, docility, facility, fertility, fragility, futility, gentility, hostility, humility, mobility, nobility, senility, stability, sterility, tranquility, utility, virility • affability, capability, countability, credibility, culpability, disability, durability, fallibility, feasibility, flexibility, gullibility, imbecility, immobility, inability, incivility, infertility, instability, legibility, liability, likability, livability, plausibility, portability, possibility, probability, readability, sensibility, sociability, suitability, tunability, usability, versatility, viability, visibility, volatility • acceptability, accessibility, accountability, adaptability, advisability, affordability, applicability, attainability, availability, believability, compatibility, deniability, dependability, desirability, electability, eligibility, excitability, illegibility, impossibility, improbability, incapability, infallibility, inflexibility, invisibility, manageability, marketability, measurability, navigability, predictability, profitability, public utility, reliability, respectability, responsibility, susceptibility, sustainability, upward mobility, variability, vulnerability

ilk \ilk\ bilk, ilk, milk, silk • corn silk, ice milk, skim milk • buttermilk, condensed milk, malted milk • cry over spilled milk

ilky \il-kē\ milky, silky

ill \il\ bill, Bill, chill, dill, drill, fill, frill, gill, grill, grille, hill, ill, Jill, kill, krill, mill, nil, Phil, pill, quill, rill, shrill, sill, skill, spill, still, swill, thrill, til, till, trill, twill, will, Will • anthill, at will, backfill, bluegill, Brazil, Catskill, Churchill, crossbill, de Mille, distill, doorsill, downhill, duckbill, dullsville, dunghill, fire drill, foothill, freewill, free will, fulfill, goodwill, gristmill, handbill, hornbill, Huntsville, ill will, instill, Knoxville, landfill, Melville, mixed grill, molehill, Nashville, pep pill, playbill, refill, roadkill, sawmill, Schuylkill, Seville, spoonbill, standstill, stock-still, storksbill, treadmill, true bill, twin bill, twist drill, unreal, until, uphill, vaudeville, waxbill, windchill, windmill • Brazzaville, Bunker Hill, Chapel Hill, chlorophyll, daffodil, de Tocqueville, double bill, espadrille, Evansville, fiberfill, fill the bill, fit to kill, if you will, Jacksonville, living will, Louisville, overfill, overkill, pepper mill, poison pill, puppy mill, rototill, San Juan Hill, sleeping pill, sugar pill, windowsill, whippoor-will • Buffalo Bill, Capitol Hill, over-the-hill, run-of-the-mill

I'll \īl\ see ILE[1]

illa¹ \ē-yə\ mantilla, tortilla • quesadilla

illa² \il-ə\ villa, Willa • Anguilla, Attila, Camilla, cedilla, chinchilla, flotilla, gorilla, guerrilla, manila, mantilla, Priscilla, scintilla, vanilla • sarsaparilla

illa³ \ē-ə\ see IA[1]

illa⁴ \ēl-yə\ see ELIA[1]

illa⁵ \ē-lə\ see ELA[1]

illable \il-ə-bəl\ billable, drillable, fillable, spillable, syllable, tillable • refillable, trisyllable • monosyllable, polysyllable

illage \il-ij\ pillage, spillage, tillage, village • global village, Greenwich Village • Potemkin village

illah \il-ə\ see ILLA[2]

illain \il-ən\ see ILLON

illar \il-ər\ see ILLER

illate \il-ət\ see ILLET
ille¹ \il\ see ILL
ille² \ē\ see EE¹
ille³ \ēl\ see EAL²
illea \il-yə\ see ILIA²
illed \ild\ build, gild, gilled, guild, skilled, willed • gold-filled, rebuild, tendriled, unskilled • overbuild, semiskilled
—*also* -ed *forms of verbs listed at* ILL
illedness \il-nəs\ see ILLNESS
illein \il-ən\ see ILLON
iller \il-ər\ chiller, filler, killer, miller, pillar, thriller, tiller • distiller, painkiller, time killer • caterpillar, lady-killer, Rototiller, techno-thriller
—*also* -er *forms of adjectives listed at* ILL
illery \il-rē\ pillory • artillery, distillery • field artillery
illes \il-ēz\ see ILLIES
illet \il-ət\ millet, skillet • distillate
illful \il-fəl\ skillful, willful • unskillful
illi¹ \il-ē\ see ILLY
illi² \ē-lē\ see EELY
illian¹ \il-ē-ən\ see ILIAN¹
illian² \il-yən\ see ILLION
illiance \il-yəns\ brilliance • resilience
illiancy \il-yən-sē\ brilliancy • resiliency
illiant \il-yənt\ see ILIENT
illick \il-ik\ see ILIC
illie \il-ē\ see ILLY
illies \il-ēz\ willies • Achilles, Antilles • Greater Antilles, Lesser Antilles
—*also* -s, -'s, *and* -s' *forms of nouns listed at* ILLY
illin \il-ən\ see ILLON
illing \il-iŋ\ billing, drilling, filling, killing, milling, shilling, willing • bone-chilling, fulfilling, painkilling, spine-chilling, top

billing, unwilling • mercy killing, self-fulfilling
—*also* -ing *forms of verbs listed at* ILL
illion \il-yən\ billion, Lillian, million, trillion, zillion • Brazilian, Castilian, civilian, cotillion, gazillion, pavilion, quadrillion, reptilian, Sicilian, vaudevillian, vermilion • crocodilian, Maximilian
illis \il-əs\ see ILLUS
illness \il-nəs\ illness, shrillness, stillness
illo¹ \il-ō\ billow, pillow, willow • Amarillo, armadillo, cigarillo, peccadillo
illo² \ē-ō\ see IO²
illon \il-ən\ Dylan, villain • penicillin
illory \il-rē\ see ILLERY
illous \il-əs\ see ILLUS
illow¹ \il-ə\ see ILLA²
illow² \il-ō\ see ILLO¹
illowy \il-ə-wē\ billowy, pillowy, willowy
ills \ilz\ Black Hills, no-frills • Alban Hills, Berkshire Hills, Chiltern Hills, Cotswold Hills, Malvern Hills, Naga Hills • Beverly Hills, Cheviot Hills, Grampian Hills
—*also* -s, -'s, *and* -s' *forms of nouns and* -s *forms of verbs listed at* ILL
illus \il-əs\ Phyllis, Willis • bacillus • amaryllis
illy \il-ē\ Billie, billy, Chile, chili, chilly, dilly, filly, frilly, hilly, Lillie, lily, Lily, Millie, really, shrilly, silly, Tilly, Willie • daylily, hillbilly • rockabilly, willy-nilly
iln¹ \il\ see ILL
iln² \iln\ kiln, Milne
ilne \iln\ see ILN²
ilo¹ \ī-lō\ Milo, phyllo, silo
ilo² \ē-lō\ kilo, phyllo

ilom \ī-ləm\ see ILUM

iloquist \il-ə-kwəst\ soliloquist, ventriloquist

iloquy \il-ə-kwē\ soliloquy, ventriloquy

ilot \ī-lət\ eyelet, islet, Pilate, pilot • bush pilot, copilot, test pilot • autopilot, Pontius Pilate • automatic pilot

ilt \ilt\ built, gilt, guilt, hilt, jilt, kilt, lilt, quilt, silt, stilt, tilt, wilt • atilt, Brunhild, full tilt, homebuilt, rebuilt, unbuilt • crazy-quilt, custom-built, jerry-built, patchwork quilt, to the hilt, Vanderbilt

ilter \il-tər\ filter, kilter, quilter • off-kilter • color filter

ilth \ilth\ filth, tilth

iltie \il-tē\ see ILTY

ilton \ilt-ᵊn\ Hilton, Milton

ilty \il-tē\ guilty, silty

ilum \ī-ləm\ phylum, xylem • asylum, subphylum

ilus \ī-ləs\ eyeless, stylus, tieless

ily¹ \ī-lē\ see YLY

ily² \il-ē\ see ILLY

im¹ \im\ brim, dim, grim, Grimm, gym, him, hymn, Jim, Kim, limb, prim, rim, scrim, skim, slim, swim, Tim, trim, vim, whim • forelimb, prelim, Purim, Sikkim • acronym, antonym, pseudonym, seraphim, synonym • Pacific Rim

im² \ēm\ see EAM¹

I'm \īm\ see IME¹

ima \ē-mə\ see EMA

image \im-ij\ image, scrimmage • self-image • father image, graven image, mirror image, spitting image, line of scrimmage

iman \ē-mən\ see EMON¹

imate \ī-mət\ climate, primate • acclimate

imb¹ \im\ see IM¹

imb² \īm\ see IME¹

imbal \im-bəl\ see IMBLE

imbale \im-bəl\ see IMBLE

imbed \imd\ brimmed, limbed, rimmed
—*also* -ed *forms of verbs listed at* IM¹

imber¹ \im-bər\ limber, timber

imber² \ī-mər\ see IMER¹

imble \im-bəl\ cymbal, nimble, symbol, thimble • peace symbol

imbo \im-bō\ bimbo, limbo • akimbo

imbre \am-bər\ see AMBAR²

ime¹ \īm\ chime, climb, clime, crime, dime, grime, I'm, lime, mime, prime, rhyme, slime, thyme, time • all-time, bedtime, big time, big-time, buy time, call time, daytime, downtime, enzyme, full-time, halftime, hate crime, in time, key lime, lead time, lifetime, longtime, lunchtime, make time, Mannheim, mark time, mealtime, meantime, nighttime, noontime, old-time, onetime, on time, parttime, pastime, peacetime, playtime, prime time, quicklime, quick time, ragtime, real time, rock climb, schooltime, seedtime, showtime, small-time, sometime, Sondheim, space-time, springtime, sublime, teatime, two-time, war crime, wartime, wind chime • Anaheim, anytime, borrowed time, central time, Christmastime, dinnertime, double-time, eastern time, Father Time, harvesttime, local time, maritime, mountain time, nursery rhyme, on a dime, overtime, pantomime, paradigm, running time, standard time, summertime, take one's time, wintertime • Alaska time, Atlantic time, at the same time, from time to time, Greenwich mean time, Pacific time, nickel-and-dime • daylight saving time, geologic time

ime² \ēm\ see EAM[1]

imeless \īm-ləs\ crimeless, timeless

imely \īm-lē\ timely • sublimely, untimely

imen \ī-mən\ hymen, Hymen, Simon

imeon \im-ē-ən\ see IMIAN

imer¹ \ī-mər\ climber, primer, rhymer, timer • big-timer, egg timer, full-timer, old-timer, part-timer, small-timer • Oppenheimer, wisenheimer

imer² \im-ər\ see IMMER

imes \ēm\ see EAM[1]

imeter \im-ət-ər\ scimitar • altimeter, perimeter

imian \im-ē-ən\ Simeon, simian • Endymion

imic \im-ik\ see YMIC

imicry \im-i-krē\ gimmickry, mimicry

imile \im-ə-lē\ simile, swimmily • facsimile

iminal \im-ən-ᵊl\ criminal • subliminal, war criminal

imitable \im-ət-ə-bəl\ illimitable, inimitable

imitar \im-ət-ər\ see IMETER

imiter \im-ət-ər\ see IMETER

imits \im-its\ Nimitz • off-limits

imity \im-ət-ē\ proximity, sublimity • anonymity, equanimity, magnanimity, unanimity

imitz \im-its\ see IMITS

imm \im\ see IM[1]

immage \im-ij\ see IMAGE

imme \i-mē\ see IMMY

immed \imd\ see IMBED

immer \im-ər\ dimmer, glimmer, grimmer, primer, shimmer, simmer, skimmer, slimmer, swimmer

immick \im-ik\ see YMIC

immickry \im-i-krē\ see IMICRY

immily \im-ə-lē\ see IMILE

immy \im-ē\ gimme, jimmy, shimmy

imn \im\ see IM[1]

imner \im-ər\ see IMMER

imon \ī-mən\ see IMEN

imp \imp\ blimp, chimp, crimp, imp, limp, primp, scrimp, shrimp, skimp, wimp • brine shrimp, rock shrimp • Colonel Blimp, fairy shrimp, tiger shrimp

impe \imp\ see IMP

imper \im-pər\ shrimper, simper, whimper

imple \im-pəl\ dimple, pimple, simple

imply \im-plē\ limply, pimply, simply

impy \im-pē\ shrimpy, skimpy, wimpy

imsy \im-zē\ flimsy, whimsy

imy \ī-mē\ grimy, limey, limy, slimy, stymie • old-timey

in¹ \in\ been, bin, chin, din, fin, Finn, gin, grin, Gwyn, in, inn, kin, Lynn, pin, shin, sin, skin, spin, thin, tin, twin, win, yin • again, akin, backspin, bearskin, begin, Benin, Berlin, blow in, Boleyn, break-in, bring in, buckskin, build in, built-in, butt in, calfskin, call in, call-in, cash in, cave-in, chagrin, check in, check-in, chime in, chip in, close in, clothespin, come in, coonskin, Corinne, crankpin, cut in, deerskin, dig in, doeskin, do in, drive-in, drop in, fade-in, fall in, fill in, fill-in, give in, goatskin, go in, hairpin, hang in, has-been, herein, horn in, kick in, kidskin, kingpin, lambskin, lay in, lead-in, linchpin, live-in, lived-in, log in, love-in, moleskin, move in, munchkin, ninepin, no-win, oilskin, phone-in, pigskin, pitch in, plug-in, plugged-in, pull in, pushpin, put in, rub in, ruin, sealskin, send in, set in, sharkskin, sheepskin, shoo-in, shut-in, sign in, sit-in, sleep in, sleep-in, sloe gin, snakeskin, sock in, stand in, stand-in, step in, stickpin, suck in, swear in, swim fin, tail fin, tailspin, take in, tenpin, therein, throw in, tie-in, tiepin, tip-in, Tonkin, topspin, trade in, trade-in, tune in, tunedin, Turin, turn in, unpin, walk-in, wear thin, weigh in, wherein, wineskin, win-win, within, work in, write-in, Yeltsin • bobby pin, born-again, candlepin, come again, cotter pin, cotton gin, deadly sin, firing pin, Ho Chi Minh, listen in, listener-in, Lohengrin, loony bin, mandolin, mortal sin, motor inn, next of kin, onionskin, paper-thin, pelvic fin, rolling pin, safety pin, set foot in, thick and thin, violin • Gulf of Tonkin, Holiday Inn, original sin, pectoral fin, rub one's nose in, Siamese twin, under one's skin • again and again • on-again off-again

in[2] \ēn\ see INE[3]

in[3] \an\ see AN[5]

in[4] \aⁿ\ Chopin, dauphin, Gauguin, Louvain, Rodin • Claude Lorrain, Saint-Germain

in[5] \ən\ see UN[1]

ina[1] \ī-nə\ china, China, Dinah, Ina, mynah • angina, bone china, Regina, stone china • Carolina, Indochina, kamaaina • North Carolina, South Carolina

ina[2] \ē-nə\ Lena, Nina, Tina • arena, Athena, Christina, czarina, Edwina, farina, Georgina, hyena, Kristina, marina, Marina, Medina, Messina, novena, patina, Regina, Rowena, subpoena • Angelina, Argentina, ballerina, Carolina, Catalina, concertina, Filipina, Katerina, ocarina, Pasadena, semolina, signorina, Wilhelmina • Herzegovina, Pallas Athena, Strait of Messina

inach \in-ich\ Greenwich, spinach

inah[1] \ē-nə\ see INA[2]

inah[2] \ī-nə\ see INA[1]

inal[1] \īn-ᵊl\ final, spinal, vinyl • doctrinal • quarterfinal, semifinal

inal[2] \ēn-ᵊl\ see ENAL

inally \īn-ᵊl-ē\ finally, spinally

inas[1] \ī-nəs\ see INUS[1]

inas[2] \ē-nəs\ see ENUS[1]

inative \in-ət-iv\ see INITIVE

inc \iŋk\ see INK

inca \iŋ-kə\ Dinka, Inca

incal \iŋ-kəl\ see INKLE

incan \iŋ-kən\ Incan, Lincoln

ince[1] \ins\ blintz, chintz, mince, prince, quince, rinse, since, wince • convince, crown prince, evince, shin splints • Port-au-Prince
—*also* -s, -'s, *and* -s' *forms of nouns and* -s *forms of verbs listed at* INT

ince[2] \ans\ see ANCE[3]

incely \in-slē\ princely, tinselly

incer \in-chər\ see INCHER

inch \inch\ cinch, clinch, finch, flinch, grinch, inch, lynch, pinch, winch • bullfinch, chaffinch, goldfinch • every inch, inch by inch, purple finch

incher \in-chər\ clincher, pincer • penny-pincher • Doberman pinscher

inching \in-chiŋ\ unflinching • penny-pinching
—*also* -ing *forms of verbs listed at* INCH

incible \in-sə-bəl\ principal, principle • invincible

incing \in-siŋ\ ginseng • convincing • unconvincing
—*also* -ing *forms of verbs listed at* INCE[1]

incipal \in-sə-bəl\ see INCIBLE

inciple \in-sə-bəl\ see INCIBLE

inck \iŋk\ see INK

incky \iŋ-kē\ see INKY

incoln \iŋ-kən\ see INCAN

inct \iŋt\ linked • distinct, extinct, instinct, precinct, succinct • indistinct • killer instinct

inction \iŋ-shən\ distinction, extinction • contradistinction

ind¹ \īnd\ bind, blind, find, grind, hind, kind, mind, rind, spined, wind • behind, confined, fly blind, inclined, mankind, refined, remind, rewind, sand-blind, snow-blind, spellbind, streamlined, unbind, unkind, unwind • ax to grind, bear in mind, blow one's mind, bring to mind, color-blind, fall behind, frame of mind, humankind, in a bind, mastermind, never mind, nonaligned, put in mind, unaligned, undersigned, well-defined, womankind • back of one's mind, piece of one's mind, presence of mind, venetian blind
—*also* -ed *forms of verbs listed at* INE¹

ind² \ind\ finned, skinned, wind • crosswind, downwind, headwind, rescind, tailwind, thick-skinned, thin-skinned, upwind, whirlwind, woodwind • in the wind, solar wind, spiny-finned • twist in the wind
—*also* -ed *forms of verbs listed at* IN¹

ind³ \int\ see INT

inda \in-də\ Linda • Lucinda, Melinda

indar \in-dər\ see INDER²

inded¹ \īn-dəd\ minded • broad-minded, fair-minded, high-minded, like-minded, small-minded, snow-blinded, strong-minded, tough-minded, weak-minded • absentminded, bloody-minded, civic-minded, evil-minded, feebleminded, narrow-minded, open-minded, simpleminded, single-minded

—*also* -ed *forms of verbs listed at* IND¹

inded² \in-dəd\ long-winded, short-winded
—*also* -ed *forms of verbs listed at* IND²

inder¹ \īn-dər\ binder, finder, grinder • bookbinder, fact finder, faultfinder, pathfinder, range finder, reminder, ring binder, sidewinder, spellbinder, stemwinder, viewfinder, organ-grinder
—*also* -er *forms of adjectives listed at* IND¹

inder² \in-dər\ cinder, hinder, Pindar, tinder

indhi \in-dē\ see INDY

indi \in-dē\ see INDY

indie \in-dē\ see INDY

inding \īn-diŋ\ binding, finding, winding • bookbinding, fact-finding, faultfinding, self-winding, spellbinding
—*also* -ing *forms of verbs listed at* IND¹

indlass \in-ləs\ see INLESS

indle \in-dᵊl\ dwindle, kindle, spindle, swindle

indless \in-ləs\ mindless, spineless

indling \ind-liŋ\ dwindling, kindling

indly¹ \in-lē\ see INLY

indly² \īn-lē\ see INELY¹

indness \īn-nəs\ blindness, fineness, kindness • night blindness, snow blindness, unkindness • color blindness, loving-kindness

indowed \in-dəd\ see INDED²

indy \in-dē\ Cindy, Hindi, indie, windy

ine¹ \īn\ brine, dine, fine, kine, line, mine, nine, pine, Rhine, rind, shine, shrine, sign, spine, stein, swine, thine, tine, twine, vine, whine, wine • A-line, airline, align, alpine, assign, at sign, baseline, beeline, benign, Bernstein, bloodline, blush wine, bovine, bowline, breadline, bustline, byline, call sign, canine, carbine, chow line, clothesline, cloud nine, coastline, combine, condign, confine, consign, cosign, cosine, dateline, deadline, decline, define, design, divine, earthshine, Einstein, enshrine, ensign, entwine, equine, feline, foul line, fräulein, frontline, front line, goal line, gold mine, grapevine, guideline, hairline, hard-line, hard pine, headline, hemline, high sign, Holstein, hotline, incline, in-line, Irvine, jawline, landline, land mine, lifeline, main line, malign, midline, moonshine, neckline, off-line, old-line, online, opine, outline, outshine, Pauline, peace sign, pipeline, pitch pine, plumb line, plus sign, porcine, pound sign, punch line, quinine, recline, red pine, refine, resign, Rhine wine, ridgeline, roofline, saline, Scotch pine, scrub pine, shoreline, sideline, skyline, snow line, straight-line, streamline, strip mine, strychnine, sunshine, supine, time-line, times sign, towline, trapline, tree line, truckline, trunk line, turbine, untwine, ursine, V sign, waistline, white pine, white wine, woodbine, yard line • alkaline, Angeline, Apennine, aquiline, asinine, auld lang syne, balloon vine, battle line, borderline, bottom-line, Byzantine, calamine, Calvin Klein, Caroline, centerline, claymore mine, columbine, concubine, conga line, Constantine, contour line, coralline, countermine, countersign, credit line, crystalline, disincline, draw the line, equal sign, finish line, firing line, Florentine, Frankenstein, gas

turbine, genuine, intertwine, iodine, knotty pine, leonine, Levantine, Liechtenstein, lodgepole pine, longleaf pine, minus sign, monkeyshine, mugho pine, on deadline, on the line, Palestine, party line, picket line, porcupine, realign, redefine, redesign, riverine, Rubenstein, saturnine, second-line, serpentine, shortleaf pine, sibylline, subalpine, sparkling wine, steam turbine, story line, table wine, timberline, toe the line, turpentine, underline, undermine, valentine, waterline, wind turbine, worry line • assembly line, elephantine, Evangeline, fall into line, Frankfurt am Main, graphic design, labyrinthine, lateral line, loblolly pine, Maginot Line, poverty line, production line, receiving line, Rembrandt van Rijn, ship of the line, sweetheart neckline, top-of-the-line • Mason-Dixon line

ine² \ēn\ bean, clean, dean, e'en, gene, Gene, glean, green, jean, Jean, Jeanne, keen, lean, lien, mean, mien, preen, queen, scene, screen, seen, sheen, spleen, teen, tween, wean • Aileen, Arlene, baleen, Benin, benzene, benzine, Bernstein, between, black bean, bovine, broad bean, caffeine, canteen, carbine, careen, Carlene, Cathleen, Charlene, chlorine, chorine, Christine, Claudine, codeine, colleen, Colleen, convene, Coreen, cuisine, Darlene, demean, dentine, Doreen, dryclean, eighteen, Eileen, Eugene, e-zine, fanzine, fifteen, fluorine, fourteen, Francine, gamine, gangrene, glassine, Helene, Hellene, Hermine, Holstein, houseclean, hygiene, Ilene, Irene, Jacqueline, Jeannine, Jolene, Justine, Kathleen, Kristine, lateen, latrine, Lorene, Lublin, machine, marine, Marlene, Maureen, Maxine, morphine, mung bean, Nadine, Nicene, nineteen, Noreen, obscene, offscreen, on-screen, Pauline, praline, preteen, pristine, protein, Racine, ravine, red bean, routine, saline, saltine, sardine, sateen, serene, Sharlene, siren, Sistine, sixteen, Slovene, snap bean, soybean, string bean, strychnine, subteen, sunscreen, thirteen, Tolkien, tureen, umpteen, unclean, unseen, vaccine, wax bean, white bean, windscreen • Aberdeen, almandine, amandine, Angeline, Argentine, Augustine, Balanchine, barkentine, Bernadine, brigantine, brilliantine, Byzantine, carotene, clandestine, columbine, Constantine, contravene, crystalline, Dramamine, drum machine, endocrine, Ernestine, evergreen, fava bean, figurine, Florentine, gabardine, gasoline, Geraldine, go-between, golden mean, guillotine, Halloween, Imogene, inbetween, intervene, jelly bean, Josephine, jumping bean, kerosene, kidney bean, lethal gene, Levantine, libertine, lima bean, limousine, M16, magazine, make the scene, mezzanine, navy bean, Nazarene, nectarine, nicotine, overseen, Philistine, pinto bean, riverine, quarantine, saccharine, San Joaquin, San Martín, serpentine, seventeen, slot machine, submarine, subroutine, tambourine, tangerine, time machine, trampoline, Vaseline, velveteen, wintergreen, wolverine • acetylene, amphetamine, aquamarine, Benedictine, elephantine, Evangeline, flying machine, gar-

banzo bean, heart-lung machine, internecine, labyrinthine, merchant marine, milling machine, mujahideen, nouvelle cuisine, pinball machine, rowing machine, simple machine, threshing machine, ultramarine, vanilla bean, vending machine, voting machine, washing machine • answering machine, antihistamine, arithmetic mean, Mary Magdalene, NC-17 • oleomargarine

ine³ \in-ē\ see INNY

ine⁴ \ē-nē\ see INI[1]

ine⁵ \ən\ see UN[1]

inea \in-ē\ see INNY

ined \īnd\ see IND[1]

inee \ī-nē\ see INY[1]

ineless \īn-ləs\ see INDLESS

inely¹ \īn-lē\ blindly, finely, kindly • divinely, unkindly

inely² \ēn-lē\ see EANLY[1]

inement \īn-mənt\ see IGNMENT

ineness \īn-nəs\ see INDNESS

iner¹ \ī-nər\ diner, finer, liner, miner, minor, shiner, Shriner, signer, whiner • airliner, cosigner, designer, eyeliner, hard-liner, headliner, jetliner, moonshiner, one-liner, recliner, refiner • Asia Minor, forty-niner • graphic designer

iner² \ē-nər\ see EANER

inery¹ \īn-rē\ finery, vinery, winery • refinery

inery² \ēn-rē\ see EANERY

ines¹ \ēn\ see INE³

ines² \ēnz\ see EENS

ines³ \īnz\ Apennines • between the lines
—*also* -s, -'s, *and* -s' *forms of nouns and* -s *forms of verbs listed at* INE[1]

inest \ī-nəst\ see INIST[1]

inet \in-ət\ see INNET

inew \in-yü\ see INUE

ing \iŋ\ bring, cling, ding, fling,

king, King, Ming, ping, ring, sing, sling, spring, sting, string, swing, thing, wing, wring, zing • back-swing, bedspring, Beijing, bite-wing, bowstring, bullring, downswing, drawstring, earring, first-string, growth ring, ham-string, handspring, heartstring, hot spring, lacewing, latchstring, left-wing, mainspring, Nanjing, offspring, plaything, redwing, right-wing, shoestring, unstring, upswing, waxwing, wellspring, wingding • à la king, anything, apron string, ding-a-ling, every-thing, fairy ring, Highland fling, innerspring, on the wing, second-string, signet ring, teething ring, underwing • buffalo wing, cedar waxwing, if anything, under one's wing

inge \inj\ binge, cringe, fringe, hinge, singe, tinge, twinge • butt hinge, impinge, infringe, syringe, unhinge • lunatic fringe

inged \iŋd\ pinged, ringed, stringed, winged

ingement \inj-mənt\ impingement, infringement

ingency \in-jən-sē\ stringency • contingency

ingent \in-jənt\ stringent • astrin-gent, contingent

inger¹ \iŋ-ər\ bringer, ringer, singer, stinger, stringer, swinger, wringer, zinger • Beijinger, first-stringer, folksinger, gunslinger, humdinger, left-winger, mud-slinger, right-winger, torch singer

inger² \iŋ-gər\ finger, linger • fore-finger, ring finger • index finger, ladyfinger, little finger, middle finger

inger³ \in-jər\ ginger, Ginger, in-jure, singer, swinger • infringer

ingery \inj-rē\ gingery, injury

inghy \iŋ-ē\ see INGY¹

inging \iŋ-iŋ\ ringing, springing, stringing, swinging • folksinging, free-swinging, gunslinging, hand-wringing, mudslinging, upbring-ing
  —*also* -ing *forms of verbs listed at* ING

ingit \iŋ-kət\ see INKET

ingle \iŋ-gəl\ jingle, mingle, shin-gle, single, tingle • Kriss Kringle • intermingle

ingli \iŋ-glē\ see INGLY

ingly \iŋ-glē\ jingly, singly, tingly, Zwingli

ingo \iŋ-gō\ bingo, dingo, gringo, jingo, lingo • flamingo, Mandingo • Santo Domingo

ings \iŋz\ Hot Springs, Palm Springs, pull strings, purse strings, see things • Coral Springs, in the wings • Colorado Springs, Saratoga Springs
  —*also* -s, -'s, *and* -s' *forms of nouns and* -s *forms of verbs listed at* ING

ingue \aŋ\ see ANG²

ingy¹ \iŋ-ē\ clingy, dinghy, springy, stringy, zingy

ingy² \in-jē\ dingy, mingy, stingy

inh \in\ see IN¹

ini¹ \ē-nē\ beanie, genie, greeny, Jeannie, meanie, sheeny, teeny, weenie, weeny, wienie • Bernini, bikini, Bikini, Cyrene, Eugenie, Houdini, linguine, Mancini, mar-tini, Mycenae, Puccini, Rossini, tahini, tankini, zucchini • fettuc-cine, Mussolini, Paganini, scalop-pine, spaghettini, string bikini, teeny-weeny, tetrazzini, tortellini, Toscanini

ini² \in-ē\ see INNY

inia \in-ē-ə\ zinnia • gloxinia, Lavinia, Sardinia, Virginia • Abyssinia, West Virginia

inian¹ \in-ē-ən\ Darwinian, Sardin-ian, Virginian • Abyssinian, Ar-

gentinian, Augustinian, Carolin-
ian, Carthaginian, Palestinian
inian² \in-yən\ see INION
inic \in-ik\ clinic, cynic • rabbinic
inical \in-i-kəl\ clinical, cynical,
pinnacle
ining \ī-niŋ\ lining, mining, shining
• declining, designing, inclining
• interlining, silver lining
—*also* -ing *forms of verbs listed at*
INE¹
inion \in-yən\ minion, pinion,
piñon • dominion, Justinian,
opinion, Sardinian • Abyssinian
inis \ī-nəs\ see INUS¹
inish \in-ish\ finish, Finnish, thin-
nish • diminish, refinish • photo
finish
inist¹ \ī-nəst\ dynast, finest
inist² \ē-nəst\ hygienist, machinist
• trampolinist • dental hygienist
initive \in-ət-iv\ definitive, infinitive • split infinitive
inity \in-ət-ē\ trinity, Trinity
• affinity, divinity, infinity, salin-
ity, sanguinity, vicinity, virginity
• femininity, masculinity
inium \in-ē-əm\ delphinium • con-
dominium
injure \in-jər\ see INGER³
injury \inj-rē\ see INGERY
ink \iŋk\ blink, brink, chink, clink,
dink, drink, fink, gink, ink, kink,
link, mink, pink, plink, rink,
shrink, sink, skink, slink, stink,
sync, think, wink, zinc • cuff link,
eyeblink, groupthink, hoodwink,
hot link, lip-synch, outthink,
preshrink, rat fink, red ink, re-
think, soft drink, uplink
• bobolink, countersink, double-
think, hyperlink, interlink, in the
pink, kitchen-sink, missing link,
on the blink, rinky-dink, salmon
pink, shocking pink
inka \iŋ-kə\ see INCA
inkable \iŋ-kə-bəl\ drinkable,

shrinkable, sinkable, thinkable
• undrinkable, unsinkable, un-
thinkable
inkage \iŋ-kij\ linkage, shrinkage
inke \iŋ-kē\ see INKY
inked \iŋt\ see INCT
inker \iŋ-kər\ clinker, drinker,
sinker, stinker, thinker, tinker
• freethinker, headshrinker, hood-
winker, nondrinker • hook line
and sinker
inket \iŋ-kət\ Tlingit, trinket
inkey \iŋ-kē\ see INKY
inkgo \iŋ-kō\ see INKO
inki \iŋ-kē\ see INKY
inkie \iŋ-kē\ see INKY
inking \iŋ-kiŋ\ freethinking, un-
blinking, unthinking • wishful
thinking
—*also* -ing *forms of verbs listed at*
INK
inkle \iŋ-kəl\ crinkle, sprinkle,
tinkle, twinkle, wrinkle • periwin-
kle, Rip van Winkle
inkling \iŋ-kliŋ\ inkling, sprinkling,
twinkling
—*also* -ing *forms of verbs listed at*
INKLE
inkly \iŋ-klē\ crinkly, tinkly,
twinkly, wrinkly
inko \iŋ-kō\ ginkgo, pinko
inks \iŋs\ see INX
inky \iŋ-kē\ dinky, inky, kinky,
pinkie, pinky, slinky, stinky
• Helsinki
inland \in-lənd\ Finland, inland
inless \in-ləs\ chinless, sinless,
skinless
inley \in-lē\ see INLY
inly \in-lē\ spindly, thinly • McKinley • Mount McKinley
inn \in\ see IN¹
innacle \in-i-kəl\ see INICAL
inned \ind\ see IND²
inner \in-ər\ dinner, inner, pinner,
sinner, skinner, spinner, thinner,
winner • beginner, blood thinner,

breadwinner, prizewinner • TV
dinner

innet \in-ət\ linnet, minute, spinet
inney \in-ē\ see INNY
inni \ē-nē\ see INI[1]
innia \in-ē-ə\ see INIA
innic \in-ik\ see INIC
innie \in-ē\ see INNY
inning \in-iŋ\ inning, spinning,
winning • beginning, blood-
thinning, breadwinning, prize-
winning • underpinning
—*also* -ing *forms of verbs listed at*
IN[1]
innish \in-ish\ see INISH
innity \in-ət-ē\ see INITY
innow \in-ō\ minnow, winnow
inny \in-ē\ finny, Guinea, mini,
Minnie, ninny, Pliny, shinny,
skinny, tinny, whinny, Winnie
• New Guinea • Papua New
Guinea
ino[1] \ī-nō\ dino, rhino, wino • al-
bino
ino[2] \ē-nō\ beano, chino, vino
• bambino, casino, Latino,
merino, neutrino • cappuccino,
concertino, Filipino, maraschino,
palomino, San Marino • San
Bernardino
ino[3] \ē-nə\ see INA[2]
iñon \in-yən\ see INION
inor[1] \in-ər\ see INNER
inor[2] \ī-nər\ see INER[1]
inot \ē-nō\ see INO[2]
inous \ī-nəs\ see INUS[1]
inscher \in-chər\ see INCHER
inse \ins\ see INCE[1]
inselly \in-slē\ see INCELY
inseng \in-siŋ\ see INCING
insk \insk\ Minsk, Pinsk
insky \in-skē\ Nijinsky, Stravinsky
inster \in-stər\ minster, spinster
• Westminster
int \int\ Clint, dint, flint, Flint,
glint, hint, lint, mint, print, quint,
splint, sprint, squint, stint, tint

• blueprint, footprint, handprint,
hoofprint, imprint, in-print, large-
print, newsprint, reprint, skin-
flint, spearmint, thumbprint,
voiceprint, wind sprint • aquatint,
fingerprint, peppermint, wun-
derkind
intage \int-ij\ mintage, vintage
• nonvintage
intain \int-ᵊn\ see INTON
inter \int-ər\ hinter, Pinter, printer,
splinter, sprinter, winter • im-
printer, line printer, midwinter
• impact printer, laser printer,
overwinter, teleprinter
inth \inth\ plinth, synth • hyacinth,
labyrinth
inting \int-iŋ\ printing • imprinting,
unstinting
—*also* -ing *forms of verbs listed at*
INT
into[1] \in-tō\ pinto, Shinto
into[2] \in-tü\ back into, break into,
bump into, buy into, check into,
come into, get into, go into, look
into, plug into, rip into, run into,
tap into, tear into • enter into,
marry into
inton \int-ᵊn\ Clinton • badminton
ints \ins\ see INCE[1]
inty \int-ē\ flinty, linty, minty,
squinty • pepperminty
intz \ins\ see INCE[1]
inue \in-yü\ sinew • continue • dis-
continue
inuous \in-yə-wəs\ sinuous • con-
tinuous • discontinuous
inus[1] \ī-nəs\ dryness, highness,
Minos, minus, shyness, sinus,
slyness • Longinus • Antoninus,
plus or minus
inus[2] \ē-nəs\ see ENUS[1]
inute \in-ət\ see INNET
inx \iŋs\ Brink's, jinx, links, lynx,
minx, sphinx • hijinks, methinks
• tiddledywinks
—*also* -s, -'s, *and* -s' *forms of*

nouns and -s forms of verbs listed at INK

iny[1] \ī-nē\ briny, heinie, piny, shiny, spiny, tiny, viny, whiny, winy • sunshiny

iny[2] \in-ē\ see INNY

inya \ē-nyə\ see ENIA[2]

inyan \in-yən\ see INION

inyl \īn-ᵊl\ see INAL[1]

io[1] \ī-ō\ bayou, bio, Clio, Io • Ohio • Cinco de Mayo

io[2] \ē-ō\ brio, Clio, Leo, Rio, trio • Trujillo

iocese \ī-ə-səs\ see IASIS

ion[1] \ī-ən\ Brian, Bryan, ion, lion, Mayan, Ryan, scion, Zion • Orion • dandelion, Paraguayan, Uruguayan

ion[2] \ē-ən\ see EAN[1]

ion[3] \ē-än\ see EON[2]

ior \īr\ see IRE[1]

iory \ī-ə-rē\ see IARY[1]

iot \ī-ət\ see IET

ioter \ī-ət-ər\ see IETER

iouan \ü-ən\ see UAN

ious \ī-əs\ see IAS[1]

ioux \ü\ see IEW

ip \ip\ blip, chip, clip, dip, drip, flip, grip, grippe, gyp, hip, lip, nip, pip, quip, rip, scrip, ship, sip, skip, slip, snip, strip, tip, trip, whip, yip, zip • airship, airstrip, backflip, blue-chip, bullwhip, catnip, cleft lip, clerkship, corn chip, courtship, death grip, drag strip, ear clip, equip, felt-tip, field trip, filmstrip, flagship, foul tip, friendship, frostnip, guilt-trip, gunship, half-slip, handgrip, hardship, harelip, horsewhip, judgeship, jump ship, kinship, let rip, longship, lordship, nonslip, palship, pink slip, road trip, rose hip, round-trip, sales slip, sideslip, spaceship, starship, steamship, tall ship, township, transship, troopship, unzip, V-chip, warship • authorship, battleship, brinkmanship, censorship, chairmanship, comic strip, crack the whip, dealership, draftsmanship, ego trip, ego-trip, fellowship, filter tip, fingertip, gamesmanship, Gaza Strip, horsemanship, internship, ladyship, landing strip, leadership, marksmanship, membership, microchip, mother ship, motor ship, ownership, paper clip, partnership, penmanship, pistol grip, pistol-whip, power strip, readership, rocket ship, scholarship, seamanship, showmanship, skinny-dip, sponsorship, sportsmanship, statesmanship, stewardship, swordsmanship, underlip, viewership, weather strip, workmanship • apprenticeship, championship, citizenship, companionship, containership, dictatorship, factory ship, Freudian slip, good-fellowship, guardianship, median strip, Möbius strip, musicianship, one-upmanship, partisanship, post-nasal drip, potato chip, receivership, rejection slip, relationship, run a tight ship, shoot from the hip, stiff upper lip • bipartisanship, nonpartisanship

ipal \ē-pəl\ see EOPLE

ipari \ip-rē\ see IPPERY

ipatus \ip-ət-əs\ see IPITOUS

ipe \īp\ gripe, hype, pipe, ripe, snipe, stripe, swipe, tripe, type, wipe • bagpipe, blood type, blowpipe, drainpipe, half-pipe, hornpipe, pitch pipe, panpipe, pinstripe, sideswipe, stovepipe, tailpipe, touch-type, unripe, windpipe • archetype, corncob pipe, guttersnipe, overripe, prototype, Teletype • daguerreotype, stereotype

iped \īpt\ striped • pin-striped

—also -ed *forms of verbs listed at* IPE

ipend \ī-pənd\ ripened, stipend

iper \ī-pər\ diaper, griper, hyper, piper, riper, sniper, viper, wiper • bagpiper, pied piper, pit viper, sandpiper • candy striper, pay the piper • stereotyper

ipety \ip-ət-ē\ snippety • serendipity

iph \if\ see IFF

iphany \if-ə-nē\ see IPHONY

ipher \ī-fər\ cipher, lifer • decipher, pro-lifer • right-to-lifer

iphon \ī-fən\ see YPHEN

iphony \if-ə-nē\ Tiffany • epiphany, polyphony

ipi \ē-pē\ see EEPY

ipid \ip-əd\ lipid • insipid

iping \ī-piŋ\ piping, striping • blood-typing

—also -ing *forms of verbs listed at* IPE

ipit \ip-ət\ see IPPET

ipitous \ip-ət-əs\ precipitous • serendipitous

ipity \ip-ət-ē\ see IPETY

iple[1] \ip-əl\ see IPPLE

iple[2] \ī-pəl\ see YPAL

ipless \ip-ləs\ dripless, lipless, zipless

ipling \ip-liŋ\ Kipling, stripling

—also -ing *forms of verbs listed at* IPPLE

ipment \ip-mənt\ shipment • equipment, transshipment

ipo \ēp-ō\ see EPOT

ipoli \ip-ə-lē\ see IPPILY

ippe[1] \ip\ see IP

ippe[2] \ip-ē\ see IPPY

ippe[3] \ēp\ see EEP

ipped \ipt\ see IPT

ippee \ip-ē\ see IPPY

ipper \ip-ər\ chipper, clipper, flipper, gripper, kipper, nipper, ripper, shipper, skipper, slipper, tipper, zipper • Big Dipper, day-tripper, horsewhipper, Yom Kippur • double-dipper, ego-tripper, lady's slipper, Little Dipper, skinny-dipper

ippery \ip-rē\ frippery, slippery

ippet \ip-ət\ snippet, whippet

ippety \ip-ət-ē\ see IPETY

ippi \ip-ē\ see IPPY

ippie \ip-ē\ see IPPY

ippily \ip-ə-lē\ Tripoli • Gallipoli

ipping \ip-iŋ\ clipping, ripping, shipping, whipping • double-dipping, skinny-dipping

—also -ing *forms of verbs listed at* IP

ipple \ip-əl\ cripple, ripple, stipple, tipple, triple • participle

ippur \ip-ər\ see IPPER

ippy \ip-ē\ dippy, drippy, hippie, hippy, lippy, nippy, Skippy, snippy, tippy, yippee, zippy • Xanthippe • Mississippi

ips \ips\ snips • eclipse, ellipse, midships • amidships, fish-and-chips • apocalypse, lunar eclipse, solar eclipse, total eclipse

—also -s, -'s, *and* -s' *forms of nouns and* -s *forms of verbs listed at* IP

ipse \ips\ see IPS

ipster \ip-stər\ hipster, tipster

ipsy \ip-sē\ see YPSY

ipt \ipt\ crypt, hipped, ripped, script • conscript, harelipped, postscript, tight-lipped, transcript, typescript • manuscript, nondescript, shooting script

—also -ed *forms of verbs listed at* IP

iptic \ip-tik\ see YPTIC

iption \ip-shən\ conniption, description, Egyptian, encryption, inscription, prescription, subscription, transcription • nonprescription

iptych \ip-tik\ see YPTIC

ique \ēk\ see EAK[1]

iquey \ē-kē\ see EAKY
iquish \ē-kish\ see EAKISH
iquitous \ik-wət-əs\ iniquitous, ubiquitous
iquity \ik-wət-ē\ antiquity, iniquity, ubiquity
iquor \ik-ər\ see ICKER[1]
ir[1] \ir\ see EER[2]
ir[2] \ər\ see EUR[1]
ira[1] \ir-ə\ see ERA[2]
ira[2] \ī-rə\ see YRA
iracle \ir-i-kəl\ see ERICAL[2]
irae \īr-ē\ see IRY
iral \ī-rəl\ spiral, viral
irant \ī-rənt\ tyrant • aspirant
irate \ir-ət\ see IRIT
irby \ər-bē\ see ERBY
irca \ər-kə\ see URKA
irce \ər-sē\ see ERCY
irch \ərch\ see URCH
irchen \ər-kən\ see IRKIN
ircon \ər-kən\ see IRKIN
ircular \ər-kyə-lər\ circular • tubercular • semicircular
ird \ərd\ bird, curd, furred, gird, heard, herd, nerd, third, word • absurd, bean curd, bellbird, blackbird, bluebird, buzzword, byword, Cape Verde, catbird, catchword, cowbird, cowherd, crossword, cussword, game bird, goatherd, good word, guide word, headword, jailbird, jaybird, kingbird, last word, lovebird, lyrebird, password, rainbird, redbird, reword, ricebird, seabird, Sigurd, shorebird, snakebird, snowbird, songbird, state bird, sunbird, surfbird, swearword, swineherd, textured, unheard, watchword, yardbird • afterword, bowerbird, butcher-bird, cedarbird, dickey bird, dirty word, early bird, fighting word, frigate bird, hummingbird, in a word, ladybird, mockingbird, ovenbird, overheard, tailorbird, thunderbird,

undergird, wading bird, weaverbird, whirlybird, word for word
—also -ed *forms of verbs listed at* EUR[1]
irder \ərd-ər\ see ERDER
irdie \ərd-ē\ see URDY
irdle \ərd-ᵊl\ see URDLE
ire[1] \īr\ briar, choir, dire, drier, fire, flier, friar, fryer, hire, ire, liar, lyre, mire, prior, pyre, shire, sire, spire, squire, tire, Tyre, wire • acquire, admire, afire, aspire, attire, backfire, barbed wire, barbwire, blow-dryer, bonfire, brushfire, bushfire, campfire, catbrier, catch fire, cease-fire, conspire, cross fire, denier, desire, empire, Empire, entire, esquire, expire, for hire, fox fire, grandsire, greenbrier, gunfire, haywire, hellfire, high-wire, hot-wire, inquire, inspire, live wire, misfire, on fire, perspire, prior, quagmire, require, respire, retire, sapphire, satire, Shropshire, snow tire, spitfire, surefire, suspire, sweetbriar, tightwire, town crier, transpire, trip wire, umpire, vampire, wildfire • amplifier, ball of fire, balloon tire, beautifier, chicken wire, like wildfire, multiplier, pacifier, play with fire, qualifier, rapid-fire, razor wire, retrofire, signifier, simplifier, star sapphire, under fire • British Empire, down-to-the-wire, identifier, intensifier, under the wire, water saffire • concertina wire, iron in the fire • Holy Roman Empire
—also -er *forms of adjectives listed at* Y[1]
ire[2] \ir\ see EER[2]
ire[3] \īr-ē\ see IRY
ire[4] \ər\ see EUR[1]
ired \īrd\ fired, spired, tired, wired • hardwired, inspired, retired
—also -ed *forms of verbs listed at* IRE[1]

ireless \īr-ləs\ tireless, wireless
ireman \īr-mən\ fireman, wireman
irement \īr-mənt\ acquirement, environment, requirement, retirement
iren \ī-rən\ Byron, Myron, siren • environ
irge \ərj\ see URGE
irgin \ər-jən\ see URGEON
iri \ir-ē\ see EARY
iriam \ir-ē-əm\ see ERIUM
iric \ir-ik\ see ERIC[2]
irile \ir-əl\ see ERAL[1]
irin \ī-rən\ see IREN
irine \ī-rən\ see IREN
iring \īr-iŋ\ firing, wiring • inspiring, retiring
    —also -ing forms of verbs listed at IRE[1]
irious \ir-ē-əs\ see ERIOUS
iris \ī-rəs\ see IRUS
irish \īr-ish\ Irish • vampirish
irit \ir-ət\ spirit • dispirit, free spirit • Holy Spirit
irium \ir-ē-əm\ see ERIUM
irius \ir-ē-əs\ see ERIOUS
irk \ərk\ see ORK[1]
irker \ər-kər\ see ORKER[1]
irkie \ər-kē\ see ERKY
irkin \ər-kən\ firkin, gherkin, jerkin, zircon
irky \ər-kē\ see ERKY
irl \ərl\ churl, curl, earl, Earl, furl, girl, hurl, Merle, pearl, Pearl, purl, squirrel, swirl, twirl, whirl • awhirl, ball girl, bat girl, cowgirl, home girl, pin curl, playgirl, salesgirl, schoolgirl, shopgirl, showgirl, spit curl, uncurl, unfurl • Camp Fire girl, chorus girl, cover girl, flower girl, pinup girl, poster girl, Valley girl • mother-of-pearl
irler \ər-lər\ curler, twirler
irley \ər-lē\ see URLY
irlie \ər-lē\ see URLY
irling \ər-liŋ\ see URLING

irlish \ər-lish\ see URLISH
irly \ər-lē\ see URLY
irm \ərm\ see ORM[1]
irma \ər-mə\ see ERMA
irmess \ər-məs\ see ERMIS
irmy \ər-mē\ see ERMY
irn \ərn\ see URN
iro[1] \ir-ō\ see ERO[3]
iro[2] \ē-rō\ see ERO[1]
iro[3] \ī-rō\ see YRO[1]
iron[1] \īrn\ iron • andiron, cast-iron, environ, flatiron, gridiron, pig iron, pump iron, steam iron, wrought iron • climbing iron, curling iron, shooting iron, waffle iron • soldering iron
iron[2] \ī-rən\ see IREN
ironment \īr-mənt\ see IREMENT
irp \ərp\ see URP
irpy \ər-pē\ chirpy • Euterpe
irque \ərk\ see ORK[1]
irr[1] \ir\ see EER[2]
irr[2] \ər\ see EUR[1]
irra \ir-ə\ see ERA[2]
irrah \ir-ə\ see ERA[2]
irrel[1] \ərl\ see IRL
irrel[2] \ər-əl\ see ERRAL
irrely \ər-lē\ see URLY
irrhous \ir-əs\ see EROUS
irring \ər-iŋ\ see URRING
irror \ir-ər\ see EARER[2]
irrup \ər-əp\ chirrup, stirrup, syrup • corn syrup, cough syrup • maple syrup
irrupy \ər-ə-pē\ chirrupy, syrupy
irrus \ir-əs\ see EROUS
irry \ər-ē\ see URRY
irs \irz\ see IERS
irse[1] \irs\ see IERCE
irse[2] \ərs\ see ERSE
irst \ərst\ see URST
irt \ərt\ see ERT[1]
irted \ərt-əd\ see ERTED
irter \ərt-ər\ see ERTER
irth \ərth\ berth, birth, dearth, earth, firth, girth, mirth, Perth, worth • childbirth, Farnsworth,

Fort Worth, give birth, on earth, rebirth, scorched-earth, self-worth, stillbirth, unearth, Woolworth, Wordsworth
• down-to-earth, pennyworth, Solway Firth, two cents' worth, virgin birth

irthless \ərth-ləs\ mirthless, worthless

irting \ərt-iŋ\ see ERTING

irtle \ərt-ᵊl\ see ERTILE

irtually \ərch-lē\ see URCHLY

irty \ərt-ē\ dirty, flirty, QWERTY, thirty

irus \ī-rəs\ Cyrus, iris, Iris, Skyros, virus • desirous, Osiris, papyrus • bearded iris, rhinovirus, rotavirus, West Nile virus

irv \ərv\ see ERVE

irving \ər-viŋ\ see ERVING

irwin \ər-wən\ see ERWIN

iry \īr-ē\ diary, eyrie, friary, miry, wiry • expiry, inquiry

is¹ \is\ see ISS

is² \iz\ see IZ¹

is³ \ē\ see EE¹

is⁴ \ēs\ see IECE

is⁵ \ish\ see ISH¹

i's \īz\ see IZE¹

isa \ē-zə\ see EZA

isable \ī-zə-bəl\ see IZABLE

isal¹ \ī-səl\ sisal • paradisal

isal² \ī-zəl\ Geisel, sisal • reprisal, revisal, surprisal • paradisal

isan \is-ᵊn\ see ISTEN

isbane \iz-bən\ see ISBON

isbon \iz-bən\ Brisbane, Lisbon

isc \isk\ see ISK

iscate \is-kət\ see ISKET

isce \is\ see ISS

iscean¹ \ī-sē-ən\ Piscean • Dionysian

iscean² \is-ē-ən\ see YSIAN¹

ische \ēsh\ see ICHE²

iscia \ish-ə\ see ITIA¹

iscible \is-ə-bəl\ see ISSIBLE

iscient \ish-ənt\ see ICIENT

isco \is-kō\ disco • Francisco • San Francisco

iscous \is-kəs\ see ISCUS

iscuit \is-kət\ see ISKET

iscus \is-kəs\ discus, viscous • hibiscus

ise¹ \ēs\ see IECE

ise² \ēz\ see EZE

ise³ \īs\ see ICE¹

ise⁴ \īz\ see IZE¹

ised¹ \īst\ see IST¹

ised² \īzd\ see IZED

isel \iz-əl\ see IZZLE

iseled \iz-əld\ see IZZLED

iseler \iz-lər\ see IZZLER

isement \īz-mənt\ chastisement, disguisement • advertisement, enfranchisement

iser \ī-zər\ see IZER

ish¹ \ish\ dish, fish, squish, swish, whish, wish • blindfish, blowfish, bluefish, bonefish, catfish, clownfish, codfish, cold fish, crawfish, crayfish, death wish, deep-dish, dogfish, finfish, flatfish, fly-fish, game fish, garfish, goldfish, goosefish, hagfish, hogfish, jewfish, kingfish, knish, lungfish, monkfish, moonfish, panfish, pipefish, redfish, rockfish, sailfish, sawfish, shellfish, side dish, spearfish, sport fish, starfish, sunfish, swordfish, toadfish, trash fish, whitefish • angelfish, anglerfish, bony fish, chafing dish, cuttlefish, flying fish, jellyfish, John Bullish, lionfish, needlefish, overfish, petri dish, pilot fish, puffer fish, silverfish • gefilte fish, kettle of fish, satellite dish, tropical fish, walking catfish

ish² \ēsh\ see ICHE²

isha \ish-ə\ see ITIA¹

isher \ish-ər\ fisher, fissure • kingfisher, well-wisher

ishi \ē-shē\ chichi • maharishi

ishing \ish-iŋ\ fly-fishing, sportfish-

ing, well-wishing
—also -ing *forms of verbs listed at*
ISH[1]
ishioner \ish-nər\ see ITIONER
ishna \ish-nə\ Krishna, Mishnah
ishnah \ish-nə\ see ISHNA
ishu \ish-ü\ see ISSUE[1]
ishy \ish-ē\ fishy, squishy, swishy
isi[1] \ē-zē\ see EASY[1]
isi[2] \ē-sē\ see EECY
isia \ē-zhə\ see ESIA[2]
isian[1] \izh-ən\ see ISION
isian[2] \ē-zhən\ see ESIAN[1]
isible \iz-ə-bəl\ risible, visible
• divisible, invisible • indivisible
isin \i-zən\ see ISON[2]
ising \ī-ziŋ\ see IZING
ision \izh-ən\ fission, vision • collision, concision, decision, derision,
division, elision, elysian, envision,
incision, Parisian, precision, pro-
vision, revision, Tunisian • cell
division, circumcision, Dionysian,
double vision, field of vision,
imprecision, indecision, long
division, short division, split
decision, subdivision, supervision,
television, tunnel vision
isional \izh-nəl\ divisional, provi-
sional
isis \ī-səs\ crisis, Isis • Dionysus,
midlife crisis
isit \iz-ət\ visit • exquisite, revisit
isite \iz-ət\ see ISIT
isitor \iz-ət-ər\ visitor • inquisitor
isive \ī-siv\ decisive, derisive, divi-
sive, incisive • indecisive
isk \isk\ bisque, brisk, disk, frisk,
risk, whisk • fly whisk, hard disk,
slipped disk • asterisk, basilisk,
compact disc, floppy disk, laser
disc, obelisk, optic disk • optical
disk, videodisc
isket \is-kət\ biscuit, brisket
iskey \is-kē\ see ISKY
iskie \is-kē\ see ISKY
isky \is-kē\ frisky, risky, whiskey

island \ī-lənd\ see IGHLAND
islander \ī-lən-dər\ see IGHLANDER
islands \ī-lənz\ see IGHLANDS
isle \īl\ see ILE[1]
isles \īlz\ see ILES
islet \ī-lət\ see ILOT
isling \iz-liŋ\ brisling, quisling
isly \iz-lē\ see IZZLY
ism \iz-əm\ ism, prism, schism
• abysm, ageism, autism, baptism,
bossism, Buddhism, charism,
cubism, czarism, dwarfism, fas-
cism, Maoism, Marxism, Nazism,
nudism, racism, sadism, sexism,
snobbism, Taoism, theism,
tourism, truism • activism,
alarmism, altruism, anarchism,
aneurysm, animism, aphorism,
archaism, atheism, barbarism,
botulism, Briticism, Calvinism,
careerism, Castroism, cataclysm,
catechism, chauvinism, classi-
cism, communism, criticism,
cynicism, Darwinism, defeatism,
despotism, dogmatism, dualism,
dynamism, egoism, egotism, elit-
ism, escapism, euphemism, exor-
cism, extremism, fatalism,
feminism, feudalism, fogyism,
formalism, futurism, globalism,
gnosticism, gradualism,
heathenism, Hebraism, hedonism,
Hellenism, heroism, Hinduism,
Hitlerism, humanism, hypnotism,
idealism, Islamism, jingoism,
journalism, John Bullism, Ju-
daism, legalism, Leninism, lyri-
cism, magnetism, mannerism,
masochism, mechanism, method-
ism, me-tooism, modernism,
monarchism, moralism, Mor-
monism, mysticism, narcissism,
nationalism, nepotism, nihilism,
NIMBYism, nomadism,
occultism, optimism, organism,
ostracism, pacifism, paganism,
pantheism, paroxysm, pessimism,

plagiarism, pointillism, populism, pragmatism, Quakerism, realism, rheumatism, satanism, Semitism, Shakerism, Shamanism, Shintoism, skepticism, socialism, solecism, solipsism, Southernism, spiritism, Stalinism, stoicism, syllogism, symbolism, terrorism, tribalism, unionism, urbanism, vandalism, veganism, vocalism, vulgarism, warlordism, witticism, Zionism • absenteeism, absolutism, Africanism, alcoholism, anachronism, Anglicanism, antagonism, astigmatism, athleticism, behaviorism, Big Brotherism, bilingualism, cannibalism, capitalism, Catholicism, commercialism, Confucianism, conservatism, consumerism, creationism, ecotourism, empiricism, ethnocentrism, evangelism, exoticism, expressionism, factionalism, fanaticism, favoritism, federalism, hooliganism, impressionism, infantilism, Keynesianism, liberalism, Lutheranism, McCarthyism, mercantilism, metabolism, militarism, minimalism, monasticism, monotheism, negativism, neo-Nazism, opportunism, pacificism, parallelism, paternalism, patriotism, perfectionism, photo-realism, postmodernism, primitivism, progressivism, protectionism, Protestantism, provincialism, puritanism, radicalism, rationalism, regionalism, revisionism, revivalism, romanticism, scholasticism, sectionalism, secularism, somnambulism, surrealism, ventriloquism • abolitionism, anti-Semitism, colloquialism, colonialism, hyperrealism, imperialism, isolationism, materialism, neoclassicism, orientalism, photojournalism, Postimpressionism,

professionalism, sensationalism, spiritualism, traditionalism, transcendentalism, universalism

ismal \iz-məl\ see YSMAL

isme¹ \īm\ see IME¹

isme² \izᵊm\ see ISM

isom \iz-əm\ see ISM

ison¹ \īs-ᵊn\ bison, Meissen, Tyson • streptomycin

ison² \iz-ᵊn\ prison, risen • arisen, imprison

isor \ī-zər\ see IZER

isory \īz-rē\ advisory • supervisory

isp \isp\ crisp, lisp, wisp • will-o-the-wisp

isper \is-pər\ crisper, lisper, whisper • stage whisper

ispy \is-pē\ crispy, wispy

isque \isk\ see ISK

iss \is\ bliss, Chris, dis, Dis, hiss, kiss, miss, sis, Swiss, this • abyss, amiss, can't-miss, dismiss, French kiss, near miss, remiss • ambergris, hit-and-miss, hit-or-miss, junior miss, reminisce

issa \is-ə\ abscissa, Larissa, Melissa

issable \is-ə-bəl\ see ISSIBLE

issal \is-əl\ see ISTLE

isse¹ \is\ see ISS

isse² \ēs\ see IECE

issed \ist\ see IST²

issel \is-əl\ see ISTLE

issible \is-ə-bəl\ kissable, miscible • admissible, municipal, omissible, permissible, transmissible • impermissible, inadmissible

issile \is-əl\ see ISTLE

ission¹ \ish-ən\ see ITION

ission² \izh-ən\ see ISION

issioner \ish-nər\ see ITIONER

issive \is-iv\ missive • derisive, dismissive, permissive, submissive, transmissive

issor \iz-ər\ scissor, whizzer

issue¹ \ish-ü\ issue, tissue • nonissue, reissue, scar tissue, take issue • Mogadishu

issue[2] \ish-ə\ see ITIA[1]

issure \ish-ər\ see ISHER

issus \is-əs\ missus, Mrs. • narcissus, Narcissus

issy \is-ē\ missy, prissy, sissy

ist[1] \īst\ Christ, heist • zeitgeist • Antichrist, poltergeist
—*also* -ed *forms of verbs listed at* ICE[1]

ist[2] \ist\ cyst, fist, gist, grist, list, Liszt, mist, schist, tryst, twist, whist, wrist • A-list, assist, blacklist, checklist, consist, desist, enlist, exist, hit list, insist, persist, playlist, resist, short list, subsist, untwist, wish list • coexist, exorcist • love-in-a-mist
—*also* -ed *forms of verbs listed at* ISS

ist[3] \ēst\ see EAST[1]

ista \ē-stə\ barista • fashionista, Sandinista • hasta la vista

istaed \is-təd\ see ISTED

istal \is-tᵊl\ Bristol, crystal, Crystal, pistil, pistol

istan \is-tən\ see ISTON

istance \is-təns\ see ISTENCE

istant \is-tənt\ see ISTENT

iste[1] \is-tē\ see ICITY[2]

iste[2] \ēst\ see EAST[1]

isted \is-təd\ closefisted, enlisted, hardfisted, limp-wristed, tight-fisted, two-fisted, unlisted • ironfisted, unassisted
—*also* -ed *forms of verbs listed at* IST[2]

istel \is-tᵊl\ see IST[2]

isten \is-ᵊn\ christen, glisten, listen

istence \is-təns\ distance • assistance, existence, insistence, long-distance, outdistance, persistence, resistance, subsistence • coexistence, go the distance, keep one's distance, nonexistence, shouting distance, striking distance • passive resistance, public assistance

istent \is-tənt\ distant • assistant,

consistent, insistent, persistent, resistant • equidistant, inconsistent, nonexistent

ister \is-tər\ blister, glister, lister, Lister, mister, sister, twister • half sister, resister, resistor, solicitor, stepsister, tongue twister, transistor • water blister

istery \is-trē\ see ISTORY

isthmus \is-məs\ see ISTMAS

isti \is-tē\ see ICITY[2]

istic \is-tik\ mystic • artistic, autistic, ballistic, fascistic, holistic, linguistic, logistic, sadistic, simplistic, sophistic, statistic, stylistic • altruistic, anarchistic, animistic, aphoristic, atavistic, atheistic, egoistic, egotistic, euphemistic, fatalistic, futuristic, hedonistic, humanistic, idealistic, inartistic, jingoistic, journalistic, legalistic, masochistic, modernistic, moralistic, narcissistic, nationalistic, nihilistic, optimistic, pessimistic, realistic, unrealistic • anachronistic, antagonistic, cannibalistic, capitalistic, characteristic, impressionistic, militaristic, opportunistic, paternalistic, propagandistic • imperialistic, materialistic

istical \is-ti-kəl\ mystical • logistical, statistical • egotistical

istich \is-tik\ see ISTIC

istics \is-tiks\ ballistics, linguistics, statistics • vital statistics
—*also* -s, -'s, *and* -s' *forms of nouns listed at* ISTIC

istie \is-tē\ see ICITY[2]

istil \is-tᵊl\ see ISTAL

istin \is-tən\ see ISTON

istine \is-tən\ see ISTON

istle \is-əl\ bristle, gristle, missal, missile, thistle, whistle • bull thistle, cruise missile, dismissal, epistle, globe thistle, wolf whistle • blow the whistle, guided missile, wet one's whistle • ballistic missile

istler \is-lər\ whistler, Whistler

istly \is-lē\ bristly, gristly, thistly
• sweet cicely

istmas \is-məs\ Christmas, isthmus

isto \is-tō\ Christo • Callisto

istol \is-tᵊl\ see ISTAL

iston \is-tən\ Kristin, piston, Tristan

istor \is-tər\ see ISTER

istory \is-trē\ history, mystery • life history, prehistory • ancient history, natural history, oral history

isty \is-tē\ see ICITY²

isus \ī-səs\ see ISIS

iszt \ist\ see IST²

it¹ \it\ bit, Brit, chit, fit, flit, git, grit, hit, it, kit, knit, lit, mitt, nit, pit, quit, sit, skit, slit, snit, spit, split, twit, whit, wit, writ, zit • a bit, acquit, admit, armpit, base hit, befit, bowsprit, Brigitte, catch it, close-knit, cockpit, commit, cool it, culprit, cut it, dimwit, dog it, emit, firelit, gaslit, get it, gill slit, half-wit, hard-hit, house-sit, legit, make it, mess kit, misfit, moonlit, mosh pit, nitwit, nut-hit, obit, omit, outfit, outwit, owe it, permit, pinch-hit, press kit, pulpit, refit, remit, rough it, sandpit, Sanskrit, starlit, submit, sunlit, switch-hit, tar pit, tidbit, tight-knit, to wit, transmit, twilit, two-bit, unfit, watch it, well-knit, with-it • babysit, benefit, bit-by-bit, cable-knit, candlelit, come off it, counterfeit, double knit, get with it, hissy fit, holy writ, hypocrite, infield hit, megahit, out of it, put to it, recommit, retrofit, step on it • banana split, bully pulpit, extra-base hit, fringe benefit, lickety-split, overcommit, sacrifice hit • jack-in-the-pulpit

it² \ē\ see EE¹

it³ \ēt\ see EAT¹

ita \ēt-ə\ cheetah, Nita, pita, Rita
• Anita, Bonita, bonito, fajita, gordita, Granita, Juanita, Lolita • senhorita, señorita • Bhagavad Gita

itable¹ \īt-ə-bəl\ citable, writable • excitable, ignitable, indictable • copyrightable, extraditable

itable² \it-ə-bəl\ see ITTABLE

itae \īt-ē\ see ITE²

itain \it-n\ see ITTEN

ital¹ \īt-ᵊl\ title, vital • entitle, recital, requital, subtitle

ital² \it-ᵊl\ see ITTLE

italist \īt-ᵊl-əst\ titlist • recitalist

itan \īt-ᵊn\ see IGHTEN

itany \it-ᵊn-ē\ Brittany, litany

itch \ich\ ditch, glitch, hitch, itch, kitsch, niche, pitch, rich, snitch, stitch, such, switch, twitch, which, witch • backstitch, bewitch, Bowditch, chain stitch, clove hitch, cross-stitch, enrich, fast-pitch, half hitch, jock itch, last-ditch, purl stitch, slow-pitch, topstitch, unhitch, whipstitch, wild pitch • bait and switch, czarevitch, featherstitch, fever pitch, perfect pitch, timber hitch, toggle switch • absolute pitch

itcher \ich-ər\ pitcher, richer, snitcher, stitcher, switcher

itchery \ich-ə-rē\ witchery • obituary

itches \ich-əz\ britches, riches • in stitches • Dutchman's-breeches
—also -s, -'s, and -s' forms of nouns and -s forms of verbs listed at ITCH

itchman \ich-mən\ pitchman, switchman

itchment \ich-mənt\ bewitchment, enrichment • self-enrichment

itchy \ich-ē\ glitchy, itchy, pitchy, twitchy, witchy

it'd \it-əd\ see ITTED

ite¹ \īt\ bight, bite, blight, bright, byte, cite, Dwight, fight, flight, fright, height, kite, knight, light, lite, might, mite, night, plight, quite, right, rite, sight, site, sleight, slight, smite, spite, sprite, Sprite, tight, trite, white, Wright, write • affright, airtight, Albright, alight, all right, all-night, aright, backbite, backlight, bauxite, birthright, black light, bobwhite, bombsight, box kite, bullfight, calcite, campsite, catfight, cockfight, contrite, cordite, daylight, delight, despite, dogfight, downright, dust mite, earthlight, excite, eyesight, fanlight, finite, firefight, firelight, first night, fistfight, flashlight, fleabite, floodlight, foresight, forthright, fortnight, frostbite, gall mite, gaslight, ghostwrite, graphite, green light, gunfight, Gunite, half-light, handwrite, headlight, highlight, hindsight, Hittite, homesite, hoplite, ignite, in-flight, incite, indict, insight, in sight, invite, klieg light, lamplight, Levite, lignite, limelight, Lucite, Luddite, midnight, moonlight, night-light, off-site, off-white, on sight, on-site, outright, penlight, playwright, polite, preflight, prizefight, pyrite, quartzite, recite, red light, requite, rewrite, searchlight, Semite, Shiite, shipwright, sidelight, sit tight, skintight, skylight, skywrite, snakebite, snow-white, sound bite, spaceflight, spotlight, stage fright, starlight, stoplight, streetlight, sunlight, Sunnite, taillight, termite, tonight, top-flight, torchlight, Twelfth Night, twilight, twinight, typewrite, unite, upright, uptight, Web site, weeknight, wheelwright, zinc white • acolyte, Ammonite, anchorite, anthracite, antiwhite, apartheid, appetite, Bakelite, bedlamite, bipartite, black-and-white, bring to light, Brooklynite, Canaanite, candlelight, Carmelite, cellulite, chestnut blight, Chinese white, copyright, disunite, divine right, dolomite, dynamite, erudite, expedite, extradite, Fahrenheit, featherlight, fight-or-flight, fly-by-night, gesundheit, gigabyte, Hashemite, Hitlerite, Houstonite, impolite, inner light, Isle of Wight, Israelite, Jacobite, Jerseyite, kilobyte, leading light, Leninite, leukocyte, lily-white, line of sight, lymphocyte, magnetite, malachite, Masonite, megabyte, Mennonite, Mr. Right, Muscovite, neophyte, out-of-sight, overbite, overflight, overnight, oversight, parasite, patent right, pilot light, plebiscite, recondite, reunite, running light, satellite, second sight, see the light, serve one right, socialite, speed of light, stalactite, stalagmite, Sydneyite, traffic light, transvestite, tripartite, troglodyte, ultralight, underwrite, urbanite, water sprite, watertight • anti-Semite, cosmopolite, electrolyte, exurbanite, go fly a kite, hermaphrodite, meteorite, Michiganite, multipartite, New Hampshirite, New Jerseyite, potato blight, property right, suburbanite, sweetness and light, Turkish delight, Wyomingite • Great Australian Bight, Pre-Raphaelite

ite² \īt-ē\ flighty, mighty, nightie • almighty, Almighty • Aphrodite, arborvitae, high and mighty

ite³ \it\ see IT¹

ite⁴ \ēt\ see EAT¹

ited \īt-əd\ see IGHTED

iteful \īt-fəl\ see IGHTFUL

itely \īt-lē\ see IGHTLY

item \īt-əm\ item • line-item • ad
infinitum, collector's item
itement \īt-mənt\ excitement,
incitement, indictment
iten \īt-ᵊn\ see IGHTEN
itener \īt-nər\ see IGHTENER
iteor \ēt-ē-ər\ see ETEOR
iter¹ \īt-ər\ biter, fighter, lighter,
miter, writer • all-nighter, back-
biter, bullfighter, dogfighter,
firefighter, ghostwriter,
gunfighter, highlighter, igniter,
inciter, lamplighter, moonlighter,
nail-biter, prizefighter, rewriter,
screenwriter, scriptwriter, sky-
writer, songwriter, speechwriter,
sportswriter, street fighter, type-
writer • candlelighter, copywriter,
fly-by-nighter, freedom fighter,
underwriter
—also -er forms of adjectives listed
at ITE¹
iter² \it-ər\ see ITTER
iter³ \ēt-ər\ see EATER¹
iterally \it-ər-lē\ see ITTERLY
ites \īts\ see IGHTS
itey \īt-ē\ see ITE⁷
ith¹ \ith\ fifth, kith, myth, pith,
smith, Smith, with • bear with,
blacksmith, do with, forthwith,
goldsmith, Goldsmith, go with,
gunsmith, herewith, hold with,
live with, locksmith, run with,
tinsmith • be friends with, come
out with, come up with, complete
with, coppersmith, dispense with,
fall in with, Granny Smith, have
done with, make off with, mega-
lith, monolith, put up with,
reckon with, run off with, silver-
smith, take up with, walk off with
• come to grips with, do away
with, get away with, get even
with, have to do with, make away
with, run away with, wipe the
floor with
ith² \ēt\ see EAT¹

ith³ \ēth\ see EATH¹
ithe¹ \īth\ blithe, lithe, scythe,
tithe, writhe
ithe² \ith\ see ITH²
ithe³ \ith\ see ITH¹
ither \ith-ər\ dither, hither, slither,
thither, whither, wither, zither
• come-hither
ithy \ith-ē\ pithy, smithy
iti \ēt-ē\ see EATY
itia¹ \ish-ə\ Alicia, Letitia, militia,
Patricia, Phoenicia • Dionysia
itia² \ē-shə\ see ESIA¹
itial \ish-əl\ see ICIAL
itian¹ \ish-ən\ see ITION
itian² \ē-shən\ see ETION¹
itiate \ish-ət\ initiate, novitiate
itic \it-ik\ critic • arthritic, granitic,
Semitic • analytic, catalytic, dyna-
mitic, paralytic, parasitic,
sybaritic • anti-Semitic, hermaph-
roditic
itical \it-i-kəl\ critical • political,
uncritical • analytical • geopoliti-
cal
itid \it-əd\ see ITTED
itimati \is-məs\ see ISTMAS
itin \it-ᵊn\ see ITTEN
iting \īt-iŋ\ biting, lighting, writing
• backbiting, bullfighting, cock-
fighting, exciting, handwriting,
infighting, inviting, nail-biting,
newswriting, playwriting, prize-
fighting, skywriting, songwriting,
typewriting
—also -ing forms of verbs listed at
ITE¹
ition \ish-ən\ fission, mission, Ti-
tian • addition, admission, ambi-
tion, attrition, audition,
beautician, clinician, cognition,
commission, condition, contri-
tion, dentition, edition, emission,
fruition, ignition, logician, magi-
cian, mortician, munition, musi-
cian, nutrition, omission,
optician, partition, patrician,

perdition, permission, petition, Phoenician, physician, position, remission, rendition, sedition, submission, suspicion, tactician, technician, tradition, transition, transmission, tuition, volition • abolition, acoustician, acquisition, admonition, air-condition, ammunition, apparition, coalition, competition, composition, decommission, definition, demolition, deposition, dietitian, Dionysian, disposition, disquisition, electrician, erudition, exhibition, expedition, exposition, extradition, imposition, in addition, inhibition, inquisition, intermission, intuition, malnutrition, mathematician, obstetrician, on commission, opposition, politician, precondition, premonition, preposition, prohibition, proposition, recognition, recondition, repetition, requisition, rescue mission, rhetorician, statistician, superstition, supposition, transposition • decomposition, dental technician, family physician, fetal position, general admission, high-definition, indisposition, juxtaposition, lotus position, open admission, out of commission, pediatrician, pocket edition, redefinition, theoretician

itional \ish-nəl\ additional, conditional, nutritional, traditional, transitional • definitional, prepositional, unconditional

itioner \i-shə-nər\ commissioner, conditioner, parishioner, petitioner, practitioner • air conditioner, nurse-practitioner • family practitioner, general practitioner

itionist \i-shə-nəst\ nutritionist • abolitionist, demolitionist, exhibitionist, prohibitionist

itious \ish-əs\ see ICIOUS¹

itis \īt-əs\ Titus • arthritis, bronchitis, bursitis, colitis, detritus, gastritis, mastitis, nephritis, neuritis, phlebitis, tinnitus • cellulitis, dermatitis, gingivitis, hepatitis, laryngitis, meningitis, sinusitis, tonsillitis, tendinitis • appendicitis, conjunctivitis, encephalitis, endocarditis, peritonitis

itish \it-ish\ British, skittish

itius \ish-əs\ see ICIOUS¹

itle \īt-ᵊl\ see ITAL¹

it'll \it-ᵊl\ see ITTLE

itness \it-nəs\ fitness, witness • eyewitness, unfitness • character witness, Jehovah's Witness

itney \it-nē\ jitney, Whitney • Mount Whitney

ito¹ \ēt-ō\ Quito, Tito, veto • bandito, bonito, burrito, graffito, mosquito • Akihito, Hirohito, incognito, pocket veto • line-item veto

ito² \ēt-ə\ see ITA

iton¹ \it-ᵊn\ see ITTEN

iton² \īt-ᵊn\ see IGHTEN

its \its\ blitz, ditz, fritz, Fritz, glitz, grits, its, it's, quits, Ritz, spitz • Auschwitz, Berlitz, kibitz, Saint Kitts • Clausewitz, Horowitz, Saint Moritz • hominy grits —*also* -s, -'s, *and* -s' *forms of nouns and* -s *forms of verbs listed at* IT¹

it's \its\ see ITS

itsch \ich\ see ITCH

itschy \ich-ē\ see ITCHY

itsy \it-sē\ see ITZY

itt \it\ see IT¹

ittable \it-ə-bəl\ habitable, hospitable, transmittable • inhospitable

ittal \it-ᵊl\ see ITTLE

ittance \it-ᵊns\ pittance • admittance, remittance

ittany \it-ᵊn-ē\ see ITANY

itte \it\ see IT¹

itted \it-əd\ fitted, it'd, pitted • committed, dim-witted, half-witted, quick-witted, sharp-witted, slow-witted, thick-witted, unfitted • uncommitted
—also -ed *forms of verbs listed at* IT[1]

ittee \it-ē\ see ITTY

itten \it-ᵊn\ bitten, Britain, Briton, kitten, Lytton, mitten, smitten, written • flea-bitten, Great Britain, hard-bitten, rewritten, unwritten

ittence \it-ᵊns\ see ITTANCE

itter \it-ər\ bitter, critter, fitter, flitter, fritter, glitter, hitter, litter, quitter, sitter, skitter, titter, twitter • aglitter, atwitter, embitter, emitter, fence-sitter, hairsplitter, house sitter, no-hitter, outfitter, pinch hitter, pipe fitter, railsplitter, switch-hitter, transmitter • babysitter, counterfeiter, heavy hitter • neurotransmitter

itterer \it-ər-ər\ fritterer, litterer

itterly \it-ər-lē\ bitterly, literally

ittery \it-ə-rē\ glittery, jittery, skittery, twittery

ittie \it-ē\ see ITTY

ittier \it-ē-ər\ Whittier
—also-er *forms of adjectives listed at* ITTY

ittiness \it-ē-nəs\ grittiness, prettiness, wittiness

itting[1] \it-iŋ\ fitting, knitting, pitting, sitting, splitting, witting • befitting, earsplitting, fence-sitting, formfitting, hairsplitting, hard-hitting, house-sitting, pipe fitting, sidesplitting, unfitting, unwitting • unremitting
—also -ing *forms of verbs listed at* IT[1]

itting[2] \it-ᵊn\ see ITTEN

ittish \it-ish\ see ITISH

ittle \it-ᵊl\ brittle, it'll, little, spittle, victual, whittle • acquittal, a little, belittle, committal, hospital, lickspittle, transmittal • Chicken Little, noncommittal • little by little

ittol \it-ᵊl\ see ITTLE

ittor \it-ər\ see ITTER

itts \its\ see ITS

itty \it-ē\ bitty, city, ditty, gritty, kitty, Kitty, pity, pretty, witty • committee, Dodge City, self-pity, Sioux City • Carson City, central city, Hello Kitty, holy city, itty-bitty, Kansas City, megacity, New York City, nitty-gritty, Quezon City, Rapid City, Salt Lake City, subcommittee • Atlantic City, Ho Chi Minh City, Long Island City, Mexico City, Panama City, Vatican City

itual \ich-ə-wəl\ ritual • habitual

ituary \ich-ə-rē\ see ITCHERY

itum \īt-əm\ see ITEM

itus \īt-əs\ see ITIS

ity[1] \it-ē\ see ITTY

ity[2] \īt-ē\ see ITE[2]

itz \its\ see ITS

itzi \it-sē\ see ITZY

itzy \it-sē\ bitsy, ditzy, glitzy, Mitzi, ritzy

iu \ü\ see EW[1]

ius[1] \ē-əs\ see EUS[1]

ius[2] \ī-əs\ see IAS[1]

iv[1] \iv\ see IVE[2]

iv[2] \ēf\ see IEF[1]

iv[3] \if\ see IFF

iv[4] \ēv\ see EAVE[1]

iva[1] \ī-və\ Godiva, saliva

iva[2] \ē-və\ diva, Eva, kiva, Neva, Shiva, viva • Geneva, yeshiva

ivable[1] \ī-və-bəl\ drivable • derivable, survivable

ivable[2] \iv-ə-bəl\ livable • forgivable

ival \ī-vəl\ rival • archival, archrival, arrival, revival, survival • adjectival

ivalent \iv-ə-lənt\ ambivalent, equivalent

ivan \iv-ən\ see IVEN
ivance \ī-vəns\ connivance, contrivance
ive[1] \īv\ chive, Clive, dive, drive, five, hive, I've, jive, live, strive, thrive • alive, archive, arrive, beehive, connive, contrive, crash-dive, deprive, derive, disk drive, endive, hard drive, high five, high-five, line drive, nosedive, revive, skin-dive, skydive, survive, swan dive, take five, test-drive • eat alive, forty-five, four-wheel drive, hyperdrive, overdrive, power-dive, scuba dive
ive[2] \iv\ give, live, sieve • forgive, outlive, relive
ive[3] \ēv\ see EAVE[1]
ivel \iv-əl\ civil, drivel, shrivel, snivel, swivel • uncivil
iven \iv-ən\ driven, given, riven, striven • forgiven
iver[1] \ī-vər\ diver, driver, fiver, striver • cabdriver, pile driver, screwdriver, skin diver, skydiver, slave driver, survivor
iver[2] \iv-ər\ flivver, giver, liver, quiver, river, shiver, sliver • almsgiver, caregiver, chopped liver, deliver, downriver, East River, Fall River, lawgiver, upriver • up the river • Indian River, sell down the river
ivers \ī-vərz\ divers
—also -s, -'s, and -s' forms of nouns listed at IVER[1]
ivery \iv-rē\ livery, shivery • delivery • general delivery, special delivery
ives \īvz\ fives, hives, Ives
—also -s, -'s, and -s' forms of nouns and -s forms of verbs listed at IVE[1]
ivet \iv-ət\ civet, divot, pivot, privet, rivet, trivet
ivi \iv-ē\ see IVVY
ivia \iv-ē-ə\ trivia • Bolivia, Olivia

ivial \iv-ē-əl\ trivial • convivial
ivid \iv-əd\ livid, vivid
ivil \iv-əl\ see IVEL
iving \iv-iŋ\ giving, living • almsgiving, caregiving, forgiving, free-living, life-giving, misgiving, thanksgiving • cost of living, unforgiving • assisted living, standard of living
—also -ing forms of verbs listed at IVE[2]
ivion \iv-ē-ən\ Vivian • Bolivian, oblivion
ivious \iv-ē-əs\ lascivious, oblivious
ivir \iv-ər\ see IVER[2]
ivity \iv-ət-ē\ activity, captivity, festivity, nativity, passivity, proclivity • conductivity, connectivity, creativity, inactivity, inclusivity, negativity, objectivity, productivity, relativity, selectivity, sensitivity, subjectivity • hyperactivity, insensitivity, overactivity • radioactivity
ivol \iv-əl\ see IVEL
ivor \ī-vər\ see IVER[1]
ivorous \iv-rəs\ carnivorous, herbivorous, omnivorous • insectivorous
ivot \iv-ət\ see IVET
ivus \ē-vəs\ see EVOUS
ivver \iv-ər\ see IVER[2]
ivvy \iv-ē\ chivy, divvy, Livy, privy, skivvy
ivy \iv-ē\ see IVVY
iwi \ē-wē\ see EEWEE
ix[1] \iks\ fix, mix, nix, six, Styx • affix, deep-six, prefix, premix, prix fixe, prolix, suffix, trail mix, transfix • cicatrix, crucifix, intermix, politics • geopolitics
—also -s, -'s, and -s' forms of nouns and -s forms of verbs listed at ICK
ix[2] \ē\ see EE[1]
ixe[1] \iks\ see IX[1]
ixe[2] \ēsh\ see ICHE[2]

ixed \ikst\ fixed, mixed, twixt
• betwixt, well-fixed
—*also* -ed *forms of verbs listed at*
IX[1]
ixen \ik-sən\ Nixon • Mason-Dixon
ixer \ik-sər\ fixer, mixer • elixir
ixie \ik-sē\ Dixie, pixie, tricksy
ixion \ik-shən\ see ICTION
ixir \ik-sər\ see IXER
ixon \ik-sən\ see IXEN
ixt \ikst\ see IXED
ixture \iks-chər\ fixture, mixture
• intermixture
iya \ē-ə\ see IA[1]
iyeh \ē-ə\ see IA[1]
iz[1] \iz\ biz, fizz, frizz, his, is, Ms.,
quiz, 'tis, whiz, wiz • gee-whiz,
pop quiz, show biz
iz[2] \ēz\ see EZE
iza[1] \ē-zə\ see EZA
iza[2] \ē-thə\ see ETHA
izable \ī-zə-bəl\ sizable • advisable
• analyzable, inadvisable, localiz-
able, recognizable
izar \ī-zər\ see IZER
izard \iz-ərd\ blizzard, gizzard,
lizard, wizard
ize[1] \īz\ guise, prize, rise, size, wise
• advise, apprise, arise, baptize,
bite-size, capsize, chastise, clock-
wise, comprise, crabwise, cross-
wise, demise, despise, devise,
disguise, door prize, downsize,
edgewise, endwise, excise, fran-
chise, full-size, high-rise, incise,
king-size, leastwise, lengthwise,
life-size, likewise, low-rise, man-
size, mid-rise, midsize, moonrise,
outsize, pint-size, queen-size,
revise, slantwise, streetwise, styl-
ize, suffice, sunrise, surmise,
surprise, twin-size, unwise • ad-
vertise, aggrandize, agonize,
amortize, analyze, atomize, au-
thorize, balkanize, booby prize,
bowdlerize, brutalize, burglarize,
canonize, capsulize, caramelize,

catalyze, catechize, cauterize,
centralize, Christianize, circum-
cise, civilize, colonize, colorize,
compromise, concertize, criticize,
crystalize, customize, demonize,
deputize, digitize, dramatize,
empathize, emphasize, energize,
enterprise, equalize, eulogize,
exercise, exorcise, fantasize,
feminize, fertilize, finalize, for-
malize, galvanize, ghettoize, glam-
orize, globalize, harmonize,
humanize, hypnotize, idolize,
immunize, improvise, itemize,
jeopardize, legalize, lionize, liq-
uidize, localize, magnetize, maxi-
mize, mechanize, memorize,
merchandise, mesmerize, mini-
mize, mobilize, modernize, mois-
turize, monetize, moralize,
motorize, neutralize, Nobel Prize,
normalize, notarize, novelize,
optimize, organize, ostracize,
otherwise, oversize, oxidize, paradise, paralyze, pasteurize, patron-
ize, penalize, penny-wise,
personalize, plagiarize, pluralize,
pocket-size, polarize, pressurize,
privatize, publicize, pulverize,
rationalize, realize, recognize,
rhapsodize, robotize, sanitize,
satirize, scandalize, scrutinize,
sensitize, sermonize, slenderize,
socialize, solemnize, specialize,
stabilize, standardize, sterilize,
stigmatize, strategize, subsidize,
summarize, supervise, symbolize,
sympathize, synchronize, synthe-
size, systemize, tantalize, televise,
tenderize, terrorize, theorize,
tranquilize, traumatize, tyrannize,
unionize, urbanize, utilize, van-
dalize, vaporize, verbalize, victim-
ize, vocalize, vulcanize, vulgarize,
weather-wise, weatherize, west-
ernize, winterize, worldly-wise
• accessorize, acclimatize,

Africanize, alphabetize, anes-
thetize, antagonize, anticlockwise,
apologize, cannibalize, capitalize,
categorize, characterize, comput-
erize, contrariwise, counterclock-
wise, criminalize, cut down to
size, decentralize, de-emphasize,
deglamorize, dehumanize, demag-
netize, democratize, demoralize,
deodorize, depressurize, desensi-
tize, disenfranchise, economize,
epitomize, evangelize, familiarize,
fictionalize, floor exercise, free
enterprise, generalize, homoge-
nize, hospitalize, hypothesize,
idealize, immobilize, immortalize,
infantilize, internalize, italicize,
legitimize, liberalize, marginalize,
metabolize, metastasize, milita-
rize, monopolize, nationalize,
naturalize, philosophize, politi-
cize, popularize, prioritize, prose-
lytize, Pulitzer prize, regularize,
reorganize, revitalize, romanti-
cize, systematize, trivialize,
visualize • Americanize, com-
partmentalize, consolation prize,
decriminalize, departmentalize,
individualize, industrialize, inter-
nationalize, legitimatize, material-
ize, memorialize, miniaturize,
private enterprise, professionalize,
psychoanalyze, revolutionize,
sensationalize, underutilize, uni-
versalize • editorialize, intellectu-
alize
—*also* -s, -'s, *and* -s' *forms of*
nouns and -s *forms of verbs listed*
at Y[1]
ize[2] \ēz\ see EZE
ized \īzd\ sized • advised, king-
sized, outsized, pearlized, queen-
sized • ill-advised, organized,

Sanforized, unadvised, under-
sized, well-advised • elasticized
—*also* -ed *forms of verbs listed at*
IZE[1]
izen[1] \īz-ᵊn\ bison • horizon
izen[2] \iz-ᵊn\ see ISON[2]
izer \ī-zər\ Dreiser, geyser, kaiser,
miser, riser, visor • adviser, divi-
sor, incisor • advertiser, appetizer,
atomizer, compromiser, ener-
gizer, equalizer, exerciser, fertil-
izer, improviser, modernizer,
moisturizer, moralizer, organizer,
pollenizer, pressurizer, stabilizer,
sterilizer, supervisor, sympathizer,
synthesizer, tenderizer, tranquil-
izer, vaporizer • popularizer,
proselytizer
izing \ī-ziŋ\ rising, sizing • uprising
• advertising, agonizing, appetiz-
ing, enterprising, merchandising,
unsurprising • self-sacrificing,
unappetizing, uncompromising
—*also* -ing *forms of verbs listed at*
IZE[1]
izo \ē-zō\ sleazo • mestizo
izon \īz-ᵊn\ see IZEN[1]
izy \it-sē\ see ITZY
izz \iz\ see IZ[1]
izzard \iz-ərd\ see IZARD
izzen \iz-ᵊn\ see ISON[2]
izzer \iz-ər\ see ISSOR
izzical \iz-i-kəl\ see YSICAL
izzie \i-zē\ see IZZY
izzle \iz-əl\ chisel, drizzle, fizzle,
grizzle, sizzle • cold chisel
izzled \iz-əld\ chiseled, grizzled
—*also* -ed *forms of verbs listed at*
IZZLE
izzler \iz-lər\ chiseler, sizzler
izzly \iz-lē\ drizzly, grisly, grizzly
izzy \iz-ē\ busy, dizzy, fizzy, frizzy,
tizzy • tin lizzie

O

o¹ \ü\ see EW¹

o² \ō\ see OW¹

oa¹ \ō-ə\ boa, Goa, Noah, Shoah • aloha, Balboa, Samoa • Krakatoa, Mauna Loa, Mount Gilboa, Shenandoah

oa² \ō\ see OW¹

oable \ü-ə-bəl\ see UABLE

oach \ōch\ broach, brooch, coach, poach, roach • approach, cockroach, encroach, reproach, stagecoach

oachable \ō-chə-bəl\ coachable • approachable • irreproachable, unapproachable

oacher \ō-chər\ cloture, poacher

oad¹ \ōd\ see ODE

oad² \òd\ see AUD¹

oader \ōd-ər\ see ODER

oadie \ōd-ē\ see ODY²

oady \ōd-ē\ see ODY²

oaf \ōf\ loaf, oaf • meat loaf • sugarloaf

oafer \ō-fər\ see OFER

oagie \ō-gē\ see OGIE

oah \ō-ə\ see OA¹

oak \ōk\ see OKE¹

oaken \ō-kən\ see OKEN

oaker \ō-kər\ see OKER

oaky \ō-kē\ see OKY

oal \ōl\ see OLE¹

oalie \ō-lē\ see OLY¹

oam \ōm\ see OME¹

oamer \ō-mər\ see OMER¹

oaming \ō-miŋ\ gloaming • Wyoming
—also -ing forms of verbs listed at OME¹

oamy \ō-mē\ foamy, homey, loamy, show-me • Naomi, Salome

oan¹ \ō-ən\ Owen, roan • Minoan, Samoan • Idahoan, protozoan • strawberry roan

oan² \ōn\ see ONE¹

oaner \ō-nər\ see ONER¹

oaning \ō-niŋ\ see ONING²

oap \ōp\ see OPE

oaper \ō-pər\ see OPER

oapy \ō-pē\ see OPI

oar \òr\ see OR¹

oard \òrd\ board, bored, chord, cord, floored, ford, Ford, gourd, hoard, horde, lord, Lord, oared, sword, toward, ward, Ward • aboard, accord, afford, award, backboard, baseboard, billboard, blackboard, breadboard, broadsword, cardboard, chalkboard, chessboard, clapboard, clipboard, concord, dart board, dashboard, discord, draft board, fjord, floorboard, headboard, inkboard, keyboard, kickboard, landlord, lapboard, nerve cord, onboard, on board, outboard, pasteboard, Peg-Board, rearward, record, reward, scoreboard, shipboard, signboard, skateboard, slumlord, snowboard, soundboard, splashboard, springboard, surfboard, switchboard, untoward, wallboard, warlord, washboard, whiteboard, whipcord • aboveboard, bottle gourd, bungee cord, centerboard, checkerboard, circuit board, clavichord, cutting board, diving board, drawing board, emery board, fiberboard, fingerboard, harpsichord, mortarboard, motherboard, overboard, overlord, paddleboard, plasterboard, room and board, sandwich board, shuffleboard, smorgasbord, sounding board, spinal cord, tape-record, teeterboard, untoward • across-the-board, bulletin board, extension cord, go by the board, ironing board, off-the-record, on-the-record, out of one's gourd, particleboard • Federal Reserve Board, platinum record • Academy Award

—also -ed forms of verbs listed at OR[1]

oarder \òrd-ər\ *see* ORDER
oarding \òrd-iŋ\ *see* ORDING[1]
oared \òrd\ *see* OARD
oarer \òr-ər\ *see* ORER
oaring \òr-iŋ\ *see* ORING
oarious \òr-ē-əs\ *see* ORIOUS
oarse \òrs\ *see* ORSE[1]
oarsman \òrz-mən\ oarsman • outdoorsman
oart \òrt\ *see* ORT[1]
oary \òr-ē\ *see* ORY
oast \ōst\ *see* OST[2]
oastal \ōs-t³l\ *see* OSTAL[1]
oaster \ō-stər\ coaster, poster, roaster, toaster • four-poster • roller-coaster, roller coaster
oat \ōt\ bloat, boat, coat, dote, float, gloat, goat, moat, mote, note, oat, quote, rote, smote, throat, tote, vote, wrote • afloat, airboat, banknote, catboat, C-note, compote, connote, coyote, cutthroat, demote, denote, devote, dovecote, dreamboat, eighth note, emote, fireboat, flatboat, footnote, frock coat, grace note, greatcoat, gunboat, half note, houseboat, housecoat, iceboat, keynote, lab coat, lifeboat, longboat, promote, rewrote, rowboat, sailboat, sauceboat, scapegoat, seed coat, sheepcote, showboat, sore throat, speedboat, steamboat, straw vote, strep throat, Sukkoth, surfboat, topcoat, towboat, trench coat, tugboat, turncoat, U-boat, unquote, wainscot, whaleboat, whole note • anecdote, antidote, assault boat, billy goat, cashmere goat, creosote, dead man's float, ferryboat, flying boat, jolly boat, miss the boat, motorboat, mountain goat, nanny goat, overcoat, paddleboat, petticoat, polo coat, powerboat, PT boat, quarter note, riverboat, rock the boat, sixteenth note, sticky note, sugarcoat, Terre Haute, undercoat, yellowthroat • Angora goat, in the same boat, lump in one's throat, torpedo boat, treasury note
oate \ō-ət\ *see* OET
oated \ōt-əd\ bloated, coated, noted, throated • devoted
—also -ed forms of verbs listed at OAT
oaten \ōt-³n\ *see* OTON
oater \ōt-ər\ boater, motor, rotor, voter • keynoter, promoter, showboater • outboard motor
oath \ōth\ *see* OWTH
oathe \ōth\ *see* OTHE
oathing \ō-thiĭ\ *see* OTHING
oating \ōt-iŋ\ coating, floating • free-floating, iceboating, sailboating, speedboating, wainscoting • motorboating, powerboating, undercoating, *—also -ing forms of verbs listed at* OAT
oaty \ōt-ē\ *see* OTE[1]
oax \ōks\ coax, hoax
—also -s, -'s, and -s' forms of nouns and -s forms of verbs listed at OKE[1]
ob[1] \äb\ blob, bob, Bob, cob, daub, fob, glob, gob, job, knob, lob, mob, nob, rob, Saab, slob, snob, sob, squab, swab, throb • corn-

cob, day job, doorknob, heart-
throb, hobnob, kebab, macabre,
Punjab, snow job • shish kebab
• thingamabob
ob[2] \ŏb\ see OBE[1]
oba \ō-bə\ jojoba • Manitoba
• Lake Manitoba
obably \äb-lē\ see OBBLY
obal \ō-bəl\ see OBLE
obar \ō-bər\ see OBER
obber \äb-ər\ bobber, clobber,
robber, slobber • hobnobber
obbery \äb-rē\ robbery, slobbery,
snobbery • highway robbery
obbie \äb-ē\ see OBBY
obbin \äb-ən\ see OBIN
obble \äb-əl\ see ABBLE[1]
obbler \äb-lər\ cobbler, gobbler
obbly \äb-lē\ probably, wobbly
obby \äb-ē\ Bobbie, Bobby,
globby, hobby, knobby, lobby,
slobby, snobby • kohlrabi, Pun-
jabi • Abu Dhabi, Hammurabi
obe[1] \ōb\ globe, Job, lobe, probe,
robe, strobe • bathrobe, disrobe,
earlobe, enrobe, lap robe, mi-
crobe, wardrobe • claustrophobe,
frontal lobe, optic lobe, techno-
phobe, xenophobe • computer-
phobe, election probe, temporal
lobe • occipital lobe
obe[2] \ō-bē\ see OBY
obeah \ō-bē-ə\ see OBIA
obee \ō-bē\ see OBY
ober \ō-bər\ sober • October
obi \ō-bē\ see OBY
obia \ō-bē-ə\ phobia • Zenobia
• acrophobia, agoraphobia, claus-
trophobia, hydrophobia, techno-
phobia, xenophobia
• arachnophobia, computerpho-
bia
obic \ō-bik\ phobic • aerobic
• acrophobic, anaerobic, claustro-
phobic, hydrophobic, technopho-
bic, xenophobic • agoraphobic,
arachnophobic, computerphobic

obile \ō-bəl\ see OBLE
obin \äb-ən\ bobbin, dobbin, robin,
Robin • round-robin, sea robin
obit \ō-bət\ obit, Tobit
oble \ō-bəl\ global, mobile, noble
• ennoble, Grenoble, ignoble,
immobile • upwardly mobile
obo \ō-bō\ hobo, oboe • bonobo
oboe \ō-bō\ see OBO
obol \äb-əl\ see ABBLE[1]
oboree \äb-ə-rē\ see OBBERY
obot \ō-bət\ see OBIT
obster \äb-stər\ lobster, mobster
• spiny lobster
oby \ō-bē\ Gobi, Kobe, Obie, Toby
• adobe, Nairobi • Okeechobee
obyn \äb-ən\ see OBIN
oc[1] \ōk\ see OKE[1]
oc[2] \äk\ see OCK[1]
oc[3] \ók\ see ALK
oca \ō-kə\ coca, mocha • tapioca
ocal \ō-kəl\ focal, local, vocal,
yokel • bifocal
ocally \ō-kə-lē\ locally, vocally
occa \äk-ə\ see AKA[1]
occer \äk-ər\ see OCKER
occie \äch-ē\ see OTCHY
occhi \ō-kē\ see ALKIE
occo \äk-ō\ socko, taco • morocco,
Morocco, sirocco
oce \ō-chē\ see OCHE[1]
ocean \ō-shən\ see OTION
ocess \äs-əs\ process • colossus,
due process, proboscis, word
process
och[1] \äk\ see OCK[1]
och[2] \ósh\ see ASH[2]
och[3] \ók\ see ALK
ocha \ō-kə\ see OCA
ochal \äk-əl\ see OCKLE
oche[1] \ō-kē\ see OKY
oche[2] \ōch\ see OACH
oche[3] \ósh\ see ASH[2]
ochee \ō-kē\ see OKY
ocher \ō-kər\ see OKER
ochi \ō-chē\ see OCHE[1]
ochle \ək-əl\ see UCKLE

ochs \äks\ see OX
ociable \ō-shə-bəl\ sociable • negotiable, unsociable • renegotiable
ocile \äs-əl\ see OSSAL
ocious \ō-shəs\ atrocious, ferocious, precocious
ock¹ \äk\ Bach, bloc, block, clock, cock, crock, doc, dock, flock, frock, hock, Jacque, Jacques, jock, knock, loch, lock, moc, mock, pock, roc, rock, schlock, shock, smock, sock, Spock, stock, wok • ad hoc, air lock, amok, armlock, Bangkok, baroque, bedrock, burdock, crew sock, deadlock, debacle, defrock, dreadlock, dry dock, epoch, flintlock, forelock, foreshock, gridlock, Hancock, hard rock, haycock, headlock, hemlock, in stock, Iraq, jazz-rock, Kazakh, kapok, kneesock, Ladakh, livestock, o'clock, oarlock, padlock, peacock, picklock, punk rock, rimrock, roadblock, rootstock, rowlock, seed stock, shamrock, Sheetrock, shell shock, sherlock, shock jock, Sirach, slickrock, Slovak, soft rock, springbok, stopcock, sunblock, ticktock, time clock, time lock, unblock, uncock, van Gogh, warlock, wedlock, windsock, woodcock • acid rock, aftershock, alarm clock, antiknock, antilock, Antioch, Arawak, banjo clock, building block, butcher-block, chockablock, chopping block, cinder block, common stock, country rock, cuckoo clock, culture shock, hammerlock, hollyhock, interlock, John Hancock, laughingstock, Little Rock, manioc, mantlerock, Offenbach, on the block, out of stock, Plymouth Rock, poppycock, preferred stock, rolling stock, septic

shock, starting block, shuttlecock, sticker shock, stumbling block, water clock, weathercock, writer's block • against the clock, around-the-clock, atomic clock, Czechoslovak, electroshock, grandfather clock, insulin shock, Mount Monadnock, out of wedlock, poison hemlock, run out the clock, turn back the clock, Vladivostok • chip off the old block
ock² \ȯk\ see ALK
ocke \äk\ see OCK¹
ocked \äkt\ concoct, dreadlocked, half-cocked, landlocked, shellshocked
—*also* -ed *forms of verbs listed at* OCK¹
ocker \äk-ər\ blocker, knocker, locker, mocker, rocker, shocker, soccer • alt-rocker, art-rocker, footlocker, punk rocker • knickerbocker • Davy Jones's locker
ockery \äk-rē\ crockery, mockery
ocket \äk-ət\ Crockett, docket, locket, pocket, rocket, socket, sprocket • air pocket, patch pocket, pickpocket, skyrocket, vest-pocket • cargo pocket, retrorocket
ockett \äk-ət\ see OCKET
ockey \äk-ē\ see OCKY
ockian \äk-ē-ən\ Hitchcockian, Slovakian • Czechoslovakian
ocking \äk-iŋ\ flocking, shocking, stocking • body stocking
—*also* -ing *forms of verbs listed at* OCK¹
ockle \äk-əl\ debacle • streptococcal
ocko \äk-ō\ see OCCO
ocks \äks\ see OX
ocky \äk-ē\ blocky, cocky, hockey, jockey, rocky, schlocky, stocky • disc jockey, field hockey, ice hockey, Iraqi, street hockey • jab-

berwocky, Miyazaki, Nagasaki,
sukiyaki, teriyaki

ocle \ō-kəl\ see OCAL

oco \ō-kō\ coco, cocoa, loco • rococo • crème de cacao, Orinoco

ocoa \ō-kō\ see OCO

ocracy \äk-rə-sē\ autocracy, bu-
reaucracy, democracy, hypocrisy,
mobocracy, plutocracy • aristoc-
racy

ocre \ō-kər\ see OKER

ocrisy \äk-rə-sē\ see OCRACY

oct \äkt\ see OCKED

octor \äk-tər\ doctor, proctor
• spin doctor, witch doctor • family doctor

ocular \äk-yə-lər\ jocular • binocu-
lar

ocus \ō-kəs\ crocus, focus, hocus
• in focus, refocus, soft-focus
• autumn crocus, hocus-pocus

ocused \ō-kəst\ see OCUST

ocust \ō-kəst\ locust • unfocused

od[1] \äd\ bod, clod, cod, Fahd, god,
mod, nod, odd, plod, pod, prod,
quad, rod, scrod, shod, sod,
squad, trod, wad • Cape Cod,
death squad, dry-shod, facade, fly
rod, hot-rod, jihad, lingcod, Nim-
rod, ramrod, Riyadh, roughshod,
seedpod, slipshod, sun god, synod,
tightwad, tripod, unshod, vice
squad • accolade, act of God,
arthropod, cattle prod, demigod,
dowsing rod, esplanade, firing
squad, flying squad, gastropod,
goldenrod, lightning rod, man of
God, Novgorod, piston rod,
promenade, son of God, spinning
rod • cephalopod, connecting rod,
divining rod, Holy Synod, Islam-
abad, Scheherazade, Upanishad

od[2] \ō\ see OW[1]

od[3] \ōd\ see ODE

od[4] \ùd\ see OOD[1]

od[5] \ȯd\ see AUD[1]

o'd \üd\ see UDE[1]

oda \ōd-ə\ coda, Rhoda, Skoda,
soda • club soda, cream soda,
pagoda • baking soda

odal \ōd-ᵊl\ modal, nodal, yodel

odden \äd-ᵊn\ Flodden, sodden,
trodden • downtrodden, untrod-
den

odder \äd-ər\ dodder, fodder,
odder, plodder, solder • flyrodder,
hot-rodder • cannon fodder,
Leningrader

oddery \äd-rē\ see AWDRY

oddess \äd-əs\ bodice, goddess
• sun goddess • demigoddess

oddish \äd-ish\ cloddish, kaddish

oddle \äd-ᵊl\ coddle, model, swad-
dle, toddle, twaddle, waddle • re-
model, role model • mollycoddle,
supermodel

oddler \äd-lər\ coddler, modeler,
toddler • mollycoddler

oddly \äd-lē\ see ODLY

oddy \äd-ē\ see ODY[1]

ode \ōd\ bode, bowed, code, goad,
load, lode, mode, node, ode, road,
rode, strode, toad, toed • abode,
anode, bar code, boatload, bus-
load, byroad, carload, cartload,
caseload, cathode, commode,
corrode, crossroad, decode,
diode, download, dress code,
encode, erode, explode, fore-
bode, freeload, geode, high road,
horned toad, implode, inroad,
lymph node, Morse code, off-
load, outmode, payload, plane-
load, railroad, shipload, side road,
Silk Road, spring-load, square-
toed, trainload, truckload, two-
toed, unload, upload, zip code • à
la mode, Comstock Lode, down
the road, electrode, episode, hit the
road, mother lode, overrode, penal
code, pigeon-toed, service road,
wagonload • area code, genetic
code, rule of the road • middle-of-
the-road, Underground Railroad

—*also* -ed *forms of verbs listed at* OW[1]

odeine \ōd-ē-ən\ see ODIAN

odel \ōd-ᵊl\ see ODAL

odeler \äd-lər\ see ODDLER

odeon \ōd-ē-ən\ see ODIAN

oder \ōd-ər\ loader, Oder, odor • breechloader, freeloader, offroader, railroader • middle-of-the-roader

oderate \äd-rət\ moderate • immoderate

odes \ōdz\ Rhodes
—*also* -s, -'s, *and* -s' *forms of nouns and* -s *forms of verbs listed at* ODE

odest \äd-əst\ modest, oddest • immodest

odeum \ōd-ē-əm\ see ODIUM

odge \äj\ see AGE[1]

odger \äj-ər\ codger, dodger, lodger, roger, Roger • Jolly Roger

odgy \äj-ē\ stodgy • demagogy

odian \ōd-ē-ən\ Cambodian, custodian, melodeon • nickelodeon

odic \äd-ik\ melodic, rhapsodic, spasmodic • episodic, periodic

odical \äd-i-kəl\ methodical • periodical

odice \äd-əs\ see ODDESS

odie \ō-dē\ see ODY[2]

odious \ōd-ē-əs\ odious • commodious, melodious

odity \äd-ət-ē\ oddity • commodity

odium \ōd-ē-əm\ podium, sodium

odius \ō-dē-əs\ see ODIOUS

odly \äd-lē\ godly, oddly • ungodly

odo \ōd-ō\ dodo • Quasimodo

odom \äd-əm\ shahdom, Sodom

odor \ōd-ər\ see ODER

odule \äj-ül\ module, lunar module, service module

ody[1] \äd-ē\ body, gaudy, Mahdi, shoddy, toddy • cell body, embody, homebody, nobody, somebody, wide-body • antibody, anybody, busybody, everybody, Irrawaddy, out-of-body, student body, underbody

ody[2] \ōd-ē\ Cody, Jodie, roadie, toady

odz \üj\ see UGE[1]

oe[1] \ō\ see OW[1]

oe[2] \ō-ē\ see OWY

oe[3] \ē\ see EE[1]

oea[1] \òi-ə\ see OIA

oea[2] \ē-ə\ see IA[1]

oeba \ē-bə\ see EBA

oebe \ē-bē\ see EBE[1]

oebel \ā-bəl\ see ABLE

oed \ōd\ see ODE

oehn \ən\ see UN[1]

oeia \ē-ə\ see IA[1]

oek \ùk\ see OOK[1]

oel \ō-əl\ Joel, Lowell, Noel • bestowal • protozoal

oeless[1] \ō-ləs\ see OLUS

oeless[2] \ü-ləs\ see EWLESS

oem \ōm\ see OME[1]

oeman \ō-mən\ see OMAN

oena \ē-nə\ see INA[2]

oentgen \en-chən\ see ENSION

oer[1] \òr\ see OR[1]

oer[2] \ü-ər\ see EWER[1]

oer[3] \ùr\ see URE[1]

oer[4] \ō-ər\ blower, grower, lower, mower, rower, slower, sower, thrower • beachgoer, churchgoer, fairgoer, flamethrower, filmgoer, glassblower, lawn mower, playgoer, snowblower, winegrower • concertgoer, moviegoer, operagoer, partygoer, whistle-blower • theatergoer

o'er \òr\ see OR[1]

oes[1] \əz\ see EUSE[1]

oes[2] \ōz\ see OSE[2]

oes[3] \üz\ see USE[2]

oesia \ē-shə\ see ESIA[1]

oesn't \əz-ᵊnt\ see ASN'T

oest \ü-əst\ see OOIST

oesus \ē-səs\ see ESIS

oet \ō-ət\ poet • inchoate, prose poet

oeuf \əf\ see UFF
oeur \ər\ see EUR[1]
oeuvre \ərv\ see ERVE
oey \ō-ē\ see OWY
of[1] \äv\ see OLVE[2]
of[2] \əv\ see OVE[1]
of[3] \òf\ see OFF[2]
ofar \ō-fər\ see OFER
ofer \ō-fər\ chauffeur, gopher, loafer, shofar • penny loafer
off[1] \äf\ coif, doff, prof, quaff, scoff • carafe, pilaf • Romanov
off[2] \òf\ cough, doff, off, scoff, trough • Azov, back off, beg off, blastoff, blow off, break off, bring off, brush-off, bug off, bump off, burn off, call off, cast-off, castoff, charge off, check off, Chekhov, cook-off, cutoff, cut off, drop-off, drop off, dust off, face-off, face off, falloff, far-off, fire off, first off, fob off, get off, give off, go off, goof-off, handoff, hand off, hands-off, haul off, head off, hold off, jump-off, kickoff, kick off, kill off, kiss-off, kiss off, knock-off, knock off, Khrushchev, laugh off, layoff, lay off, leadoff, lead off, leave off, liftoff, make off, nod off, palm off, pass off, payoff, pay off, peel off, pick off, play-off, pull off, push off, put off, reel off, rip-off, rip off, rub off, runoff, sawed-off, seal off, sell off, sell-off, send-off, set off, show-off, show off, shrug off, shut off, sign off, sound off, spin-off, standoff, stave off, swear off, takeoff, take off, teed off, tee off, tell off, throw off, tick off, tip-off, touch off, trade-off, turnoff, turn off, well-off, work off, write off • better-off, cooling-off, Gorbachev, hit it off, level off, Molotov, Nabokov, polish off, Pribilof, taper off • beat the pants off, beef Stroganoff, knock one's socks off,

power take-off, Rachmaninoff • Mexican standoff, Rimsky-Korsakov
offal[1] \äf-əl\ see AFEL
offal[2] \ò-fəl\ see AWFUL
offaly \òf-ə-lē\ see AWFULLY
offee \ò-fē\ coffee, toffee • Mr. Coffee
offer[1] \äf-ər\ coffer, offer, scoffer • counteroffer
offer[2] \òf-ər\ coffer, offer, scoffer • counteroffer
offin \ò-fən\ coffin, often, soften • every so often
offle \ò-fəl\ see AWFUL
oft[1] \òft\ croft, loft, oft, soft • aloft, choir loft, hayloft • Microsoft, semisoft, undercroft
—*also* -ed *forms of verbs listed at* OFF[2]
oft[2] \äft\ see AFT[1]
often \ò-fən\ see OFFIN
ofty \òf-tē\ lofty, softy
og[1] \äg\ blog, bog, clog, cog, flog, fog, frog, grog, hog, jog, log, nog, Prague, slog, smog • agog, backlog, bullfrog, defog, eggnog, footslog, groundhog, hedgehog, ice fog, leapfrog, photog, prologue, road hog, sandhog, tree frog, unclog, warthog, whole hog, Yule log • analog, analogue, catalog, demagogue, dialogue, epilogue, leopard frog, monologue, pedagogue, pollywog, synagogue, travelogue, waterlog • card catalogue
og[2] \òg\ blog, bog, clog, dog, fog, frog, hog, jog, log, smog • backlog, bird dog, bulldog, bullfrog, corn dog, coydog, defog, groundhog, guide dog, gundog, hangdog, hedgehog, hotdog, ice fog, lapdog, leapfrog, prologue, road hog, sandhog, sheepdog, sled dog, top dog, tree frog, warthog, watchdog, whole-hog, wild dog, wolf

dog, Yule log • analog, analogue, attack dog, catalog, chili dog, dialogue, dog-eat-dog, epilogue, hearing dog, leopard frog, monologue, police dog, pollywog, prairie dog, shaggy-dog, travelogue, underdog, water dog, working dog • card catalog, Eskimo dog, Shetland sheepdog

og³ \ōg\ see OGUE¹

oga \ō-gə\ toga, yoga • Conestoga, hatha yoga

ogan \ō-gən\ shogun, slogan • Mount Logan

oge \üzh\ see UGE²

ogel \ō-gəl\ see OGLE¹

ogeny \äj-ə-nē\ progeny • misogyny

oger¹ \äj-ər\ see ODGER

oger² \ȯg-ər\ see OGGER²

ogey¹ \ō-gē\ see OGIE

ogey² \u̇g-ē\ see OOGIE

oggan \äg-ən\ see OGGIN

oggar \äg-ər\ see OGGER¹

ogger¹ \äg-ər\ blogger, jogger, lager, logger • defogger • cataloger

ogger² \ȯg-ər\ auger, augur, jogger, logger • defogger, hotdogger • cataloger

oggin \äg-ən\ noggin • toboggan, Volkswagen • Copenhagen

oggle \äg-əl\ boggle, goggle, joggle, toggle • boondoggle • synagogal

oggy¹ \äg-ē\ boggy, foggy, groggy, smoggy, soggy

oggy² \ȯg-ē\ doggy, foggy, soggy

ogh¹ \ōg\ see OGUE¹

ogh² \ōk\ see OKE¹

ogh³ \äk\ see OCK¹

ogh⁴ \ō\ see OW¹

ogi \ō-gē\ see OGIE

ogian \ō-jən\ see OJAN

ogic \äj-ik\ logic • biologic, chronologic, demagogic, geologic, mythologic

ogical \äj-i-kəl\ logical • illogical

• astrological, biological, chronological, cosmological, ecological, geological, mythological, pathological, pedagogical, psychological, seismological, technological, theological, zoological • archaeological, dermatological, ideological, sociological

ogie \ō-gē\ bogey, bogie, dogie, fogy, hoagie, logy, stogie, yogi • pierogi

ogle¹ \ō-gəl\ Gogol, ogle

ogle² \äg-əl\ see OGGLE

ogna¹ \ō-nə\ see ONA¹

ogna² \ō-nē\ see ONY¹

ogna³ \ōn-yə\ see ONIA²

ogne \ōn\ see ONE¹

ogned \ōnd\ see ONED¹

ogo \ō-gō\ go-go, logo, Togo

ographer \äg-rə-fər\ biographer, cryptographer, discographer, photographer • choreographer, oceanographer, videographer • cinematographer

ography \äg-rə-fē\ biography, cryptography, discography, filmography, geography, photography, typography • bibliography, choreography, oceanography • autobiography, cinematography

ogress \ō-grəs\ ogress, progress

ogue¹ \ōg\ brogue, rogue, vogue, Vogue

ogue² \äg\ see OG¹

ogue³ \ȯg\ see OG²

oguish \ō-gish\ roguish, voguish

ogun \ō-gən\ see OGAN

ogyny \äj-ə-nē\ see OGENY

oh \ō\ see OW¹

oha \ō-ə\ see OA¹

ohl \ōl\ see OLE¹

ohm \ōm\ see OME¹

ohn \än\ see ON¹

ohns \änz\ see ONZE

ohn's \onz\ see ONZE

ohnson \än-sən\ Johnson • Wisconsin

ohr \òr\ see OR[1]

oi[1] \ä\ see A[1]

oi[2] \òi\ see OY

oia \òi-ə\ Goya, olla • sequoia, Sequoya • paranoia

oic \ō-ik\ stoic • echoic, heroic • Cenozoic, Mesozoic • Paleozoic

oice \òis\ choice, Joyce, voice • invoice, of choice, pro-choice, rejoice • with one voice • multiple-choice

oiced \òist\ see OIST

oicer \òi-sər\ pro-choicer, rejoicer

oid[1] \òid\ Floyd, Freud, void • android, avoid, deltoid, devoid, factoid, Negroid, ovoid, rhomboid, schizoid, steroid, tabloid, thyroid, typhoid • anthropoid, asteroid, celluloid, hemorrhoid, humanoid, Mongoloid, null and void, overjoyed, paranoid, planetoid, trapezoid, unalloyed, unemployed • underemployed
—*also* -ed *forms of verbs listed at* OY

oid[2] \ä\ see A[1]

oidal \òid-[1]\ adenoidal, asteroidal, trapezoidal

oie \ä\ see A[1]

oif \äf\ see OFF[1]

oign \òin\ see OIN[1]

oil \òil\ boil, broil, coil, foil, Hoyle, loyal, oil, roil, royal, soil, spoil, toil • airfoil, charbroil, coal oil, corn oil, despoil, disloyal, embroil, fish oil, fuel oil, gargoyle, hard-boil, palm oil, parboil, recoil, snake oil, subsoil, tinfoil, topsoil, trefoil, turmoil • baby oil, castor oil, desert soil, drying oil, holy oil, hydrofoil, linseed oil, London broil, mineral oil, neat's-foot oil, olive oil, peanut oil, prairie soil, quatrefoil, rapeseed oil, safflower oil, salad oil, soybean oil • canola oil, coconut oil, cod-liver oil, cottonseed oil, in-

duction coil, sesame oil, vegetable oil • burn the midnight oil

oilage \òi-lij\ soilage, spoilage

oile[1] \äl\ see AL[1]

oile[2] \òil\ see OIL

oiled \òild\ oiled • hard-boiled, soft-boiled, uncoiled, well-oiled
—*also* -ed *forms of verbs listed at* OIL

oiler \òi-lər\ boiler, broiler, spoiler, toiler • potboiler, steam boiler • double boiler

oiling \òi-liŋ\ boiling, broiling
—*also* -ing *forms of verbs listed at* OIL

oilus \òi-ləs\ see OYLESS

oin[1] \òin\ coin, groin, join, loin • adjoin, Burgoyne, conjoin, Des Moines, enjoin, purloin, rejoin, sirloin • tenderloin

oin[2] \a[n]\ see IN[4]

oine \än\ see ON[1]

oines \òin\ see OIN[1]

oing[1] \ō-iŋ\ Boeing, going, knowing, rowing, sewing, showing • churchgoing, foregoing, free-flowing, glassblowing, mind-blowing, ongoing, outgoing, seagoing • concertgoing, easygoing, moviegoing, oceangoing, theatergoing, thoroughgoing, whistle-blowing • to-ing and fro-ing
—*also* -ing *forms of verbs listed at* OW[1]

oing[2] \ü-iŋ\ doing • undoing, wrongdoing • evildoing, nothing doing
—*also* -ing *forms of verbs listed at* EW[1]

oing[3] \ō-ən\ see OAN[1]

o-ing \ō-iŋ\ see OING[1]

oint[1] \òint\ joint, point • anoint, appoint, ballpoint, butt joint, checkpoint, clip joint, dew point, end point, flash point, grade point, gunpoint, hinge joint, hip joint, juke joint, knifepoint, lap joint, match point, midpoint, pen point, pinpoint, standpoint, viewpoint • at gunpoint, at knifepoint, boiling point, breaking point, brownie point, cardinal point, case in point, counterpoint, disappoint, focal point, freezing point, knuckle joint, melting point, miter joint, Montauk Point, needlepoint, out of joint, point-to-point, pressure point, sticking point, talking point, to the point, turning point, vantage point • beside the point, decimal point, percentage point, vanishing point

oint² \ant\ see ANT⁵

ointe \ant\ see ANT⁵

ointed \oint-əd\ jointed, pointed • disjointed, loose-jointed • disappointed, double-jointed, self-appointed, well-appointed
—*also* -ed *forms of verbs listed at* OINT¹

ointing \oin-tiŋ\ disappointing, finger-pointing
—*also* -ing *forms of verbs listed at* OINT¹

ointment \oint-mənt\ ointment • anointment, appointment • disappointment • fly in the ointment

oir¹ \īr\ see IRE¹

oir² \är\ see AR³

oir³ \oir\ see OYER

oir⁴ \or\ see OR¹

oire¹ \är\ see AR³

oire² \oir\ see OYER

oire³ \or\ see OR¹

ois¹ \ä\ see A¹

ois² \oi\ see OY

ois³ \ois\ see OICE

oise¹ \äz\ 'twas, vase, was • vichyssoise
—*also* -s, -'s, *and* -s' *forms of nouns and* -s *forms of verbs listed at* A¹

oise² \oiz\ noise, poise • turquoise, white noise

—*also* -s, -'s, *and* -s' *forms of nouns and* -s *forms of verbs listed at* OY

oise³ \oi-zē\ see OISY

oist \oist\ foist, hoist, joist, moist, voiced • unvoiced
—*also* -ed *forms of verbs listed at* OICE

oister \oi-stər\ cloister, oyster, roister • seed oyster

oisy \oi-zē\ Boise, noisy

oit¹ \oit\ adroit, Detroit, exploit

oit² \āt\ see ATE¹

oit³ \ō-ət\ see OET

oit⁴ \ä\ see A¹

oite \ät\ see OT¹

oiter \oit-ər\ goiter, loiter • Detroiter • reconnoiter

oivre \äv\ see OLVE¹

oix¹ \ä\ see A¹

oix² \oi\ see OY

oiz \ois\ see OISE²

ojan \ō-jən\ Trojan • theologian

ok¹ \äk\ see OCK¹

ok² \ək\ see UCK¹

ok³ \ok\ see ALK

oka \ō-kə\ see OCA

oke¹ \ōk\ bloke, broke, choke, cloak, coke, Coke, croak, folk, joke, oak, poke, Polk, smoke, soak, spoke, stoke, stroke, woke, yoke, yolk • ad hoc, awoke, backstroke, baroque, breaststroke, brushstroke, chain-smoke, convoke, cowpoke, downstroke, evoke, heatstroke, in-joke, invoke, keystroke, kinfolk, kinsfolk, live oak, menfolk, pin oak, presoak, provoke, red oak, revoke, scrub oak, sidestroke, slowpoke, sunstroke, townsfolk, upstroke, white oak • artichoke, Bolingbroke, fisherfolk, go for broke, masterstroke, okeydoke, poison oak, Roanoke, thunderstroke, womenfolk

oke² \ō-kē\ see OKY

oke[3] \ō\ see OW[1]

oke[4] \ùk\ see OOK[1]

okee \ō-kē\ see OKY

okel \ō-kəl\ see OCAL

oken \ō-kən\ broken, oaken, spoken, token, woken • awoken, betoken, heartbroken, housebroken, outspoken, plainspoken, soft-spoken, unbroken • by the same token

oker \ō-kər\ broker, croaker, joker, ocher, poker, smoker, stoker • chain-smoker, draw poker, pawnbroker, stockbroker, stud poker • mediocre, power broker, red-hot poker

okey \ō-kē\ see OKY

oki \ō-kē\ see OKY

oko \ō-kō\ see OCO

oky \ō-kē\ croaky, folkie, hokey, jokey, Loki, poky, smoky • Great Smoky • hokeypokey, karaoke • Okefenokee

ol[1] \ōl\ see OLE[1]

ol[2] \äl\ see AL[1]

ol[3] \ȯl\ see ALL[1]

ola \o-lə\ cola, Lola • Angola, canola, Ebola, gondola, granola, Tortola, Victrola, viola, Viola • ayatollah, gladiola, Gorgonzola, Hispaniola, Osceola, Pensacola

olable \ō-lə-bəl\ see OLLABLE

olace \äl-əs\ see OLIS

olan \ō-lən\ see OLON

oland \ō-lənd\ see OWLAND

olar[1] \ō-lər\ see OLLER

olar[2] \äl-ər\ see OLLAR

olas \ō-ləs\ see OLUS

old[1] \ōld\ bold, bowled, cold, fold, gold, hold, mold, mould, old, scold, sold, soled, told • age-old, ahold, all told, behold, billfold, blindfold, blue mold, bread mold, choke hold, controlled, cuckold, eightfold, enfold, fivefold, fool's gold, foothold, foretold, fourfold, green mold, handhold, head cold, household, ice-cold, knock cold, leaf mold, ninefold, on hold, potholed, scaffold, sheepfold, sixfold, slime mold, stone-cold, stronghold, take hold, tenfold, threefold, threshold, toehold, twofold, unfold, untold, uphold, withhold • centerfold, common cold, fingerhold, hundredfold, manifold, marigold, scissors hold, sevenfold, stranglehold, thousandfold, throttlehold • as good as gold, blow hot and cold, lo and behold, marsh marigold, out in the cold

—*also* -ed *forms of verbs listed at* OLE[1]

old[2] \ȯld\ see ALD[1]

oldan \ōl-dən\ see OLDEN

olden \ōl-dən\ golden, olden • beholden, embolden

older[1] \ōl-dər\ boulder, folder, holder, shoulder, smolder • beholder, bondholder, cardholder, householder, jobholder, landholder, leaseholder, penholder, placeholder, pot holder, shareholder, slaveholder, stockholder, toolholder • officeholder, titleholder

—*also* -er *forms of adjectives listed at* OLD[1]

older[2] \äd-ər\ see ODDER

oldie \ōl-dē\ see OLDY

olding \ōl-diŋ\ folding, holding, molding, scolding • hand-holding, landholding, scaffolding, slaveholding

—*also* -ing *forms of verbs listed at* OLD[1]

oldster \ōl-stər\ see OLSTER

oldt \ōlt\ see OLT[1]

oldy \ōl-dē\ moldy, oldie • golden oldie

ole[1] \ōl\ bowl, coal, Cole, dole, droll, foal, goal, hole, knoll, mole, pole, Pole, poll, role, roll, scroll,

Seoul, shoal, sol, sole, soul, stole, stroll, toll, troll, vole, whole • airhole, armhole, atoll, bankroll, beanpole, bedroll, black hole, blowhole, bunghole, cajole, charcoal, console, control, creole, Creole, drumroll, egg roll, enroll, extol, eyehole, field goal, fishbowl, flagpole, foxhole, hard coal, half sole, hellhole, insole, keyhole, knothole, loophole, manhole, maypole, Mongol, Nicolle, North Pole, parole, patrol, payroll, peephole, pinhole, porthole, pothole, ridgepole, Sheol, ski pole, South Pole, spring roll, tadpole, unroll, washbowl, wormhole • buttonhole, camisole, casserole, coffee roll, cubbyhole, Dover sole, escarole, exit poll, finger hole, fumarole, honor roll, innersole, in the hole, Jackson Hole, jelly roll, kaiser roll, lemon sole, methanol, on the whole, oriole, ozone hole, pigeonhole, protocol, rabbit hole, rigmarole, rock and roll, Seminole, totem pole, water hole • ace in the hole, cholesterol, Costa del Sol, Haitian Creole, magnetic pole

ole[2] \ō-lē\ see OLY[1]

ole[3] \ȯl\ see ALL[1]

olean \ō-lē-ən\ see OLIAN

oled \ōld\ see OLD[1]

oleful \ōl-fəl\ doleful, soulful

olely \ō-lē\ see OLY[1]

olemn \äl-əm\ see OLUMN

oleon \ō-lē-ən\ see OLIAN

oler[1] \ō-lər\ see OLLER

oler[2] \äl-ər\ see OLLAR

oless \ō-ləs\ see OLUS

oleum \ō-lē-əm\ see OLIUM

oley \ō-lē\ see OLY[1]

olf[1] \älf\ golf, Rolf • Adolph, Randolph, Rudolph, Lake Rudolf • miniature golf

olf[2] \əlf\ see ULF

olga \äl-gə\ Olga, Volga

oli \ō-lē\ see OLY[1]

olia \ō-lē-ə\ Mongolia • Anatolia, melancholia • Inner Mongolia, Outer Mongolia

olian \ō-lē-ən\ aeolian, Mongolian, napoleon, Napoleon, Tyrolean

olic \äl-ik\ colic, frolic, rollick • bucolic, symbolic, systolic • alcoholic, apostolic, chocoholic, diabolic, hyperbolic, melancholic, shopaholic, vitriolic, workaholic

olicking \ä-lik-iŋ\ frolicking, rollicking

olid \äl-əd\ solid, squalid, stolid • semisolid

olin[1] \äl-ən\ see OLLEN[5]

olin[2] \ō-lən\ see OLON

olis \ō-əs\ braless, solace, Wallace, Wallis • Cornwallis

olish \äl-ish\ polish • abolish, demolish • apple-polish, spit-andpolish

olity \äl-ət-ē\ see ALITY[1]

olium \ō-lē-əm\ linoleum, petroleum

olk[1] \elk\ see ELK[1]

olk[2] \ōk\ see OKE[1]

olk[3] \əlk\ see ULK

olk[4] \ȯk\ see ALK

olkie \ō-kē\ see OKY

olky \ō-kē\ see OKY

oll[1] \ōl\ see OLE[1]

oll[2] \äl\ see AL[1]

oll[3] \ȯl\ see ALL[1]

olla[1] \äl-ə\ see ALA[2]

olla[2] \ȯi-ə\ see OIA

ollable \ō-lə-bəl\ controllable • inconsolable, uncontrollable

ollack \äl-ək\ see OLOCH

ollah[1] \ō-lə\ see OLA

ollah[2] \äl-ə\ see ALA[2]

ollah[3] \əl-ə\ see ULLAH

ollar \äl-ər\ collar, dollar, holler, Mahler, scholar, squalor • bluecollar, dog collar, flea collar, halfdollar, sand dollar, shawl collar,

top dollar, white-collar • Eurodol-
lar, petrodollar • clerical collar
ollard \äl-ərd\ collard, collared,
hollered
olled \ōld\ see OLD[1]
ollee \ō-lē\ see OLY[1]
ollege \äl-ij\ see OWLEDGE
ollen[1] \ō-lən\ see OLON
ollen[2] \əl-ə\ see ULLAH
ollen[3] \əl-ən\ see ULLEN
ollen[4] \ó-lən\ see ALLEN
ollen[5] \äl-ən\ Colin, pollen
oller \ō-lər\ bowler, molar, polar,
poller, roller, solar, stroller
• bankroller, comptroller, con-
troller, high roller, logroller,
steamroller • rock and roller
ollet \äl-ət\ wallet • whatchama-
callit
ollett \äl-ət\ see OLLET
olley \äl-ē\ see OLLY[1]
ollick \äl-ik\ see OLIC
ollicking \ä-lik-iŋ\ see OLICKING
ollie \äl-ē\ see OLLY[1]
ollin \äl-ən\ see OLLEN[5]
olling \ō-liŋ\ bowling • high-
rolling, logrolling • exit polling
—*also* -ing *forms of verbs listed at*
OLE[1]
ollis \äl-əs\ see OLIS
ollity \äl-ət-ē\ see ALITY[1]
ollo \äl-ō\ see OLLOW[1]
ollop \äl-əp\ dollop, polyp, scallop,
trollop, wallop • bay scallop, sea
scallop
ollow[1] \äl-ō\ follow, hollow, swallow, wallow • Apollo, barn swallow, cliff swallow, tree swallow
ollow[2] \äl-ə\ see ALA[2]
ollower \äl-ə-wər\ follower, wal-
lower • camp follower
ollster \ōl-stər\ see OLSTER
olly[1] \äl-ē\ Bali, Cali, collie, Dalí,
dolly, folly, golly, Halle, holly,
jolly, Mali, Molly, Ollie, Polly,
Raleigh, trolley, volley • Denali,
finale, Kigali, Nepali, Somali,

Svengali, tamale • melancholy,
Mexicali
olly[2] \ó-lē\ see AWLY
olm \ōm\ see OME[1]
olman \ōl-mən\ dolmen • patrol-
man
olmen \ōl-mən\ see OLMAN
olmes \ōmz\ Holmes
—*also* -s, -'s, *and* -s' *forms of*
nouns and -s *forms of verbs listed*
at OME[1]
olo \ō-lō\ bolo, polo, solo • Marco
Polo, water polo
oloch \äl-ək\ Moloch, rowlock
ologist \äl-ə-jəst\ biologist, ecolo-
gist, gemologist, geologist,
mythologist, neurologist, oncolo-
gist, psychologist, seismologist,
zoologist • anthropologist, ar-
chaeologist, cardiologist, climatol-
ogist, cosmetologist,
dermatologist, Egyptologist, ento-
mologist, immunologist, musicol-
ogist, ophthalmologist,
ornithologist
ology \äl-ə-jē\ anthology, apology,
astrology, biology, chronology,
cosmology, doxology, ecology,
geology, mythology, pathology,
psychology, seismology, technol-
ogy, theology, zoology • anthro-
pology, archaeology, cardiology,
climatology, cosmetology, crimi-
nology, dermatology, Egyptology,
etymology, genealogy, ideology,
immunology, methodology, mineralogy, musicology, numerology,
ophthalmology, ornithology,
pharmacology, physiology, Scien-
tology, sociology, terminology
• microbiology, nanotechnology,
paleontology
olon \ō-lən\ bowline, Colin, colon,
Nolan, stolen, swollen • semi-
colon
olonel \ərn-ᵊl\ see ERNAL
olonist \äl-ə-nəst\ colonist, Stalinist

olor[1] \ō-lər\ see OLLER
olor[2] \äl-ər\ see OLLAR
olored \əl-ərd\ colored, dullard • tricolored
olp \ōp\ see OPE
olph \älf\ see OLF[1]
olster \ōl-stər\ bolster, holster, oldster, pollster • upholster
olt[1] \ōlt\ bolt, colt, dolt, jolt, molt, volt • dead bolt, revolt, spring bolt, unbolt • thunderbolt
olt[2] \ólt\ see ALT
olta \äl-tə\ see ALTA
oltish \ōl-tish\ coltish, doltish
oluble \äl-yə-bəl\ soluble, voluble • insoluble • indissoluble
olumn \äl-əm\ column, slalom, solemn • fifth column • giant slalom, spinal column, steering column
olus \ō-ləs\ snowless, toeless • gladiolus
olve[1] \älv\ salve, solve • absolve, devolve, dissolve, evolve, involve, resolve, revolve
olve[2] \äv\ of, salve, Slav, suave • Gustav, thereof, whereof • Stanislav, unheard-of, well-thought-of, Yugoslav
oly[1] \ō-lē\ goalie, holy, lowly, mole, slowly, solely • cannoli, frijole, unholy • guacamole, ravioli, roly-poly
oly[2] \äl-ē\ see OLLY[1]
olyp \äl-əp\ see OLLOP
om[1] \äm\ balm, bomb, calm, from, Guam, mom, palm, prom, psalm, qualm, tom • A-bomb, aplomb, ashram, becalm, bee balm, buzz bomb, car bomb, dive-bomb, dotcom, embalm, firebomb, grande dame, H-bomb, imam, Islam, napalm, noncom, phenom, pogrom, pom-pom, salaam, sitcom, stink bomb, therefrom, time bomb, tom-tom, wigwam • atom bomb, cardamom, CD-ROM,

cherry bomb, cluster bomb, diatom, intercom, lemon balm, letter bomb, neutron bomb, Peeping Tom, royal palm, sago palm, soccer mom, supermom, telecom, Uncle Tom, Vietnam • atomic bomb, coconut palm, Dar es Salaam, hydrogen bomb, Omar Khayyám
om[2] \ōm\ see OME[1]
om[3] \üm\ see OOM[1]
om[4] \əm\ see UM[1]
om[5] \ùm\ see UM[2]
om[6] \óm\ see AUM[1]
oma \ō-mə\ chroma, coma, Roma • aroma, diploma, glaucoma, lymphoma, Tacoma • carcinoma, melanoma, Oklahoma
omac \ō-mik\ see OMIC[2]
omace \äm-əs\ see OMISE
omaly \äm-ə-lē\ homily • anomaly
oman \ō-mən\ bowman, foeman, omen, Roman, showman, snowman, yeoman
omany \äm-ə-nē\ see OMINY
omas \äm-əs\ see OMISE
omb[1] \ōm\ see OME[1]
omb[2] \üm\ see OOM[1]
omb[3] \äm\ see OM[1]
omb[4] \əm\ see UM[1]
omba \äm-bə\ see AMBA
ombe[1] \ōm\ see OME[1]
ombe[2] \üm\ see OOM[1]
ombe[3] \äm\ see OM[1]
ombed \ümd\ see OOMED
omber[1] \äm-ər\ bomber • dive-bomber, embalmer
omber[2] \ō-mər\ see OMER[1]
ombic \ō-mik\ see OMIC[2]
ombie \äm-bē\ zombie • Abercrombie
ombing \ō-miŋ\ see OAMING
ombo[1] \äm-bō\ combo, mambo
ombo[2] \əm-bō\ see UMBO
ombre \äm-bər\ see OMBER[2]
ome[1] \ōm\ chrome, comb, dome, foam, gnome, home, loam, ohm,

poem, roam, Rome, tome • at-home, beachcomb, bring home, Cape Nome, down-home, genome, hot comb, Jerome, rest home, rhizome, shalom, Stockholm, syndrome • catacomb, chromosome, close to home, Down syndrome, fine-tooth comb, foster home, funeral home, honeycomb, metronome, mobile home, monochrome, motor home, nursing home, onion dome, polychrome, Reye's syndrome, soldiers' home, stay-at-home, Styrofoam • detention home, Mercurochrome, X chromosome, Y chromosome

ome² \ō-mē\ see OAMY

ome³ \əm\ see UM¹

omely \əm-lē\ see UMBLY²

omen \ō-mən\ see OMAN

omenal \äm-ən-ᵊl\ see OMINAL

omene \äm-ə-nē\ see OMINY

omer¹ \ō-mər\ homer, Homer, roamer • beachcomber, misnomer

omer² \əm-ər\ see UMMER

omery \əm-ə-rē\ see UMMERY

omet \äm-ət\ comet, grommet, vomit

ometer \äm-ət-ər\ barometer, chronometer, kilometer, micrometer, odometer, pedometer, speedometer, tachometer, thermometer

ometry \äm-ə-trē\ geometry, optometry • plane geometry, trigonometry

omey \ō-mē\ see OAMY

omi \ō-mē\ see OAMY

omic¹ \äm-ik\ comic • atomic, Islamic • anatomic, diatomic, economic, ergonomic, gastronomic, metronomic, subatomic, tragicomic

omic² \ō-mik\ gnomic • Potomac

omical \äm-i-kəl\ comical

• anatomical, astronomical, economical

omics \äm-iks\ comics • economics, ergonomics • home economics

omily \äm-ə-lē\ see OMALY

ominal \äm-ən-ᵊl\ nominal • abdominal, phenomenal

ominance \äm-nəns\ dominance, prominence • predominance

ominant \äm-nənt\ dominant, prominent • predominant

omine \äm-ə-nē\ see OMINY

ominence \äm-nəns\ see OMINANCE

ominent \äm-nənt\ see OMINANT

oming¹ \əm-iŋ\ coming, numbing, plumbing • becoming, forthcoming, have coming, homecoming, incoming, mind-numbing, oncoming, shortcoming, upcoming • Second Coming, unbecoming, up-and-coming
—also -ing forms of verbs listed at UM¹

oming² \ō-miŋ\ see OAMING

omini \äm-ə-nē\ see OMINY

ominy \äm-ə-nē\ hominy • ignominy • anno Domini

omise \äm-əs\ pomace, promise, Thomas • Saint Thomas • breach of promise, doubting Thomas • lick and a promise

omit \äm-ət\ see OMET

omma \äm-ə\ see AMA²

ommel¹ \äm-əl\ pommel, Rommel

ommel² \əm-əl\ pommel, pummel • Beau Brummell

ommet \äm-ət\ see OMET

ommie \äm-ē\ see AMI¹

ommon \äm-ən\ Brahman, common, shaman • in common • Tutankhamen

ommy¹ \äm-ē\ see AMI¹

ommy² \əm-ē\ see UMMY

omo \ō-mō\ Como, promo • majordomo

omon \ō-mən\ see OMAN

omp¹ \ämp\ champ, chomp, clomp,

pomp, romp, stamp, stomp,
swamp, tramp, tromp, whomp

omp² \əmp\ see UMP

ompass \əm-pəs\ compass, rumpus
• encompass

omper \äm-pər\ romper, stamper,
stomper

ompey \äm-pē\ see OMPY

ompt \aunt\ see OUNT²

ompy \äm-pē\ Pompey, swampy

on¹ \än\ ban, Bonn, con, dawn,
don, Don, drawn, faun, fawn,
gone, John, Jon, khan, on, pawn,
prawn, Ron, spawn, swan, wan,
yawn, yon, yuan • aeon, add-on,
Amman, anon, Anton, argon,
Argonne, Aswan, Avon, bank on,
baton, big on, bonbon, boron,
bouillon, bring on, build on,
bygone, caisson, call on, catch on,
Ceylon, chevron, chew on, chif-
fon, chignon, clip-on, come-on,
cordon, coupon, crampon,
crayon, crouton, Dacron, dead-
on, Dear John, doggone, dog-
goned, Don Juan, eon, far-gone,
foregone, Freon, futon, Gibran,
Golan, go on, hand on, hands-on,
hang on, head-on, high on, hit on,
hogan, hold on, Hunan, icon,
Inchon, ion, Ivan, jargon, keen
on, krypton, Leon, let on, lock
on, log on, look on, Luzon, Milan, moron, neon, neuron, neutron, Nippon, nylon, odds-on,
Oman, Orlon, pecan, peon, pho-
ton, pick on, piton, plankton,
pompon, proton, Pusan, put-on,
pylon, python, Qur'an, radon, rag
on, rayon, right-on, Saint John,
Saipan, salon, San Juan, shaman,
sign on, sit on, slip-on, snap-on,
solon, spot on, stand on, stuck on,
sweet on, Szechwan, Taiwan, take
on, Teflon, Tehran, toucan, Tristan, try on, Tucson, turned-on,
turn on, upon, wait on, walk-on,

wonton, work on, Yukon,
Yvonne, zircon • Abidjan, aileron,
amazon, Amazon, and so on,
Aragon, autobahn, Avalon, Baby-
lon, Barbizon, bear down on, beat
up on, biathlon, call upon, caril-
lon, carry-on, carry on, check up
on, come upon, cyclotron, decathlon, early on, echelon, elec-
tron, epsilon, fall back on,
Fuji-san, Genghis Khan, go back
on, going on, goings-on, Grand
Teton, hanger-on, helicon, hexa-
gon, hold out on, Kazakhstan,
Kublai Khan, Kyrgyzstan, Lake
Huron, lay eyes on, Lebanon,
leprechaun, lexicon, liaison, load
up on, make good on, marathon,
marzipan, mastodon, miss out on,
myrmidon, octagon, off and on,
omicron, Oregon, Pakistan, pan-
theon, paragon, Parmesan,
Parthenon, pentagon, pentathlon,
Phaethon, pick up on, polygon,
put-upon, Ramadan, ride herd on,
Rubicon, run low on, set eyes on,
set foot on, silicon, sneak up on,
talkathon, Teheran, telethon,
triathlon, undergone, upsilon,
walkathon, walk out on, whereupon, woebegone • Agamemnon,
automaton, Azerbaijan,
Bellerophon, emoticon, get a
move on, keep an eye on, oxy-
moron, phenomenon, pteran-
odon, Saskatchewan, set one's
heart on, set one's sights on, sine
qua non, t'ai chi ch'uan, take it
out on, turn one's back on, zoo-
plankton • a leg to stand on, put
one's finger on, throw cold water
on, ultramarathon

on² \ōn\ fond, ton • baton, bouillon, Dijon, Gabon, Lyon, salon
• filet mignon

on³ \ȯn\ Bonn, brawn, dawn,
Dawn, drawn, faun, fawn, gone,

lawn, on, pawn, prawn, Sean, spawn, Vaughn, won, yawn • add-on, Argonne, begone, bygone, clip-on, come-on, dead-on, dog-gone, far-gone, foregone, hands-on, head-on, odds-on, put-on, Quezon, run-on, slip-on, snap-on, turned-on, turn-on, turn on, upon, walk-on, whereon, with-drawn • Ben-Gurion, carry-on, goings-on, hanger-on, leprechaun, put-upon, undergone, whereupon, woebegone

on⁴ \ōn\ see ONE¹

on⁵ \ən\ see UN¹

ona¹ \ō-nə\ Jonah, Mona • bologna, Bologna, corona, kimono, Leona, Pamplona, persona, Pomona, Ramona, Verona • Arizona, Barcelona, Desdemona

ona² \än-ə\ see ANA¹

oña \ōn-yə\ see ONIA²

onachal \än-i-kəl\ see ONICAL

onae \ō-nē\ see ONY¹

onah \ō-nə\ see ONA¹

onal \ōn-ᵊl\ tonal, zonal • hormonal

onald \än-ᵊld\ Donald, Ronald • MacDonald

onant \ō-nənt\ see ONENT

onas \ō-nəs\ see ONUS²

onc \äŋk\ see ONK¹

once¹ \äns\ see ANCE²

once² \əns\ see UNCE

onch¹ \äŋk\ see ONK¹

onch² \änch\ see AUNCH¹

oncha \äŋ-kə\ see ANKA

oncho \än-chō\ honcho, poncho, rancho

onco \äŋ-kō\ bronco, Franco

ond¹ \änd\ blond, bond, fond, frond, pond, wand • abscond, ash-blond, beyond, fishpond, gourmand, junk bond, millpond, respond • bottle blond, correspond, savings bond, vagabond, Walden Pond • back of beyond,

slough of despond, strawberry blond
—*also* -ed *forms of verbs listed at* ON¹

ond² \ōⁿ\ see ON²

ond³ \ónt\ see AUNT¹

onda \än-də\ Fonda, Honda, Rhonda, Wanda • Golconda, Rwanda, Uganda • anaconda

ondant \än-dənt\ see ONDENT

onday \ən-dē\ see UNDI

ondays \ən-dēz\ see UNDAYS

ondda \än-də\ see ONDA

onde \änd\ see OND¹

ondeau \än-dō\ see ONDO

ondent \än-dənt\ despondent, respondent • correspondent

onder¹ \än-dər\ condor, maunder, ponder, squander, wander, yonder • responder, transponder
—*also* -er *forms of adjectives listed at* OND¹

onder² \ən-dər\ see UNDER

ondly \än-lē\ see ANLY

ondo \än-dō\ condo, rondo • glissando • accelerando

ondor \än-dər\ see ONDER¹

ondrous \ən-drəs\ see UNDEROUS

one¹ \ōn\ blown, bone, clone, cone, crone, drone, flown, groan, grown, hone, Joan, known, loan, lone, moan, mown, own, phone, prone, Rhône, roan, Saône, scone, sewn, shone, shown, sown, stone, throne, thrown, tone, zone • alone, atone, backbone, bemoan, birthstone, bloodstone, bluestone, breastbone, brimstone, brownstone, calzone, Capone, cell phone, cheekbone, cologne, Cologne, colon, Colón, condone, corn pone, curbstone, cyclone, dethrone, dial tone, disown, drop zone, earphone, earth tone, end zone, enthrone, fieldstone, firestone, flagstone, flyblown, full-blown, gallstone, gemstone, gravestone, grindstone, hailstone, handblown, headphone, headstone, hearthstone, high-flown, hip bone, homegrown, hormone, ingrown, in stone, intone, jawbone, keystone, limestone, lodestone, long bone, milestone, millstone, moonstone, nose cone, outgrown, outshone, ozone, pay phone, pinecone, postpone, Ramon, rhinestone, sandstone, shinbone, Shoshone, snow cone, soapstone, strike zone, T-bone, tailbone, thighbone, time zone, tombstone, touchstone, touchtone, trombone, turnstone, twotone, Tyrone, unknown, war zone, well-known, whalebone, whetstone, windblown, wishbone • anklebone, Barbizon, baritone, buffer zone, Canal Zone, chaperon, cinder cone, cobblestone, collarbone, comfort zone, cornerstone, cortisone, crazy bone, cuttlebone, Dictaphone, free-fire zone, frigid zone, funny bone, gramophone, growth hormone, herringbone, hold one's own, ice-cream cone, kidney stone, knucklebone, leave alone, let alone, megaphone, microphone, minestrone, monotone, neutral zone, on one's own, overblown, overgrown, overthrown, overtone, Picturephone, provolone, saxophone, silicone, sousaphone, speakerphone, stand-alone, stepping-stone, telephone, temperate zone, torrid zone, traffic cone, twilight zone, undertone, vibraphone, xylophone, Yellowstone • accident-prone, Asunción, close to the bone, eau de cologne, fire-and-brimstone, radiophone, Rosetta stone, sine qua non, strawberry roan, testosterone, videophone • philosopher's stone, Ponce de León, Sierra Leone

one² \ō-nē\ see ONY¹
one³ \än\ see ON¹
one⁴ \ən\ see UN¹
one⁵ \ȯn\ see ON³
onean \ō-nē-ən\ see ONIAN¹
oned¹ \ōnd\ boned, toned • earth-toned, high-toned, pre-owned, rawboned, two-toned • cobble-stoned
   —also -ed *forms of verbs listed at* ONE¹
oned² \än\ see ON¹
onely \ōn-lē\ lonely, only • eyes-only
onement \ōn-mənt\ atonement, postponement • Day of Atonement
onent \ō-nənt\ component, exponent, opponent, proponent
oneous \ō-nē-əs\ see ONIOUS
oner¹ \ō-nər\ boner, cloner, donor, groaner, loaner, loner, owner, stoner • landowner, shipowner • telephoner
oner² \ȯn-ər\ see AWNER¹
onerous \än-ə-rəs\ onerous, sonorous
ones \ōnz\ Jones • bare-bones, Dow Jones • Davy Jones, lazy-bones, make no bones • skull and crossbones
   —also -s, -'s, *and* -s' *forms of nouns and* -s *forms of verbs listed at* ONE¹
oney¹ \ō-nē\ see ONY¹
oney² \ən-ē\ see UNNY
oney³ \ü-nē\ see OONY
ong¹ \äŋ\ gong, prong, tong • Da Nang, Hong Kong, Mah-Jongg, Mekong, ping-pong, sarong • billabong, Pyongyang, Sturm und Drang, Vietcong
ong² \ȯŋ\ bong, gong, long, prong, song, strong, thong, throng, tong, wrong • along, Armstrong, belong, birdsong, chaise longue, daylong, ding-dong, dugong, fight

song, folk song, furlong,
Haiphong, headlong, headstrong,
Hong Kong, hour-long, lifelong,
livelong, Mekong, monthlong,
nightlong, oblong, part-song,
Ping-Pong, prolong, sarong, side-
long, singsong, so long, swan
song, theme song, torch song,
weeklong, work song, yearlong
• all along, before long, billabong,
come along, cradlesong, drinking
song, get along, go along, run
along, sing-along, siren song,
string along, summerlong, taga-
long, Vietcong

ong[3] \əŋ\ see UNG[1]

ong[4] \u̇ŋ\ see UNG[2]

onga \äŋ-gə\ conga, Tonga
• chimichanga

onge \ənj\ see UNGE

onged \ȯŋd\ pronged, wronged
• multipronged
—also -ed *forms of verbs listed at*
ONG[2]

onger[1] \əŋ-gər\ hunger, younger
• fearmonger, fishmonger, scare-
monger, warmonger • gossipmon-
ger, rumormonger,
scandalmonger

onger[2] \ən-jər\ see UNGER[1]

ongery \əŋ-grē\ hungry • ironmon-
gery

ongful \ȯŋ-fəl\ wrongful, songful

ongish \ȯŋ-ish\ longish, strongish

ongo \äŋ-gō\ bongo, Congo • Belgian Congo, Pago Pago

ongous \əŋ-gəs\ see UNGOUS

ongue[1] \əŋ\ see UNG[1]

ongue[2] \ȯŋ\ see ONG[2]

ongy \ən-jē\ see UNGY

onhomous \än-ə-məs\ see ONYMOUS

oni \ō-nē\ see ONY[1]

onia[1] \ō-nē-ə\ Estonia, Franconia,
Laconia, Slavonia, zirconia
• Amazonia, Babylonia, Caledonia, Catalonia, Macedonia, Patagonia • New Caledonia

onia[2] \ō-nyə\ doña, Sonia • ammo-
nia, begonia, Bologna, Estonia,
Franconia, Laconia, pneumonia,
Slavonia • Babylonia, Caledonia,
Catalonia, Macedonia, Patagonia
• double pneumonia, New Caledonia, walking pneumonia

onial \ō-nē-əl\ baronial, colonial
• ceremonial, Dutch Colonial,
matrimonial, testimonial

onian[1] \ō-nē-ən\ Bostonian, dra-
conian, Estonian, Houstonian,
Jacksonian, Miltonian, Newtonian, Wilsonian • Amazonian,
Arizonian, Babylonian, calypson-
ian, Catalonian, Ciceronian,
Emersonian, Hamiltonian, Jeffersonian, Macedonian, Oregonian,
Patagonian, Washingtonian

onian[2] \ō-nyən\ Bostonian, Eston-
ian, Franconian, Houstonian,
Miltonian, Newtonian, Nixonian,
Slavonian • Amazonian, Arizon-
ian, Babylonian, Ciceronian,
Emersonian, Jeffersonian, Mace-
donian, Oregonian, Patagonian,
Washingtonian

onic \än-ik\ chronic, conic, phonic,
sonic, tonic • bionic, bubonic,
cyclonic, demonic, harmonic,
iconic, Ionic, ironic, laconic,
Masonic, mnemonic, moronic,
planktonic, platonic, sardonic,
Slavonic, subsonic, symphonic,
tectonic, Teutonic • catatonic,
electronic, embryonic, histrionic,
Housatonic, philharmonic, poly-
phonic, quadraphonic, super-
sonic, ultrasonic • stereophonic

onica \än-i-kə\ Monica • harmonica, Veronica • electronica, glass
harmonica, Santa Monica, Thes-
salonica

onical \än-i-kəl\ chronicle, conical,
monocle • canonical

onicle \än-i-kəl\ see ONICAL

onics \än-iks\ onyx, phonics

- bionics, tectonics • electronics, plate tectonics
—*also* -s, -'s, *and* -s' *forms of nouns listed at* ONIC
onika \än-i-kə\ see ONICA
oning[1] \än-iŋ\ awning
—*also* -ing *forms of verbs listed at* ON[1]
oning[2] \ō-niŋ\ jawboning, landowning
—*also* -ing *forms of verbs listed at* ONE[1]
onion \ən-yən\ see UNION
onious \ō-nē-əs\ Antonius, erroneous, felonious, harmonious, Petronius, Polonius • acrimonious, ceremonious, parsimonious, sanctimonious
• unceremonious
onis[1] \ō-nəs\ see ONUS[2]
onis[2] \än-əs\ see ONUS[1]
onish \än-ish\ admonish, astonish
• leprechaunish
onishment \än-ish-mənt\ admonishment, astonishment
onium \ō-nē-əm\ euphonium, plutonium • pandemonium, Pandemonium
onius \ō-nē-əs\ see ONIOUS
onja \ō-nyə\ see ONIA[2]
onk[1] \äŋk\ bonk, bronc, conch, conk, honk, plonk, wonk, zonk
• honky-tonk
onk[2] \əŋk\ see UNK
onkey[1] \äŋ-kē\ see ONKY
onkey[2] \əŋ-kē\ see UNKY
onky \äŋ-kē\ donkey, wonky, yanqui
onless \ən-ləs\ see UNLESS
only \ōn-lē\ see ONELY
onment \ōn-mənt\ see ONEMENT
onn[1] \än\ see ON[1]
onn[2] \ȯn\ see ON[3]
onna[1] \ȯn-ə\ Donna, fauna, sauna
• prima donna
onna[2] \än-ə\ see ANA[1]
onne[1] \än\ see ON[1]

onne[2] \ən\ see UN[1]
onne[3] \ȯn\ see ON[3]
onner \än-ər\ see ONOR[1]
onnet \än-ət\ bonnet, sonnet
• bluebonnet, sunbonnet, warbonnet • bee in one's bonnet
onnie \än-ē\ see ANI[1]
onnish \än-ish\ see ONISH
onnor \än-ər\ see ONOR[1]
onny[1] \än-ē\ see ANI[1]
onny[2] \ən-ē\ see UNNY
ono[1] \ō-nō\ kimono, pro bono
ono[2] \ō-nə\ see ONA[1]
ono[3] \än-ō\ see ANO[1]
onocle \än-i-kəl\ see ONICAL
onomist \än-ə-məst\ agronomist, economist • home economist
onomous \än-ə-məs\ see ONYMOUS
onomy \än-ə-mē\ agronomy, astronomy, autonomy, economy, gastronomy, taxonomy
• Deuteronomy
onor[1] \än-ər\ goner, honor, yawner
• dishonor, O'Connor • Afrikaner, maid of honor, marathoner, point of honor, weimaraner • Legion of Honor, matron of honor, Medal of Honor
onor[2] \ō-nər\ see ONER[1]
onorous \än-ə-rəs\ see ONEROUS
ons[1] \änz\ see ONZE
ons[2] \ōⁿ\ see ON[2]
onsil \än-səl\ see ONSUL
onsin \än-sən\ see OHNSON
onson \än-sən\ see OHNSON
onsul \än-səl\ consul, tonsil • proconsul
ont[1] \ənt\ blunt, brunt, bunt, front, grunt, hunt, punt, runt, shunt, stunt, want • affront, beachfront, cold front, confront, forefront, home front, lakefront, manhunt, shorefront, storefront, up-front, warm front, witch hunt • battlefront, oceanfront, riverfront, waterfront • scavenger hunt
ont[2] \änt\ see ANT[2]

ont³ \ȯnt\ see AUNT¹

on't \ōnt\ don't, won't

ontal¹ \änt-ᵊl\ horizontal • peri-
odontal

ontal² \ənt-ᵊl\ see UNTLE

ontas \änt-əs\ see ONTUS

onte¹ \änt-ē\ see ANTI¹

onte² \än-tā\ see ANTE¹

onted \ȯnt-əd\ vaunted, wonted
• undaunted
—also -ed forms of verbs listed at
AUNT¹

onter \ənt-ər\ see UNTER

onth \ənth\ month • billionth,
millionth, trillionth, twelvemonth
• gazillionth

ontil \änt-ᵊl\ see ONTAL¹

onto \än-tō\ see ANTO

ontra \än-trə\ contra, mantra

ontre \änt-ər\ see AUNTER¹

ontus \änt-əs\ Pontus • Pocahontas

onty \änt-ē\ see ANTI¹

onus¹ \än-əs\ Cronus, Faunus
• Adonis

onus² \ō-nəs\ bonus, Cronus,
Jonas, onus, slowness • Adonis

ony¹ \ō-nē\ bony, crony,
phony, pony, Sony, stony, Toni,
Tony • baloney, bologna, cow
pony, Giorgione, Marconi, Mo-
roni, Shoshone, spumoni, tortoni
• abalone, acrimony, alimony,
ceremony, hegemony, macaroni,
matrimony, minestrone, one-trick
pony, patrimony, pepperoni,
provolone, sanctimony, Shetland
pony, testimony, zabaglione
• phony-baloney • dramatis per-
sonae

ony² \än-ē\ see ANI¹

onya \ō-nyə\ see ONIA²

onymist \än-ə-məst\ see ONOMIST

onymous \än-ə-məs\ anonymous,
autonomous, synonymous

onymy \än-ə-mē\ see ONOMY

onyon \ən-yən\ see UNION

onyx \än-iks\ see ONICS

onze \änz\ bronze • long johns,
Saint John's • Afrikaans
—also -s, -'s, and -s' forms of
nouns and -s forms of verbs listed
at ON¹

oo¹ \ü\ see EW¹

oo² \ō\ see OW¹

oob \üb\ see UBE

oober \ü-bər\ see UBER

ooby \ü-bē\ booby, ruby, Ruby

ooch¹ \üch\ brooch, mooch,
pooch, smooch

ooch² \ōch\ see OACH

oocher \ü-chər\ see UTURE

oochy \ü-chē\ smoochy • penuche,
Vespucci

ood¹ \ùd\ good, hood, should,
stood, wood, would • basswood,
boxwood, boyhood, brushwood,
childhood, cordwood, corkwood,
deadwood, dogwood, driftwood,
falsehood, feel-good, firewood,
for good, girlhood, greenwood,
hardwood, heartwood, ironwood,
knighthood, make good, man-
hood, Mount Hood, no-good,
pinewood, plywood, priesthood,
pulpwood, redwood, rosewood,
sainthood, Sherwood, softwood,
statehood, stinkwood, Talmud,
Wedgwood, wifehood, withstood,
wormwood • adulthood, bache-
lorhood, brotherhood, candle-
wood, cedarwood, cottonwood,
fatherhood, Hollywood, knock on
wood, likelihood, livelihood,
maidenhood, motherhood, neigh-
borhood, parenthood, Robin
Hood, sandalwood, sisterhood, to
the good, tulipwood, understood,
widowhood, womanhood • blood
brotherhood, grandparenthood,
misunderstood, second childhood,
unlikelihood

ood² \ōd\ see ODE

ood³ \üd\ see UDE¹

ood⁴ \əd\ see UD¹

ooded[1] \əd-əd\ blue-blooded, cold-blooded, full-blooded, half-blooded, hot-blooded, pure-blooded, red-blooded, star-studded, warm-blooded
—*also* -ed *forms of verbs listed at* UD[1]

ooded[2] \ùd-əd\ hooded, wooded

ooder[1] \üd-ər\ see UDER

ooder[2] \əd-ər\ see UDDER

oodle \üd-ᵊl\ doodle, feudal, noodle, poodle, strudel • caboodle, canoodle, toy poodle • Yankee-Doodle

oodoo \üd-ü\ doo-doo, hoodoo, kudu, voodoo • in deep doo-doo

oods \ùdz\ hoods • backwoods, dry goods, piece goods, white goods • bill of goods, piney woods • consumer goods, Lake of the Woods • deliver the goods
—*also* -s, -'s, *and* -s' forms of nouns listed at OOD[1]

oodsman \ùdz-mən\ woodsman • backwoodsman, ombudsman

oody[1] \üd-ē\ broody, Judy, moody, Rudy, Trudy

oody[2] \ùd-ē\ goody, hoody, woody

oody[3] \əd-ē\ see UDDY[1]

ooer \ü-ər\ see EWER[1]

ooey \ü-ē\ see EWY

oof[1] \üf\ goof, hoof, poof, proof, roof, spoof, woof • aloof, bombproof, childproof, crush-proof, fireproof, flameproof, foolproof, forehoof, germproof, greaseproof, heatproof, leakproof, lightproof, moonroof, pickproof, rainproof, reproof, rustproof, shockproof, soundproof, stainproof, sunroof, windproof • bulletproof, burglarproof, gable roof, gambrel roof, hit the roof, ovenproof, shatterproof, tamperproof, through the roof, waterproof, weatherproof • burden of proof, idiotproof

oof[2] \ùf\ hoof, poof, roof, woof

• moon roof • cloven hoof, gable roof, gambrel roof, hit the roof, through the roof

oof[3] \ōf\ see OAF

oof[4] \üv\ see OVE[3]

oofer[1] \ü-fər\ roofer, twofer

oofer[2] \ùf-ər\ hoofer, woofer

oofy \ü-fē\ goofy, Sufi

ooga \ü-gə\ see UGA

ooge \üj\ see UGE[1]

ooger \ùg-ər\ see UGUR

oogie \ùg-ē\ bogey, boogie • boogie-woogie

oo-goo \ü-gü\ see UGU

ooh \ü\ see EW[1]

ooi \ü-ē\ see EWY

ooist \ü-əst\ doest • tattooist, voodooist
—*also* -est *forms of adjectives listed at* EW[1]

ook[1] \ùk\ book, brook, cook, Cook, crook, hook, look, nook, rook, shook, took • bankbook, checkbook, cookbook, e-book, forsook, fishhook, guidebook, handbook, hymnbook, Innsbruck, logbook, matchbook, mistook, Mount Cook, notebook, outlook, partook, phrase book, pothook, prayer book, schoolbook, scrapbook, sketchbook, songbook, stylebook, textbook, unhook, wordbook, workbook, yearbook • buttonhook, comic book, donnybrook, grappling hook, inglenook, off the hook, overlook, overtook, picture book, pocketbook, pocket book, pressure-cook, pruning hook, Sandy Hook, storybook, talking book, tenterhook, undertook • audiobook, coloring book, gobbledygook, ring off the hook, telephone book • by hook or by crook

ook[2] \ük\ see UKE

ooka \ü-kə\ yuca • bazooka, palooka

ooke \ük\ see OOK[1]

ooker \ük-ər\ booker, cooker, looker, snooker • good-looker, onlooker • pressure cooker

ookery \ük-ə-rē\ cookery, rookery

ookie \ük-ē\ bookie, cookie, hooky, rookie • fortune cookie

ooking \ük-iŋ\ booking, cooking • good-looking • forward-looking, solid-looking
—*also* -ing *forms of verbs listed at* OOK[1]

ooklet \ük-lət\ booklet, brooklet

ooks[1] \üks\ deluxe
—*also* -s, -'s, *and* -s' *forms of nouns and* -s *forms of verbs listed at* UKE

ooks[2] \ùks\ Brooks, crux, looks • deluxe • on tenterhooks
—*also* -s, -'s, *and* -s' *forms of nouns and* -s *forms of verbs listed at* OOK[1]

ooky[1] \ü-kē\ kooky, spooky • bouzouki, Kabuki

ooky[2] \ük-ē\ see OOKIE

ool[1] \ül\ cool, drool, fool, fuel, ghoul, mule, pool, rule, school, spool, stool, tool, you'll, yule • air-cool, B-school, carpool, church school, cesspool, day school, edge tool, footstool, gene pool, grade school, high school, homeschool, Kabul, misrule, Mosul, old school, prep school, preschool, refuel, retool, self-rule, step stool, synfuel, tide pool, toadstool, trade school, uncool, unspool, whirlpool • April fool, blow one's cool, boarding school, charter school, ducking stool, grammar school, Istanbul, Liverpool, machine tool, magnet school, middle school, minuscule, molecule, motor pool, nursery school, overrule, private school, public school, reform school, ridicule, summer school, Sunday

school, training school, vestibule, wading pool • finishing school, junior high school, parochial school, primary school, senior high school • alternative school, secondary school

ool[2] \ùl\ see UL[1]

oola \ü-lə\ see ULA

oole \ül\ see OOL[1]

oolean \ü-lē-ən\ see ULEAN

ooled \üld\ bejeweled, unschooled
—*also* -ed *forms of verbs listed at* OOL[1]

ooler \ü-lər\ cooler, ruler • carpooler, grade-schooler, high schooler, homeschooler, preschooler, wine cooler • middle schooler, watercooler

oolie \ü-lē\ see ULY

oolish \ü-lish\ foolish, ghoulish, mulish

oolly[1] \ü-lē\ see ULY

oolly[2] \ùl-ē\ see ULLY[2]

oom[1] \üm\ bloom, boom, broom, doom, flume, fume, gloom, groom, loom, plume, room, spume, tomb, vroom, whom, womb, zoom • abloom, assume, backroom, ballroom, barroom, bathroom, bedroom, boardroom, bridegroom, chat room, checkroom, classroom, cloakroom, coatroom, consume, costume, courtroom, darkroom, entomb, exhume, greenroom, guardroom, headroom, heirloom, homeroom, Khartoum, legroom, legume, lunchroom, men's room, mushroom, perfume, playroom, poolroom, pressroom, presume, restroom, resume, schoolroom, showroom, sickroom, stateroom, stockroom, storeroom, sunroom, throne room, washroom, weight room, whisk broom, workroom • baby boom, banquet room, birthing room, elbow room, family room, ladies' room, living room, locker-room, nom de plume, powder room, rumpus room, sitting room, sonic boom, standing room, waiting room, women's room • lower the boom, master bedroom, recovery room • emergency room, recreation room

oom² \ùm\ see UM²

oomed \ümd\ plumed • well-groomed
—*also* -ed *forms of verbs listed at* OOM[1]

oomer \ü-mər\ see UMER

oomily \ü-mə-lē\ doomily, gloomily

ooming¹ \ü-mən\ see UMAN

ooming² \ü-miη\ see UMING

oomy \ü-mē\ bloomy, boomy, doomy, gloomy, roomy • costumey

oon¹ \ün\ boon, Boone, coon, croon, dune, goon, hewn, June, loon, moon, noon, prune, rune, soon, spoon, swoon, strewn, tune • attune, baboon, balloon, bassoon, blue moon, buffoon, Calhoun, Cancún, cartoon, cocoon, commune, doubloon, dragoon, festoon, fine-tune, forenoon, full moon, half-moon, harpoon, high noon, immune, impugn, Kowloon, lagoon, lampoon, maroon, monsoon, Neptune, new moon, Pashtun, platoon, pontoon, raccoon, rough-hewn, saloon, soupspoon, teaspoon, tribune, tycoon, typhoon, Walloon • afternoon, Brigadoon, Cameroon, dessertspoon, greasy spoon, harvest moon, honeymoon, importune, macaroon, opportune, picayune, Saskatoon, silver spoon, tablespoon • contrabassoon, inopportune, over the moon, trial balloon

oon² \ōn\ see ONE¹

oona \ü-nə\ see UNA

oonal \ün-ᵊl\ see UNAL

oone \ün\ see OON¹

ooner \ü-nər\ crooner, lunar, schooner, tuner • harpooner • honeymooner, prairie schooner

oonery¹ \ün-rē\ buffoonery, lampoonery

oonery² \ü-nə-rē\ see UNARY

ooney \ü-nē\ see OONY

oonie \ü-nē\ see OONY

ooning \ü-niη\ ballooning, cartooning, cocooning
—*also* -ing *forms of verbs listed at* OON¹

oonish \ü-nish\ buffoonish, cartoonish

oonless \ün-ləs\ moonless, tuneless

oons \ünz\ afternoons, loony tunes
—*also* -s, -'s, *and* -s' *forms of nouns and* -s *forms of verbs listed at* OON¹

oony \ü-nē\ loony, Moonie, moony, puny, Zuni • cartoony

oop \üp\ coop, coupe, croup, droop, dupe, goop, group, hoop, loop, poop, scoop, sloop, snoop, soup, stoop, swoop, troop, troupe, whoop • age-group, blood group, duck soup, in-group, newsgroup, pea soup, playgroup, recoup, regroup, war whoop • alley-oop, Betty Boop, bird's-nest soup, for a loop, Guadeloupe, Hula Hoop, nincompoop, paratroop, pressure group, support group • alphabet soup, knock for a loop, mock turtle soup

o-op \üp\ see OOP

oopee \ü-pē\ see OOPY

ooper \ü-pər\ blooper, Cooper, looper, scooper, stupor, super, trooper, trouper • storm trooper • party pooper, paratrooper, pooper-scooper, super-duper

oops \ùps\ oops, whoops

oopy \ü-pē\ droopy, groupie, loopy, snoopy, Snoopy, soupy, whoopee

oor¹ \ȯr\ see OR¹

oor² \u̇r\ see URE¹

oorage¹ \u̇r-ij\ moorage • sewerage

oorage² \ȯr-ij\ see ORAGE²

oore¹ \ȯr\ see OR¹

oore² \u̇r\ see URE¹

oored \ȯrd\ see OARD

oorer \ȯr-ər\ see ORER

oori \u̇r-ē\ see URY¹

ooring¹ \ȯr-iŋ\ see ORING

ooring² \u̇r-iŋ\ see URING

oorish \u̇r-ish\ boorish, Moorish

oorly \u̇r-lē\ see URELY

oorman \ȯr-mən\ see ORMAN

oors \ȯrz\ drawers, yours • Azores, indoors, outdoors • out-of-doors
—also -s, -'s, and -s' forms of nouns and -s forms of verbs listed at OR¹

oorsman \ȯrz-mən\ see OARSMAN

oort \ȯrt\ see ORT¹

oosa \ü-sə\ see USA¹

oose¹ \üs\ see USE¹

oose² \üz\ see USE²

ooser¹ \ü-sər\ see USER

ooser² \ü-zər\ see USER

oosey \ü-sē\ see UICY

oosh¹ \üsh\ see OUCHE

oosh² \u̇sh\ see USH²

oost \üst\ boost, juiced, roost • self-induced
—also -ed forms of verbs listed at USE¹

oosy \ü-zē\ see OOZY

oot¹ \u̇t\ foot, put, root, soot • afoot, barefoot, bigfoot, Blackfoot, board foot, clubfoot, cube root, hard put, input, kaput, on foot, output, Rajput, shot put, square root, taproot, trench foot, uproot • arrowroot, athlete's foot, hand and foot, pussyfoot, tenderfoot, underfoot

oot² \üt\ see UTE

oot³ \ət\ see UT¹

ooted¹ \üt-əd\ booted, fruited, muted • deep-rooted, jackbooted, reputed
—also -ed forms of verbs listed at UTE

ooted² \u̇t-əd\ clubfooted, deep-rooted, flat-footed, fleet-footed, four-footed, heavy-footed, light-footed, slow-footed, surefooted, web-footed • cloven-footed
—also -ed forms of verbs listed at OOT¹

ooter¹ \u̇t-ər\ footer, putter • shot-putter • pussyfooter

ooter² \üt-ər\ see UTER

ooth¹ \üth̲\ smooth, soothe

ooth² \üth\ booth, Booth, Ruth, sleuth, tooth, truth, youth • bucktooth, dogtooth, Duluth, eyetooth, half-truth, in truth, milk tooth, sweet tooth, tollbooth, uncouth, untruth • baby tooth, snaggletooth, wisdom tooth • moment of truth, projection booth, telephone booth

oothe \üth̲\ see OOTH¹

oothed \ütht\ sleuthed, toothed • buck-toothed, gap-toothed • saber-toothed, snaggletoothed

oothless \üth-ləs\ see UTHLESS

ootie \üt-ē\ see OOTY¹

ooting¹ \u̇t-iŋ\ footing • off-putting, war footing
—also -ing forms of verbs listed at OOT¹

ooting² \üt-iŋ\ see UTING

ootle \üt-ᵊl\ see UTILE

ootless \üt-ləs\ fruitless, rootless

oots \üts\ grassroots, Vaduz
—also -s, -'s, and -s' forms of nouns and -s forms of verbs listed at UTE

ootsie \u̇t-sē\ footsie, tootsie

ooty¹ \üt-ē\ beauty, booty, cootie, cutie, duty, fruity, snooty, sooty • agouti, Djibouti • Funafuti, heavy-duty, tutti-frutti

ooty² \ət-ē\ see UTTY
oove \üv\ see OVE³
oover \ü-vər\ see OVER³
oovy \ü-vē\ groovy, movie • B movie
ooze \üz\ see USE²
oozer \ü-zər\ see USER
oozle \ü-zəl\ see USAL
oozy \ü-zē\ choosy, floozy, newsy, oozy, Susie, woozy • Jacuzzi
op¹ \äp\ bop, chop, clop, cop, crop, drop, flop, fop, glop, hop, lop, mop, plop, pop, prop, shop, slop, sop, stop, swap, top, whop • Aesop, airdrop, a pop, atop, backdrop, backstop, bakeshop, bebop, bellhop, benchtop, big top, blacktop, bookshop, cartop, cash crop, clip-clop, coin-op, cooktop, co-op, cough drop, desktop, dewdrop, doorstop, doo-wop, dry mop, dust mop, eavesdrop, field crop, flattop, flip-flop, gumdrop, hardtop, high-top, hilltop, hip-hop, hockshop, housetop, laptop, name-drop, nonstop, one-stop, palmtop, pawnshop, pit stop, poptop, post-op, pre-op, ragtop, raindrop, rooftop, root crop, sharecrop, shortstop, snowdrop, sweatshop, sweetshop, tank top, teardrop, thrift shop, tip-top, treetop, truck stop, workshop • barbershop, beauty shop, belly flop, blow one's top, body shop, carrottop, channel-hop, coffee shop, countertop, cover crop, drag-and-drop, island-hop, lollipop, machine shop, mom-and-pop, mountaintop, photo op, set up shop, soda pop, tabletop, techno-pop, teenybop, turboprop, union shop, whistle-stop, window-shop • comparison shop
op² \ō\ see OW¹
opal \ō-pəl\ opal • Constantinople
ope \ōp\ cope, dope, grope, hope,

Hope, lope, mope, nope, ope, pope, Pope, rope, scope, slope, soap, taupe • downslope, elope, fly dope, jump rope, North Slope, skip rope, tightrope, towrope • antelope, cantaloupe, envelope, forlorn hope, gyroscope, horoscope, interlope, isotope, microscope, misanthrope, periscope, slippery slope, stethoscope, telescope • Cape of Good Hope, kaleidoscope, oscilloscope, pay envelope, stereoscope
opean \ō-pē-ən\ see OPIAN
opee \ō-pē\ see OPI
opence \əp-əns\ see UPPANCE
oper \ō-pər\ coper, soaper • eloper • interloper
opey \ō-pē\ see OPI
oph \ōf\ see OAF
ophe¹ \ō-fē\ see OPHY
ophe² \óf\ see OFF²
opher \ō-fər\ see OFER
ophie \ō-fē\ see OPHY
ophir \ō-fər\ see OFER
ophy \ō-fē\ Sophie, strophe, trophy
opi \ō-pē\ dopey, Hopi, mopey, ropy, soapy
opia \ō-pē-ə\ myopia, utopia • cornucopia, Ethiopia
opian \ō-pē-ən\ Aesopian, utopian • Ethiopian
opic¹ \äp-ik\ topic, tropic • Aesopic, myopic, subtropic • gyroscopic, microscopic, misanthropic, philanthropic, semitropic, telescopic • kaleidoscopic, stereoscopic
opic² \ō-pik\ tropic • myopic • Ethiopic
opical \äp-i-kəl\ topical, tropical • subtropical
oplar \äp-lər\ see OPPLER
ople \ō-pəl\ see OPAL
opol \ō-pəl\ see OPAL
opolis \äp-ə-ləs\ acropolis, metropolis, necropolis • megalopolis

opoly \äp-ə-lē\ choppily, floppily, sloppily • monopoly, Monopoly, vox populi

opped \äpt\ see OPT

opper \äp-ər\ chopper, copper, dropper, hopper, proper, shopper, stopper, swapper, whopper • clodhopper, eavesdropper, eyedropper, eyepopper, grasshopper, heart-stopper, hip-hopper, improper, jaw-dropper, job-hopper, leafhopper, name-dropper, sharecropper, showstopper, woodchopper • teenybopper, window-shopper

oppily \äp-ə-lē\ see OPOLY

oppiness \äp-ē-nəs\ choppiness, sloppiness

opping \äp-iŋ\ hopping, sopping, topping, whopping • eye-popping, heart-stopping, jaw-dropping, jobhopping, name-dropping, outcropping, showstopping • channel-hopping
—*also* -ing *forms of verbs listed at* OP[1]

oppler \äp-lər\ Doppler, poplar

oppy \äp-ē\ choppy, copy, floppy, gloppy, poppy, sloppy, soppy • jalopy, serape • photocopy

ops \äps\ chops, copse, tops • Cheops, cyclops, Cyclops, eyedrops, Pelops • lick one's chops • from the housetops, triceratops
—*also* -s, -'s, *and* -s' *forms of nouns and* -s *forms of verbs listed at* OP[1]

opse \äps\ see OPS

opsy \äp-sē\ autopsy, biopsy

opt \äpt\ opt, topped • adopt, close-cropped, co-opt • carrottopped
—*also* -ed *forms of verbs listed at* OP[1]

opter \äp-tər\ copter • adopter, helicopter

optic \äp-tik\ Coptic, optic • fiberoptic

option \äp-shən\ option • adoption

opuli \äp-ə-lē\ see OPOLY

opus \ō-pəs\ opus • Canopus, Mount Scopus • magnum opus

opy[1] \ō-pē\ see OPI

opy[2] \äp-ē\ see OPPY

oque[1] \ōk\ see OKE[1]

oque[2] \äk\ see OCK[1]

oque[3] \ōk\ see ALK

or[1] \ȯr\ boar, Boer, bore, chore, core, corps, door, drawer, floor, for, fore, four, gore, Gore, lore, Moore, more, nor, o'er, oar, or, ore, poor, pore, pour, roar, score, shore, snore, soar, sore, spoor, spore, store, swore, Thor, tor, tore, war, wore, yore, your, you're • abhor, adore, and/or, as for, ashore, backdoor, Bangor, bedsore, before, bookstore, box score, call for, candor, captor, centaur, chain store, closed-door, cold sore, condor, decor, deplore, dime-store, Dior, done for, donor, downpour, drugstore, Dutch door, encore, explore, eyesore, fall for, Fillmore, flexor, folklore, footsore, fourscore, French door, full-bore, galore, go for, ground floor, hard-core, ignore, implore, indoor, in for, in-store, Lahore, lakeshore, Lenore, look for, Luxor, memoir, mentor, Mysore, Nestor, next-door, offshore, onshore, outdoor, phosphor, rancor, rapport, raptor, Realtor, restore, savior, seafloor, seashore, sector, señor, sensor, Seymour, smoothbore, s'more, sophomore, stand for, storm door, subfloor, Tagore, take for, temblor, tensor, therefore, threescore, Timor, topdrawer, trapdoor, uproar, vendor, what's more, wherefore, wild boar, woodlore • albacore, allosaur, alongshore, anymore, archosaur, at death's door, at one's door, Baltimore, Bangalore, bargain for, Barrymore, canker sore, carnivore, close the door, come in for, commodore, corridor, dinosaur, door-to-door, double door, Eastern shore, East Timor, Ecuador, either-or, Eleanor, elector, evermore, except for, forest floor, from the floor, furthermore, general store, go in for, guarantor, herbivore, heretofore, in line for, Labrador, man-of-war, matador, metaphor, meteor, Minotaur, more and more, Mount Rushmore, Mount Tabor, nevermore, omnivore, picador, pinafore, pompadour, predator, reservoir, saddle sore, Salvador, semaphore, Singapore, stand up for, stevedore, stick up for, struggle for, superstore, sycamore, take the floor, Theodore, to die for, troubadour, tug-of-war, two-by-four, uncalled-for, underscore • ambassador, conquistador, conservator, convenience store, Corregidor, department store, El Salvador, esprit de corps, foot in the door, forevermore, go to bat for, have it in for, insectivore, legislator, national seashore, revolving door, San Salvador, toreador, tyrannosaur • administrator, lobster thermidor, variety store

or² \ər\ see EUR¹

ora \òr-ə\ aura, Cora, Dora, flora, Flora, hora, Laura, Lora, Nora, Torah • Andorra, angora, aurora, fedora, Gomorrah, Lenora, menorah, Pandora, remora, señora, Sonora • Bora-Bora, Leonora, Simchas Torah

orable \òr-ə-bəl\ horrible, pourable, storable • adorable, deplorable, restorable

orace \òr-əs\ see AURUS

orage¹ \är-ij\ forage, porridge
orage² \òr-ij\ forage, porridge, storage • cold storage
orah \òr-ə\ see ORA
oral \òr-əl\ aural, choral, coral, floral, laurel, Laurel, moral, oral, quarrel • amoral, immoral, mayoral, monaural • electoral
oram \òr-əm\ see ORUM
orative \òr-ət-iv\ pejorative, restorative
oray \ə-rē\ see URRY
orb \òrb\ orb • absorb • reabsorb
orc \òrk\ see ORK²
orca \òr-ka\ orca • Majorca
orce \òrs\ see ORSE¹
orced \òrst\ see ORST¹
orceful \òrs-fəl\ see ORSEFUL
orcement \òr-smənt\ see ORSEMENT
orcer \òr-sər\ coarser, hoarser • enforcer
orch \òrch\ porch, scorch, torch • blowtorch, sunporch • sleeping porch
orcher \òr-chər\ scorcher, torture
orchid \òr-kəd\ forked, orchid
ord¹ \òrd\ see OARD
ord² \ərd\ see IRD
ord³ \òr\ see OR¹
ordan \òrd-ᵊn\ see ARDEN²
ordant \òrd-ᵊnt\ mordant • discordant
orde \òrd\ see OARD
orded \òrd-əd\ see ARDED²
ordent \òrd-ᵊnt\ see ORDANT
order \òrd-ər\ boarder, border, hoarder, order • back order, court order, disorder, gag order, in order, keyboarder, mail-order, on order, recorder, reorder, sailboarder, short-order, skateboarder, snowboarder, surfboarder, to order, transborder, word order • flight recorder, holy order, in short order, law-and-order, made-to-order, money order, mood disorder, pecking

order, tape recorder, wire
recorder • eating disorder, panic
disorder, restraining order
ordered \órd-ərd\ bordered, ordered • disordered, well-ordered
—*also* -ed *forms of verbs listed at*
ORDER
orders \órd-ərz\ marching orders
—*also* -s, -'s, *and* -s' *forms of*
nouns and -s *forms of verbs listed*
at ORDER
ordid \órd-əd\ see ARDED[2]
ording[1] \órd-iŋ\ hoarding • recording, rewarding, skateboarding
• tape recording, weatherboarding
—*also* -ing *forms of verbs listed at*
OARD
ording[2] \ərd-iŋ\ see ERDING
ordion \órd-ē-ən\ accordion, Ed-
wardian
ordon \órd-ᵊn\ see ARDEN[2]
ordure \ór-jər\ see ORGER
ordy \ərd-ē\ see URDY
ore[1] \ór-ē\ see ORY
ore[2] \úr\ see URE[1]
ore[3] \ər-ə\ see OROUGH[1]
ore[4] \ór\ see OR[1]
oreal \ór-ē-əl\ see ORIAL
orean \ór-ē-ən\ see ORIAN
oreas \ór-ē-əs\ see ORIOUS
ored \órd\ see OARD
orehead \ór-əd\ see ORRID
oreign[1] \är-ən\ see ARIN
oreign[2] \ór-ən\ see ORIN[1]
oreigner \ór-ə-nər\ see ORONER
orem \ór-əm\ see ORUM
oreman \ór-mən\ see ORMAN
oronce \ór-ɔn(t)s\ see AWRENCE
oreous \ór-ē-əs\ see ORIOUS
orer \ór-ər\ borer, corer, floorer,
horror, poorer, pourer, scorer,
snorer, sorer • adorer, corn borer,
explorer • Sea Explorer
ores[1] \ór-əs\ see AURUS
ores[2] \órz\ see OORS
orest \ór-əst\ see ORIST
orester \ór-ə-stər\ see ORISTER

oreum \ór-ē-əm\ see ORIUM
oreward \ór-wərd\ see ORWARD
oreword \ór-wərd\ see ORWARD
orey \ór-ē\ see ORY
orf \órf\ see ORPH
org[1] \órg\ Borg, morgue • cyborg
org[2] \ór-ē\ see ORY
organ \ór-gən\ gorgon, Morgan,
organ • hand organ, house organ,
mouth organ, pipe organ, reed
organ, sense organ • barrel organ
orge \órj\ forge, George, gorge
• disgorge, engorge, Fort George,
Lake George, Lloyd George
• Royal Gorge • Olduvai Gorge
orger \ór-jər\ forger, ordure
orgi \ór-gē\ see ORGY
orgia \ór-jə\ Borgia, Georgia
orgon \ór-gən\ see ORGAN
orgue \órg\ see ORG[1]
orgy \ór-gē\ corgi, porgy
ori \ór-ē\ see ORY
oria \ór-ē-ə\ Gloria • euphoria,
Peoria, Pretoria, Victoria • Lake
Victoria • phantasmagoria
orial \ór-ē-əl\ boreal, oriole • arbo-
real, armorial, authorial, corpo-
real, factorial, manorial,
marmoreal, memorial, pictorial,
sartorial, tutorial • curatorial,
dictatorial, editorial, equatorial,
immemorial, janitorial, professo-
rial, senatorial, territorial • am-
bassadorial, conspiratorial,
gubernatorial, prosecutorial, time
immemorial
oriam \ór-ē-əm\ see ORIUM
orian \ór-ē-ən\ Dorian • Azorean,
Gregorian, historian, praetorian,
stentorian, Victorian
• dinosaurian, Ecuadorean,
Labradorean, Salvadorean, Singa-
porean • salutatorian, valedicto-
rian
oric \ór-ik\ caloric, euphoric, folk-
loric, historic, phosphoric
• metaphoric, meteoric,

noncaloric, prehistoric, sopho-
moric • phantasmagoric

orical \òr-i-kəl\ historical, rhetori-
cal • allegorical, categorical,
metaphorical, oratorical

orid \òr-əd\ see ORRID

oriel \òr-ē-əl\ see ORIAL

orin[1] \òr-ən\ chlorine, foreign,
Lauren, Orrin, warren, Warren
• Andorran

orin[2] \är-ən\ see ARIN

orine \òr-ən\ see ORIN[1]

oring \òr-iŋ\ boring, flooring,
roaring • outpouring, rip-roaring,
wood-boring
—*also* -ing *forms of verbs listed at*
OR[1]

öring \ər-iŋ\ see URRING

oriole \òr-ē-əl\ see ORIAL

orious \òr-ē-əs\ Boreas, glorious
• censorious, laborious, notori-
ous, uproarious, uxorious, vain-
glorious, victorious • meritorious

oris \òr-əs\ see AURUS

orish \ùr-ish\ see OORISH

orist \òr-əst\ florist, forest, poorest,
sorest • Black Forest, deforest,
folklorist, reforest • Petrified
Forest

orister \òr-ə-stər\ chorister,
forester

ority \òr-ət-ē\ authority, majority,
minority, priority, seniority,
sonority, sorority • inferiority,
superiority

orium \òr-ē-əm\ emporium • audi-
torium, cafetorium, crematorium,
in memoriam, moratorium, sana-
torium

ork[1] \ərk\ clerk, Dirk, irk, jerk,
Kirk, lurk, murk, perk, quirk,
shirk, smirk, Turk, work • art-
work, at work, beadwork,
berserk, brickwork, brushwork,
casework, clockwork, Dunkirk,
earthwork, file clerk, firework,
footwork, framework, Grand

Turk, groundwork, guesswork,
handwork, homework, house-
work, ironwork, knee-jerk, leg-
work, lifework, make-work,
network, outwork, patchwork,
piecework, rework, roadwork,
salesclerk, schoolwork, Selkirk,
stonework, teamwork, town
clerk, waxwork, woodwork,
young Turk • Atatürk, basket-
work, bodywork, busywork,
cabinetwork, city clerk, clean-
and-jerk, handiwork, leather-
work, masterwork, metalwork,
needlework, out of work, over-
work, paperwork, piece of work,
shipping clerk, social work, soda
jerk, wickerwork

ork[2] \òrk\ cork, Cork, dork, fork,
pork, quark, stork, torque, York
• bulwark, Cape York, New York,
North York, pitchfork, salt pork,
uncork, wood stork

orked \òr-kəd\ see ORCHID

orker[1] \ər-kər\ lurker, shirker,
worker • caseworker,
dockworker, farmworker, field-
worker, ironworker, networker,
pieceworker, steelworker, tear-
jerker, woodworker
• autoworker, metalworker, social
worker, wonder-worker

orker[2] \òr-kər\ corker, porker
• New Yorker

orkie \òr-kē\ see ORKY

orking \ər-kiŋ\ hardworking, net-
working, tear-jerking, woodwork-
ing • metalworking,
wonder-working
—*also* -ing *forms of verbs listed at*
ORK[1]

orky \òr-kē\ dorky, Gorky, porky,
Yorkie

orl \ərl\ see IRL

orld \ərld\ world • dreamworld,
free world, New World, old-
world, Old World, real-world,

third world • afterworld, brave new world, Disney World, in the world, netherworld, otherworld, underworld • for all the world, man of the world, out of this world • on top of the world
—*also* -ed *forms of verbs listed at* IRL

orled \ərld\ see ORLD

orm¹ \ərm\ firm, germ, perm, squirm, term, worm • affirm, bookworm, budworm, confirm, cutworm, deworm, earthworm, flatworm, glowworm, heartworm, hookworm, hornworm, inchworm, infirm, long-term, midterm, pinworm, ringworm, roundworm, short-term, silkworm, tapeworm, webworm • pachyderm, reconfirm

orm² \ȯrm\ dorm, form, norm, storm, swarm, warm • aswarm, barnstorm, brainstorm, by storm, conform, deform, dust storm, firestorm, free-form, hailstorm, ice storm, inform, landform, lifeform, lukewarm, perform, platform, preform, rainstorm, re-form, reform, sandstorm, snowstorm, transform, waveform, windstorm • chloroform, cruciform, land reform, thunderstorm, uniform • cuneiform, dress uniform, magnetic storm, quadratic form

ormal \ȯr-məl\ formal, normal • abnormal, informal, subnormal • paranormal, semiformal

ormally \ȯr-mə-lē\ formally, formerly, normally, stormily • abnormally, informally • paranormally

orman \ȯr-mən\ doorman, foreman, Foreman, Mormon, Norman • longshoreman

ormant \ȯr-mənt\ dormant • informant

ormative \ȯr-mət-iv\ formative, normative • informative, transformative

orme \ȯrm\ see ORM²

ormed \ȯrmd\ deformed, informed, malformed, unformed • well-informed
—*also* -ed *forms of verbs listed at* ORM²

ormer \ȯr-mər\ dormer, former, warmer • barnstormer, benchwarmer, brainstormer, heartwarmer, informer, performer, reformer, transformer

ormerly \ȯr-mə-lē\ see ORMALLY

ormily \ȯr-mə-lē\ see ORMALLY

orming \ȯr-miŋ\ brainstorming, heartwarming, housewarming, performing • habit-forming
—*also* -ing *forms of verbs listed at* ORM²

ormity \ȯr-mət-ē\ conformity, deformity, enormity • nonconformity, uniformity

ormless \ȯrm-ləs\ formless, gormless

ormon \ȯr-mən\ see ORMAN

ormy \ȯr-mē\ see ORMY

orn¹ \ȯrn\ born, borne, corn, horn, morn, mourn, scorn, shorn, sworn, thorn, torn, warn, worn • acorn, adorn, airborne, bighorn, blackthorn, blue corn, boxthorn, broomcorn, buckthorn, bullhorn, Cape Horn, careworn, Dearborn, dehorn, earthborn, field corn, firethorn, firstborn, flint corn, foghorn, forewarn, forlorn, freeborn, French horn, greenhorn, hawthorn, Hawthorne, highborn, inborn, longhorn, lovelorn, newborn, outworn, popcorn, pronghorn, ramshorn, reborn, saxhorn, seaborne, shipborne, shoehorn, shopworn, shorthorn, skyborne, soilborne, stillborn, sweet corn, tick-borne, timeworn, tinhorn, tricorne, unborn, unworn, well-born, well-worn, wind-borne • barleycorn, Capricorn, English horn, flügelhorn, foreign-born, hunting horn, Matterhorn, peppercorn, powder horn, saddle horn, unicorn, waterborne, weatherworn • Indian corn, Little Bighorn, Texas longhorn • to the manner born, to the manor born

orn² \ərn\ see URN

ornament \ȯr-nə-mənt\ ornament, tournament

orne \ȯrn\ see ORN¹

orned \ȯrnd\ horned, thorned • unadorned
—also -ed forms of verbs listed at ORN¹

orner \ȯr-nər\ corner, scorner, Warner • kitty-corner

orney \ər-nē\ see OURNEY¹

ornful \ȯrn-fəl\ mournful, scornful

orning \ȯr-niŋ\ morning, mourning, warning
—also -ing forms of verbs listed at ORN¹

ornment \ərn-mənt\ see ERNMENT

orny \ȯr-nē\ corny, thorny

oro \ər-ə\ see OROUGH¹

oroner \ȯr-ə-nər\ coroner, foreigner

orough¹ \ər-ə\ borough, burro, burrow, furrow, ore, thorough • Gainsborough, Greensboro • Edinburgh, kookaburra

orough² \ər-ō\ see URROW¹

orous \ȯr-əs\ see AURUS

orp \ȯrp\ gorp, warp

orpe \ȯrp\ see ORP

orph \ȯrf\ dwarf, morph • Düsseldorf

orphan \ȯr-fən\ orphan • endorphin

orpheus \ȯr-fē-əs\ Morpheus, Orpheus

orphin \ȯr-fən\ see ORPHAN

orpoise \ȯr-pəs\ see ORPUS

orps \ȯr\ see OR¹

orpsman \ȯr-mən\ see ORMAN

orpus \ȯr-pəs\ porpoise • habeas corpus

orque \ȯrk\ see ORK²

orquer \ȯr-kər\ see ORKER²

orr \ȯr\ see OR¹

orra¹ \är-ə\ see ARA¹

orra² \ȯr-ə\ see ORA

orrah¹ \ȯr-ə\ see ORA

orrah² \är-ə\ see ARA¹

orran¹ \är-ən\ see ARIN

orran² \ȯr-ən\ see ORIN¹

orrence \ȯr-əns\ see AWRENCE

orrel \ȯr-əl\ see ORAL

orrent \ȯr-ənt\ torrent, warrant • abhorrent, death warrant, search warrant

orrer \ȯr-ər\ see ORER

orres \ȯr-əs\ see AURUS

orrest \ȯr-əst\ see ORIST

orrible \ȯr-ə-bəl\ see ORABLE

orrid \ȯr-əd\ florid, horrid, torrid

orridge¹ \är-ij\ see ORAGE¹

orridge² \ȯr-ij\ see ORAGE²

orrie¹ \är-ē\ see ARI¹

orrie² \ȯr-ē\ see ORY

orrier \ȯr-ē-ər\ see ARRIOR

orrin¹ \är-en\ see ARIN

orrin² \ȯr-ən\ see ORIN¹

orris¹ \är-əs\ Juárez, Maurice, morris, Morris • Benares, Polaris

orris² \ȯr-əs\ see AURUS

orror \ȯr-ər\ see ORER

orrow¹ \är-ō\ borrow, morrow, sorrow, taro • bizarro, Pizarro, saguaro, tomorrow • Kilimanjaro

orrow² \är-ə\ see ARA¹

orry¹ \är-ē\ see ARI¹

orry² \ər-ē\ see URRY

ors \ȯrz\ see OORS

orsal \ȯr-səl\ see ORSEL

orse¹ \ȯrs\ coarse, course, force, hoarse, horse, Morse, Norse, source • clotheshorse, concourse, crash course, dark horse, dead horse, discourse, divorce, endorse, enforce, golf course, gut course, high horse, iron horse, midcourse, of course, one-horse, packhorse, racecourse, racehorse, recourse, remorse, resource, sawhorse, sea horse, unhorse, warhorse, Whitehorse, workhorse • charley horse, Crazy Horse, harness horse, hobbyhorse, mini-course, pommel horse, quarter horse, reinforce, rocking horse, saddle horse, stalking horse, telecourse, tour de force, Trojan horse, vaulting horse, watercourse • collision course, matter of course, obstacle course, par for the course • Arabian horse

orse² \ərs\ see ERSE

orseful \ȯrs-fəl\ forceful • remorse-ful, resourceful

orsel \ȯr-səl\ dorsal, morsel

orseman \ȯr-smən\ horseman, Norseman

orsement \ȯr-smənt\ endorsement, enforcement • reinforcement

orsen \ərs-³n\ see ERSON

orset \ȯr-sət\ corset, Dorset

orsion \ȯr-shən\ see ORTION

orst¹ \ȯrst\ forced
—*also* -ed *forms of verbs listed at* ORSE¹

orst² \ərst\ see URST

ort¹ \ȯrt\ court, fort, forte, port, quart, short, snort, sort, sport, thwart, tort, torte, wart • abort, airport, athwart, Bridgeport, carport, cavort, cohort, comport, consort, contort, deport, disport, distort, effort, escort, exhort, export, extort, fall short, for short, Gulfport, home port, in short, Newport, passport, presort, pur-port, report, re-sort, resort, retort, seaport, sell short, Shreveport, spaceport, spoilsport, support, transport • davenport, heliport,

hold the fort, life-support, non-support, of a sort, worrywart • pianoforte, the long and short

ort² \ȯr\ see OR¹

ort³ \ərt\ see ERT¹

ortage \ȯrt-ij\ portage, shortage • reportage

ortal \ȯrt-³l\ chortle, mortal, portal • immortal

ortar \ȯrt-ər\ see ORTER

orte¹ \ȯrt\ see ORT¹

orte² \ȯrt-ē\ see ORTY

orted \ȯrt-əd\ assorted, purported • self-supported
—*also* -ed *forms of verbs listed at* ORT¹

orter \ȯrt-ər\ mortar, porter, Porter, quarter, shorter, sorter • exporter, headquarter, importer, reporter, supporter, transporter • brick-and-mortar • athletic supporter

orteur \ȯrt-ər\ see ORTER

orth¹ \ȯrth\ forth, fourth, north, North • bring forth, call forth, thenceforth • and so forth, back and forth, Firth of Forth

orth² \ərth\ see IRTH

orthless \ərth-ləs\ see IRTHLESS

orthy \ər-thē\ earthy, worthy • air-worthy, blameworthy, crashwor-thy, newsworthy, noteworthy, praiseworthy, roadworthy, sea-worthy, trustworthy, unworthy • creditworthy

ortie \ȯrt-ē\ see ORTY

orting \ȯrt-iŋ\ sporting • nonsport-ing • self-supporting
—*also* -ing *forms of verbs listed at* ORT¹

ortion \ȯr-shən\ portion, torsion • apportion, contortion, distor-tion, extortion, proportion • dis-proportion, in proportion, reapportion

ortionate \ȯr-shnət\ extortionate, proportionate • disproportionate

ortionist \ȯr-shnist\ contortionist,
extortionist
ortis \ȯrt-əs\ mortise, tortoise
• rigor mortis
ortise \ȯrt-əs\ see ORTIS
ortive \ȯrt-iv\ abortive, supportive
ortle \ȯrt-ᵊl\ see ORTAL
ortly \ȯrt-lē\ courtly, portly,
shortly
ortment \ȯrt-mənt\ assortment,
comportment, deportment
ortoise \ȯrt-əs\ see ORTIS
orts \ȯrts\ quartz, shorts, sports
• boxer shorts, out of sorts, un-
dershorts • Bermuda shorts, bicycle shorts
—*also* -s, -'s, *and* -s' *forms of
nouns and* -s *forms of verbs listed
at* ORT¹
ortunate \ȯrch-nət\ fortunate
• importunate, unfortunate
orture \ȯr-chər\ see ORCHER
orty \ȯrt-ē\ forty, shorty, sporty
• pianoforte
orum \ȯr-əm\ forum, quorum
• decorum • indecorum • sanctum
sanctorum
orus \ȯr-əs\ see AURUS
orward \ȯr-wərd\ forward, fore-
word, shoreward • bring forward,
fast-forward, flash forward,
henceforward, look forward, put
forward, set forward, straightfor-
ward, thenceforward
ory \ȯr-ē\ dory, glory, gory, Laurie,
Lori, quarry, sorry, story, Tory
• backstory, fish story, ghost
story, Old Glory, short story, sob
story • allegory, auditory, bedtime
story, category, cover story, cre-
matory, desultory, dilatory, dor-
mitory, horror story, hunky-dory,
inventory, Lake Maggiore, lauda-
tory, lavatory, mandatory, migra-
tory, Montessori, morning glory,
offertory, oratory, predatory,
prefatory, promissory, promon-

tory, purgatory, repertory, statu-
tory, territory, transitory • accu-
satory, ambulatory, celebratory,
compensatory, conservatory,
dedicatory, defamatory, deposi-
tory, derogatory, exculpatory,
explanatory, exploratory, inflam-
matory, laboratory, masturba-
tory, obligatory, observatory,
preparatory, reformatory, regula-
tory, repository, revelatory, respi-
ratory • anticipatory,
discriminatory, hallucinatory
orze \ȯrz\ see OORS
os¹ \äs\ boss, dross, floss, gloss,
toss • Argos, chaos, cosmos, De-
los, emboss, en masse, Eros, ku-
dos, Lagos, Laos, Madras, Naxos,
pathos, Patmos, Pharos, ringtoss
• albatross, coup de grâce, demitasse, dental floss, gravitas, semigloss
os² \ō\ see OW¹
os³ \ōs\ see OSE¹
os⁴ \ȯs\ see OSS¹
osa \ō-sə\ Xhosa • Formosa, mi-
mosa
osable \ō-zə-bəl\ disposable, op-
posable, reclosable
osal \ō-zəl\ Mosel • disposal, pro-
posal
osch \äsh\ see ASH²
oschen \ō-shən\ see OTION
osco \äs-kō\ see OSCOE
oscoe \äs-kō\ Bosco, Roscoe • fiasco
ose¹ \ōs\ Bose, close, dose, gross
• Carlos, cosmos, dextrose, en-
gross, fructose, glucose, lactose,
maltose, morose, pathos, sucrose,
Sukkoth, up close, verbose
• adios, bellicose, cellulose, coma-
tose, diagnose, grandiose, Helios,
lachrymose, megadose, overdose,
varicose • metamorphose
ose² \ōz\ chose, close, clothes,
doze, froze, hose, nose, pose,

prose, rose, Rose • Ambrose,
arose, bedclothes, bulldoze, com-
pose, depose, dextrose, disclose,
dispose, dog rose, enclose, expose,
foreclose, fructose, glucose, im-
pose, Mount Rose, nightclothes,
oppose, plainclothes, primrose,
propose, pug nose, repose, rock-
rose, suppose, transpose, tuberose
• Berlioz, cabbage rose, cellulose,
China rose, Christmas rose,
damask rose, decompose, diagnose, indispose, interpose, juxta-
pose, on the nose, panty hose,
predispose, presuppose, shovel-
nose, swaddling clothes, thumb
one's nose, underclothes
• evening primrose, follow one's
nose, look down one's nose, metamorphose, overexpose, pay
through the nose, superimpose,
under one's nose
—*also* -s, -'s, *and* -s' *forms of
nouns and* -s *forms of verbs listed
at* OW[1]
ose[3] \üz\ *see* USE[2]
osed \ōzd\ closed • composed,
exposed, hard-nosed, opposed,
pug-nosed, supposed • indisposed,
shovel-nosed, well-disposed
—*also* -ed *forms of verbs listed at*
OSE[2]
osee \ō-zē\ *see* OSY
osel \ō-zəl\ *see* OSAL
osen \ōz-ᵊn\ chosen, frozen • deep-
frozen, quick-frozen
oser[1] \ō-zər\ brownnoser, bull-
dozer, composer, disposer
oser[2] \ü-zər\ *see* USER
oset \äz-ət\ *see* OSIT
osey \ō-zē\ *see* OSY
osh[1] \ȯsh\ *see* ASH[2]
osh[2] \ōsh\ *see* OCHE[2]
oshed[1] \äsht\ galoshed
—*also* -ed *forms of verbs listed at*
ASH[1]
oshed[2] \ȯsht\ *see* ASHED[1]

oshen \ō-shən\ *see* OTION
osher \äsh-ər\ *see* ASHER[1]
osible \ō-zə-bəl\ *see* OSABLE
osier \ō-zhər\ *see* OSURE
osily \ō-zə-lē\ cozily, nosily, rosily
osing \ō-ziŋ\ closing • disclosing,
imposing, self-closing, supposing
—*also* -ing *forms of verbs listed at*
OSE[2]
osion \ō-zhən\ corrosion, erosion,
explosion, implosion
osis \ō-səs\ cirrhosis, hypnosis,
meiosis, mitosis, neurosis, osmo-
sis, prognosis, psychosis, sclerosis
• diagnosis, halitosis, symbiosis
• cystic fibrosis, tuberculosis
• mononucleosis
osit \äz-ət\ closet, posit • compos-
ite, deposit
osite \äz-ət\ *see* OSIT
osius \ō-shəs\ *see* OCIOUS
osive \ō-siv\ corrosive, explosive,
implosive, purposive • high explosive
osk \äsk\ mosque • kiosk
oso[1] \ō-sō\ mafioso, virtuoso
• concerto grosso
oso[2] \ü-sō\ *see* USOE
osophy \äs-ə-fē\ philosophy, theos-
ophy
osque \äsk\ *see* OSK
oss[1] \ȯs\ boss, cross, floss, gloss,
loss, moss, Ross, sauce, toss
• across, Blue Cross, brown sauce,
club moss, crisscross, emboss,
Greek cross, lacrosse, pathos,
peat moss, Red Cross, ringtoss,
tau cross, uncross, white sauce
• albatross, applesauce, at a loss,
béarnaise sauce, Celtic cross, chili
sauce, come across, dental floss,
double-cross, get across, hoisin
sauce, Iceland moss, Irish moss,
Latin cross, Maltese cross, Mor-
nay sauce, motocross, Navy
Cross, Northern Cross, papal
cross, reindeer moss, run across,

semigloss, Southern Cross, Spanish moss, tartar sauce, underboss • pectoral cross, sign of the cross, Worcestershire sauce • stations of the cross

oss² \ōs\ see OSE¹

oss³ \äs\ see OS¹

ossa \äs-ə\ see ASA¹

ossal \äs-əl\ docile, fossil, jostle, tassel, wassail • apostle, colossal

osse¹ \äs\ see OS¹

osse² \äs-ē\ see OSSY¹

osse³ \ȯs\ see OSS¹

ossed \ȯst\ see OST³

osser \ȯ-sər\ Chaucer, saucer • double-crosser, flying saucer

ossil \äs-əl\ see OSSAL

ossity \äs-ət-ē\ atrocity, ferocity, monstrosity, pomposity, precocity, velocity, verbosity, viscosity • animosity, curiosity, generosity, grandiosity, reciprocity, virtuosity • religiosity

ossly \ȯs-lē\ costly, crossly

osso \ō-sō\ see OSO¹

ossos \äs-əs\ see OCESS

ossum \äs-əm\ blossom, possum • opossum, play possum

ossus \äs-əs\ see OCESS

ossy¹ \äs-ē\ Aussie, bossy, glossy, posse, quasi

ossy² \ȯ-sē\ Aussie, bossy, mossy

ost¹ \äst\ accost • Pentecost
—*also* -ed *forms of verbs listed at* OS¹

ost² \ōst\ boast, coast, ghost, host, most, post, roast, toast • almost, at most, bedpost, compost, doorpost, endmost, foremost, French toast, gatepost, goalpost, Gold Coast, lamppost, milepost, pot roast, rearmost, rib roast, seacoast, signpost, Slave Coast, topmost, utmost • at the most, Barbary Coast, bottommost, coast-to-coast, command post, easternmost, Holy Ghost, inner-

most, Ivory Coast, melba toast, northernmost, outermost, parcel post, southernmost, trading post, uppermost, uttermost, whipping post • from coast to coast, give up the ghost, Mosquito Coast, Washington Post
—*also* -ed *forms of verbs listed at* OSE¹

ost³ \ȯst\ cost, frost, lost • accost, defrost, exhaust, hoarfrost, Jack Frost, star-crossed • holocaust, Pentecost, permafrost,
—*also* -ed *forms of verbs listed at* OSS¹

ost⁴ \əst\ see UST¹

ostal¹ \ōs-t³l\ coastal, postal • bicoastal

ostal² \äs-t³l\ see OSTEL

oste \ōst\ see OST²

ostel \äs-t³l\ hostile • youth hostel • Pentecostal

oster¹ \äs-tər\ foster, Foster, roster • impostor • paternoster

oster² \ȯs-tər\ foster, Foster, roster

oster³ \ō-stər\ see OASTER

ostic \äs-tik\ acrostic, agnostic • diagnostic

ostile \äs-t³l\ see OSTEL

ostle \äs-əl\ see OSSAL

ostly¹ \ōst-lē\ ghostly, mostly

ostly² \ȯs-lē\ see OSSLY

oston \ȯs-tən\ Austen, Austin, Boston

ostor \äs-tər\ see OSTER¹

ostrum \äs-trəm\ nostrum, rostrum

osure \ō-zhər\ closure, crosier • composure, disclosure, enclosure, exposure, foreclosure • time exposure • overexposure, underexposure

osy \ō-zē\ cozy, dozy, mosey, nosy, posy, prosy, rosy • ring-around-the-rosy

osz \ȯsh\ see ASH²

oszcz \ȯsh\ see ASH²

ot¹ \ät\ blot, bot, clot, cot, dot, got,

hot, jot, knot, lot, Lot, naught,
not, plot, pot, rot, Scot, Scott,
shot, slot, sot, spot, squat, swat,
tot, trot, watt, Watt, what, yacht
• Alcott, allot, a lot, a shot, big
shot, blind spot, bloodshot, boy-
cott, buckshot, cannot, cheap
shot, crackpot, despot, dogtrot,
dovecote, dry rot, dunk shot,
earshot, feedlot, fiat, forgot, foul
shot, fox-trot, gunshot, have-not,
hotshot, jackpot, jump shot,
kumquat, long shot, mascot, mug
shot, Pequot, Pol Pot, potshot,
Rabat, red-hot, reef knot, robot,
root rot, Sadat, sandlot, sexpot,
Shabbat, shallot, sheepcote, slap
shot, slingshot, slipknot, snapshot,
soft spot, somewhat, square knot,
stinkpot, stockpot, subplot,
sunspot, sweet spot, teapot, tin-
pot, upshot, wainscot, whatnot,
white-hot, woodlot • aeronaut,
apricot, aquanaut, argonaut,
astronaut, booster shot, Camelot,
caveat, chamber pot, chimney
pot, coffeepot, cosmonaut, coun
terplot, diddley-squat, flowerpot,
granny knot, hit the spot, Hotten-
tot, Huguenot, juggernaut, kilo-
watt, Lancelot, like a shot, like as
not, lobster pot, megawatt, melting pot, microdot, monocot,
ocelot, on the spot, parking lot,
patriot, Penobscot, piping hot,
polka dot, scattershot, tie the
knot, touch-me-not, Windsor
knot • as like as not, by a long
shot, compatriot, forget-me-not,
Gordian knot, hit the jackpot,
penalty shot, stevedore knot,
whether or not • all over the lot
• Johnny-on-the-spot
ot² \ō\ see OW[1]
ot³ \ȯt\ see OAT
ot⁴ \ȯt\ see OUGHT[1]
ôt \ō\ see OW[1]

ota \ōt-ə\ quota • Carlota, Dakota,
iota, Lakota, Toyota • Minnesota,
North Dakota, Sarasota, South
Dakota
otable \ōt-ə-bəl\ notable, potable,
quotable
otal \ōt-ᵊl\ total • subtotal, sum
total • anecdotal
otany \ät-ᵊn-ē\ botany, cottony
• monotony
otary \ōt-ə-rē\ coterie, rotary
otas \ō-təs\ see OTUS
otch \äch\ blotch, botch, crotch,
notch, scotch, Scotch, splotch,
swatch, watch • bird-watch,
deathwatch, hopscotch,
Sasquatch, stopwatch, top-notch,
wristwatch • butterscotch
otchman \äch-mən\ Scotchman,
watchman
otchy \äch-ē\ blotchy, boccie,
splotchy • hibachi, Karachi • Lib-
erace, mariachi
ote¹ \ōt-ē\ throaty • coyote, peyote
• Don Quixote
ote² \ōt\ see OAT
ote³ \ät\ see OT[1]
oted \ōt-əd\ see OATED
oten \ōt-ᵊn\ see OTON
oter \ōt-ər\ see OATER
oterie \ōt-ə-rē\ see OTARY
oth¹ \ȯth\ broth, cloth, froth,
moth, sloth, swath • breechcloth,
clothes moth, dishcloth, face-
cloth, ground cloth, ground sloth,
hawk moth, loincloth, oilcloth,
sailcloth, scotch broth, silk moth,
sphinx moth, washcloth • gypsy
moth, luna moth, Ostrogoth,
tablecloth, three-toed sloth, tiger
moth, two-toed sloth
oth² \äth\ Goth, sloth, swath • Ostrogoth, Visigoth
oth³ \ōs\ see OSE[1]
oth⁴ \ȯt\ see OAT
oth⁵ \ōth\ see OWTH
othe \ōth\ clothe, loathe • unclothe

other[1] \ətẖ-ər\ brother, mother, other, rather, smother • another, big brother, blood brother, den mother, each other, godmother, grandmother, half brother, queen mother, stepbrother, stepmother • fairy godmother

other[2] \ätẖ-ər\ see ATHER[1]

otherly \ətẖ-ər-lē\ brotherly, motherly, southerly • grandmotherly

othes \ōz\ see OSE[2]

othing \ō-tẖiŋ\ clothing, loathing • betrothing, unclothing • underclothing • wolf in sheep's clothing

otho \ō-tō\ see OTO

oti[1] \ōt-ē\ see OTE[1]

oti[2] \ȯt-ē\ see AUGHTY[1]

otiable \ō-shə-bəl\ see OCIABLE

otic \ät-ik\ aquatic, chaotic, despotic, erotic, exotic, hypnotic, narcotic, neurotic, psychotic, quixotic, robotic • idiotic, patriotic, symbiotic • antibiotic

otice \ōt-əs\ see OTUS

otics \ät-iks\ robotics • aeronautics, astronautics
—*also* -s, -'s, *and* -s' *forms of nouns listed at* OTIC

otid \ät-əd\ see OTTED

otile \ōt-ᵊl\ see OTAL

oting[1] \ōt-iŋ\ see OATING

oting[2] \ät-iŋ\ see OTTING

otinous \ät-ᵊn-əs\ see OTONOUS

otion \ō-shən\ Goshen, lotion, motion, notion, ocean, potion • commotion, demotion, devotion, emotion, Laotian, promotion, slow-motion • Arctic Ocean, locomotion, Nova Scotian, set in motion, Southern Ocean • Antarctic Ocean, Atlantic Ocean, Indian Ocean, Pacific Ocean

otional \ō-shnəl\ devotional, emotional, promotional • unemotional

otis \ōt-əs\ see OTUS

otive \ōt-iv\ motive, votive • emotive • automotive, locomotive

otl \ät-ᵊl\ see OTTLE

otle \ät-ᵊl\ see OTTLE

otley \ät-lē\ see OTLY

otly \ät-lē\ hotly, motley

oto \ō-tō\ photo • de Soto, in toto, Kyoto, Lesotho • telephoto, Yamamoto

otomy \ät-ə-mē\ dichotomy, lobotomy

oton \ōt-ᵊn\ oaten • Lofoten, verboten

otonous \ät-ᵊn-əs\ rottenness • monotonous

otor \ōt-ər\ see OATER

otory \ōt-ə-rē\ see OTARY

ots \äts\ Graz, lots, Scots • age spots, ersatz • call the shots • connect-the-dots, hit the high spots
—*also* -s, -'s, *and* -s' *forms of nouns and* -s *forms of verbs listed at* OT[1]

otsman \ät-smən\ Scotsman, yachtsman

ott \ät\ see OT[1]

otta \ät-ə\ see ATA[1]

ottage \ät-ij\ cottage, wattage

ottal \ät-ᵊl\ see OTTLE

otte[1] \ät\ see OT[1]

otte[2] \ȯt\ see OUGHT[1]

otted \ät-əd\ knotted, potted, spotted • besotted, unspotted • polka-dotted
—*also* -ed *forms of verbs listed at* OT[1]

otten \ät-ᵊn\ cotton, gotten, rotten • au gratin, forgotten, ill-gotten • misbegotten, sauerbraten

ottenness \ät-ᵊn-əs\ see OTONOUS

otter \ät-ər\ blotter, daughter, hotter, otter, plotter, potter, Potter, Qatar, rotter, spotter, squatter, swatter, Tatar, totter, trotter, water • backwater, bathwater, boycotter, breakwater, Clearwater, deepwater, dishwater, floodwater, flyswatter, freshwater, globe-trotter, groundwater, headwater, hot water, ice water, jerkwater, meltwater, rainwater, saltwater, sea otter, seawater, tap water, tidewater, tread water, white-water • above water, alma mater, holy water, in deep water, mineral water, river otter, running water, soda water, teetertotter, tonic water, underwater • dead in the water, fish out of water, hell or high water

ottery \ät-ə-rē\ lottery, pottery, tottery, watery

ottid \ät-əd\ see OTTED

ottie \ät-ē\ see ATI[1]

otting \ät-iŋ\ jotting • globe-trotting, wainscoting
—also -ing forms of verbs listed at OT[1]

ottle \ät-ᵊl\ bottle, mottle, throttle, wattle • squeeze bottle • Aristotle, at full throttle, spin the bottle, vacuum bottle • Quetzalcoatl

otto[1] \ät-ō\ see ATO[1]

otto[2] \ot-ō\ see AUTO[1]

ottom \ät-əm\ see ATUM[1]

otty \ät-ē\ see ATI[1]

otun \ōt-ᵊn\ see OTON

oture \ō-chər\ see OACHER

otus \ōt-əs\ lotus, notice, Otis

oty \ot-ē\ see AUGHTY[1]

otyl \ät-ᵊl\ see OTTLE

ou[1] \ō\ see OW[1]

ou[2] \ü\ see EW[1]

ou[3] \aú\ see OW[2]

oubled \əb-əld\ see UBBLED

ouble \əb-əl\ see UBBLE

oubly \əb-lē\ see UBBLY[1]

oubt \aút\ see OUT[3]

oubted \aút-əd\ see OUTED

oubter \aút-ər\ see OUTER[2]

ouc[1] \ü\ see EW[1]

ouc[2] \ük\ see UKE

ouc[3] \úk\ see OOK[1]

ouce \üs\ see USE[1]

oucester[1] \äs-tər\ see OSTER[1]

oucester[2] \os-tər\ see OSTER[2]

ouch[1] \üch\ see OOCH[1]

ouch[2] \üsh\ see OUCHE

ouch[3] \əch\ see UTCH

ouch[4] \aúch\ couch, crouch, grouch, ouch, pouch, slouch, vouch • studio couch

ouche \üsh\ swoosh, whoosh

ouchy[1] \əch-ē\ see UCHY

ouchy[2] \aú-chē\ grouchy, pouchy, slouchy

oud[1] \üd\ see UDE[1]

oud[2] \aúd\ boughed, bowed, cloud, crowd, loud, proud, shroud • aloud, becloud, do proud, enshroud, out loud, Saint Cloud, unbowed • funnel cloud, mushroom cloud, overcloud, overcrowd, thundercloud
—also -ed forms of verbs listed at OW[2]

ou'd \üd\ see UDE[1]

ouda \üd-ə\ see UDA

oudy \aúd-ē\ see OWDY

oue \ü\ see EW[1]

ouf \üf\ see OOF[1]

ouffe \üf\ see OOF[1]

oug \aú\ see UH

ouge[1] \üj\ see UGE[1]

ouge[2] \üzh\ see UGE[2]

ough[1] \ō\ see OW[1]

ough[2] \ü\ see EW[1]

ough[3] \aú\ see OW[2]

ough[4] \äk\ see OCK[1]

ough[5] \əf\ see UFF

ough[6] \of\ see OFF[2]

ougham[1] \ōm\ see OME[1]

ougham[2] \üm\ see OOM[1]

oughed \aúd\ see OUD[2]

oughen \əf-ən\ see UFFIN

ougher \əf-ər\ see UFFER

oughie \əf-ē\ see UFFY

oughly \əf-lē\ see UFFLY

oughs \ōz\ see OSE[1]

ought[1] \ot\ bought, brought, caught, dot, fought, fraught, naught, ought, sought, taught, taut, thought, wrought

• distraught, forethought, hand-
wrought, onslaught, self-taught,
store-bought, unsought, untaught
• aeronaut, afterthought, aquanaut, argonaut, astronaut, cosmonaut, juggernaut, overwrought,
second thought

ought² \aut\ see OUT³

oughy¹ \ō-ē\ see OWY

oughy² \ü-ē\ see EWY

ouie \ü-ē\ see EWY

ouille \ü-ē\ see EWY

ouis \ü-ē\ see EWY

ouk \ük\ see UKE

ouki \ü-kē\ see OOKY¹

oul¹ \ōl\ see OLE¹

oul² \ül\ see OOL¹

oul³ \aul\ see OWL²

ould¹ \ōld\ see OLD¹

ould² \ud\ see OOD¹

oulder \ōl-dər\ see OLDER¹

ouldered \ōl-dərd\ shouldered
• round-shouldered
—*also* -ed *forms of verbs listed at*
OLDER¹

ouldest \ud-əst\ couldest,
shouldest, wouldest

ouldn't \ud-³nt\ couldn't,
shouldn't, wouldn't

oule¹ \ü-lē\ see ULY

oule² \ül\ see OOL¹

ouled \ōld\ see OLD¹

oulee \ü-lē\ see ULY

ouleh¹ \ü-lə\ see ULA

ouleh² \ü-lē\ see ULY

ouli \ü-lē\ see ULY

oulie \ü-lē\ see ULY

ouling \au-liŋ\ see OWLING²

oulish \ü-lish\ see OOLISH

ou'll¹ \ül\ see OOL¹

ou'll² \ul\ see UL¹

oulle \ül\ see OOL¹

oulli \ü-lē\ see ULY

oully \au-lē\ see OWLY²

oult \ōlt\ see OLT¹

oum \üm\ see OOM¹

oun¹ \aun\ see OWN²

oun² \ün\ see OON¹

ounce \auns\ bounce, flounce,
ounce, pounce, trounce • an-
nounce, denounce, pronounce,
renounce • dead-cat bounce, fluid
ounce, mispronounce

ouncer \aun-sər\ bouncer • an-
nouncer

ound¹ \ünd\ wound • flesh wound
—*also* -ed *forms of verbs listed at*
OON¹

ound² \aund\ bound, crowned,
found, ground, hound, mound,
pound, round, sound, wound
• abound, aground, all-round,
around, astound, background,
bloodhound, campground,
chowhound, compound, con-
found, coonhound, dachshund,
deerhound, dumbfound, earth-
bound, eastbound, elkhound,
expound, fairground, fogbound,
foot-pound, foreground, foxhound, gain ground, greyhound,
Greyhound, hardbound, high
ground, homebound,
housebound, icebound, impound,
inbound, lose ground, newfound,
northbound, outbound, play-
ground, profound, rebound,
redound, renowned, resound,
rockbound, rock hound, snow-
bound, southbound, spellbound,
staghound, stone-ground, storm-
bound, surround, unbound, un-
sound, westbound, wolfhound,
year-round • aboveground,
Afghan hound, all-around, basset
hound, battleground, been
around, belowground, break new
ground, breeding ground, bring
around, common ground, dump-
ing ground, fool around, get
around, go around, hang around,
horse around, kick around, mess
around, muscle-bound, Nootka
Sound, off the ground, on the

ground, outward-bound, paper-bound, proving ground, Puget Sound, push around, runaround, screw around, spiral-bound, staging ground, stand one's ground, stick around, stomping ground, surround sound, turnaround, turn around, ultrasound, underground, wraparound • Albemarle Sound, English foxhound, Irish wolfhound, Long Island Sound, McMurdo Sound, merry-go-round, Prince William Sound, run rings around, Russian wolfhound, Scottish deerhound • happy hunting ground, run circles around, throw one's weight around
—*also* -ed *forms of verbs listed at* OWN[2]

oundary \aùn-drē\ see OUNDRY

ounded \aùn-dəd\ bounded, grounded, rounded • confounded, unbounded, unfounded, well-founded, well-grounded, well-rounded
—*also* -ed *forms of verbs listed at* OUND[2]

ounder \aùn-dər\ bounder, flounder, founder, grounder, pounder, sounder

ounding \aùn-diŋ\ grounding, sounding • astounding, high-sounding, resounding
—*also* -ing *forms of verbs listed at* OUND[2]

oundless[1] \ün-ləs\ see OONLESS

oundless[2] \aùn-ləs\ boundless, groundless

oundly \aùnd-lē\ roundly, soundly • profoundly

oundness \aùn-nəs\ roundness, soundness

oundry \aùn-drē\ boundary, foundry

ounds[1] \ünz\ see OONS

ounds[2] \aùnz\ zounds • out-of-bounds • by leaps and bounds

—*also* -s, -'s, *and* -s' *forms of nouns and* -s *forms of verbs listed at* OUND[2]

oundsman \aùnz-mən\ see OWNSMAN

ounge \aùnj\ lounge, scrounge • cocktail lounge

ounger[1] \aùn-jər\ lounger, scrounger

ounger[2] \əŋ-gər\ see ONGER[1]

ounker \əŋ-kər\ see UNKER

ount[1] \änt\ see ANT[2]

ount[2] \aùnt\ count, fount, mount • account, amount, discount, dismount, recount, remount, surmount, viscount • body count, catamount, paramount, Rocky Mount, tantamount • call to account, checking account, expense account, on no account, savings account • Sermon on the Mount, take into account

ountable \aùnt-ə-bəl\ countable • accountable, discountable, surmountable • insurmountable, unaccountable

ountain \aùnt-ʔn\ fountain, mountain • drinking fountain, soda fountain

ountie \aùnt-ē\ see OUNTY

ounting \aùnt-iŋ\ mounting • accounting
—*also* -ing *forms of verbs listed at* OUNT[2]

ounty \aùnt-ē\ bounty, county, Mountie

oup[1] \ōp\ see OPE

oup[2] \ü\ see EW[1]

oup[3] \üp\ see OOP

oupe[1] \ōp\ see OPE

oupe[2] \üp\ see OOP

ouper \ü-pər\ see OOPER

oupie \ü-pē\ see OOPY

ouple \əp-əl\ see UPLE[1]

ouplet \əp-lət\ see UPLET

oupy \ü-pē\ see OOPY

our[1] \ȯr\ see OR[1]

our² \ur\ see URE¹
our³ \aur\ see OWER²
our⁴ \är\ see AR³
our⁵ \ər\ see EUR¹
oura \ur-ə\ see URA
ourable \or-ə-bəl\ see ORABLE
ourbon \ər-bən\ see URBAN
ource \ors\ see ORSE¹
ourceful \ors-fəl\ see ORSEFUL
ourd \ord\ see OARD
ourde \urd\ see URED¹
ou're¹ \or\ see OR¹
ou're² \ü-ər\ see EWER¹
ou're³ \ur\ see URE¹
ou're⁴ \ər\ see EUR¹
oured \ord\ see OARD
ourer¹ \or-ər\ see ORER
ourer² \ur-ər\ see URER
ourg \ur\ see URE¹
ourge¹ \ərj\ see URGE
ourge² \orj\ see ORGE
ourger \ər-jər\ see ERGER
ouri \ur-ē\ see URY¹
ourier¹ \ur-ē-ər\ courier • couturier
ourier² \ər-ē-ər\ see URRIER
ouring¹ \or-iŋ\ see ORING
ouring² \ur-iŋ\ see URING
ourish \ər-ish\ flourish, nourish
• amateurish
ourist \ur-əst\ see URIST
ourly \aur-lē\ dourly, hourly,
sourly • half-hourly
ourn¹ \orn\ see ORN¹
ourn² \ərn\ see URN
ournal \ərn-°l\ see ERNAL
ournament \or-nə-mənt\ see ORNA-
MENT
ourne \orn\ see ORN¹
ourney¹ \ər-nē\ Bernie, Ernie,
gurney, journey, tourney • attorney • district attorney
ourney² \or-nē\ see ORNY
ournful \orn-fəl\ see ORNFUL
ourning \or-niŋ\ see ORNING
ournment \ərn-mənt\ see ERNMENT
ours¹ \orz\ see OORS
ours² \ärz\ see ARS

ours³ \aurz\ ours • all hours
• after-hours
—*also* -s, -'s, *and* -s' *forms of
nouns and* -s *forms of verbs listed
at* OWER²
ours⁴ \ur\ see URE¹
ourse \ors\ see ORSE¹
ourt¹ \ort\ see ORT¹
ourt² \urt\ see URT¹
ourth \orth\ see ORTH¹
ourtier \or-chər\ see ORCHER
ourtly \ort-lē\ see ORTLY
oury \aur-ē\ see OWERY
ous¹ \ü\ see EW¹
ous² \üs\ see USE¹
ousa¹ \ü-sə\ see USA¹
ousa² \ü-zə\ see USA²
ousal \au-zəl\ spousal, tousle
• arousal, carousal
ouse¹ \üs\ see USE¹
ouse² \aus\ blouse, douse, grouse,
house, Klaus, Laos, louse, mouse,
souse, spouse, Strauss • alehouse,
bathhouse, Bauhaus, birdhouse,
boathouse, book louse,
bunkhouse, clubhouse, court-
house, crab louse, deer mouse,
delouse, doghouse, dollhouse,
dormouse, espouse, farmhouse,
field house, field mouse, fire-
house, flophouse, full house, fun
house, greenhouse, guardhouse,
guesthouse, head louse, hothouse,
house mouse, icehouse, jailhouse,
keep house, lighthouse, long-
house, madhouse, nuthouse,
outhouse, penthouse, playhouse,
poorhouse, ranch house, road-
house, roughhouse, roundhouse,
row house, ruffed grouse, school-
house, smokehouse, statehouse,
steak house, storehouse,
teahouse, titmouse, tollhouse,
Toll House, town house, tree
house, warehouse, wheelhouse,
White House, wood louse, work-
house • boardinghouse, body

louse, cat and mouse, coffee-
house, countinghouse, country
house, customhouse, halfway
house, house-to-house, manor
house, meetinghouse, Mickey
Mouse, motherhouse, on the
house, open house, opera house,
pocket mouse, powerhouse,
rooming house, slaughterhouse,
station house, sugarhouse, sum-
merhouse, Westinghouse • bring
down the house, man of the
house

ouse³ \aůz\ blouse, browse, douse,
dowse, drowse, house, mouse,
rouse, spouse • arouse, carouse,
delouse, espouse, rehouse, roughhouse, warehouse
—*also* -s, -'s, *and* -s' *forms of
nouns and* -s *forms of verbs listed
at* OW²

ouse⁴ \üz\ see USE²

ousel \aů-zəl\ see OUSAL

ouser \aů-zər\ mouser, schnauzer,
trouser, wowser • carouser • rab-
ble-rouser

ousin \əz-³n\ see OZEN¹

ousing \aů-ziŋ\ housing, rousing
• rabble-rousing
—*also* -ing *forms of verbs listed at*
OUSE³

ousle¹ \ü-zəl\ see USAL

ousle² \aů-zəl\ see OUSAL

ousse \üs\ see USE¹

ousseau \ü-sō\ see USOE

oust¹ \aůst\ Faust, joust, oust,
roust
—*also* -ed *forms of verbs listed at*
OUSE²

oust² \üst\ see OOST

ouste \üst\ see OOST

ousy \aů-zē\ see OWSY

out¹ \ü\ see EW¹

out² \üt\ see UTE

out³ \aůt\ bout, clout, doubt,
drought, flout, gout, grout, lout,
out, pout, rout, route, scout,
shout, snout, spout, sprout, stout,
tout, trout • about, act out, all-out,
back out, bailout, bail out, bawl
out, bear out, beat out, blackout,
black out, blot out, blowout,
bombed-out, bow out, Boy Scout,
breakout, break out, breechclout,
bring out, brook trout, brownout,
brown trout, bug out, burned-out,
burnout, burn out, butt out, buy-
out, buy out, campout, cast out,
checkout, check out, chill out,
clear out, closeout, come out,
cookout, cop out, Cub Scout,
cutout, cut out, devout, die out,
dig out, dine out, dish out, dole
out, downspout, draw out,
dropout, drop out, dry out,
dugout, eke out, en route, fade-
out, fake out, fallout, fall out,
farm out, far-out, fill out, find out,
flake out, flameout, flame out,
flat-out, flunk out, foldout, foul
out, freak-out, freaked-out, get
out, Girl Scout, give out, go out,
grind out, gross-out, gross out,
handout, hand out, hangout, hide-
out, holdout, hold out, iron out,
kick out, knockout, knock out,
lake trout, layout, lights-out, line
out, lock out, lookout, look out,
lose out, make out, max out, miss
out, no doubt, nose out, opt out,
pan out, pass out, payout, phase-
out, phase out, pick out, pig out,
printout, print out, psych-out, pull
out, punch out, put out, roll out,
rub out, rule out, run out, sack
out, Sea Scout, sea trout, sellout,
sell out, set out, shell out, shoot-
out, shout-out, shutout, shut out,
sick-out, sign out, sit out, sleep
out, smoke out, sold-out, spaced-
out, space out, speak out, spell
out, stakeout, stake out, standout,
stand out, step out, stick out,
stressed-out, strikeout, strike out,

strung out, sweat out, takeout,
take out, talk out, thought-out,
throughout, throw out, time-out,
trade route, tryout, try out, tune
out, turnout, turn out, veg out,
wait out, walkout, walk out,
washout, wash out, watch out,
way-out, wear out, weird out,
whiteout, wigged-out, wimp out,
wiped out, wipeout, wipe out,
without, workout, work out,
worn-out, write out, zone out,
zonked-out • autoroute, bring
about, brussels sprout, Cape Lookout, carryout, carry out, cast
about, come about, cutthroat
trout, down-and-out, duke it out,
Eagle Scout, falling-out, figure
out, gadabout, go about, hammer
out, have it out, how about, just
about, long-drawn-out, odd man
out, out-and-out, rainbow trout,
roustabout, runabout, rural route,
sauerkraut, set about, speckled
trout, spit it out, talent scout,
waterspout • day in day out, eat
one's heart out, knock-down drag-
out, stick one's neck out • techni-
cal knockout
oute¹ \üt\ see UTE
oute² \aût\ see OUT³
outed \aût-əd\ snouted
• undoubted
—*also* -ed *forms of verbs listed at*
OUT³
outer¹ \üt-ər\ see UTER
outer² \aût-ər\ doubter, outer,
shouter, stouter • devouter
outh¹ \üth\ see OOTH²
outh² \aûth\ mouth, south • bad-
mouth, Deep South, loudmouth,
trench mouth • blabbermouth,
cottonmouth, hand-to-mouth,
motormouth, word-of-mouth
• down in the mouth • from the
horse's mouth • put one's foot in
one's mouth

outherly \əth-ər-lē\ see OTHERLY
outhful \üth-fəl\ see UTHFUL
outi \üt-ē\ see OOTY¹
outing \aût-iŋ\ outing, scouting
—*also* -ing *forms of verbs listed at*
OUT³
outre \üt-ər\ see UTER
outrement \ü-trə-mənt\ see UTRI-
MENT
outs \aûts\ bean sprouts • here-
abouts, on the outs, thereabouts,
whereabouts
—*also* -s, 's, *and* -s' *forms of nouns
and* -s *forms of verbs listed at* OUT³
ou've \üv\ see OVE³
ouver \ü-vər\ see OVER³
oux \ü\ see EW¹
ouy \ē\ see EE¹
ouzel \ü-zəl\ see USAL
ov¹ \äf\ see OFF¹
ov² \òf\ see OFF²
ova \ō-və\ nova • Jehovah
• Casanova, supernova
• Navratilova
ovable \ü-və-bəl\ movable, prov-
able • disprovable, immovable,
improvable, removable
ovah \ō-və\ see OVA
oval \ü-vəl\ approval, removal
• disapproval
ove¹ \əv\ dove, glove, love, of,
shove • above, as of, dream of,
foxglove, in love, kind of, make
love, out of, rock dove, short of,
tough love, truelove • afoul of,
ahead of, all kinds of, all sorts of,
because of, become of, boxing
glove, by means of, by way of,
dispose of, get wind of, have none
of, in case of, in light of, in place
of, inside of, in spite of, instead
of, in terms of, in view of, la-
dylove, make fun of, make use of,
mourning dove, on top of, outside
of, puppy love, turtledove, unheard-of, well-thought-of • alongside of, at the hands of, in

advance of, in behalf of, in favor of, in the face of, in the light of, in the wake of, make the most of, on account of, on behalf of, on the heels of, push comes to shove, regardless of • at the mercy of, in defiance of, irrespective of

ove² \ōv\ clove, cove, dove, drove, grove, Jove, mauve, rove, stove, strove, trove, wove • alcove, cookstove, mangrove, woodstove • Franklin stove, interwove, treasure trove • potbellied stove

ove³ \üv\ groove, move, prove, you've • approve, disprove, improve, remove, reprove • disapprove, on the move

ovel¹ \äv-əl\ grovel, novel • graphic novel

ovel² \əv-əl\ grovel, hovel, shovel • steam shovel • power shovel

ovement \üv-mənt\ movement • improvement

oven \ō-vən\ cloven, coven, woven • Beethoven, handwoven, plainwoven • interwoven

over¹ \əv-ər\ cover, hover, lover, plover • bedcover, discover, dustcover, gill cover, ground cover, hardcover, recover, slipcover, softcover, uncover • blow one's cover, undercover

over² \ō-vər\ clover, Dover, Grover, over, rover • all over, blow over, boil over, bowl over, chew over, comb-over, crossover, flyover, get over, go over, hand over, hangover, holdover, hold over, in clover, knock over, layover, lay over, leftover, look over, moreover, once-over, Passover, pass over, pick over, popover, pullover, pull over, pushover, put over, red clover, rollover, run over, sea rover, spillover, stopover, strikeover, sweet clover, takeover, take over, talk over,

tide over, turnover, turn over, voice-over, walk over, warmed-over, watch over, work over • carryover, Strait of Dover • over and over

over³ \ü-vər\ Hoover, louver, mover • earthmover, maneuver, remover, Vancouver • people mover

over⁴ \äv-ər\ see AVER¹

overt \ō-vərt\ covert, overt

overy \əv-rē\ discovery, recovery

ovey \ə-vē\ covey • lovey-dovey

ovie \ü-vē\ see OOVY

ovo \ō-vō\ Provo • de novo

ow¹ \ō\ beau, blow, bow, bro, crow, do, doe, dough, floe, flow, foe, fro, glow, go, grow, hoe, Jo, joe, Joe, know, lo, low, mow, no, o, O, oh, owe, Poe, pro, roe, row, schmo, sew, show, slow, snow, so, sow, stow, Stowe, though, throe, throw, toe, tow, whoa, woe, yo • aglow, ago, airflow, air show, although, archfoe, argot, a throw, backhoe, Bardot, below, bestow, big toe, Bordeaux, bravo, callow, chateau, cockcrow, cornrow, corn snow, crossbow, Cousteau, Day-Glo, death row, Defoe, deathblow, elbow, fencerow, forego, forgo, freak show, free throw, game show, Glasgow, goslow, gung ho, Hankow, heave-ho, hedgerow, hello, horse show, ice floe, ice show, inflow, in tow, Io, Jane Doe, jim crow, Joe Blow, John Doe, Juneau, kayo, KO, lie low, light show, longbow, Luchow, macho, mallow, Marlowe, marrow, merlot, minnow, mojo, Monroe, Moscow, mudflow, nono, no-show, nouveau, oboe, outflow, outgrow, oxbow, plateau, pronto, quiz show, rainbow, red snow, regrow, repo, road show, Rousseau, scarecrow, sideshow, skid row, ski tow, Soho, so-so, sourdough, stone's throw, tableau, talk show, tiptoe, Thoreau, trade show, trousseau, uh-oh, van Gogh, wallow, widow, willow, winnow, yarrow • afterglow, aikido, Angelo, apropos, art deco, art nouveau, audio, barrio, bay window, Bilbao, black widow, blow-by-blow, bone marrow, Borneo, buffalo, Buffalo, bungalow, calico, cameo, centimo, CEO, Cicero, curio, do-si-do, domino, dynamo, embryo, Eskimo, French window, hammer throw, hammertoe, high and low, HMO, horror show, Idaho, in a row, indigo, in the know, Jericho, Lake Tahoe, little toe, long-ago, Longfellow, Mario, medico, Mexico, mistletoe, Monaco, Navajo, NCO, oleo, on tiptoe, overflow, overgrow, overthrow, patio, piccolo, Point Barrow, polio, pompano, portico, quid pro quo, radio, ratio, rococo, rodeo, Romeo, rose window, Scorpio, semipro, show window, sloppy joe, so-and-so, status quo, stereo, stop-and-go, studio, tallyho, tangelo, tic-tac-toe, TKO, to-and-fro, Tokyo, touch-and-go, tupelo, UFO, undergo, undertow, vertigo, video, zydeco • Antonio, Arapaho, arpeggio, at one's elbow, bull's-eye window, centesimo, clock radio, Geronimo, get-up-and-go, go with the flow, Guantánamo, home video, lothario, magnifico, medicine show, New Mexico, oregano, Ozark Plateau, picture window, politico, portfolio, pussy willow, Rosario, Sarajevo, scenario, simpatico, talk radio, tennis elbow • archipelago, braggadocio, dog and pony show, ex officio, gener-

alissimo, impresario, oratorio, Paramaribo, variety show

ow² \aủ\ bough, bow, brow, chow, ciao, cow, Dow, how, Howe, Lao, Mao, now, ow, plow, pow, prow, row, scow, slough, sow, Tao, thou, vow, wow • allow, and how, as how, avow, bowwow, cacao, cash cow, chowchow, chow chow, Cracow, Dachau, endow, eyebrow, Hankow, highbrow, hoosegow, Jungfrau, know-how, kowtow, Kraków, lowbrow, luau, Macao, mau-mau, meow, Moscow, nohow, Palau, powwow, sea cow, snowplow, somehow, Spandau • anyhow, cat's meow, disallow, disavow, here and now, Hu Jintao, Krakatau, middlebrow, sacred cow • crème de cacao, Guinea-Bissau • holier-than-thou, Oberammergau

ow³ \óv\ see OFF²

owa \ō-və\ see OVA

owable¹ \ō-ə-bəl\ knowable, showable • unknowable

owable² \aủ-ə-bəl\ plowable • allowable

owal¹ \ō-əl\ see OEL

owal² \aủl\ see OWL²

owan \ō-ən\ see OAN¹

oward¹ \òrd\ see OARD

oward² \aủrd\ see OWERED

owd¹ \üd\ see UDE¹

owd² \aủd\ see OUD²

owdah \aủd-ə\ see AUDE³

owder \aủd-ər\ chowder, louder, powder, prouder • black powder, gunpowder, tooth powder • chili powder, curry powder, talcum powder

owdown \ō-daủn\ lowdown, showdown, slowdown

owdy \aủd-ē\ Audi, cloudy, dowdy, howdy, rowdy • cum laude • magna cum laude, summa cum laude

owe \ō\ see OW[1]
owed[1] \ōd\ see ODE
owed[2] \aud\ see OUD[2]
owel \aul\ see OWL[2]
oweling \au-liŋ\ see OWLING[2]
owell[1] \aul\ see OWL[2]
owell[2] \ō-əl\ see OEL
owen \ō-ən\ see OAN[1]
ower[1] \or\ see OR[1]
ower[2] \aur\ bower, cower, dour, flour, flower, glower, hour, our, plower, power, scour, shower, sour, tower • air power, bellflower, bell tower, black power, brainpower, coneflower, cornflower, devour, disk flower, empower, firepower, fire tower, Glendower, great power, half hour, horsepower, man-hour, manpower, mayflower, moonflower, pasqueflower, ray flower, rush hour, safflower, sea power, starflower, state flower, strawflower, sunflower, wallflower, watchtower, wildflower, willpower, world power • candlepower, cauliflower, fanning tower, cooling tower, Devils Tower, disempower, Eisenhower, flower power, gillyflower, happy hour, hydropower, ivory tower, overpower, passionflower, person-hour, quarter hour, staying power, superpower, sweet-and-sour, thundershower, trumpet flower, waterpower, water tower, whisky sour, zero hour • balance of power, eleventh hour, kilowatt-hour
ower[3] \ō-ər\ see OER[4]
owered \aurd\ coward, flowered, Howard, powered • high-powered • ivory-towered, underpowered
—*also* -ed *forms of verbs listed at* OWER[2]
owering \au-riŋ\ flowering, towering • nonflowering

—*also* -ing *forms of verbs listed at* OWER[2]
owery \aur-ē\ dowry, floury, flowery, Maori, showery
owhee \ō-ē\ see OWY
owie \au-ē\ Maui, zowie
owing \ō-iŋ\ see OING[1]
owl[1] \ōl\ see OLE[1]
owl[2] \aul\ bowel, foul, fowl, growl, howl, jowl, owl, prowl, scowl, towel, trowel, vowel, yowl • avowal, barn owl, barred owl, beach towel, befoul, horned owl, night owl, peafowl, screech owl, tea towel, wildfowl • disavowal, disembowel, guinea fowl, jungle fowl, on the prowl, snowy owl, spotted owl, Turkish towel, waterfowl • throw in the towel • neither fish nor fowl
owland \ō-lənd\ lowland, Poland, Roland
owledge \äl-ij\ college, knowledge • acknowledge
owler[1] \ō-lər\ see OLLER
owler[2] \au-lər\ growler, howler, prowler, scowler
owless \ō-ləs\ see OLUS
owline \ō-lən\ see OLON
owling[1] \ō-liŋ\ see OLLING
owling[2] \au-liŋ\ growling, howling, toweling
—*also* -ing *forms of verbs listed at* OWL[2]
owlock \äl-ək\ see OLOCH
owly[1] \ō-lē\ see OLY[1]
owly[2] \au-lē\ foully, growly, jowly
owman \ō-mən\ see OMAN
ow-me \ō-mē\ see OAMY
own[1] \ōn\ see ONE[1]
own[2] \aun\ Braun, brown, clown, crown, down, drown, frown, gown, noun, town • back down, bear down, boil down, boomtown, breakdown, break down, bring down, Cape Town, Charlestown, clampdown, clamp

down, closedown, comedown, come down, cooldown, countdown, count down, cow town, crackdown, crack down, crosstown, cut down, downtown, dress down, dumb down, facedown, first down, Freetown, Georgetown, ghost town, go down, hand down, hands-down, hold down, hometown, Jamestown, knockdown, knock down, lay down, letdown, let down, lie down, live down, look down, lowdown, markdown, mark down, meltdown, melt down, midtown, nightgown, nutbrown, phase down, pipe down, play down, pronoun, pull-down, renown, rubdown, rundown, set down, shakedown, shake down, shoot down, showdown, shutdown, shut down, slap down, slowdown, splashdown, splash down, strike down, strippeddown, sundown, swansdown, take down, tear down, thumbs-down, top-down, touchdown, touch down, trade down, turndown, turn down, uptown, Von Braun, wear down, weigh down, wind down, write down, Youngstown • Allentown, broken-down, Chinatown, common noun, dressing gown, eiderdown, go to town, hand-me-down, proper noun, shantytown, simmer down, thistledown, Tinseltown, trickledown, Triple Crown, tumbledown, up and down, up-and-down, upside down, water down, watered-down • bring the house down, let one's hair down, man-about-town, nervous breakdown, put one's foot down

ownded \aún-dəd\ see OUNDED
ownding \aún-diŋ\ see OUNDING
owned[1] \ōnd\ see ONED[1]
owned[2] \aúnd\ see OUND[2]
owner[1] \ō-nər\ see ONER[1]
owner[2] \ü-nər\ see OONER
owner[3] \aú-nər\ downer • downtowner
owness \ō-nəs\ see ONUS[2]
ownia \ō-nē-ə\ see ONIA[1]
ownie \aú-nē\ see OWNY
owning \ō-niŋ\ see ONING[2]
ownish \aú-nish\ brownish, clownish
ownsman \aúnz-mən\ groundsman, townsman
owny \aú-nē\ brownie, browny, downy, townie
owper \ü-pər\ see OOPER
owry \aúr-ē\ see OWERY
owse \aúz\ see OUSE[3]
owser \aú-zər\ see OUSER
owster \ō-stər\ see OASTER
owsy \aú-zē\ blousy, blowsy, drowsy, frowsy, lousy, mousy
owth \ōth\ both, growth, loath, oath, quoth • old-growth, outgrowth • overgrowth, undergrowth • Hippocratic oath
owy \ō-ē\ blowy, Chloe, doughy, Joey, showy, snowy • echoey
owys \ō-əs\ see OIS[3]
ox \äks\ box, fox, Fox, Knox, lox, ox, pox • bandbox, black box, boom box, boondocks, Botox, cowpox, detox, dreadlocks, firebox, Fort Knox, gearbox, gray fox, hatbox, icebox, in-box, jewel box, jukebox, lockbox, mailbox, matchbox, musk ox, out-box, outfox, red fox, sandbox, smallpox, soapbox, squawk box, strongbox, toolbox, unbox, voice box, workbox, Xerox • arctic fox, ballot box, bobby socks, chatterbox, chicken pox, equinox, flying fox, music box, orthodox, Orthodox, paradox, sentry box, shadowbox, silver fox, tinderbox, window box, witness-box • dialog

box, Greek Orthodox, heterodox,
idiot box, jack-in-the-box, Pandora's box, penalty box, unortho-
dox • Eastern Orthodox,
safe-deposit box
—*also* -s, -'s, *and* -s' *forms of
nouns and* -s *forms of verbs listed
at* OCK[1]

oxer \äk-sər\ boxer, Boxer • kick-
boxer • bobby-soxer

oxie \äk-sē\ see OXY

oxy \äk-sē\ boxy, foxy, moxie,
proxy • epoxy • orthodoxy • un-
orthodoxy

oy \ȯi\ boy, buoy, cloy, coy, joy,
Joy, koi, oy, ploy, poi, Roy, soy,
toy, Troy • ahoy, alloy, annoy, ball
boy, batboy, B-boy, beachboy,
bellboy, bell buoy, bok choy,
borzoi, busboy, carboy, choirboy,
convoy, cowboy, decoy, deploy,
destroy, doughboy, employ, enjoy,
envoy, Hanoi, homeboy, houseboy,
killjoy, Leroy, life buoy, McCoy,
newsboy, pageboy, page boy, Que-
moy, Saint Croix, schoolboy, stock
boy, Tolstoy, tomboy, viceroy
• Adonai, altar boy, attaboy, bully-
boy, cabin boy, corduroy, hoi
polloi, Illinois, Iroquois, mama's
boy, office boy, overjoy, paperboy,
poster boy, Tinkertoy, whipping
boy • delivery boy, Helen of Troy

oya \ȯi-ə\ see OIA

oyable \ȯi-ə-bəl\ employable, en-
joyable • unemployable

oyal[1] \īl\ see ILE[1]

oyal[2] \ȯil\ see OIL

oyalist \ȯi-ə-ləst\ loyalist, royalist

oyalty \ȯil-tē\ loyalty, royalty • dis-
loyalty

oyance \ȯi-əns\ annoyance, clair-
voyance, flamboyance
—*also* -s, -'s, *and* -s' *forms of
nouns listed at* OYANT

oyant \ȯi-ənt\ buoyant • clairvoy-
ant, flamboyant

oyce \ȯis\ see OICE

oyd \ȯid\ see OID[1]

oyed \ȯid\ see OID[1]

oyer \ȯir\ foyer • destroyer

oyes \ȯiz\ see OISE[2]

oying \ȯiŋ\ see AWING

oyle \ȯil\ see OIL

oyless \ȯi-ləs\ joyless, Troilus

oyment \ȯi-mənt\ deployment,
employment, enjoyment • rede-
ployment, self-employment, un-
employment

oyne \ȯin\ see OIN[1]

oyo \ȯi-ə\ see OIA

oyster \ȯi-stər\ see OISTER

oz[1] \əz\ see EUSE[1]

oz[2] \ȯz\ see AUSE[1]

oz[3] \ōz\ see OSE[2]

oze \ōz\ see OSE[2]

ozen[1] \əz-ᵊn\ cousin, dozen • first
cousin • baker's dozen, second
cousin • a dime a dozen

ozen[2] \ōz-ᵊn\ see OSEN

ozer \ō-zər\ see OSER[1]

ozily \ō-zə-lē\ see OSILY

ozo[1] \ō-sō\ see OSO[1]

ozo[2] \ō-zō\ see OSO[2]

ozy \ō-zē\ see OSY

ozzle \äz-əl\ Basel, Basil, nozzle,
schnozzle

U

u \ü\ see EW[1]

ua \ä\ see A[1]

uable \ü-ə-bəl\ chewable, doable, viewable • renewable, undoable • nonrenewable

ual \ü-əl\ see UEL[1]

uan \ü-ən\ bruin, ruin, yuan

uancy \ü-ən-sē\ see UENCY

uant \ü-ənt\ see UENT

uart \ùrt\ see URT[1]

ub \əb\ chub, club, cub, drub, dub, flub, grub, hub, nub, pub, rub, schlub, scrub, shrub, snub, stub, sub, tub • bathtub, book club, brew pub, glee club, health club, hot tub, hubbub, nightclub, war club, washtub, yacht club • billy club, country club, overdub, service club, syllabub • Beelzebub

uba \ü-bə\ Cuba, scuba, tuba • Aruba, saxtuba

ubal \ü-bəl\ nubile, ruble, tubal

uban \ü-bən\ see EUBEN

ubbard \əb-ərd\ cupboard • Mother Hubbard

ubber \əb-ər\ blubber, rubber, scrubber • foam rubber, landlubber, nightclubber • money-grubber

ubbery \əb-rē\ blubbery, rubbery, shrubbery

ubbily \əb-ə-lē\ bubbly, grubbily

ubbing \əb-iŋ\ drubbing, rubbing • *also* -ing *forms of verbs listed at* UB

ubble \əb-əl\ bubble, double, Hubble, rubble, stubble, trouble • abubble, redouble, soap bubble • body double, borrow trouble, daily double, on the double

ubbled \əb-əld\ bubbled, doubled, troubled • redoubled, untroubled

ubbly[1] \əb-lē\ bubbly, doubly, stubbly

ubbly[2] \əb-ə-lē\ see UBBILY

ubby \əb-ē\ chubby, clubby, grubby, hubby, scrubby, shrubby, stubby, tubby

ube \üb\ boob, cube, lube, rube, tube • boob tube, Danube, flashcube, jujube, test tube • bouillon cube, breathing tube, down the tube, inner tube

uben \ü-bən\ see EUBEN

ubens \ü-bənz\ Rubens —*also* -s, -'s, *and* -s' *forms of nouns listed at* EUBEN

uber \ü-bər\ goober, tuber

uberance \ü-brəns\ exuberance, protuberance

uberant \ü-brənt\ exuberant, protuberant • overexuberant

uberous \ü-brəs\ see UBRIS

ubic \ü-bik\ cubic • cherubic

ubile \ü-bəl\ see UBAL

uble \ü-bəl\ see UBAL

ubric \ü-brik\ Kubrick, rubric

ubrious \ü-brē-əs\ lugubrious, salubrious

ubris \ü-brəs\ hubris, tuberous

ubtile \ət-ᵊl\ see UTTLE

uby \ü-bē\ see OOBY

uca \ü-kə\ see OOKA

ucat \ək-ət\ see UCKET

ucca[1] \ü-kə\ see OOKA

ucca[2] \ək-ə\ see UKKA

uccal \ək-əl\ see UCKLE

ucci \ü-chē\ see OOCHY

uccor \ək-ər\ see UCKER

ucculence \ək-yə-ləns\ see UCULENCE

uce \üs\ see USE[1]

uced \üst\ see OOST

ucence \üs-³ns\ nuisance • translucence

ucer \ü-sər\ juicer • producer, seducer

uch[1] \ich\ see ITCH

uch[2] \ük\ see UKE

uch[3] \əch\ see UTCH

uche[1] \ü-chē\ see OOCHY

uche[2] \üch\ see OOCH[1]

uche[3] \üsh\ see OUCHE

ucher \ü-chər\ see UTURE

uchin \ü-shən\ see UTION

uchy \əch-ē\ duchy, touchy • archduchy, grand duchy

ucian \ü-shən\ see UTION

ucible \ü-sə-bəl\ crucible • deducible, inducible, producible, reducible • irreducible, reproducible

ucifer \ü-sə-fər\ crucifer, Lucifer

ucive \ü-siv\ see USIVE

uck[1] \ək\ buck, Buck, chuck, cluck, duck, guck, luck, muck, pluck, puck, Puck, schmuck, shuck, snuck, struck, stuck, suck, truck, tuck, yuck • amentruck, dead duck, dumbstruck, dump truck, fire truck, hard luck, lameduck, moonstruck, mukluk, potluck, roebuck, sawbuck, shelduck, stagestruck, starstruck, sunstruck, unstuck, upchuck, woodchuck • Daffy Duck, Habakkuk, horror-struck, Keokuk, ladder truck, megabuck, motortruck, muckamuck, nip and tuck, pass the buck, Peking duck, pickup truck, push one's luck, sitting duck, thunderstruck

uck[2] \ùk\ see OOK[1]

ukar \ək-ər\ see UCKER

ucker \ək-ər\ pucker, shucker, succor, sucker, trucker, tucker • bloodsucker, goatsucker, sapsucker, seersucker, shark sucker

ucket \ək-ət\ bucket, ducat

• lunch-bucket, Nantucket, Pawtucket, rust bucket • kick the bucket • drop in the bucket

uckle \ək-əl\ buckle, chuckle, knuckle, suckle, truckle • bareknuckle, pinochle, swashbuckle, unbuckle • honeysuckle

uckled \ək-əld\ cuckold, knuckled • bare-knuckled
—also -ed forms of verbs listed at UCKLE

uckling \ək-liŋ\ duckling, suckling • swashbuckling • ugly duckling
—also -ing forms of verbs listed at UCKLE

uckold \ək-əld\ see UCKLED

ucks \əks\ see UX[1]

uckus \ük-əs\ ruckus, Sukkoth

ucky \ək-ē\ ducky, lucky, mucky, plucky, sucky, yucky • Kentucky, unlucky • happy-go-lucky

uct \əkt\ duct • abduct, bile duct, conduct, construct, deduct, destruct, induct, instruct, obstruct • aqueduct, deconstruct, reconstruct, self-destruct, viaduct
—also -ed forms of verbs listed at UCK[1]

uctable \ək-tə-bəl\ see UCTIBLE

uctible \ək-tə-bəl\ deductible, destructible • indestructible, nondeductible

uction \ək-shən\ suction • abduction, conduction, construction, deduction, destruction, induction, instruction, obstruction, production, reduction, seduction • coproduction, deconstruction, introduction, liposuction, mass production, reconstruction, reproduction, self-destruction

uctive \ək-tiv\ conductive, constructive, deductive, destructive, inductive, instructive, obstructive, productive, reductive, seductive • nonproductive, reconstructive, reproductive, self-destructive,

unconstructive, unproductive
• counterproductive

uctor \ək-tər\ conductor, instructor • nonconductor • semiconductor, superconductor

uculence \ək-yə-ləns\ succulence, truculence

ucy \ü-sē\ see UICY

ud¹ \əd\ blood, bud, crud, cud, dud, flood, Judd, mud, scud, spud, stud, thud • bad blood, blue blood, earbud, full-blood, half-blood, leaf bud, lifeblood, new blood, oxblood, pure-blood, redbud, rosebud, shed blood, smell blood, sweat blood • dragon's blood, flesh and blood, flower bud, in cold blood, in the bud • stick-in-the-mud

ud² \üd\ see UDE¹

ud³ \u̇d\ see OOD¹

uda \üd-ə\ Buddha, Gouda, Judah • Barbuda, Bermuda • barracuda

udah \üd-ə\ see UDA

udal \üd-ᵊl\ see OODLE

udd¹ \u̇d\ see OOD¹

udd² \əd\ see UD¹

udded \əd-əd\ see OODED¹

udder \əd-ər\ rudder, shudder, udder

uddha \üd-ə\ see UDA

uddhist \üd-əst\ see UDIST¹

uddie \əd-ē\ see UDDY¹

udding \əd-iŋ\ budding, —also -ing forms of verbs listed at UD¹

uddle \əd-ᵊl\ cuddle, fuddle, huddle, muddle, puddle • befuddle

uddly \əd-lē\ cuddly, Dudley

uddy¹ \əd-ē\ bloody, buddy, Buddy, cruddy, muddy, ruddy, study • case study, work-study • buddy-buddy, fuddy-duddy, understudy

uddy² \u̇d-ē\ see OODY²

ude¹ \üd\ brood, crude, dude, feud, food, hued, Jude, lewd, mood, nude, prude, rude, shrewd, snood, 'tude, who'd, you'd • allude, blood feud, collude, conclude, delude, denude, elude, exclude, exude, fast-food, Gertrude, health food, include, intrude, junk food, nonfood, plant food, postlude, preclude, prelude, protrude, seafood, seclude, subdued, unglued • altitude, amplitude, aptitude, attitude, certitude, comfort food, finger food, fortitude, frankenfood, gratitude, interlude, lassitude, latitude, longitude, magnitude, multitude, platitude, rectitude, servitude, solitude • beatitude, ineptitude, ingratitude, natural food, vicissitude

ude² \üd-ə\ see UDA

udel \üd-ᵊl\ see OODLE

udeness \üd-nəs\ see UDINOUS

udent \üd-ᵊnt\ prudent, student • imprudent, nonstudent

uder \üd-ər\ brooder, Tudor • intruder —also -er forms of adjectives listed at UDE¹

udge¹ \əj\ budge, drudge, fudge, grudge, judge, nudge, sludge, smudge, trudge • adjudge, begrudge, misjudge, prejudge

udge² \üj\ see UGE¹

udgeon \əj-ən\ bludgeon • curmudgeon

udgie \əj-ē\ see UDGY

udgy \əj-ē\ budgie, pudgy, sludgy, smudgy

udi \ü-dē\ see OODY¹

udie \ü-dē\ see OODY¹

udinous \üd-nəs\ crudeness, rudeness, shrewdness • multitudinous

udist¹ \üd-əst\ Buddhist, nudist —also -est forms of adjectives listed at UDE¹

udist² \u̇d-əst\ see OULDEST

udity \üd-ət-ē\ crudity, nudity

udley \əd-lē\ see UDDLY
udly \əd-lē\ see UDDLY
udo \üd-ō\ judo, pseudo
udor \üd-ər\ see UDER
udsman \ùdz-mən\ see OODSMAN
udu \üd-ü\ see OODOO
udy[1] \ü-dē\ see OODY[1]
udy[2] \əd-ē\ see UDDY[1]
ue[1] \ü\ see EW[1]
ue[2] \ā\ see AY[1]
ued \üd\ see UDE[1]
ueghel \ü-gəl\ see UGAL
uel[1] \ü-əl\ crewel, cruel, dual, duel,
fuel, gruel, jewel, Jewel • accrual,
refuel, renewal, synfuel • biofuel,
diesel fuel, fossil fuel
uel[2] \ül\ see OOL[1]
uely \ü-lē\ see ULY
uence \ü-əns\ affluence, conflu-
ence, congruence, influence,
pursuance • incongruence
—*also* -s, -'s *and* -s' *forms of
nouns listed at* UENT
uency \ü-ən-sē\ fluency, truancy
• congruency
ueness \ü-nəs\ see EWNESS
uent \ü-ənt\ fluent, truant • affluent,
congruent, effluent • incongruent
uer \ü-ər\ see EWER[1]
uerile \ùr-əl\ see URAL
ues \üz\ see USE[2]
uesman \üz-mən\ see EWSMAN
uesome \ü-səm\ gruesome, two-
some
uesy \ü-zē\ see OOZY
uet \ü-ət\ bluet, cruet, suet • con-
duit, intuit
uette \et\ see ET[1]
uey \ü-ē\ see EWY
uff \əf\ bluff, buff, cuff, duff, fluff,
gruff, guff, huff, luff, muff, puff,
rough, ruff, scruff, scuff, slough,
snuff, stuff, tough • cream puff,
earmuff, enough, feedstuff, food-
stuff, french cuff, handcuff, hang
tough, hot stuff, kid stuff, Pine
Bluff, rebuff • blindman's buff,

call one's bluff, off-the-cuff,
overstuff, powder puff, strut one's
stuff, up to snuff
uffe[1] \üf\ see OOF[1]
uffe[2] \ùf\ see OOF[2]
uffed \əft\ tuft
—*also* -ed *forms of verbs listed at* UFF
uffel \əf-əl\ see UFFLE
uffer \əf-ər\ bluffer, buffer, duffer,
puffer, suffer • candlesnuffer,
stocking stuffer
—*also* -er *forms of adjectives listed
at* UFF
uffet \əf-ət\ buffet, tuffet
uffin \əf-ən\ muffin, puffin,
roughen, toughen • English muffin, ragamuffin
uffle \əf-əl\ duffel, muffle, ruffle,
scuffle, shuffle, snuffle, truffle
• kerfuffle, reshuffle
uffled \əf-əld\ unruffled
—*also* -ed *forms of verbs listed at*
UFFLE
uffly \əf-lē\ gruffly, roughly
uffy \əf-ē\ fluffy, huffy, puffy,
scruffy, stuffy, toughie
ufi \ü-fē\ see OOFY
ufous \ü-fəs\ doofus, Rufus
uft \əft\ see UFFED
ufus \ü-fəs\ see UFOUS
ug \əg\ bug, chug, Doug, drug,
dug, hug, jug, lug, mug, plug, pug,
rug, shrug, slug, smug, snug, thug,
tug, ugh • bear hug, bedbug,
debug, earplug, firebug, fireplug,
humbug, june bug, nondrug,
prayer rug, sea slug, spark plug,
stinkbug, throw rug, unplug, wall
plug • antidrug, doodlebug, gateway drug, jitterbug, ladybug,
lightning bug, litterbug, mealy-
bug, pull the plug, scatter rug,
shutterbug, toby jug, water bug,
wonder drug • miracle drug,
prescription drug • oriental rug
uga \ü-gə\ beluga, Tortuga • Chat-
tanooga

ugal \ü-gəl\ Brueghel, bugle, frugal

ugar \ù́g-ər\ see UGUR

uge[1] \üj\ huge, scrooge, stooge
• deluge, refuge • centrifuge, subterfuge

uge[2] \üzh\ Bruges, luge, rouge
• deluge, refuge • Baton Rouge

ugel \ü-gəl\ see UGAL

uges \üzh\ see UGE[2]

ugger[1] \əg-ər\ bugger, mugger, plugger, slugger, smugger, snugger • debugger, tree hugger

ugger[2] \ù́g-ər\ see UGUR

uggery \əg-rē\ thuggery • skulduggery

uggie \əg-ē\ see UGGY

uggish \əg-ish\ sluggish, thuggish

uggle \əg-əl\ juggle, smuggle, snuggle, struggle

uggler \əg-lər\ juggler, smuggler

uggy \əg-ē\ buggy, muggy • beach buggy, dune buggy, swamp buggy • baby buggy, horse-and-buggy

ugh[1] \əg\ see UG

ugh[2] \ü\ see EW[1]

ughes \üz\ see USE[2]

ugle \ü-gəl\ see UGAL

ugli \ə-glē\ see UGLY

uglia \ù́l-yə\ see ULIA

ugly \əg-lē\ smugly, snugly, ugly

ugn \ün\ see OON[1]

ugner \ü-nər\ see OONER

ugu \ü-gü\ fugu, goo-goo

ugur \ù́g-ər\ booger, sugar • blood sugar, brown sugar, cane sugar • maple sugar

uhl \ül\ see OOL[1]

uhr[1] \ər\ see EUR[1]

uhr[2] \ù́r\ see URE[1]

ührer \ù́r-ər\ see URER

ui[1] \ā\ see AY[1]

ui[2] \ē\ see EE[1]

uice \üs\ see USE[1]

uiced \üst\ see OOST

uicer \ü-sər\ see UCER

uicy \ü-sē\ juicy, Lucy • Watusi

uid \ü-id\ druid, fluid

uidance \īd-ᵊns\ see IDANCE

uide \īd\ see IDE[1]

uided \īd-əd\ see IDED

uider \īd-ər\ see IDER[1]

uidon \īd-ᵊn\ see IDEN

uiker \ī-kər\ see IKER

uild \ild\ see ILLED

uilder \il-dər\ see ILDER[1]

uilding \il-diŋ\ see ILDING

uile \īl\ see ILE[1]

uiler \ī-lər\ see ILAR

uilleann \i-lən\ see ILLON

uilt \ilt\ see ILT

uimpe \amp\ see AMP[3]

uin[1] \ü-ən\ see UAN

uin[2] \ən\ see UN[1]

uin[3] \aⁿ\ see IN[4]

uing \ü-iŋ\ see OING[2]

uint \ü-ənt\ see UENT

uir \ù́r\ see URE[1]

uirdly \ù́r-lē\ see URELY

uisance \üs-ᵊns\ see UCENCE

uise[1] \üz\ see USE[2]

uise[2] \īz\ see IZE[1]

uiser \ü-zər\ see USER

uish \ü-ish\ see EWISH

uisne \ü-nē\ see OONY

uiste \is-tē\ see ICITY[2]

uit[1] \ü-ət\ see UET

uit[2] \üt\ see UTE

uitable \üt-ə-bəl\ see UTABLE

uite \üt\ see UTE

uited \üt-əd\ see OOTED[1]

uiter \üt-ər\ see UTER

uiting \üt-iŋ\ see UTING

uitless \üt-ləs\ see OOTLESS

uitor \üt-ər\ see UTER

uitous \ü-ət-əs\ circuitous, fortuitous, gratuitous

uits \üts\ see OOTS

uittle[1] \üt-ᵊl\ see UTILE

uittle[2] \ət-ᵊl\ see UTTLE

uity[1] \ü-ət-ē\ acuity, annuity, congruity, gratuity • ambiguity, continuity, incongruity, ingenuity • discontinuity

uity[2] \üt-ē\ see OOTY[1]

uk¹ \ük\ see UKE
uk² \ùk\ see OOK¹
uk³ \ək\ see UCK¹
ukar \ə-kər\ see UCKER
uke \ük\ cuke, duke, fluke, kook, Luke, nuke, Nuuk, puke, snook, spook, uke • archduke, Chinook, Dubuque, Farouk, grand duke, Kirkuk, rebuke • antinuke, Pentateuch
uki¹ \ü-kē\ see OOKY¹
uki² \ù-kē\ see OOKIE
ukka \ək-ə\ pukka, yucca
ukker \ək-ər\ see UCKER
ukkoth \ùk-əs\ see UCKUS
ul¹ \ùl\ bull, full, pull, wool, you'll • armful, bagful, bellpull, brimful, carful, chock-full, cupful, earful, eyeful, fistful, forkful, glassful, handful, houseful, in full, John Bull, mouthful, pailful, pit bull, plateful, potful, roomful, spoonful, steel wool, tankful, truckful, trunkful • barrelful, basketful, bellyful, bucketful, closetful, cock-and-bull, Istanbul, shovelful, Sitting Bull, tableful • dyed-in-the-wool
ul² \ül\ see OOL¹
ul³ \əl\ see ULL¹
ula \ü-lə\ Beulah, hula, moola • Missoula • Ashtabula, Pascagoula
ular \ü-lər\ see OOLER
ulch \əlch\ gulch, mulch
ule¹ \ü-lē\ see ULY
ule² \ül\ see OOL¹
ulean \ü-lē-ən\ Julian • Herculean
uled \üld\ see OOLED
ulep \ü-ləp\ see ULIP
uler \ü-lər\ see OOLER
ules \ülz\ Jules
—also -s, -'s, and -s' forms of nouns and -s forms of verbs listed at OOL¹
ulet \əl-ət\ see ULLET¹
uley¹ \ü-lē\ see ULY

uley² \ùl-ē\ see ULLY²
ulf \əlf\ golf, gulf, Gulf • engulf • Beowulf
ulgar \əl-gər\ see ULGUR
ulge \əlj\ bulge • divulge, indulge • overindulge
ulgur \əl-gər\ bulgur, vulgar
ulhas \əl-əs\ see ULLUS
uli \ùl-ē\ see ULLY²
ulia \ül-yə\ Julia • Apulia
ulie \ü-lē\ see ULY
ulip \ü-ləp\ julep, tulip • mint julep
ulish \ü-lish\ see OOLISH
ulk \əlk\ bulk, hulk, skulk, sulk, yolk
ulky \əl-kē\ bulky, sulky
ull¹ \əl\ cull, dull, gull, hull, lull, mull, null, scull, skull • annul, mogul, numskull, seagull • herring gull, laughing gull, monohull, multihull, Sitting Bull
ull² \ùl\ see UL¹
ulla¹ \ü-lə\ see ULA
ulla² \əl-ə\ see ULLAH
ullah \əl-ə\ Gullah, mullah, Sulla • medulla • ayatollah
ullan \əl-ən\ see ULLEN
ullard \əl-ərd\ see OLORED
ullate \əl-ət\ see ULLET¹
ulle \ül\ see OOL¹
ullein \əl-ən\ see ULLEN
ullen \əl-ən\ mullein, sullen
uller \əl-ər\ see OLOR¹
ulles \əl-əs\ see ULLUS
ullet¹ \əl-ət\ bullet, gullet, mullet • dodge a bullet, magic bullet, silver bullet
ullet² \ùl-ət\ bullet, pullet
ulley \ùl-ē\ see ULLY²
ullis \əl-əs\ see ULLUS
ullitt \ùl-ət\ see ULLET²
ullus \əl-əs\ Dulles • Catullus
ully¹ \əl-ē\ gully, sully
ully² \ùl-ē\ bully, fully, gully, pulley, woolly
ulp \əlp\ gulp, pulp • wood pulp
ulse \əls\ dulse, pulse • convulse, impulse, repulse

ulsion \əl-shən\ compulsion, convulsion, emulsion, expulsion, impulsion, propulsion, repulsion, revulsion • jet propulsion, self-propulsion

ulsive \əl-siv\ compulsive, convulsive, impulsive, propulsive, repulsive • anticonvulsive

ult \əlt\ cult • adult, consult, exult, insult, occult, result, subcult, tumult • catapult, difficult •

ultant \əlt-°nt\ consultant, exultant, resultant

ultch \əlch\ see ULCH

ultery \əl-trē\ see ULTRY

ultry \əl-trē\ sultry • adultery

ulture \əl-chər\ culture, vulture • subculture • agriculture, aquaculture, counterculture, horticulture, turkey vulture

ulu \ü-lü\ lulu, Sulu, Zulu • Honolulu

uly \ü-lē\ coolie, coolly, duly, Julie, newly, Thule, truly • Grand Coulee, unduly, unruly, yours truly

um[1] \əm\ bum, chum, come, crumb, drum, dumb, from, glum, gum, hum, mum, numb, plum, plumb, rum, scum, slum, some, strum, sum, swum, them, thrum, thumb, yum • bass drum, bay rum, beach plum, become, dum-dum, eardrum, green thumb, ho-hum, how come, humdrum, income, outcome, pond scum, side drum, snare drum, steel drum, succumb, therefrom, to come, Tom Thumb, tom-tom, yum-yum • apart from, aside from, bubblegum, chewing gum, kettledrum, kingdom come, overcome, rule of thumb, sugarplum, Tweedledum •

um[2] \üm\ broom, groom, room • ballroom, barroom, bathroom, bedroom, chat room, checkroom, classroom, cloakroom, coatroom, courtroom, darkroom, headroom, homeroom, lunchroom, men's room, mushroom, push broom, rec room, restroom, schoolroom, stateroom, sunroom, washroom, weight room, workroom • breathing room, dining room, dressing room, elbow room, family room, ladies' room, locker room, sitting room, standing room, waiting room, wiggle room

um[3] \üm\ see OOM[1]

uma \ü-mə\ puma, Yuma • Montezuma, Petaluma

uman \ü-mən\ crewman, human, Newman, Truman, Yuman • acumen, illumine, inhuman, nonhuman, prehuman, subhuman • superhuman

umanous \ü-mə-nəs\ see UMINOUS

umb \əm\ see UM[1]

umbar \əm-bər\ see UMBER[1]

umbed \əmd\ unplumbed
—*also* -ed *forms of verbs listed at* UM[1]

umbel \əm-bəl\ see UMBLE

umber[1] \əm-bər\ Humber, lumbar, lumber, number, slumber, umber • call number, cucumber, encumber, outnumber, prime number • sea cucumber • atomic number, 800 number, serial number

umber[2] \əm-ər\ see UMMER

umbered \əm-bərd\ numbered • unnumbered
—*also* -ed *forms of verbs listed at* UMBER[1]

umberland \əm-bər-lənd\ Cumberland • Northumberland

umbing \əm-iŋ\ see OMING[1]

umble \əm-bəl\ bumble, crumble, fumble, grumble, humble, jumble, mumble, rumble, stumble, tumble • rough-and-tumble

umbler \əm-blər\ bumbler, grumbler, tumbler

umbling \əm-bliŋ\ tumbling
—also -ing *forms of verbs listed at*
UMBLE

umbly[1] \əm-blē\ crumbly, grumbly,
humbly, mumbly, rumbly

umbly[2] \əm-lē\ dumbly, numbly

umbness \əm-nəs\ numbness
• alumnus

umbo \əm-bō\ gumbo, jumbo
• Colombo • mumbo jumbo

umbria \əm-brē-ə\ Cumbria
• Northumbria

ume \üm\ see OOM[1]

umed \ümd\ see OOMED

umely \ü-mə-lē\ see OOMILY

umen \ü-mən\ see UMAN

umer \ü-mər\ bloomer, Bloomer,
boomer, humor, roomer, rumor,
Sumer, tumor • consumer, cos-
tumer • baby boomer, gallows
humor

umerous \üm-rəs\ see UMOROUS

umerus \üm-rəs\ see UMOROUS

umey \ü-mē\ see OOMY

umf \əmf\ see UMPH

umi \ü-mē\ see OOMY

umin \ü-mən\ see UMAN

umine \ü-mən\ see UMAN

uming \ü-miŋ\ blooming
• everblooming, time-consuming,
unassuming
—also -ing *forms of verbs listed at*
OOM[1]

uminous \ü-mə-nəs\ luminous
• bituminous, voluminous

ummary \əm-ə-rē\ see UMMERY

ummate \əm-ət\ see UMMET

ummel \əm-əl\ see OMMEL[2]

ummell \əm-əl\ see OMMEL[2]

ummer \əm-ər\ bummer, drummer,
mummer, plumber, strummer,
summer • latecomer, midsummer,
newcomer • Indian summer
—also -er *forms of adjectives listed*
at UM[1]

ummery \əm-ə-rē\ summary, sum-
mery • Montgomery

ummet \əm-ət\ plummet, summit

ummie \əm-ē\ see UMMY

ummit \əm-ət\ see UMMET

ummox \əm-əks\ flummox, lum-
mox

ummy \əm-ē\ chummy, crummy,
dummy, gummy, mommy,
mummy, rummy, scummy,
slummy, tummy, yummy • gin
rummy

umness \əm-nəs\ see UMBNESS

umnus \əm-nəs\ see UMBNESS

umor \ü-mər\ see UMER

umorous \üm-rəs\ humerus, hu-
morous, numerous

umous \ü-məs\ humus • posthu-
mous

ump \əmp\ bump, chump, clump,
dump, grump, hump, jump, lump,
plump, pump, rump, slump,
stump, sump, thump, trump, ump
• air pump, broad jump, heat
pump, high jump, long jump, ski
jump, speed bump, sump pump
• bungee jump, vacuum pump
• hop skip and jump

umper \əm-pər\ bumper, dumper,
jumper, pumper, stumper • broad
jumper, high jumper, long
jumper, ski jumper, smoke
jumper, tub-thumper • bungee
jumper • bumper-to-bumper

umph \əmf\ humph • galumph,
harrumph

umpish \əm-pish\ lumpish, plump-
ish

umpkin \əŋ-kən\ see UNKEN

umple \əm-pəl\ crumple, rumple

umps \əms\ dumps, mumps
• goose bumps
—also -s, -'s, and -s' forms of
nouns listed and -s forms of verbs listed
at UMP

umption \əm-shən\ gumption
• assumption, consumption, pre-
sumption, resumption

umptious \əm-shəs\ bumptious,

scrumptious, sumptuous • pre-sumptuous

umptuous[1] \əm-chəs\ sumptuous • presumptuous

umptuous[2] \əm-shəs\ see UMPTIOUS

umpus \əm-pəs\ see OMPASS

umpy \əm-pē\ bumpy, dumpy, grumpy, jumpy, lumpy, stumpy

umus \ü-məs\ see UMOUS

umy \ü-mē\ see OOMY

un[1] \ən\ bun, done, Donne, fun, gun, hon, Hun, none, nun, one, pun, run, shun, son, spun, stun, sun, ton, won • A-1, air gun, begun, big gun, blowgun, Bull Run, burp gun, Chaplin, dry run, earned run, end run, first-run, flashgun, godson, grandson, hand-gun, hard-won, hired gun, home run, homespun, long run, out-done, outgun, outrun, popgun, redone, rerun, short run, shotgun, six-gun, speargun, spray gun, squirt gun, stepson, stun gun, top gun, trial run, undone, V-1, well-done, zip gun • Algonquin, anti-gun, Bofors gun, Browning gun, Gatling gun, hit-and-run, jump the gun, kiloton, machine-gun, machine gun, megaton, midnight sun, one-on-one, one-to-one, on the run, overdone, overrun, pellet gun, radar gun, ride shotgun, riot gun, smoking gun, squirrel gun, tommy gun, underdone, water gun • son of a gun, submachine gun

un[2] \ün\ see OON[1]

una \ü-nə\ Luna, tuna • Altoona, kahuna, vicuña

uña[1] \ü-nə\ see UNA

uña[2] \ün-yə\ see UNIA

unal \ün-ᵊl\ communal, tribunal

unar \ü-nər\ see OONER

unary \ü-nə-rē\ buffoonery, fes-toonery, lampoonery

unc \ənk\ see UNK

uncan \əŋ-kən\ see UNKEN

unce \əns\ dunce, once
—*also* -s, -'s, *and* -s' *forms of nouns and* -s *forms of verbs listed at* ONT[1]

unch \ənch\ brunch, bunch, crunch, hunch, lunch, munch, punch, scrunch • box lunch, free lunch, keypunch • counterpunch, one-two punch, out to lunch, rabbit punch, sucker punch

unche \ənch\ see UNCH

uncher \ən-chər\ cowpuncher, keypuncher • counterpuncher, number cruncher

unchy \ən-chē\ crunchy, punchy

uncle \əŋ-kəl\ uncle • carbuncle, granduncle, great-uncle, say uncle

unct \əŋt\ adjunct, defunct
—*also* -ed *forms of verbs listed at* UNK

unction \əŋ-shən\ function, junc-tion • compunction, conjunction, dysfunction, injunction, malfunc-tion

uncture \əŋ-chər\ juncture, punc-ture • acupuncture

und[1] \ənd\ fund • dachshund, hedge fund, refund, rotund, slush fund, trust fund • cummerbund, underfund • mutual fund
—*also* -ed *forms of verbs listed at* UN[1]

und[2] \au̇nd\ see OUND[2]

undae \ən-dē\ see UNDI

undant \ən-dənt\ abundant, redun-dant • overabundant, superabun-dant

unday \ən-dē\ see UNDI

undays \ən-dēz\ Mondays, Sun-days, undies
—*also* -s *and* -s' *forms of nouns listed at* UNDI

under \ən-dər\ blunder, funder, plunder, thunder, under, wonder • asunder, down under, go under, plow under, snow under

- knuckle under, steal one's thunder • build a fire under
underous \ən-drəs\ thunderous, wondrous
undi \ən-dē\ Monday, sundae, Sunday • Bay of Fundy, salmagundi • coatimundi
undies \ən-dēz\ see UNDAYS
undle \ən-dᵊl\ bundle, trundle
undy \ən-dē\ see UNDI
une \ün\ see OON¹
uneau \ü-nō\ see UNO
uneless \ün-ləs\ see OONLESS
uner \ü-nər\ see OONER
unes \ünz\ see OONS
ung¹ \əŋ\ clung, dung, flung, hung, lung, rung, slung, sprung, strung, stung, sung, swung, tongue, wrung, young • among, black lung, far-flung, forked tongue, hamstrung, high-strung, iron lung, low-slung, unsung, with young • Aqua-Lung, bite one's tongue, egg foo yong, hold one's tongue, mother tongue
ung² \ûn\ Jung, Sung
ungal \ən-gəl\ see UNGLE
unge \ənj\ grunge, lunge, plunge, sponge • expunge • take the plunge
unger¹ \ən-jər\ plunger, sponger
unger² \əŋ-gər\ see ONGER¹
ungle \əŋ-gəl\ bungle, fungal, jungle • asphalt jungle
ungous \əŋ-gəs\ fungus • humongous
ungry \ən-grē\ see ONGERY
ungus \əŋ-gəs\ see UNGOUS
ungy \ən-jē\ grungy, spongy
unha \ü-nə\ see UNA
uni \ü-nē\ see OONY
unia \ün-yə\ petunia, vicuña
unic \ü-nik\ eunuch, Munich, Punic, runic, tunic
unich \ü-nik\ see UNIC
union \ən-yən\ bunion, onion • Paul Bunyan

unis \ü-nəs\ see EWNESS
unish¹ \ən-ish\ Hunnish, punish
unish² \ü-nish\ see OONISH
unity \ü-nət-ē\ unity • community, disunity, immunity, impunity • opportunity
unk \əŋk\ bunk, chunk, clunk, drunk, dunk, flunk, funk, gunk, hunk, junk, monk, plunk, punk, shrunk, skunk, slunk, spunk, stunk, sunk, thunk, trunk • chipmunk, debunk, Podunk, preshrunk, punch-drunk, slam dunk • cyberpunk, steamer trunk
unked \əŋt\ see UNCT
unken \ən-kən\ Duncan, drunken, pumpkin, shrunken, sunken
unker \əŋ-kər\ bunker, clunker, hunker, junker • debunker, spelunker
unkie \əŋ-kē\ see UNKY
unkin \əŋ-kəm\ see UNCAN
unky \əŋ-kē\ chunky, clunky, donkey, flunky, funky, gunky, hunky, junkie, junky, monkey, skunky, spunky • grease monkey
unless \ən-ləs\ runless, sunless
unn \ən\ see UN¹
unned \ənd\ see UND¹
unnel \ən-ᵊl\ funnel, tunnel • wind tunnel
unner \ən-ər\ gunner, runner, stunner • base runner, forerunner, front-runner, gunrunner, roadrunner, rumrunner • machine gunner
unnery \ən-rē\ gunnery, nunnery
unning \ən-in\ cunning, running, stunning • baserunning, gunrunning, rum-running • blockaderunning, in the running • hit the ground running, out of the running
—also -ing forms of verbs listed at UN¹
unnion \ən-yən\ see UNION
unnish \ən-ish\ see UNISH¹

unny \ən-ē\ bunny, funny, honey, money, runny, sonny, sunny • blood money, Bugs Bunny, dust bunny, pin money, prize money, seed money, smart money, unfunny • for one's money, funny money, on the money, pocket money, spending money • run for one's money

uno \ü-nō\ Bruno, Juneau, Juno • numero uno

unt \ənt\ see ONT[1]

untal \ənt-ᵊl\ see UNTLE

unter \ənt-ər\ bunter, hunter, punter • foxhunter, headhunter, witch-hunter • bounty hunter, fortune hunter

unting \ənt-iŋ\ bunting • foxhunting, head-hunting, witch-hunting —*also* -ing *forms of verbs listed at* ONT[1]

untle \ənt-ᵊl\ frontal • disgruntle

unwale \ən-ᵊl\ see UNNEL

uny \ü-nē\ see OONY

unyan \ən-yən\ see UNION

uoy[1] \ü-ē\ see EWY

uoy[2] \ȯi\ see OY

uoyance \ü-əns\ see OYANCE

uoyant \ȯi-ənt\ see OYANT

up \əp\ cup, pup, sup, up, yup • act up, add up, backup, back up, bang-up, bear up, beat-up, beat up, blowup, blow up, bone up, bound up, breakup, break up, bring up, brush up, buck up, buildup, build up, built-up, bulk up, buy up, catch-up, chalk up, checkup, choose up, clam up, cleanup, clean up, close-up, close up, come up, cough up, crack-up, curl up, cut up, dial-up, dial up, dig up, doll up, do up, draw up, dream up, dress up, dried-up, drive-up, drum up, dry up, dustup, face up, fed up, fill up, fix up, flare-up, foul-up, foul up, frame-up, gang up, gear up,

getup, get up, giddap, give up, grown-up, grow up, hang-up, hang up, hard up, heads-up, hiccup, hitch up, holdup, hold up, hole up, hookup, hook up, hung up, hyped-up, juice up, keep up, lay-up, lead-up, leg up, letup, let up, line up, linkup, lockup, look up, louse up, made-up, makeup, make up, markup, matchup, mix-up, mixed-up, mop-up, one-up, pass up, pay up, pickup, pick up, pileup, pinup, play up, pop-up, pull-up, pump up, push-up, rack up, rake up, ramp up, re-up, ring up, roll up, roundup, round up, run-up, scare up, screwup, screw up, setup, set up, sew up, shake-up, shape up, shook-up, show up, shut up, sign up, sit-up, size up, slipup, slip up, smashup, souped-up, speak up, speedup, spiffed-up, spit up, stack up, stand-up, start-up, steam up, step up, stepped-up, stickup, stick up, strike up, sum up, sunup, take up, talk up, teacup, throw up, thumbs-up, tie-up, toss-up, touch-up, trade up, trumped-up, tune-up, turn up, use up, wait up, wake up, warm-up, washed-up, windup, work up, wrap-up • belly-up, bottom-up, buckle up, bundle up, buttercup, butter up, cover-up, cover up, Dixie cup, double up, follow-up, giddyup, higher-up, hurry up, lighten up, live it up, measure up, open up, pick-me-up, power up, runner-up, shoot-'em-up, suction cup • sunny-side up

upboard \əb-ərd\ see UBBARD

upe \üp\ see OOP

upel \ü-pəl\ see UPLE[2]

uper \ü-pər\ see OOPER

upi \ü-pē\ see OOPY

upid \ü-pəd\ Cupid, stupid

upil \ü-pəl\ see UPLE[2]

uple[1] \əp-əl\ couple, supple • quadruple, quintuple, sextuple, uncouple

uple[2] \ü-pəl\ pupil, scruple • quadruple, quintuple, sextuple

uplet \əp-lət\ couplet • quadruplet, quintuplet, sextuplet

uplicate \ü-pli-kət\ duplicate • quadruplicate

upor \ü-pər\ see OOPER

uppance \əp-əns\ threepence, twopence

upper \əp-ər\ supper, upper • Last Supper, Lord's Supper • builder-upper, fixer-upper

uppie \əp-ē\ see UPPY

upple[1] \üp-əl\ see UPLE[2]

upple[2] \əp-əl\ see UPLE[1]

uppy \əp-ē\ guppy, puppy, yuppie • hush puppy, mud puppy

upt \əpt\ abrupt, bankrupt, corrupt, disrupt, erupt • developed, interrupt
—also -ed forms of verbs listed at UP

uq \ük\ see UKE

uque \ük\ see UKE

ur[1] \ȯr\ see OR[1]

ur[2] \u̇r\ see URE[1]

ur[3] \ər\ see EUR[1]

ura \u̇r-ə\ Jura, Kura • bravura, tempura • coloratura

urable \u̇r-ə-bəl\ curable, durable • endurable, incurable, insurable • unendurable, uninsurable

urae \u̇r-ē\ see URY[1]

urah \u̇r-ə\ see URA

ural \u̇r-əl\ mural, neural, plural, puerile, rural, Ural • extramural, intramural, semirural

urance \u̇r-əns\ assurance, endurance, insurance • health insurance, life insurance, reassurance, self-assurance

urate \u̇r-ət\ curate, turret

urb \ərb\ see ERB

urban \ər-bən\ bourbon, Durban, turban, turbine, urban • steam turbine, suburban, wind turbine

urber \ər-bər\ Berber • disturber

urbia \ər-bē-ə\ Serbia • exurbia, suburbia

urbine \ər-bən\ see URBAN

urble \ər-bəl\ see ERBAL

urch \ərch\ birch, church, lurch, perch, search • Christchurch, research

urchly \ərch-lē\ churchly, virtually

urd[1] \u̇rd\ see URED[1]

urd[2] \ərd\ see IRD

urder \ərd-ər\ see ERDER

urdle \ərd-ᵊl\ curdle, girdle, hurdle

urdy \ərd-ē\ birdie, sturdy, wordy • hurdy-gurdy, Mesa Verde, Monteverdi

ure[1] \u̇r\ Boer, boor, cure, dour, ewer, fewer, lure, moor, Moore, poor, pure, Ruhr, sewer, skewer, sure, tour, your, you're • abjure, allure, amour, assure, brochure, cocksure, conjure, contour, demure, detour, dirt-poor, endure, ensure, Exmoor, for sure, grandeur, impure, insure, land-poor, manure, mature, obscure, procure, secure, tenure, unmoor, unsure, velour • amateur, aperture, connoisseur, curvature, epicure, forfeiture, haute couture, immature, insecure, manicure, overture, pedicure, portraiture, premature, reassure, saboteur, signature, sinecure, soup du jour, temperature, to be sure, troubadour, Yom Kippur • caricature, entrepreneur, expenditure, imprimatur, investiture, literature, miniature, musculature, nomenclature

ure[2] \u̇r-ē\ see URY[1]

urean \u̇r-ē-ən\ see URIAN

ureau \u̇r-ō\ see URO

ured[1] \u̇rd\ gourd, Kurd • assured, steward • self-assured • out of one's gourd, underinsured

—*also* -ed *forms of verbs listed at* URE[1]

ured[2] \ərd\ see IRD

urely \ùr-lē\ poorly, purely, surely • securely • prematurely

ureous \ùr-ē-əs\ see URIOUS

urer \ùr-ər\ führer, furor, juror • insurer
—*also* -er *forms of adjectives listed at* URE[1]

urety \ùr-ət-ē\ see URITY

urey \ùr-ē\ see URY[1]

urf \ərf\ serf, surf, turf • windsurf • Astroturf, bodysurf, channel surf, surf and turf

urgative \ər-gə-tiv\ see URGATIVE

urge \ərj\ dirge, merge, purge, splurge, surge, urge, verge • converge, diverge, emerge, resurge, submerge, upsurge • reemerge

urgence \ər-jəns\ see ERGENCE

urgency \ər-jən-sē\ see ERGENCY

urgent \ər-jənt\ urgent • convergent, detergent, divergent, emergent, insurgent, resurgent • counterinsurgent

urgeon \ər-jən\ burgeon, sturgeon, surgeon, virgin • tree surgeon • plastic surgeon

urger[1] \ər-gər\ burger, burgher • cheeseburger, hamburger, Limburger • Luxembourger, veggie burger

urger[2] \ər-jər\ see ERGER

urgery \ərj-rē\ see ERJURY

urgh[1] \ər-ə\ see OROUGH[1]

urgh[2] \ər-ō\ see URROW[1]

urgher \ər-gər\ see URGER[1]

urgic \ər-jik\ see ERGIC

urgical \ər-ji-kəl\ surgical • liturgical • metallurgical

urgor \ər-gər\ see URGER[1]

urgy \ər-jē\ clergy • dramaturgy, metallurgy

uri \ùr-ē\ see URY[1]

urial \er-ē-əl\ see ARIAL

urian \ùr-ē-ən\ Arthurian, centu-

rion, Manchurian, Missourian • Canterburian, epicurean

urible \ùr-ə-bəl\ see URABLE

urie \ùr-ē\ see URY[1]

urier[1] \er-ē-ər\ see ERRIER

urier[2] \ùr-ē-ər\ see OURIER[1]

uriere \ùr-ē-ər\ see OURIER[1]

uring \ùr-iŋ\ during, mooring, touring • alluring, enduring
—*also* -ing *forms of verbs listed at* URE[1]

urion \ùr-ē-ən\ see URIAN

urious \ùr-ē-əs\ curious, furious, spurious • incurious, injurious, luxurious

uris \ùr-əs\ see URUS

urist \ùr-əst\ jurist, purist, tourist • manicurist, pedicurist • caricaturist
—*also* -est *forms of adjectives listed at* URE[1]

urity \ùr-ət-ē\ purity • impurity, maturity, obscurity, security • immaturity, insecurity • Social Security

urk \ərk\ see ORK[1]

urka \ər-kə\ burka, circa, Gurkha

urke \ərk\ see ORK[1]

urker \ər-kər\ see ORKER[1]

urkey \ər-kē\ see ERKY

urkha \ər-kə\ see URKA

urki \ər-kē\ see ERKY

urky \ər-kē\ see ERKY

url \ərl\ see IRL

urled \ərld\ see ORLD

urlin \ər-lən\ see ERLIN

urling \ər-liŋ\ hurling, sterling
—*also* -ing *forms of verbs listed at* IRL

urlish \ər-lish\ churlish, girlish

urly \ər-lē\ burly, curly, early, pearly, squirrely, surly, swirly, twirly, whirly

urman \ər-mən\ see ERMAN

urn \ərn\ Bern, burn, churn, earn, fern, learn, spurn, stern, tern, turn, urn, yearn • adjourn, astern, concern, discern, downturn, heartburn, Hepburn, intern, in turn, kick turn, Lucerne, nocturne, return, sojourn, sunburn, unlearn, upturn, U-turn, windburn • Arctic tern, in return, out of turn, overturn, slash-and-burn, taciturn, unconcern • at every turn, from stem to stern • point of no return

urnable \ər-nə-bəl\ burnable • discernible, returnable
• indiscernible, nonreturnable

urnal \ərn-ᵊl\ see ERNAL

urne \ərn\ see URN

urned \ərnd\ burned • concerned, sunburned, unearned, unlearned, windburned
—*also* -ed *forms of verbs listed at* URN

urner \ər-nər\ burner, earner • afterburner

urney \ər-nē\ see OURNEY[1]

urnian \ər-nē-ən\ see ERNIAN

urnish \ər-nish\ burnish, furnish

urnt \ərnt\ see EARNT

uro \ùr-ō\ bureau, euro, Euro
• politburo, travel bureau, weather bureau

uror \ùr-ər\ see URER

urore \ùr-ər\ see URER

urous \ùr-əs\ see URUS

urp \ərp\ burp, chirp, perp, slurp, twerp • Antwerp, usurp

urr \ər\ see EUR[1]

urra[1] \ùr-ə\ see URA

urra[2] \ər-ə\ see OROUGH[1]

urragh \ər-ə\ see OROUGH[1]

urral \ər-əl\ see ERRAL

urrant \ər-ənt\ see URRENT

urray \ər-ē\ see URRY

urre \ər\ see EUR[1]

urred \ərd\ see IRD

urrence \ər-əns\ deterrence, occurrence, recurrence, transference
—*also* -s, -'s, *and* -s' *forms of nouns listed at* URRENT

urrent \ər-ənt\ currant, current, weren't • concurrent, crosscurrent, deterrent, recurrent, rip current • countercurrent, undercurrent

urret \ùr-ət\ see URATE

urrey \ər-ē\ see URRY

urrian \ùr-ē-ən\ see URIAN

urrie \ər-ē\ see URRY

urrier \ər-ē-ər\ blurrier, courier, furrier, worrier

urring \ər-iŋ\ stirring
—*also* -ing *forms of verbs listed at* EUR[1]

urrish \ər-ish\ see OURISH

urro[1] \ər-ə\ see OROUGH[1]

urro[2] \ər-ō\ see URROW[1]

urrow[1] \ər-ō\ borough, burgh, burro, burrow, furrow, thorough
• Marlborough

urrow[2] \ər-ə\ see OROUGH[1]

urry \ər-ē\ blurry, curry, flurry, furry, hurry, Murray, scurry, surrey, Surrey, worry • in a hurry

ursary \ərs-rē\ cursory, nursery
• day nursery • anniversary

urse \ərs\ see ERSE

ursed \ərst\ see URST

ursery \ərs-rē\ see URSARY

ursion \ər-zhən\ see ERSION[1]

ursive \ər-siv\ see ERSIVE

ursory \ərs-rē\ see URSARY

urst \ərst\ burst, cursed, first, Hearst, thirst, worst • accursed, at first, cloudburst, feetfirst, headfirst, knockwurst, outburst, starburst, sunburst • liverwurst, microburst
—*also* -ed *forms of verbs listed at* ERSE

ursy[1] \ər-sē\ see ERCY

ursy[2] \əs-ē\ see USSY

urt[1] \ùrt\ Frankfurt

urt[2] \ərt\ see ERT[1]

urtain \ərt-ᵊn\ see ERTAIN

urtal \ərt-ᵊl\ see ERTILE

urter \ərt-ər\ see ERTER

urtive \ərt-iv\ see ERTIVE
urtle \ərt-ᵊl\ see ERTILE
urton \ərt-ᵊn\ see ERTAIN
urus \ùr-əs\ Arcturus, sulfurous • Epicurus
urve \ərv\ see ERVE
urved \ərvd\ see ERVED
urvy \ər-vē\ curvy, nervy, scurvy • topsy-turvy
ury[1] \ùr-ē\ Curie, fury, jury • grand jury, Missouri
ury[2] \er-ē\ see ARY[1]
urze \ərz\ see ERS[1]
urzy \ər-zē\ see ERSEY
us[1] \əs\ bus, cuss, fuss, Gus, muss, plus, pus, Russ, thus, truss, us • airbus, discuss, school bus, surplus • blunderbuss, minibus, motor bus, trolleybus
us[2] \ü\ see EW[1]
us[3] \ùsh\ see OUCHE
us[4] \üz\ see USE[2]
usa[1] \ü-sə\ Sousa • Medusa • Appaloosa, Tuscaloosa
usa[2] \ü-zə\ Sousa • Medusa • Arethusa
usable \ü-zə-bəl\ usable • excusable, reusable, unusable • inexcusable, nonreusable
usae \ü-sē\ see UICY
usal \ü-zəl\ bamboozle, perusal, refusal
usc \əsk\ see USK
uscan \əs-kən\ Tuscan • Etruscan
uscle \əs-əl\ see USTLE
use[1] \üs\ Bruce, deuce, goose, juice, loose, moose, mousse, noose, puce, ruse, Russ, schuss, Seuss, sluice, spruce, truce, use, Zeus • abstruse, abuse, adduce, blue spruce, burnoose, caboose, chartreuse, conduce, cut loose, deduce, diffuse, disuse, excuse, footloose, hang loose, induce, misuse, mongoose, obtuse, Orpheus, papoose, Perseus, produce, profuse, Proteus, recluse, reduce,

refuse, reuse, Sanctus, seduce, slip noose, snow goose, Theseus, turn loose, vamoose • Belarus, Betelgeuse, cook one's goose, fast and loose, flag of truce, introduce, mass-produce, Mother Goose, Odysseus, overuse, Prometheus, reproduce, Syracuse • Canada goose, hypotenuse
use[2] \üz\ blues, booze, bruise, choose, cruise, Druze, fuse, Hughes, lose, Meuse, muse, news, ooze, ruse, schmooze, snooze, use, whose • abuse, accuse, amuse, bad news, chartreuse, confuse, defuse, diffuse, enthuse, excuse, infuse, masseuse, misuse, peruse, refuse, reuse, short fuse, suffuse, transfuse • Betelgeuse, disabuse, Newport News, overuse, p's and q's, Santa Cruz, Syracuse, Veracruz • Goody Two-shoes, hypotenuse
—*also* -s, -'s, *and* -s' *forms of nouns and* -s *forms of verbs listed at* EW[1]
used \üzd\ used • confused • underused
—*also* -ed *forms of verbs listed at* USE[2]
user \ü-zər\ boozer, bruiser, cruiser, loser, user • abuser, accuser, end user • battle cruiser, cabin cruiser
ush[1] \əsh\ blush, brush, crush, flush, gush, hush, lush, mush, plush, rush, shush, slush, squush, thrush • bulrush, bum's rush, gold rush, hairbrush, hush-hush, nailbrush, onrush, paintbrush, sagebrush, scrub brush, song thrush, straight flush, toothbrush, wood thrush • Hindu Kush, royal flush, underbrush
ush[2] \ùsh\ bush, Bush, mush, push, shush, squoosh, swoosh, whoosh • ambush, bell push, rosebush,

spicebush, thornbush • burning
bush, Hindu Kush • beat around
the bush

usher[1] \əsh-ər\ crusher, gusher,
usher
  —*also* -er *forms of adjectives listed
  at* USH[1]

usher[2] \ush-ər\ pusher • ambusher

ushi \ush-ē\ see USHY[2]

ushing \əsh-iŋ\ onrushing, un-
blushing
  —*also* -ing *forms of verbs listed at*
  USH[1]

ushy[1] \əsh-ē\ brushy, gushy,
mushy, plushy, slushy

ushy[2] \ush-ē\ bushy, cushy, mushy,
pushy, sushi

usi \ü-sē\ see UICY

usian \ü-zhən\ see USION

usible[1] \ü-sə-bəl\ see UCIBLE

usible[2] \ü-zə-bəl\ see USABLE

usie \ü-zē\ see OOZY

usil \ü-zəl\ see USAL

using \əs-iŋ\ busing • antibusing
  —*also* -ing *forms of verbs listed at*
  US[1]

usion \ü-zhən\ fusion • allusion,
collusion, conclusion, confusion,
contusion, delusion, exclusion,
illusion, inclusion, infusion, intru-
sion, profusion, protrusion, seclusion, transfusion, Venusian
• Andalusian, disillusion, maloc-
clusion • foregone conclusion
• optical illusion

usive \ü-siv\ abusive, allusive,
conclusive, conducive, delusive,
effusive, elusive, exclusive, inclusive, intrusive, reclusive • all-
inclusive, inconclusive,
unobtrusive

usk \əsk\ brusque, dusk, husk,
musk, tusk

usker \əs-kər\ busker • cornhusker

uskie \əs-kē\ see USKY

uskin \əs-kən\ see USCAN

usky \əs-kē\ dusky, husky, musky

uso \ü-sō\ see USOE

usoe \ü-sō\ Rousseau, trousseau,
whoso • Caruso • Robinson Crusoe

usque \əsk\ see USK

uss[1] \us\ puss, wuss • chartreuse,
sourpuss • glamour-puss, octopus,
platypus

uss[2] \üs\ see USE[1]

uss[3] \əs\ see US[1]

ussate \əs-ət\ see USSET

usse \üs\ see USE[1]

ussel \əs-əl\ see USTLE

ussell \əs-əl\ see USTLE

usset \əs-ət\ gusset, russet

ussia \əsh-ə\ Prussia, Russia • Be-
lorussia

ussian \əsh-ən\ see USSION

ussing \əs-iŋ\ see USING

ussion \əsh-ən\ Prussian, Russian
• concussion, discussion, percus-
sion • Belorussian, repercussion

ussle \əs-əl\ see USTLE

ussy \əs-ē\ fussy, mussy

ust[1] \əst\ bust, crust, dust, gust,
just, lust, must, rust, thrust, trust
• adjust, august, bloodlust, dis-
gust, distrust, encrust, entrust, in-
trust, leaf rust, mistrust, moon-
dust, piecrust, robust, sawdust,
stardust, unjust • antitrust, bite
the dust, cosmic dust, readjust,
upper crust, wanderlust
  —*also* -ed *forms of verbs listed at*
  US[1]

ust[2] \əs\ see US[1]

ust[3] \üst\ see OOST

ustable \əs-tə-bəl\ see USTIBLE

ustard \əs-tərd\ custard, mustard
  —*also* -ed *forms of verbs listed at*
  USTER

usted \əs-təd\ busted • disgusted
• maladjusted, well-adjusted
  —*also* -ed *forms of verbs listed at*
  UST[1]

uster \əs-tər\ bluster, buster, cluster, Custer, duster, fluster, luster,
muster • adjuster, blockbuster,

crop duster, gangbuster, lackluster, pass muster • broncobuster, filibuster

ustful \əst-fəl\ lustful, trustful • distrustful, mistrustful

usth \əst\ see UST[1]

ustible \əs-tə-bəl\ adjustable, combustible • incombustible

ustin \əs-tən\ Justin • Augustine

ustine \əs-tən\ see USTIN

ustle \əs-əl\ bustle, hustle, muscle, mussel, Russell, rustle, trestle, tussle • corpuscle, outhustle, outmuscle

ustor \əs-tər\ see USTER

ustrious \əs-trē-əs\ illustrious, industrious

usty \əs-tē\ busty, crusty, dusty, gusty, lusty, musty, rusty, trusty

usy \iz-ē\ see IZZY

ut[1] \ət\ but, butt, cut, glut, gut, hut, jut, mutt, nut, putt, rut, shut, smut, soot, strut, what • abut, all but, beechnut, brush cut, buzz cut, catgut, chestnut, clean-cut, clear-cut, crew cut, crosscut, doughnut, haircut, jump cut, kick butt, lug nut, peanut, pignut, pine nut, precut, putt-putt, rebut, shortcut, somewhat, walnut, wing nut, woodcut • betel nut, brazil nut, butternut, coconut, hazelnut, lychee nut, scuttlebutt, undercut, uppercut • director's cut, open-and-shut

ut[2] \ü\ see EW[1]

ut[3] \üt\ see UTE

ut[4] \u̇t\ see OOT[1]

utable \üt-ə-bəl\ suitable • immutable, inscrutable • executable, indisputable, irrefutable, substitutable

utal \üt-ᵊl\ see UTILE

utan \üt-ᵊn\ gluten, Newton, Putin, Teuton • Rasputin • highfalutin

utant \üt-ᵊnt\ mutant • disputant, pollutant

utch \əch\ clutch, crutch, dutch, Dutch, hutch, much, such, touch • and such, as such, retouch, soft touch, so much, too much • a bit much, common touch, Midas touch, overmuch, pretty much, such and such

utchy \əch-ē\ see UCHY

ute \üt\ boot, brute, butte, chute, coot, cute, flute, fruit, hoot, jute, Jute, loot, lute, moot, mute, newt, root, rout, route, scoot, shoot, snoot, soot, suit, toot, Ute • acute, astute, bear fruit, Beirut, breadfruit, Canute, commute, compute, cube root, deaf-mute, dilute, dispute, en route, flight suit, grapefruit, hip boot, hirsute, impute, jackboot, jumpsuit, lawsuit, minute, offshoot, Paiute, pantsuit, playsuit, pollute, pursuit, reboot, recruit, refute, salute, Silk Route, snowsuit, spacesuit, sport-ute, square root, star fruit, statute, strong suit, sunsuit, sweat suit, swimsuit, take root, taproot, to boot, tracksuit, trade route, transmute, tribute, uproot, wet suit • absolute, Aleut, arrowroot, attribute, autoroute, bathing suit, birthday suit, bitterroot, bodysuit, business suit, constitute, contribute, destitute, disrepute, dissolute, execute, follow suit, gingerroot, hot pursuit, institute, kiwifruit, leisure suit, malamute, overshoot, parachute, passion fruit, persecute, point-and-shoot, prosecute, resolute, rural route, substitute, troubleshoot • electrocute, forbidden fruit, reconstitute, redistribute, telecommute

uted \üt-əd\ see OOTED[1]

utee \üt-ē\ see OOTY[1]

utely \üt-lē\ acutely, minutely • absolutely, resolutely

uten \üt-ᵊn\ see UTAN
uteness \üt-nəs\ cuteness, muti-
nous
utenous \üt-nəs\ see UTENESS
uteous \üt-ē-əs\ beauteous, du-
teous
uter \üt-ər\ cuter, neuter, hooter,
looter, pewter, scooter, suitor,
tutor • commuter, computer,
freebooter, jump shooter,
peashooter, polluter, recruiter,
sharpshooter, six-shooter, straight
shooter, trapshooter • motor
scooter, persecutor, prosecutor,
troubleshooter • microcomputer,
minicomputer, telecommuter
utes \üts\ see OOTS
uteus \üt-ē-əs\ see UTEOUS
uth¹ \üt\ see UTE
uth² \üth\ see OOTH²
uther \ə-thər\ see OTHER¹
uthful \üth-fəl\ truthful, youthful
• untruthful
uthless \üth-ləs\ ruthless, toothless
uti \üt-ē\ see OOTY¹
ution \ü-shən\ see UTION
utical \üt-i-kəl\ cuticle • pharma-
ceutical
uticle \üt-i-kəl\ see UTICAL
utie \üt-ē\ see OOTY¹
utiful \üt-i-fəl\ beautiful, dutiful
utile \üt-ᵊl\ brutal, futile, tootle
utin \üt-ᵊn\ see UTAN
utine \üt-ᵊn\ see UTAN
uting \üt-iŋ\ sharpshooting, trap-
shooting
—also -ing forms of verbs listed at
UTE
utinous¹ \üt-ᵊn-əs\ glutinous, muti-
nous
utinous² \üt-nəs\ see UTENESS
utiny \üt-ᵊn-ē\ mutiny, scrutiny
ution \ü-shən\ Aleutian, Confu-
cian, dilution, locution, pollution,
solution • absolution, attribution,
constitution, contribution, desti-
tution, dissolution, distribution,

elocution, evolution, execution,
institution, persecution, prosecu-
tion, resolution, restitution, retri-
bution, revolution, substitution
• electrocution, joint resolution,
redistribution
utionary \ü-shə-ner-ē\ evolutionary, revolutionary
utist \üt-əst\ cutest, flutist • abso-
lutist
utl \ü-tᵊl\ see UTILE
utland \ət-lənd\ Jutland, Rutland
utlass \ət-ləs\ cutlass, gutless
utless \ət-ləs\ see UTLASS
utney \ət-nē\ chutney, gluttony
uton \üt-ⁿ\ see UTAN
utor \üt-ər\ see UTER
utriment \ü-trə-mənt\ nutriment
• accoutrement
uts \əts\ see UTZ
utsy \ət-sē\ gutsy, klutzy
utt \ət\ see UT¹
uttal \ət-ᵊl\ see UTTLE
utte \üt\ see UTE
uttee \ət-ē\ see UTTY
utter¹ \ət-ər\ butter, clutter, cutter,
flutter, gutter, mutter, putter,
shutter, splutter, sputter, stutter,
utter • aflutter, haircutter, stone-
cutter, woodcutter • bread and
butter, cookie-cutter, paper cutter
utter² \ùt-ər\ see OOTER¹
uttery \ət-ə-rē\ buttery, fluttery
utti¹ \üt-ē\ see OOTY¹
utti² \ùt-ē\ see OOTY²
utting \ùt-iŋ\ see OOTING¹
uttle \ət-ᵊl\ scuttle, shuttle, subtle
• rebuttal, space shuttle
utton \ət-ᵊn\ button, glutton, mut-
ton, Sutton • hot-button, push-
button, unbutton • belly button,
on the button, panic button
uttony \ət-nē\ see UTNEY
utty \ət-ē\ gutty, nutty, putty,
rutty, smutty
uture \ü-chər\ future, moocher,
suture • wave of the future

uty \üt-ē\ see OOTY[1]

utz \əts\ klutz, nuts • blood-and-guts, spill one's guts
—also -s, -'s, and -s' forms of nouns and -s forms of verbs listed at UT[1]

utzy \ət-sē\ see UTSY

uu \ü\ see EW[1]

uvian \ü-vē-ən\ Peruvian, Vesuvian • antediluvian

uvion \ü-vē-ən\ see UVIAN

ux[1] \əks\ crux, flux, tux • big bucks, deluxe, influx • Benelux, megabucks,
—also -s, -'s, and -s' forms of nouns and -s forms of verbs listed at UCK[1]

ux[2] \úks\ see OOKS[2]

uxe[1] \üks\ see OOKS[1]

uxe[2] \úks\ see OOKS[2]

uxe[3] \əks\ see UX[1]

uxion \ək-shən\ see UCTION

uy \ī\ see Y[1]

uygur \ē-gər\ see EAGER

uyot \ē-ō\ see IO[2]

uyp \īp\ see IPE

uz[1] \üts\ see OOTS

uz[2] \úz\ see USE[2]

uze \üz\ see USE[2]

uzz \əz\ see EUSE[1]

uzzi \ü-zē\ see OOZY

uzzle \əz-əl\ guzzle, muzzle, nuzzle, puzzle • crossword puzzle, jigsaw puzzle

uzzler \əz-lər\ guzzler, muzzler, puzzler • gas-guzzler

uzzy \əz-ē\ fuzzy, muzzy, scuzzy

Y

y[1] \ī\ aye, Bligh, buy, by, bye, chai, cry, die, dry, dye, eye, fie, fly, fry, guy, Guy, hi, high, i, I, lie, lye, my, nigh, pi, pie, ply, pry, rye, scythe, shy, sigh, sky, Skye, sly, spry, spy, sty, Thai, thigh, thy, tie, try, vie, why, wry, wye, Y • air-dry, ally, anti, apply, awry, aye-aye, Bacchae, Baha'i, banzai, Belgae, belie, black eye, blackfly, black tie, blow-dry, blowfly, bone-dry, bonsai, botfly, Brunei, buckeye, bull?s-eye, bye-bye, cockeye, come by, comply, cow pie, crane fly, cream pie, cross-eye, decry, deep-fry, deerfly, defy, Delphi, deny, drip-dry, drive-by, drop by, Dubai, Eli, espy, face fly, firefly, flyby, fly high, freeze-dry, fruit fly, gadfly, get by, GI, glass eye, go by, good-bye, gun-shy, Haggai, Hawkeye, hereby, hi-fi, hog-tie, horn fly, horsefly, house-fly, imply, jai alai, July, Karzai, Kaui, Kenai, knee-high, Lehigh, let fly, Levi, magpie, Masai, mayfly, medfly, mind's eye, Mumbai, nearby, necktie, outcry, panfry, pigsty, pinkeye, Popeye, pop fly, potpie, put by, quasi, rabbi, red-eye, rely, reply, retry, rib eye, run dry, sand fly, sci-fi, screw eye, semi, shanghai, Shanghai, shut-eye, Sinai, sky-high, small-fry, stand by, standby, stir-fry, string tie, supply, swear by, test-fly, thereby, tie-dye, tongue-tie, Transkei, twist tie, two-ply, untie, vat dye, Versailles, whereby, whitefly, white tie, wise guy • abide by, Adonai, alibi, alkali, amplify, beautify, bolo tie, butterfly, by-and-by, by the bye, calcify, certify, Chou En-lai, citify, clarify, classify, codify, crucify, cut-and-dry, cutie-pie, DIY, damselfly, dandify, deify, dignify, do-or-die, dragonfly, eagle eye, edify, evil eye, falsify, fortify, Gemini, gentrify, glorify, gratify, Haggai, high and dry, horrify, junior high, justify, kiss good-bye, liquefy, Lorelei, lull-aby, magnify, Malachi, misapply, modify, mollify, mortify, Mount Sinai, multi-ply, multiply, mum-mify, mystify, nazify, notify, nuclei, nullify, occupy, on standby, on the fly, ossify, over-buy, overfly, overlie, pacify, Paraguay, passerby, petrify, preachify, prettify, private eye, prophesy, purify, putrefy, qualify, quantify, ratify, RBI, reapply, rectify, resupply, robber fly, runner's high, Russify, samurai, sanctify, satisfy, scarify, Busing Eye, senior high, shepherd's pie, shoofly pie, signify, simplify, specify, speechify, stratify, stul-tify, stupefy, sweetie pie, Tene-brae, terrify, testify, tsetse fly, tumble dry, typify, uglify, under-lie, unify, Uruguay, verify, vilify, vivify, yuppify, zombify • aniline dye, a priori, beatify, decertify, declassify, demystify, detoxify, disqualify, dissatisfy, diversify, electric eye, electrify, exemplify, Helvetii, humidify, identify, inten-sify, misclassify, money supply, oversupply, personify, preoccupy, revivify, see eye to eye, solidify, undersupply, water supply • de-humidify, misidentify, oversim-plify • in the blink of an eye, modus operandi

y² \ē\ see EE¹

yable \ī-ə-bəl\ see IABLE¹

yad \ī-əd\ dryad, naiad, triad • jere-miad

yan \ī-ən\ see ION¹

yant \ī-ənt\ see IANT

yatt \ī-ət\ see IET

yber \ī-bər\ see IBER

ybia \i-bē-ə\ see IBIA

yce \īs\ see ICE¹

yche \ī-kē\ see IKE¹

ycin \is-ᵊn\ see ISON¹

ycle¹ \ī-kəl\ cycle, Michael • cell cycle, life cycle, recycle, song cycle • business cycle, carbon cycle, Exercycle, kilocycle, mega-cycle, motorcycle, unicycle

ycle² \ik-əl\ see ICKLE

ycler \ik-lər\ see ICKLER

yde \īd\ see IDE¹

ydia \i-dē-ə\ see IDIA

ydian \id-ē-ən\ see IDIAN

ydney \id-nē\ see IDNEY

ye \ī\ see Y¹

yeable \ī-ə-bəl\ see IABLE¹

yed \īd\ see IDE¹

yer \īr\ see IRE¹

yeth \ī-əth\ see IATH¹

yfe \īf\ see IFE¹

yg \ig\ see IG

ygamous \ig-ə-məs\ see IGAMOUS

ygamy \ig-ə-mē\ see IGAMY

ygian \i-jən\ Phrygian, pidgin, pigeon, smidgen • clay pigeon, religion, rock pigeon, stool pi-geon, wood pigeon • homing pigeon • carrier pigeon, passenger pigeon

ying \ī-iŋ\ crying, flying, lying, trying • high-flying, low-lying, outlying, undying • terrifying, underlying
—*also* -ing *forms of verbs listed at* Y¹

yke \īk\ see IKE²

ylan \il-ən\ see ILLON

yle \īl\ see ILE¹

ylem \ī-ləm\ see ILUM
yler \ī-lər\ see ILAR
ylet \ī-lət\ see ILOT
ylic \il-ik\ see ILIC
yling \ī-liŋ\ see ILING[1]
yllable \il-ə-bəl\ see ILLABLE
yllic \il-ik\ see ILIC
yllis \il-əs\ see ILLUS
yllo[1] \ē-lō\ see ILO[2]
yllo[2] \ī-lō\ see ILO[1]
ylum \ī-ləm\ see ILUM
ylus \ī-ləs\ see ILUS
yly \ī-lē\ dryly, highly, shyly, slyly, smiley, Wiley, wily, wryly
ym \im\ see IM[1]
ymbal \im-bəl\ see IMBLE
ymbol \im-bəl\ see IMBLE
yme \īm\ see IME[1]
ymen \ī-mən\ see IMEN
ymer \ī-mər\ see IMER[1]
ymic \im-ik\ gimmick, mimic
ymie \ī-mē\ see IMY
ymion \im-ē-ən\ see IMIAN
ymity \im-ət-ē\ see IMITY
ymn \im\ see IM[1]
ymph \imf\ lymph, nymph
ynah \ī-nə\ see INA[1]
ynast \ī-nəst\ see INIST[1]
ynch[1] \inch\ see INCH
ynch[2] \iŋk\ see INK
yness \ī-nəs\ see INUS[1]
ynic \in-ik\ see INIC
ynical \in-i-kəl\ see INICAL
ynn \in\ see IN[1]
ynth \inth\ see INTH
ynx \iŋs\ see INX
yp \ip\ see IP
ypal \ī-pəl\ disciple • archetypal, prototypal
ype \īp\ see IPE
yper \ī-pər\ see IPER
yph \if\ see IFF
yphen \ī-fən\ hyphen, siphon
yphic \if-ik\ see IFIC
yphony \if-ə-nē\ see IPHONY
yping \ī-piŋ\ see IPING
ypo \ī-pō\ hypo, typo

ypse \ips\ see IPS
ypsy \ip-sē\ gypsy, Gypsy, tipsy
ypt \ipt\ see IPT
yptian \ip-shən\ see IPTION
yptic \ip-tik\ cryptic, triptych
 • ecliptic, elliptic • apocalyptic
yra \ī-rə\ Ira, Lyra, Myra • Elmira, Elvira, hegira, Palmyra
yrant \ī-rənt\ see IRANT
yre \īr\ see IRE[1]
yria \ir-ē-ə\ see ERIA[1]
yriad \ir-ē-əd\ see ERIOD
yric \ir-ik\ see ERIC[2]
yrical \ir-i-kəl\ see ERICAL[2]
yrie \ir-ē\ see EARY
yril \ir-əl\ see ERAL[1]
yrna \ər-nə\ see ERNA
yro[1] \ī-rō\ Cairo, gyro, Gyro, tyro
yro[2] \ir-ō\ see ERO[3]
yron \īr-ən\ see IREN
yros \ī-rəs\ see IRUS
yrrh \ər\ see EUR[1]
yrrhic \ir-ik\ see ERIC[2]
yrrhus \ir-əs\ see EROUS
yrtle \ərt-ᵊl\ see ERTILE
yrup \ər-əp\ see IRRUP
yrupy \ər-ə-pē\ see IRRUPY
yrus \ī-rəs\ see IRUS
ysch \ish\ see ISH[1]
ysia \ish-ə\ see ITIA[1]
ysian[1] \is-ē-ən\ Odyssean
 • Dionysian
ysian[2] \ish-ən\ see ITION
ysian[3] \izh-ən\ see ISION
ysian[4] \ī-sē-ən\ see ISCEAN[1]
ysical \iz-i-kəl\ physical, quizzical
 • nonphysical • metaphysical
ysm \iz-əm\ see ISM
ysmal \iz-məl\ dismal • abysmal, baptismal • cataclysmal
yson \īs-ᵊn\ see ISON[1]
yss \is\ see ISS
yssean \is-ē-ən\ see YSIAN[1]
yst \ist\ see IST[2]
ystal \is-tᵊl\ see ISTAL
yster \ī-stər\ see EISTER[1]
ystery \is-trē\ see ISTORY

ystic \is-tik\ see ISTIC
ystical \is-ti-kəl\ see ISTICAL
ysus[1] \ē-səs\ see ESIS
ysus[2] \ī-səs\ see ISIS
yte \īt\ see ITE[1]
ythe[1] \ī\ see Y[1]

ythe[2] \īth\ see ITHE[1]
ytic \it-ik\ see ITIC
ytical \it-i-kəl\ see ITICAL
ytton \it-ᵊn\ see ITTEN
yx \iks\ see IX[1]
yze \īz\ see IZE[1]